The constitutional question is of paramount importance in the political and nationalist agenda of late twentieth-century Europe. Arguments focus on the best form of constitutional organization: democracy versus autocracy, unitary versus federal organization, pluralism versus intolerance, centralism versus regionalism, national sovereignty versus European. Professor van Caenegem's new book addresses these fundamental questions by analysing different models of constitutional government through a historical perspective, assessing why some models were established and others rejected. The book's approach is pragmatic and chronological: constitutionalism is explained not as a paradigm devised by a team of jurists, but as the result of many centuries of trial and error. The narrative begins in the early Middle Ages and concludes with contemporary debates, taking as its focus the main European countries, the United States, and finally the former Soviet Union. Special attention is devoted to the rise of the rule of law, and of constitutional, parliamentary and federal forms of government. The Anglo-American contribution to the ascendancy of present-day liberal democracy is underlined, but the latter's rejection by twentieth-century totalitarian regimes also receives extensive treatment. The epilogue discusses the future of liberal democracy as a universal model.

# AN HISTORICAL INTRODUCTION TO WESTERN
## CONSTITUTIONAL LAW

# AN HISTORICAL
# INTRODUCTION
# TO WESTERN
# CONSTITUTIONAL LAW

R. C. van CAENEGEM

*University of Ghent*

CAMBRIDGE
UNIVERSITY PRESS

Published by the Press Syndicate of the University of Cambridge
The Pitt Building, Trumpington Street, Cambridge CB2 1RP
40 West 20th Street, New York, NY 10011–4211, USA
10 Stamford Road, Oakleigh, Melbourne 3166, Australia

First published 1995

Printed in Great Britain at the University Press, Cambridge

*A catalogue record for this book is available from the British Library*

*Library of Congress cataloguing in publication data*
Caenegem, R. C. van.
An historical introduction to western constitutional law / R. C. van Caenegem.
p.      cm.
Includes bibliographical references.
ISBN 0 521 47115 X (hardcover). — ISBN 0 521 47693 3 (pbk.)
1. Europe — Constitutional history.   I. Title.
KJC4431.C34   1995
342.4′029 — dc20
[344.0229]   94–16814   CIP


ISBN 0 521 47115 X hardback
ISBN 0 521 47693 3 paperback

VN

# Contents

vii

# Preface

Whereas until recently economic problems seemed to dominate the public mind, the debate on the best way of organizing the state has now also come to the fore. Recent momentous developments in Europe have focused attention on such fundamental options as democracy versus autocracy, politics versus ideology, unitary versus federal organization, pluralism versus intolerance, centralism versus regionalism, national sovereignty versus European unity, the bureaucratic welfare state versus individual freedom and a market economy, and a Bill of Rights versus parliamentary omnipotence: in 1990–1 alone I counted six books or pamphlets on 'Britain's constitutional future' and a 'Bill of Rights for Britain'. Third World countries are also interested, as they realize that economic progress is hard to achieve in a backward political regime. Leading economic historians such as Douglass North, one of the 1993 Nobel Prize winners for economics, have shown that the free market alone does not ensure prosperity, but that a stable political and legal organization is also necessary; the role played by a liberal constitution in the industrial take-off in Europe some two hundred years ago was indeed conspicuous.

Today's constitutional debate would be shallow without a knowledge of the historical antecedents. It would be preposterous to imagine that we were the first to discern the fundamental options, and foolish not to try and learn from the experiences of the past. The question as to how the state ought to be constituted has led to fierce debates in lecture halls and violent clashes on the battlefield, and it is to these antecedents that this book is devoted: not the articles of arid treaties and constitutions, but the dreams and achievements of scholars and nations. It is hoped that placing the great constitutional debate of our time in an historical perspective may help to illuminate it.

The readers to whom this short book is addressed consist of law students in various countries who want to place their own constitution, which is part of their curriculum, in an international and historical perspective, but who lack the time and the languages to read the relevant national legal histories. I also address myself to the members of the legal profession, politicians and political observers who wonder how the present constitutional diversity came about, and I am convinced that the general educated public, which follows the struggles for constitutional change in many parts of the world, will appreciate a – not too abstruse or technical – book that shows why these problems arose and how our ancestors handled them.

Writing a short but comprehensive survey of a wide subject entails sacrificing detail to main issues and nuance to summary description; it also means ignoring lively debates among successive schools of interpretation in favour of a presentation of the facts and the *communis opinio*. It was impossible, for example, to present here the arguments of the orthodox, the revisionist and the anti-revisionist approaches to Tudor and Stuart history that have enlivened scholarly debate since the late 1960s. Nor could I enter into the vigorous discussions on the real significance of the Bismarck era for German and European history. I can only apologize to the specialists of these countries and periods for my brief presentation, and refer the reader to the relevant works in the bibliography for further enlightenment.

*Ghent*                                                            R. C. VAN CAENEGEM

# CHAPTER I

# Introduction

## AN 'INTELLIGIBLE FIELD OF STUDY'

Constitutional law may be considered the most important part of public law, beside criminal, fiscal and administrative law, and the law of nations, and it seems advisable at the outset carefully to define our field of study.

### Definition of the subject

The concept of public law is itself somewhat problematic. It is true that Roman law expressly distinguished *ius privatum* and *ius publicum*, but the latter appears, on closer examination, not quite to cover the same ground as present-day notions of public law. Indeed, we read in Justinian's Institutes that '*publicum ius est, quod ad statum rei Romanae spectat, privatum quod ad singulorum utilitatem pertinet*' (1, 1, 4) ('public law is concerned with the Roman state, private law belongs to the utility of individuals'), and the Digest, the most important part of Justinian's *Corpus Iuris Civilis*, goes on to explain that '*publicum ius in sacris, in sacerdotibus, in magistratibus consistit*' (1, 1, 1, 2) ('public law concerns sacred things, priests and magistrates'). This definition is, to modern lawyers, incomplete as it omits, *inter alia*, criminal law. Elsewhere the *Corpus Iuris* mentions *ius publicum* in a sense that reminds us of the modern notion of public order: for example where the Digest (28, 1, 3) explains that the form of a testament is a matter '*non privati, sed publici iuris*'.

The rise of the patrimonial concept of the state in the Middle Ages meant that this fundamental dichotomy was lost. The rights of kings and manorial lords were not essentially distinguished from other rights to rank, possession and income, and fell under the jurisdiction of the same law courts as what today would be considered private-law cases. This is not surprising in a world where a kingdom was treated as family estate, divided among the king's heirs, given in dowry to his daughters or mortgaged. It is typical that medieval translators render *magistratus* in texts from Antiquity as *seigniories* and that the *coutumiers*, or books of customary law of the fifteenth century, ignore the *publicum–privatum* dichotomy: chapters on the organization of the law courts are mixed with matters which to us are of a purely private character.

The impact of the revival of the study of Roman law[1] soon made itself felt, and in the thirteenth century Bracton's famous *Treatise on the laws and customs of England* mentions the distinction between *ius publicum* and *ius privatum*, following the aforementioned passage of the Institutes.[2] The theoretical elaboration of this dichotomy in subsequent centuries has had no immediate impact on legal practice and has even left some countries completely untouched. It has for many centuries failed to have any impact on French jurists, and only gained influence there around the middle of the seventeenth century, when the opposition was clearly perceived between *res publica* and private interests. It is therefore not surprising that the teaching of public law in French universities did not start until the second half of the eighteenth century.[3] This contributed to a general recognition of the distinction between private and public law, which in the Middle Ages had been familiar only to Roman lawyers. In the Low Countries Philip Wielant (*d.* 1520) was the first jurist to make the distinction expressly, in his *Practyke Civile*, where he linked public law to the common good, including such matters as the imposition of taxes and the construction of harbours and fortifications.

For a long time European law was indivisible, without special courts for constitutional and administrative cases – a state of affairs that still prevails to some extent in England. The reason was political, as public law was associated with a strong monarchy, and the resistance to the rise of a distinct public law (with courts of its own) was part and parcel of the liberal fight against absolutism. The unity of the law was the palladium of freedom and equality, whereas the

---

[1] See R. C. van Caenegem, *An historical introduction to private law* (Cambridge, 1992), 45–84, and the bibliography there.
[2] Ed. S. Thorne, II (Cambridge, Mass., 1968), 25–6. Glanvill, in the late twelfth century distinguished the *causae seculares* in *criminalia* and *civilia* (I, I) (ed. G. D. G. Hall, London, 1965, 3).
[3] G. Chevrier, 'Remarques sur l'introduction et les vicissitudes de la distinction du "jus privatum" et du "jus publicum" dans les œuvres des anciens juristes français', *Archives de philosophie du droit* (n.s.) I (1952), 5–77.

emergence of public law beside and above private law was an expression of absolutism and the inaccessibility of the *raison d'état*[4] invoked by the prince who was *legibus solutus*, 'not bound by the laws'. Eventually public law was fully recognized as a separate branch in most countries, although measures were taken to prevent the rise of kings or bureaucrats operating above the heads of the citizens and outside the control of the judges. The absolutist idea that matters of public law ought to be removed from the jurisdiction of ordinary courts was most strikingly expressed in Prussia in 1653 where it was said in so many words that 'Regierungssachen sind keine Justizsachen' ('the business of the government is no judicial matter').

The definition of public law as a separate field was on the other hand also sustained by the struggle for the autonomy of private law as a sphere that was immune from the dreaded omnipotence of the state. If public law had to be left to the state, the least one could do was to define its terrain as exactly as possible and to safeguard as much as possible the sphere of the free individual, i.e. private law. The more sharply the limits of public law were drawn, the safer would the citizen be from the tentacles of political power. Whereas the older legal order had encompassed everyone, both governors and governed, modern Europe produced a new system, containing two co-existing legal worlds, that of the relations between monarch and subjects, and that of the relations between the citizens mutually.[5] It is because of these political overtones that the distinction between public and private law is even today much debated and in no way evident to everyone. Hence the reservation of conflicts on these matters to important courts such as the Court of Cassation in Belgium and the Tribunal des Conflits in France.

Until the nineteenth century, and even beyond, English doctrine proudly maintained that, unlike the Continent, England knew no separate public law or public-law courts: the traditional common law assumed that the law was indivisible in the sense that the same body of rules applied to the government and its agents as well as to private citizens. This position, defended by the famous Oxford professor A. V. Dicey (*d.* 1922), was difficult to maintain when it became clear

---

[4] The expression *ragion di stato* appeared in Italy in the first decades of the sixteenth century and gained wide acceptance thanks to Giovanni Botero's book *Della ragion di stato*, of 1589.

[5] See on all this D. Grimm, 'Zur politischen Funktion der Trennung von öffentlichem und privatem Recht in Deutschland' in D. Grimm (ed.), *Recht und Staat der bürgerlichen Gesellschaft* (Frankfurt, 1987), 84–103.

that England too was producing a vast body of administrative law and numerous special tribunals dealing, *inter alia*, with the new situation created by the welfare state. It remains clear, however, that even today public law is not a familiar or important category in English legal thinking.[6]

All these developments are reflected in the teaching in the universities. Public law, particularly the *ius publicum internum*, was treated sporadically in the Middle Ages, and more generally from the sixteenth century onwards, in the framework of the lectures on Roman, canon and feudal law. Here the students became familiar with the problems concerning *regalia* (royal rights), the relations between state and Church and between ruler and subjects. Aspects of constitutional law were moreover studied in the light of Aristotelian theory; in fact the two disciplines – public law and political theory – were not clearly distinguished until the seventeenth century. Interest in public law was greatest in Germany, partly because of the complicated structure of the Holy Roman Empire. Chairs for public law were founded in several mainly Lutheran universities in the first half of the seventeenth century;[7] textbooks on public law began to appear around the same time.[8]

In the southern Netherlands the Austrian government was keen on the modernization of the legal curriculum in the University of Leuven, and particularly on the introduction of public law. Consequently *ius publicum* was intermittently recognized as a teaching subject, but, because of resistance from traditional and clerical circles, no permanent chair of public law was founded there in the course of the eighteenth century.[9] The same applied to France, so that in the face of the resistance of the law faculties the government took the initiative to found a chair for *droit public*. This took place in 1773, not in the universities, but in the Collège de France, which depended directly on the crown. The measure was taken partly to attract young

[6] We cannot enter into this complicated question here, but see W. Robson, *Justice and administrative law* (London, 1928) and the remarks in P. Stein and J. Shand, *Legal values in western society* (Edinburgh, 1974), 34 and in J. H. Baker, *An introduction to English legal history* (3rd edn, London, 1990), 172, 174–5. See also P. P. Craig, *Public law and democracy in the United Kingdom and the United States of America* (Oxford, 1990).

[7] See on all this the fundamental book of M. Stolleis, *Geschichte des öffentlichen Rechts in Deutschland*, I: *Reichspublizistik und Policeywissenschaft 1600–1800* (Munich, 1988).

[8] D. Otto, *De iure publico imperii Romani* (Wittenberg, 1616); C. Mantz, *Summa iuris publici* (Ingolstadt, 1623); D. Arumaeus, *Discursus academici de iure publico* (Jena, 1620–3).

[9] P. Godding, 'La distinction entre droit public et droit privé dans les Pays-Bas Méridionaux avant 1800', *Rapports belges au VIIᵉ Congrès international de droit comparé* (Brussels, 1966), 1–24.

Frenchmen who used to study this discipline in foreign universities.[10]

The teaching of legal history is another indication of the separate and secondary role of public as compared to private law. In Belgian universities, for example, several generations of lawyers have heard lectures on the historical introduction to civil law (or to the Civil Code), but not until the late 1960s were courses provided on the historical introduction to public law.[11] This example may serve as one among many proofs of Heyen's thesis that the 'civil origin of modern legal history has overshadowed research on the history of public law'.[12] It is not by chance that the monumental *Handbuch* edited from 1973 by Professor H. Coing for the Max-Planck-Institut für Europäische Rechtsgeschichte in Frankfurt[13] concerns private and not public law (recent plans of the Institute aim at remedying this state of affairs).

This situation goes back a long way. To the learned jurists of the Middle Ages and those of Modern Times the exact contents and structure of private law were no problem: persons, things and obligations had from the start been the subject of classic expositions and lectures. Public law was different, for it had to get along without ordered and comprehensive treatises. Lawyers groped painfully towards a clear view of the exact field of public law and its component parts. Its doctrine has for a long time found much of its inspiration, as I said before, in political theory as well as in the *Corpus Iuris*.

As public law is the law of the state, it is not amiss to say a few words about the latter term. The old Latin *status* has only acquired its present meaning in the course of many centuries. At first *status* simply meant 'situation'. Thus the *Corpus Iuris* speaks of the *status rei Romanae* and medieval charters of the *status regni*, meaning the state of the Roman republic or the state of the kingdom: monks who received gifts from monarchs promised to pray *pro statu regni* ('for the welfare of the kingdom'). Gradually the second substantive was dropped and 'state' acquired its present meaning. Thus Accursius, in the first half of the

---

[10] See the chapter by H. Coing, 'Die juristische Fakultät und ihr Lehrprogramm' in H. Coing (ed.), *Handbuch der Quellen und Literatur der neueren europäischen Privatrechtsgeschichte*, II: *Neuere Zeit (1500–1800)*, I: *Wissenschaft* (Munich, 1977), 3–102.

[11] The present author was appointed to give this course in the University of Ghent in 1968, where the teaching led to two textbooks, which can be seen as forerunners to the present work, i.e. R. C. van Caenegem, *Over koningen en bureaucraten. Oorsprong en ontwikkeling van de hedendaagse politieke instellingen* (2nd edn, Amsterdam, 1980) and R. C. van Caenegem, *Geschiedkundige inleiding tot het recht*, II: *Publiekrecht* (Brussels, 1988).

[12] See the Preface in E. V. Heyen (ed.), *Geschichte der Verwaltungsrechtswissenschaft* (Frankfurt, 1982).

[13] See above, n. 10.

thirteenth century, in his gloss on Digest 1, 1, 1, 2, talks of public law existing *ad statum conservandum, ne pereat* ('to preserve the state so that it shall not perish'). The modern usage has the advantage that the term can be used for states of various regimes and not only *regna* (kingdoms). Thus it can be used for democracies, where the other historic term, 'domination' (*seigneurie, gosudarstvo*), would be less appropriate. It is not by chance that the expression 'state of the kingdom' has lost the second word, because in the course of the centuries the state has become more important than the monarchy. Originally the kingdom belonged to the king, but in the eighteenth century the opposite position was reached, and the king belonged to the state: Frederick the Great of Prussia called himself the 'servant of the state'.

### Geographical framework

We shall focus our attention on the European tradition, whose impact on the modern world was paramount. We include, however, two great powers which are wholly or partly situated outside the European frontiers, the United States of America and the Union of Soviet Socialist Republics (now the Commonwealth of Independent States). The reason is obvious. The people in the United States who drafted the Constitution were Europeans who had crossed the Atlantic, or their descendants, and whose ties with Europe in general and the United Kingdom in particular were very close: the two main sources of inspiration of the founding fathers were the English common law and the European Enlightenment. The Soviet Union also belonged in many ways to the European world: its main constitutional developments have taken place in the European part of its territory and the ideological basis of the Soviet state was the philosophy of a German nineteenth-century philosopher. Both the American and the Soviet experience have been largely inspired by Western-European creativity. As the fundamental laws of the United States, Western Europe and the Soviet Union have deeply influenced the rest of the world, their historical study is a contribution to the understanding of constitutional realities, tendencies and problems of the present world.

We shall, as was pointed out, pay attention to the English and American experience as well as the continental. This is all the more natural as we are not faced here with the profound and fundamental difference between common law and civil law, which is characteristic of private law.[14] The English constitutional evolution was not essentially distinct from that of the Continent. There were differences in timing and accent, but the main ingredients such as monarchy, feudalism, absolutism, parliaments, constitutions, bureaucratization and the welfare state were common. The absence from the English common law of the *Corpus Iuris Civilis*, which was so vital a factor in the private field, was unimportant for constitutional development, as medieval parliaments were just as vital in common-law as in civil-law countries; absolutism flourished in Tudor England in spite of the predominance of the common law, and republicanism flourished in the Italian city-states in spite of the predominance of the *leges* of the Roman emperors.

### Chronological limits

Our story starts with the new world that rose in the early Middle Ages from the collapse of the Roman empire in the West. It is in those countries that, under the aegis of the Latin Church, the Roman-Germanic world which led in unbroken continuity to modern Europe took shape. If our *terminus a quo* is, therefore, roughly the fifth century AD, our *terminus ad quem* is our own time. This introduction is, however, a work of legal history and not of comparative law. New experimental creations which are still going on and are hotly debated – such as the 'Constitution' of the European Community and the coming shape of the ex-Soviet Union – will therefore not be studied in any systematic way. The public law of the Third Reich and the Soviet Constitutions, down to the one of 1977, belong to the past and are therefore included. The national-socialist and communist regimes, which collapsed in 1945 and 1989, were the two main twentieth-century adversaries of the western liberal model, and the study of their political organization falls therefore within the scope of this book. Their defeat has ensured the survival, possibly for a long time, of the constitutional and parliamentary form of government. The Constitution of the French Fifth Republic will not be studied, as it is of recent date and broke in an important way with those of the Third and Fourth Republics. The same applies to the Constitution of the German Federal Republic, which is very much a phenomenon of our own

---

[14] In the present author's *Historical introduction to private law* (see above n. 1) an attempt was made to explain the parallel, but very different development of both systems.

time. As our narrative, encompassing fifteen centuries, unfolds, the following main periods will easily be distinguished.

The 350 years from the fifth to the middle of the eighth century were the era of the tribal monarchy. Germanic peoples conquered the West Roman empire, removed its last emperor and divided its territory into semi-nomadic kingdoms, which were often at war with each other. The exercise of authority in this 'Time of Troubles' took on a very different shape from the imperial bureaucracy of the empire. Efforts to keep up the appearances of the past were of no avail: Greek and Roman Antiquity was gone forever. It had, however, not yet been replaced by a new order.

Between the middle of the eighth and the late ninth century the Carolingian dynasty made an impressive effort to give this rudderless society a new sense of direction and confidence. In the field of public law Charlemagne's extensive and forcefully governed empire made great and creative strides. His crowning as Roman emperor indicated a restoration of the normal situation. Henceforth Western Europe considered itself on an equal footing with Byzantium: both had an emperor, a spiritual leader and a capital – Constantinople was a real one already, Aachen was supposed to develop into one.

The 'First Europe' collapsed in the course of the ninth century. On the Continent the tenth and eleventh centuries witnessed political division and extreme fragmentation. Political life became a small-scale affair. In some areas the seigniory – land and peasants in a radius of often no more than 5 km, around a feudal castle – became the only operative entity in public law. The kingdom and in some cases even the duchies and counties had lost all relevance to the daily exercise of public authority. Life was dominated by feudalism and seigniories; the political institutions of the state, as we conceive them, were weakened or, in some regions, extinct. As there was often no authority to compel the feudal lords, entrenched in their castles, a situation of permanent anarchy prevailed in many areas.

The reaction to this intolerable state of affairs led, around AD I 100, to a rebirth of monarchical power and of a true state administration. Profiting from an economic and intellectual leap forward, the *Fürstenstaat*, i.e. the kingdoms, duchies and counties led by powerful rulers, organized itself and tamed the feudal lords and their 'adulterine' castles: the power of the state was re-established and respected. The nascent sovereign monarchies used their new human and financial resources to build the semi-bureaucratic administration of the later

Middle Ages. The familiar nation states of Europe have arisen in those centuries, even though they were not yet 'absolute': their freedom of action was still limited by imperial and papal authority and the power of proud barons and towns. These limitations were thrown off in the classic age of absolutism, from the sixteenth to the eighteenth century. The Reformation put an end to the universal authority of the papal curia, and the Roman empire became a national, German monarchy. Urban autonomy was a medieval relic and national parliaments disappeared or became administrative cogs in the machinery of the state. It was the age when an archbishop of Canterbury under Henry VIII could say *'ira regis mors est'* ('the wrath of the king means death') and Louis XIV could say *'L'Etat c'est moi'*. This classic royal absolutism was no universal model, nor did it last forever. In many countries it was sooner or later either transformed into a constitutional and parliamentary monarchy or into the modernized regime of the so-called 'enlightened despots'. Elsewhere the monarchy itself was abolished and replaced by a republican Constitution.

The nineteenth century reaped the fruits of these developments. It was dominated by the liberal idea of a constitutional and parliamentary form of government headed either by a king or a president (who was a sort of republican monarch). This ideal was attained in numerous, but not all, countries. In Central Europe the monarchy, which eventually became constitutional, steered clear of real parliamentary control. The government did not depend on the representatives of the people, nor was it accountable to them but to the ruler, whose personal impact on the politics of the nation remained considerable.

In the twentieth century this liberal model of the state was violently contested. Where constitutional and parliamentary practices had already grown solid roots, the liberal state maintained itself, though not without the replacement of oligarchic by democratic parliaments and moves towards the welfare state. In countries where the liberal tradition was recent and feeble, the nineteenth-century model was severely weakened or even eliminated. This was most marked in Russia, where the tsar, notwithstanding some minor concessions in the early twentieth century, remained an autocratic ruler of a type that was hardly imaginable elsewhere in Europe. In the course of the one year 1917 the country moved from Ancient-Regime autocracy to a soviet state and proletarian dictatorship. A radical rejection of parliamentary democracy also took place in several other countries where constitutionalism and parliamentarianism had no solid historical foundations. In Italy, Portugal and last but not least, Germany, the multi-party parliamentary regime was temporarily abolished, together with the constitutional freedoms, which were considered factors of internal division and national weakness: dictatorial regimes of a rightist complexion were established instead. Sooner or later both the right-wing dictatorships and the monolithic soviet model collapsed and western-style democracy has been vindicated.

### MAIN THEMES

During the past fifteen centuries the constitutional debate has concerned a number of main issues, which we shall now briefly introduce. It is advisable to keep them in mind as a background to the vicissitudes which the nations have at various moments encountered.

### *Monarchy, aristocracy, democracy*

The conflict between monarchy, aristocracy (or oligarchy) and democracy, i.e. between the rule of one person, that of the notables – few in number (in Greek, *oligoi*) and deemed the best (in Greek, *aristoi*) – and that of the people (in Greek, *demos*) is an ever present leitmotiv. After the great Germanic migrations, the monarchy was established everywhere as the personal rule of a member of a thaumaturgic family protected by God (or even descended from some Germanic deity). These kings had stepped forward from the ranks of the leading warriors and landowners, whose support they needed. Those notables, however, all needed the king to guarantee the political continuity of the nation. They consequently were from time to time moved to replace a decrepit dynasty by a younger, promising leading lineage: this was the fate in the kingdom of the Franks of both the Merovingian and the Carolingian dynasties. The balance of power between the crown and the big landowners, the 'barons' of the feudal age, was fragile. In post-Carolingian France the feudal top tried to live without a king: public authority was fragmented *ad infinitum* and every landowning castellan was his own sovereign. This anarchy was, as we have seen, untenable, and the monarchy revived, bringing the barons back under the authority of the crown. Soon it was the turn of the monarchy to push its luck too far in its autocratic endeavour to reduce the nobles and knights to mere subservience: baronial revolts and civil war were the consequence. The monarchy underwent this late-medieval ordeal victoriously and managed to establish its absolute authority, albeit only for the time being. Indeed, it was soon challenged by another sort of notables, not the mailed warriors of bygone days, but the urban bourgeoisie, whose talent and wealth led to economic, and eventually political power. In the northern Netherlands first, and then in England, this new breed of *aristoi* managed to get hold of the state and to run it on their own, either dispensing with kings altogether or in collaboration with a subdued monarchy, bound by the law. This model was imitated elsewhere and led to the classic liberal regimes, where the notables and not the crowned heads held the reins of power.

Except in a few free cities, the plebeian masses had no part in this power game, even though medieval urban militias were occasionally used by kings against barons, and the mob sometimes proved useful to the bourgeoisie when old-fashioned kings had to be toppled. Not until the twentieth century did ordinary people discover that they did not need 'their betters' to run the state, just as the bourgeoisie had previously realized that it could manage without a royal lord and master.

The traditional crowned heads were an extraneous element, imposed from on high. This was not the case with the leaders who stepped forward from the ranks of the common people and were acclaimed by them: Caesars, popular heroes and demagogues. After the dethronement of the oligarchs, democracy can develop in two directions. It can govern itself through elected representatives, committees and judges, even through referendums in which all citizens take part on an equal footing. Alternatively, it can transfer power by way of a plebiscite to a charismatic leader, who conducts an anti-oligarchic, populist policy and founds a Caesarist 'democracy'. Various mixed solutions are also possible, the Constitution of the United States being an interesting example. Here the element of Caesarism, i.e. the personal rule of a president elected by the people from their own ranks, is combined with the indirect democracy of the Senate and the House of Representatives, who can keep possible dictatorial tendencies of the White House in check. At the same time the sacrosanct Constitution, guarded by the judicature, protects everyone against abuse of power by either president or Congress. The old Soviet Union could best be described as an oligarchy supported by plebiscite, as the Communist Party was a co-opted, self-perpetuating elite and its elections a ritual show of popular adherence.

## The legitimation of power

Max Weber's theory about the three forms of legitimate government – charismatic, traditional and rational – is supported by historical evidence. Personal rule is indeed often legitimized, i.e. accepted as justified by the community, through the extraordinary impact of a charismatic leader. Such a figure is rare and cannot create permanent institutions.[15] His successors – often descendants, but devoid of the exceptional gifts of the predecessor – nevertheless share his prestige and that of his lineage. Their authority is based on tradition and frequently also on a religious doctrine which preaches obedience to the powers that be.[16] This traditionalism, usually based on heredity, has the advantage of stability, as it avoids power struggles at every succession. The disadvantage is that it may produce unsuitable rulers, making the quality of the government depend on biological chance and the random results of the genetic code. This inadequate method of selection eventually gave way to a more rational formula, which attributes power to the most dynamic and hopefully ablest politicians, chosen by the people, and officials selected for their academic qualifications (according to cognoscible legal rules excluding unwritten customs and obscure usages). That history has indeed known, from earliest times till our own day, numerous examples of great loyalty, fanatical faith and blind devotion to 'superior' figures needs no further comment. It is striking, however, that people in the Middle Ages and Modern Times have for so long had such a deep veneration for their traditional rulers that they became as it were struck with paralysis when a break with this 'crust of ancient custom' became imperative: even the most enterprising popular leaders often shrank from the brink and did not dare launch a frontal attack on their legitimate prince. Thus, to quote an example from the feudal world, the count of Flanders, Philip of Alsace, who was ready to give battle against his suzerain, King Philip Augustus of France, refrained at the

---

[15] See some recent remarks in R. C. van Caenegem, 'Max Weber: historian and sociologist' in R. C. van Caenegem, *Legal history: a European perspective* (London, 1991), 201–22.

[16] For example: 'Let every soul be subject unto the higher powers, for there is no power but of God: the powers that be are ordained of God' (Paul, Rom. 13:1) and 'Servants, be subject to your masters with all fear; not only to the good and gentle, but also to the forward' (1 Peter 2:18).

last minute from attacking an anointed head and feudal overlord, and gave up the fight (Boves on the Somme, AD 1185). Something similar happened in the urban world when the revolt of Ghent, conducted by James van Artevelde (*d.* 1345) against the count of Flanders and the latter's suzerain, the king of France, ended in failure, *inter alia*, because no solution was found for the question of legitimacy. Similarly, some forty years later, at the time of the English peasants' revolt, it became clear that no legitimate alternative could be devised for the traditional monarchy, even though, in 1381, it was in the hands of the incompetent and tyrannical Richard 11.

After the elimination of the old-style monarchies Europe entered upon a phase of rational and bureaucratic government, although the lure of charismatic leaders remained real enough, even in our own century: witness French Caesarism and leaders of the Duce, Caudillo or Führer-type in Italy, Spain and Germany.

### The sovereign nation state

Among all the social units known to historic Europe the nation state eventually became paramount. It left other formations, some of which were large (empire, papal Church) and others smaller (tribe, kinship, feudal group, regional or urban solidarity), far behind. It is only in our time that supranational as well as regional institutions have again become important.

The nation states had different origins. Some were the political organization of ancient nations. Thus the Old English kingdom became the common framework for the Angles and the Saxons, whom the Venerable Bede already called the *gens Anglorum* (the English nation): in this case ethnic group and state coincided. In France also ethnic unity largely prevailed, although it was not so clear cut as in England; yet, generally speaking, the French state coincided with the French people. At the other end of the spectrum we find states which were anything but ethnically homogeneous. They were the product of dynastic state builders, who united mixed populations under one sceptre: the Habsburg lands are the most notorious model of such a political multinational. Whenever state and nationality did not coincide, tension was liable to arise, leaving scars that are today still painfully visible. The peoples of the Danubian Monarchy went their separate ways after the First World War. In Belgium, consisting of the southern, amputated half of the Burgundian Netherlands and of the prince-bishopric of Liège, the two cultural communities, Dutch-speaking Flanders and French-speaking Wallonia, have moved towards a federal solution. The fate of the old Soviet Union, itself the heir of Imperial Russia, and of Yugoslavia, an artificial post-World War creation, hangs in the balance. In contrast to these centrifugal developments the divergence between state and nationhood has also led to centripetal reactions, i.e. the desire to unite in one vast state all the elements of one people which had become politically estranged through historical vicissitudes: the classic example here is Hitler's aim of reuniting the whole *Deutschtum* in one great Reich.

The states which have been, from the twelfth century till our own day, the fundamental units in European politics, were not only national, they also became sovereign. This meant that they did not consider themselves bound by supranational laws or subject to supranational institutions, so that they freely decided about their own international politics, including war and peace. They were *superior*, sovereign, i.e. higher than any other authority. The *superioritas* of these states did not only concern other states, but had an internal dimension as well, as their citizens were subjected completely and solely to the national lawgiver, the national government and the national judicature, without recourse to any outside authority. This came about because the two overriding structures of the medieval world, the empire and the papacy, had been largely or completely eliminated. When these sovereign states were moreover ruled by absolute autocrats, the subjects were utterly trapped, and emigration was their only way out, although even that escape route was sometimes forbidden by jealous governments.

National sovereignty arose effectively in the twelfth century. The French king Louis VI, for example, in 1124 scornfully resisted the planned intervention in his kingdom by the Roman emperor – German king, Henry V. Less than two centuries later the sharp conflict between King Philip the Fair and Pope Boniface VIII dramatically demonstrated France's emancipation from the papacy. The legal notion of sovereignty also took shape in the twelfth century, when jurists maintained that '*rex est imperator in regno suo*' ('the king is emperor in his kingdom'). This fiction meant that every royal government was sovereign within the national boundaries, as there was no authority above that of an emperor.[17]

---

[17] The theory was soon accepted in official documents. Thus Pope Innocent III in the decretal *Per venerabilem* of 1203 states that the king of France 'recognizes no superior in temporal

This sovereign power may have been useful in medieval times, when the monarchy had an uphill struggle to establish law and order. Afterwards it became a recipe for endless conflicts, and the slaughter of two World Wars – both started as European wars and for national motives – was needed to bring Europe to its senses and to curtail national sovereignty through the creation of a European government, law courts and parliament.

## *The* Rechtsstaat *and the separation of powers*

On the Continent *Rechtsstaat* is a widely used term for a state where the government is bound by the law in its dealings with the citizens: its power is in other words limited by the individual rights of the people. That the citizens are bound by the law in their contacts with each other is obvious: if this were not the case there would be anarchy. The idea that the rulers also have to operate under the law was for a long time not obvious at all; it was in fact frequently rejected on principle. Some scholars distinguish the *Rechtsstaat* from the *Verfassungsstaat* ('law-based state' and 'constitutional state'). The latter concerns the specific liberties guaranteed by the Constitution, the former refers to the duty of the governors always to act legally. As this implies that they should respect individual rights and freedoms, one can say that the *Verfassungsstaat* is included in the wider notion of the *Rechtsstaat*.

Some authors go a step further and make a distinction between the formal and the material *Rechtsstaat*. In the former the authorities are bound by the rules of positive law, in the latter they (and this includes the legislature) are also bound by the dictates of justice. In a material *Rechtsstaat* the rulers must not only act according to the law, but the law itself must respect the rules of justice. The attractiveness of this idea is obvious: numerous rules in Nazi Germany, for example, belonged formally speaking to the positive law of the Third Reich, but offended justice and even humanity. Unfortunately the notion of the material *Rechtsstaat* is difficult to apply in practice, as public opinion is often divided on the content and the criteria of justice: whereas some people believe that fiscal laws which confiscate more than half a citizen's earnings are manifestly unjust, others maintain that every income above average is an injustice and should be taxed accordingly. I shall therefore limit my considerations to the formal *Rechtsstaat*.

matters'. See on all this S. Mochi Onori, *Fonti canonistiche dell' idea moderna dello stato* (Milan, 1951), 162 ff., and W. Ullmann, *Law and politics in the Middle Ages* (s.l., 1975), 102 ff.

The opposite of the *Rechtsstaat* is the *Polizeistaat* ('police state') or the *Machtsstaat* ('state based on might'), where the arbitrary will of the persons in power prevails and the rulers do not have to observe legal norms. In the one case the citizens are governed by laws rather than by people, in the other the opposite applies.

A judiciary which is independent of the political and administrative authorities is an essential element of the *Rechtsstaat*. Only the judges can in conscience and complete freedom reprimand the government and even force it to obey the law and redress injustice. A judiciary which is in the hands of the government would turn the *Rechtsstaat* into a hypocritical farce. Hence the separation of powers – a fruit of eighteenth-century theory – is an inseparable element of the rule of law. It not only provides for a separate and independent judiciary, but it also separates legislative from executive power, the daily activity of the government having another aim than that of the lawgiver, whose work should be more concerned with the long term.

The word *Rechtsstaat* is of relatively recent date, as it appeared in the early nineteenth century in Germany;[18] it became widespread after Robert von Mohl's *Die Polizeiwissenschaft nach den Grundsätzen des Rechtsstaates* (published in three volumes, Tübingen, 1832–4) and Otto Bähr's *Der Rechtsstaat. Eine publizistische Skizze*, of 1864. The term was adopted literally in the Dutch language where it appeared for the first time in 1870, in a text dealing with Thorbecke, the father of the liberal Dutch Constitution of 1848. In France the phrase *Etat de droit* is recent: although it sporadically appeared shortly before the Second World War, it is only now coming into general use. The English equivalent would be the rule of law[19] (and the *Rechtsstaat* could be described as 'the state where the rule of law prevails', the 'state under law' or the 'law-based state'). Thus A. V. Dicey, author of the authoritative *Law of the Constitution* (1885), described it as 'the absolute supremacy or predominance of regular law as opposed to arbitrary power'.[20]

---

[18] In C. T. Welcker's *Die letzten Gründe von Recht, Staat und Strafe*, I (Giessen, 1813), 25. See A. M. Donner, *Werkt de rechtsstaatsidee bureaucratie in de hand?* (Amsterdam, 1984) 3.

[19] The phrase 'rule of law' was given wide circulation by the Oxford constitutionalist Dicey, who borrowed it from W. E. Hearn (*d.* 1888), first dean of the Law Faculty of Melbourne and author of *The government of England. Its structure and its development* (London, 1867). See H. W. Arndt, 'The origin of Dicey's concept of the rule of law', *Australian Law Journal* 31 (1957), 117–23.

[20] See on all this E. Angermann, *Robert von Mohl 1799–1875. Leben und Werk eines altliberalen Staatsgelehrten* (Neuwied, 1962); A. Funk, *Polizei und Rechtsstaat. Die Entwicklung des staatlichen Gewaltmonopols in Preussen 1848–1914* (Frankfurt, 1986); *Handwörterbuch zur deutschen Rechtsgeschichte*

## History of the rule of law

The fundamental notion of the *Rechtsstaat* or the rule of law was, of course, not conceived out of the blue and introduced without resistance. It was, in fact, the fruit of political conflict and scholarly disputes stretching over many centuries. We believe that three main lines of development can be distinguished: political struggle, the writings of the jurists and treatises of the political theorists.

Around AD 1200 there began in Western Europe a series of documents of the Magna Carta type, which would eventually lead to the modern Declarations of Human Rights. King John's Great Charter of Liberties of 1215 was but one among many similar documents, which were granted at various moments and in numerous countries by kings and other rulers. Their common core was an undertaking by the crown to observe a precisely formulated code of behaviour towards their subjects or, in other words, to respect their rights and liberties, as specified in the charters. The latter were sometimes issued in the course of peaceful negotiations, but others were the result of revolt and military pressure. In some cases the ruler intended honestly to observe them, in others they were no more than manoeuvres to gain time until the royal power was strong enough to suppress the rebels. All those documents were rooted in the feudal world and clearly based on the principle that even crowned heads had to respect certain legal norms and individual rights, rejecting arbitrary rule. Among the main sources were the feudal right of resistance and the feudal principle that a vassal could, by the judgment of his fellow vassals, obtain justice even against his own overlord and in the latter's court. This was clearly an important ingredient of the *Rechtsstaat* idea. Modern absolutism has admittedly curtailed medieval constitutionalism, but in seventeenth-century England the Magna Carta tradition finally won the day. One of the fruits of the Glorious Revolution was the Bill of Rights of 1689 and its logical conclusion, the Act of Settlement of 1701, which proclaimed the independence of the judicature from the government.[21] The repercussions of these English

---

IV (Berlin, 1990), 367–75 (by M. Stolleis); R. C. van Caenegem, 'The *Rechtsstaat* in historical perspective' in R. C. van Caenegem, *Legal history: a European perspective* (London, 1991), 185–99; K. W. Nörr, *Eher Hegel als Kant. Zum Privatrechtsverständnis im 19. Jahrhundert* (Paderborn, 1991).

[21] The principle still stands today, but it should be understood that the judges concerned are those in the top courts (High Court, Court of Appeal, House of Lords), numbering less than 150 altogether, and not the large number of magistrates throughout the country, who are under the lord chancellor's authority.

developments on the American and European Constitutions are well known and will be studied in detail later.

The learned lawyers also have discussed whether public authority – imperial or royal – stood under or above the law. A few examples of contradictory attitudes may suffice here. Some jurists, such as Jean Bodin (*d.* 1596), were resolutely in favour of absolutism, i.e. the theory that the prince was not bound by the laws, as he could make and unmake them and could not bind himself (Dig. 1, 4, 1). The logic of this thesis was aptly formulated as follows in Bodin's *Six livres de la République*: 'It is necessary that the sovereign should in no way be subjected to somebody else's command and that he should be able to give laws to the subjects and abolish useless laws in order to make others. This cannot be done by anyone who is bound by laws or under other people's command: that is why the [Roman] law says that the prince is free from the power of the laws'. It is interesting to note Bodin's appeal to royal power as a tool for modernization and the abolition of outdated, medieval rules. Other jurists, such as Henry de Bracton (*d.* 1268), author of a famous treatise on the English common law, were resolutely in favour of the opposite theory, that the king was 'under God and under the law'. His opinion was shared by François Hotman (*d.* 1590), a countryman but adversary of Bodin, who, commenting on the Digest 1, 3, 31, wrote that its political consequences were deplorable, as they would make imperial power *infinitum, immensum et . . . absolutum*. This would lead to 'the most disgusting servitude', delivering the nations to the whims of 'any demented or monstrous tyrant'.

There was a third group, amongst whom we may count the glossator Accursius (*d.* 1260), who accepted, on the authority of Roman law, that the emperor was indeed *legibus solutus* ('not bound by the laws'), but that nevertheless he more than anyone else was expected to obey the laws, as his own position was based on them. Since, however, the Roman Constitution knew of no authority above the emperor and since no one could sit in judgment over himself or be judged by someone of lower rank, there was no institutional possibility to force an emperor who failed freely to obey the law. This interpretation, implied in Accursius' gloss on the aforementioned passage in the Digest, viewed the *legibus solutus* principle as an organizational rather than a substantial problem.[22] Many pronouncements on this

---

[22] B. Tierney, '"The prince is not bound by the law". Accursius and the origins of the modern state', *Comparative Studies in Society and History* 5 (1962), 378–400.

age-old question could be quoted here, but we will limit ourselves to a few of the most striking. Around 1300 Giles of Rome maintained that it was 'better to be governed by a king than by the law' and that kings ought to be *super justitiam legalem* ('above justice based on the law'). Jean Bodin put it even more starkly when he wrote that the law 'was nothing else but the command of the highest power', adding that 'majesty is the highest power over citizens and subjects, and not bound by the law'. He voiced the opinion of many civilians and canonists who, beginning with Azo (*d.* 1230), had placed emperors and kings above the law, calling the monarch *origo iuris* ('the origin of the law') and *viva et animata lex* ('the living and animated law'), or even *tamquam quidem corporalis Deus* ('as it were a bodily God'). Baldus (*d.* 1400) went so far as to write *'imperator est ipsum imperium'* ('the emperor is the empire itself'), a foretaste of the famous '*L'Etat c'est moi*'. Charondas le Caron (*d.* 1617) was more on Accursius' wavelength when he wrote that kings ought to obey the law if they did not want to become tyrants, but that they were 'exempt from the sanctions of the laws because their persons were not subjected to any judge, as they recognized God only as their sovereign and the sole judge of their actions'. The jurists also held that the divinely appointed kings combined the three powers – legislative, executive and judicial – in their own hands. All this was changed radically by the American and French Revolutions, which introduced the separation of powers and based the right to govern not on the will of God but of the people. In the seventeenth and eighteenth centuries the jurists of the Natural Law School – Grotius (*d.* 1645), Pufendorf (*d.* 1694) and especially Wolff (*d.* 1754) – defended the idea that all human beings were born with certain rights, which ought to be safe from any legislative or governmental encroachment. This placed them among the defenders of the *Verfassungsstaat*, where various human rights are guaranteed by the Constitution.

A third line of development can be found in theological and philosophical reflection. The Church Fathers already defended the notion that positive law ought not to contravene God's will. As St Ambrose (*d.* 397) squarely put it: *'non legibus rex solutus est'* ('the king is not free from the laws') – no doubt with the famous passage from the Digest in mind. The canonists, who vehemently defended the papal primacy, nevertheless reminded their readers that 'it is allowed to no one to act against natural law'. An imposing line of philosophers, beginning with Marsilius of Padua (*d.* 1342), defended points of view irreconcilable with unfettered government. According to Marsilius, the ruler is bound by the law, as he is a citizen exercising a governmental function and liable to be called to account for his deeds 'as any subject who has broken the law'. Famous modern thinkers in this line are Johannes Althusius (*d.* 1638), John Locke (*d.* 1704) and Montesquieu (*d.* 1755). Locke maintained that liberty can only exist when the relations between citizen and state are precisely established by laws which cannot be changed unilaterally by those in power. This could best be realized by the separation of powers, whose best-known theoretical defender was Montesquieu. Locke believed that even after the contractual transfer of political power from the people to the monarch (the idea of the Roman *lex regia*), the contracting parties maintained their rights and liberties. Hence his thesis that 'the legislative or supreme authority cannot assume to itself a power to rule by extemporary arbitrary decrees, but is bound to dispense justice and decide the rights of the subject by promulgated standing laws, and known authorized judges'. And again: 'For all the power the government has, being only for the good of society, as it ought not to be arbitrary and at pleasure, so it ought to be exercised by promulgated and established law, that both the people may know their duty and be safe and secure within the limits of the law, and the rulers too kept within their bounds'.

It is noteworthy that as Montesquieu was giving the theory of the separation of powers and the supremacy of the law its classic expression, another French philosopher, J. J. Rousseau (*d.* 1778), defended the opposite view. According to him no resistance could be tolerated to a government based on the *volonté générale*, which meant that whosoever governed in the name of the people could disregard existing laws. It was the old idea of the state being above the law, but adapted to a new, democratic age. As the sixteenth-century absolutist authors had used *princeps legibus solutus* to defend the modern *Fürstenstaat* against feudalism and privileges, so Rousseau's ideas sustained the onslaught of the masses on 'their betters'. His pronouncements were unambiguous: 'the sovereign being formed by the individuals who compose him, has no interest contrary to theirs, nor could he have, since it is impossible that the body wants to do harm to all its limbs . . . and it cannot harm any one of them in particular'. Hence: 'whosoever refuses to obey the general will, shall be forced to by the whole body: which only means that he will be forced to be free'. Thus at the threshold of the modern world the old polemic about *princeps legibus solutus* was revived and placed in a new perspective.

## The welfare state

So far we have talked about the limits imposed on political power in order to safeguard the citizen's freedom in the framework of a reliable system of law, binding on everyone. In social terms this is the prosperous and careful *paterfamilias*, who is prepared to go about his business freely and responsibly. The *liber homo* of Magna Carta was such a person, and so was the enterprising bourgeois of the liberal state. He, and not the state, was supposed to create wealth: it was not the government's task to be a universal entrepreneur and employer. Some groups, however, were forgotten in this picture: the serfs ignored by Magna Carta and the proletariat left out in the nineteenth century. What was the real significance of constitutional freedom for the have nots who owned only the air they breathed and were at the mercy of the iron laws of economics? To them a strong state, which looked after their welfare, seemed more desirable, for it could guarantee them bread, work and social security. The 'caring state' or welfare state does not see its only role in the creation of a legal framework for a flourishing *laissez-faire*, but wants to intervene in economic life, create or at least stimulate prosperity, distribute equally and provide for everyone an existence that is not only legally but also economically safe. It is, however, clear that if the state is supposed to look after everything and everyone, everybody will come to depend on the state and its political and bureaucratic elites. It is only in the twentieth century that, apart from some isolated forerunners, these social and economic concerns found their way into the Constitutions: the right to employment, medical care and education.

The welfare state is a modern phenomenon, but the caring state is much older. Early medieval kings considered it their Christian duty to protect the oppressed and the poor, particularly widows and orphans. The capitularies of the Carolingian kings contain numerous measures for the protection of the *pauperes* against the rapacity of the *potentes*, and we know that Louis the Pious started a large-scale enquiry at the beginning of his reign in order to give back to oppressed peasants the land or the free status of which they had been deprived. Thus also the count of Flanders, Charles the Good, murdered in 1127, had taken measures against urban hoarders of grain, who let the poor die of hunger on the doorsteps of their stone houses. The French king Louis IX is famous for his protection of needy widows and orphans. Other rulers, however, sided with the rich and powerful and neglected their duty of protection. The state was often in the hands of the powerful and wealthy, and if it was the duty of that state to protect the weak, it had to protect them against itself. In other words, the powerful were supposed to protect the weak against the powerful! No wonder that the weak were often left to their fate. Absolute monarchs spent lavishly on the luxuries of court life and on dynastic wars, while smallholders were crushed by a variety of charges and even died of hunger (as happened in the glorious day of the Sun King). Restricted suffrage and the elitist parliaments it produced until well into the nineteenth century were not much better: social history tells a tale of oppression of the poor, harsh punishments for even minor theft, imprisonment for debt in gaols that were insanitary and murderous. As Magna Carta had protected the feudal landowners but not their serfs, thus the liberal Constitutions protected the bourgeoisie but had little to offer the destitute who depended on it. The English workhouse was there to save people from starvation, but also to make life so mean that the inmates might well prefer any job in any factory to the workhouse. In the twentieth century, when the salaried masses acquired a solid impact on politics, the situation changed, and farmers, workers, tenants and disabled and unemployed people were protected by the state. Through political, mainly parliamentary action, they learned to look after themselves instead of counting on the goodwill of others.

All these developments suggest that in the course of the centuries the state has adopted three attitudes towards the problem of inequality. In the Old European age legal as well as economic inequality was openly and unashamedly accepted, and the political top sided with the upper classes. During the liberal age equality in law became a question of principle, and the state treated all citizens as equal, since they were all equal before the law: the courts turned a blind eye on the divide between rich and poor. In the twentieth century governments and parliaments have again openly recognized the existing social and economic inequality, but this time with the avowed aim of protecting the weaker groups and taking their side in many respects.

The history of the welfare state goes back to the eighteenth century and the enlightened monarchs. It is indeed both in the governmental initiatives and the theoretical works of that age, particularly in German lands, that we find the belief that the state ought to care for the material, cultural and moral well-being of the people, from the cradle to the grave. The enlightened king, the 'first servant of the state', was responsible for that policy. He knew what was best for his subjects, because his position and education gave him a wider and correcter understanding of the needs of society. He had to look after the welfare of the citizens, who were in no position to decide for themselves: 'everything for the people, nothing by the people'! Whereas in the past the king had the religious duty to look after the souls of his subjects, to protect the Church and to prosecute the heretics, henceforth it was his rational task to build a welfare state. This eighteenth-century line of thought was continued in the nineteenth: William I in the kingdom of the Netherlands and Bismarck in Germany – with his *Kulturkampf* and his system of social security – come to mind. It is not always understood that this tradition was continued in the socialist countries of the twentieth century, where until recently the almighty and omnipresent state, led by the moral and intellectual elite of the Communist Party, was supposed to lead the toiling masses to a bright material and moral future. In present-day Western Europe the two tendencies coexist, and an attempt is made to combine a liberal Constitution and a free-market economy with the welfare state and the bureaucratization it implies.

### The importance of constitutional law

The debate on the best political organization of society has been going on for centuries, and never more so than today. Concern with public law in general and constitutional law in particular has never disappeared from western consciousness.[23] The following synopsis may illustrate its importance for the generations that succeeded each other since the Middle Ages.

Innumerable political conflicts, national and international, were caused by struggles for the Constitution. The first major conflict

---

[23] Law and the settlement of disputes as practised in the West are held in little regard in some other great civilizations, such as China and Japan, where 'the harmony of the world demands that disputes be solved through conciliation and where the law, good for the barbarians, should only intervene in criminal matters, if there is no hope for redemption for the criminal' (R. David, *Les avatars d'un comparatiste* (Paris, 1982), 241). Cf. the remarks in H. Coing, 'Das Recht als Element der europäischen Kultur', *Historische Zeitschrift* 238 (1984), 4, 14.

which shook the medieval world was the Investiture Struggle. It concerned the opposing claims of *sacerdotium* and *regnum*, priesthood and kingship. In modern parlance it concerned the relationship between ideology and the state. Was it proper for the government to control the country's religion and its role in the life of the nation, or did the Church belong to a higher, supranational order, which was not linked to any particular state, let alone subjected to it? The war between Emperor Henry IV and Pope Gregory VII was waged again in other times and with other arguments between Boniface VIII and Philip the Fair, and Clement VII and Henry VIII. It also divided the Lutherans, who accepted the protection of the ruler, and the Calvinists, who wanted the 'saints' to dominate the state.

Several urban revolts, some being aimed at kings and lords, others at local oligarchies, were caused by the desire for democracy. Numerous peasant revolts were supposed to re-establish the 'good old law' which had been perverted by evil men. And popular resistance in the medieval kingdoms led to the limitation of arbitrary rule both by the proclamation of charters of liberties and through the impact of parliament. In Modern Times a series of great national revolts were aimed against tyrannical governments, which attempted to brush aside medieval Constitutions and to introduce 'absolute', i.e. unfettered, autocracy. The chain is well known, leading from the revolt of the Low Countries against Philip II of Spain, the English rising against Charles I, the American War of Independence and the French Revolution of 1789 to the February Revolution of 1917 in Russia, which toppled the regime of the tsars.[24]

After the First World War Europe became involved in a dramatic conflict between the defenders of liberal democracy and the dictatorships of right and left, which dominated most of the century and was only resolved in its last decade. All these contests concerned, of course, the struggle for political power, but it is undeniable that the preference

---

[24] See the classic analysis by C. Brinton, *The anatomy of revolution* (3rd edn, New York, 1965). It is surprising that the author ignores the Dutch revolt and starts with the English Puritans of the seventeenth century. A similar oversight occurs in L. Stone, 'The results of the English revolutions of the seventeenth century' in J. G. A. Pocock (ed.), *Three British Revolutions: 1641, 1688, 1776* (Princeton, 1980), 24, who writes of the events of 1640–60 as England's only 'Great Revolution' and 'the first in the history of Western Civilization since the fall of Rome'. He does, however, refer to the Low Countries on p. 94, where he speaks of England having 'a social configuration very different from that of any country in Europe, except Holland'. Similarly C. Hill, 'A bourgeois revolution', in the same volume, p. 134, writes that England in the late seventeenth century was a freer country than any in Europe, 'except possibly the bourgeois Netherlands'.

for a particular form of government also motivated the parties. Consequently these wars and revolts often led to the solemn proclamation of fundamental charters which were expected to establish a better Constitution and to preserve the newly gained rights and liberties. Legal awareness had deep roots in western society and the question of legitimacy was taken very seriously. Also the strength of protest against unlawful behaviour betrays western attachment to, and faith in, the law as the cornerstone of society.

It is, however, not only on the battlefield that constitutional debate was settled: theologians, philosophers and jurists have for centuries taken part in it. During the First Middle Ages, until *c.* 1100, Holy Writ and the Fathers of the Church were the main sources of inspiration. We refer to such biblical figures as Melchisedek and David, to symbols and images such as the *civitas terrena* and the *civitas Dei* (the earthly city and the city of God), and the theory of the two swords, both granted by God, the temporal one being wielded by the princes and the (higher) spiritual sword by the clergy. A rational, scholarly analysis of political forms was undertaken in the Second Middle Ages, under the impact of Aristotle. Authors such as Marsilius of Padua subjected public law to a critical examination and posed questions about the *raison d'être* of the state and about the role of the people and the clergy in public life.

Numerous jurists have also taken part in the debate, and each of the main legal systems that coexisted in Old European society has contributed some specific element to it. Feudal law was important because it viewed kings not merely as rulers and heads of state, but also as feudal lords who were bound to their vassals by contracts, which created mutual rights and obligations. Feudal tenants had claims as well as duties, and if a lord treated his vassals/subjects unlawfully, they were freed from their obligations and empowered to resist their unjust suzerain (*ius resistendi*). Ever since the twelfth century Europe has never been without treatises on feudal law where this vassal relationship between governors and governed was expounded.

Roman law, which in the twelfth century embarked upon its conquest of the western legal mind, was the voice of imperial centralization and absolutism. At least from the days of Frederick I Barbarossa (*d.* 1190) its impact on the thoughts and actions of medieval kings was unmistakable. It belonged to a world which had never heard of feudalism, and was in fact opposed to everything feudal society held dear. Rome knew of no autonomous sources of legitimate authority: concentration, not diffusion of power, was her leading principle. The *Corpus Iuris* preached unilateral subjection to the ruler, new laws issued according to his pleasure (no question here of the consensus of the tenants in chief) and a bureaucracy dependent on the central government (instead of local chiefs whose independence was guaranteed by landed wealth and hereditary tenure). The *Corpus Iuris* was an inexhaustible source of inspiration for the advocates of the modern *Fürstenstaat* as against the 'feudal anarchy'. Their adversaries, however, who preferred urban autonomy and strong parliaments, also managed to find arguments in Justinian's law book. This seeming contradiction is understandable when it is realized that medieval jurists did not hesitate to quote authoritative pronouncements out of context and were not averse to fictions. Thus the *Corpus Iuris* said that 'what concerns all should be approved by all', an excellent argument for parliamentarianism, as it suggested that on business that concerned all the people the king had to consult them or their representatives and obtain their approval. That, in fact, the phrase in question had – in the *Corpus* – nothing to do with public law (which would anyhow have been absurd in the late Roman empire), but dealt with the organization of tutelage and the role of all the tutors, did not bother the jurists.[25] Nor did they shun fictions: they not only, as we have seen, proclaimed kings to be 'emperors in their own kingdoms', but even promoted the free city state to a (collective) emperor, which was a way of saying that it was a sovereign power. As Bartolus put it: *'civitas sibi princeps est'* ('the city is its own emperor'). However strange this way of thinking and arguing may seem to us, it betrays the ambition to approach the problems of public life by legal analysis and with arguments from the great Roman law books.

The canonists also, who were interested in the papacy and its relations with the empire, made a specific contribution to the debate on public law. Ever since the Investiture Struggle they searched ancient authors and ransacked whole libraries to find authoritative pronouncements on the legal bases of papal imperial doctrines. The classic writers of the twelfth and thirteenth centuries built a juridical foundation for the papal claim to independence from emperors and kings and to universal authority over the Latin Church. Some of those jurists became popes themselves and could implement in governmental

---

[25] See some recent remarks by A. Gouron, 'Aux origines médiévales de la maxime *Quod omnes tangit'*, *Histoire du droit social. Mélanges en hommage à Jean Imbert* (Paris, 1989), 277–86.

practice what they had taught in their lectures and books. However, the classic curialism of the twelfth and thirteenth centuries provoked resistance among some theologians and jurists, who viewed the papacy as an office of the Church and subordinate to it. The commonalty of the 'people of God' spoke through the ecumenical council, which according to the conciliarists wielded the highest authority. Their ideas became popular and were put to the practical test during the conciliar period, in the late fourteenth and the first half of the fifteenth century. Several councils were held in southern Germany, Switzerland and Italy, where numerous representatives from many countries, both clerics and laymen, gathered in what can be described as the earliest form of a European parliament. Afterwards curial centralism gained the upper hand again; a state of affairs that was accentuated by the Council of Trent (1545–63), so that the conciliar movement was shelved for four centuries, until the Second Vatican Council (1962–5).

In England the common lawyers added a distinct and important note to the debate. Their great moment came in the seventeenth century, when the struggle between Stuart absolutism and Parliament divided the country. Among the most important voices heard in the conflict were those of Sir Edward Coke (*d.* 1634), possibly the most learned lawyer of all time, Francis Bacon (*d.* 1626), John Selden (*d.* 1654) and Matthew Hale (*d.* 1676). One of their striking contentions maintained that no one – certainly not the crown, but not even Parliament – was above the common law, and that it belonged to the judges to decide whether a particular Act of Parliament was contrary to its fundamental principles. In their struggle against royal 'sovereignty' they appealed to history, some of them evoking the legend of a free Anglo-Saxon England which had been conquered and oppressed by the Normans, subjected to the 'Norman Yoke' and deprived of her ancient laws and traditions. Others, like Coke, limited themselves to strictly legal arguments and looked for precedents in medieval court rolls, such as judgments declaring new laws null and void for being incompatible with the common law, to support their thesis. It is noteworthy that they did not appeal to modern natural law, which was even then taking shape on the Continent; the more or less mythological common law from England's medieval past had to serve in that capacity. In the following century American lawyers attacking the tyranny of the mother country would appeal both to the common law and to natural law.

On the Continent in the eighteenth century natural law was a mighty weapon against the Ancient Regime and absolute kingship. Numerous jurists took part in the debate on the fundamental conception of the state and defended a rational system, based not on an anointed monarch but on a community of free citizens who accepted a wise 'first servant of the state', an administrator rather than a ruler. This ideal was widespread in the lands of the 'enlightened despots'. Elsewhere, particularly in France, the aim was to hand over the government to the people or at least their elected representatives: the king and his ministers were expected to carry out the will of the nation as expressed through the National Assembly. Here again jurists played a considerable role; the French Revolution carried on a great debate on the law in general and public law in particular.

### Rectilinear or cyclical development

Thanks to modern research we are in a position to survey fifteen centuries of western public law. The picture has, however, been interpreted in very different ways. Some scholars – particularly in the nineteenth century – saw history as a rectilinear march forward of a great idea: the progress of freedom. The famous Oxford professor and bishop, William Stubbs (*d.* 1901), for example, saw a continuous development from the pristine liberty in the Germanic forests via the medieval assemblies towards the apex of the Victorian parliamentary monarchy: the final achievement of history and a universal model. Modern Europe was the ultimate realization of a potential that had been present ever since the collapse of late Roman despotism. Other believers in a linear, ascending development, a secularized Providential History, place the progress of reason in the forefront. They see the march of political institutions in the light of a steady emancipation from religious foundations and metaphysical speculation towards systems based on critical rational thought and devised to create the greatest happiness for the greatest number in this world.

Others discern a cyclical pattern. They point at the succession of freedom, followed by oppression and the restoration of freedom through revolt, followed by a new cycle of oppression and rebellion. They point at the free Frankish peasantry, the seigniories of the feudal age, the peasant revolts of the fourteenth century and their merciless oppression by kings and knights. Powerful towns, sometimes allied with the discontented peasantry, also went through cycles of autonomy and subjection: the mighty town of Ghent, which repeatedly revolted against the counts of Flanders in the fourteenth, fifteenth and sixteenth centuries, was invariably conquered, but always emerged more powerful than before, until the final capitulation to the army of Philip II in 1584. The ups and downs of the legislative and the executive power in post-revolutionary France is another example of this modern version of the wheel of fortune: all-powerful legislature at the time of the National Convention, all-powerful executive under Napoleon Bonaparte, all-powerful parliament in the Third and Fourth Republics, and a powerful president and government under the Fifth. The scale of political life also went through similar cycles: from the large-scale empire of Charlemagne to the minute castellanies of the Mâconnais two centuries later, followed by the large modern nation states, and even, under French or German hegemony, European superstates.

Some authors are keen on discovering the laws of history and have tried ever since the time of G. Vico (*d.* 1744), to do in the social sciences what Galileo, Newton and Leibniz did for the physical universe. They see recurrences and true laws of nature. Such is, for example, the succession from monarchy to oligarchy, followed by a plebeian reaction and the establishment of democracy which, after internal strife, results in the rule of a dictatorial saviour and a new autocracy, ready for the next succession of revolts. It is undeniable that this pattern frequently repeated itself in Rome and in medieval and modern Europe.

Another mechanism which we can observe with some regularity tends to push an original idea to its extreme logical consequence and thereby turns an institution that made sense at the beginning into an irrelevant absurdity. The starting point of the papal theocracy, the Gregorian Reform, made sense in the context of the eleventh century. It reacted against the inappropriate subjection of religious life and institutions to kings and other lay lords. To be efficacious this Church movement had to be centrally led and co-ordinated, hence papal centralism. In the course of some two centuries this initial idea was worked out in so many directions and pushed to such extremes that a theocracy arose which stood at the head of the whole of western society, condemned emperors and kings, received whole countries as fiefs of the Holy See and reduced their kings to vassals. The pope, the representative of Christ, had become a universal legislator, judge and teacher, who controlled, *ratione peccati*, the souls even of the crowned heads. Eventually the nations baulked at this draining away of their political substance, and the fall of the old-style theocracy came with the tragedy of Boniface VIII, shortly after his great triumph during the Holy Year of 1300.

The absolute monarchy is another example. It must have been useful in the sixteenth and seventeenth centuries, when it was imperative to establish peace in England after the Wars of the Roses, and in France after the *guerres de religion*, and when post-medieval Europe needed laws for a modern society. But afterwards this extreme form of personal arbitrary rule became an unbearable anachronism.

The sovereign nation state was another of these notions that led, when pushed to its logical extreme, to the most fatal consequences. One can understand that the state, the political expression of the nation, wanted to be free to look after its own interest, without outside interference either from the empire or the papacy or from neighbouring powers. Nations have their own priorities and aims, and should be free to realize them, but when this is done outside any legal order and without any supranational authority, the result is anarchy, where might is right and the national interest the sole criterion. In spite of the jurists' laudable attempts to work out a law of nations, the sovereign states have turned modern Europe into a jungle, with disastrous consequences for that continent and the world.

The state as universal employer and entrepreneur is another idea that was pushed to extremes. Here again one can understand governments trying to stimulate the economy, protect nascent industries, and even build their own armaments factories, but when the state, instead of sticking to its essential political tasks, takes over whole industries, and commerce and banking as well, and becomes one huge entrepreneur and universal employer controlling capital, production and distribution, the idea has run riot.

Similarly, some scholars view Stalinism as the logical, extreme outcome of Leninism, as it carried the dictatorship of the proletariat to excesses which, though not originally envisaged, nevertheless represented a foreseeable if not inevitable stage in the development of the Bolshevik Party.

Imperialism is another case in point. One can see the advantages of great empires, gathering many tribes, nations and cities in one large complex, enjoying stability and the prosperity produced by a large market. Some of these great empires were miracles of organization and had started from humble beginnings: Latium was not at the centre of classical civilization and England was a middle-sized island off the European shore. But here again, once the engine was in full swing, it did not know when to stop. Expansion was followed by expansion and conquest by conquest, as when the Emperor Claudius, who had no wars on his hands at that moment, decided to occupy Celtic Britain just to keep his troops busy. When eventually these great empires stopped providing cultural or economic advantages and only served to enrich the dominating centre and exploit the conquered provinces, disintegration set in.

Finally, there is the idea that the state is an instrument of ideology and that the temporal sword is obliged to impose *manu militari* a specific religion or ideology and to prosecute dissidents, called heretics or deviationists. Here again the primitive idea is understandable in its cultural context. The gods of the tribe were the guardians of its success, so impiety was a public danger. And when the monarchy was based on the one true religion, anything which undermined the latter was a menace to the former. Also, judicial proceedings might be preferable to mob lynching. But when a fully fledged organization, the Inquisition, was instituted to prosecute every new idea or interpretation of the sacred books and to pry into every act and every thought of every individual, a crazy extreme was reached whose terrorizing flames stifled creativity. Nobody knows how many pyres were needed to convince people that to fight the free expression of ideas was not only inhuman but a handicap to the general welfare. This leads one to the reflection that man is often in danger of producing powerful institutions which eventually lead a life of their own, beyond his control and thus enslave him to his own creatures.

Theories about continuity and progress, recurrences and laws of history have not convinced everyone. Some scholars see catastrophes and sudden mutations at work rather than a great providential design; they stress the unforeseen character of many constitutional changes. The Norman occcupation of England in 1066 was a sharp breach in continuity; it halted the normal development of the Old English monarchy, one of the best organized in Europe, and led to a feudal militarist regime and a great loss of freedom for the native population. It was an external event and in no way in the normal line of expectation. And whereas the French Revolution of 1789 could be seen as a long overdue process of modernization under the influence of the British example, what happened after the coup of 10 August 1792 and the Terror was quite out of character with the philosophical climate, and a bloody disappointment of the high hopes of the very civilized eighteenth century. Changes have so often had the wrong effect and so many revolutions have eaten their own children that a chaotic vision of history seems justified. So many forms of government have been tried and discarded, and so often statesmen have stumbled or blundered from one experiment to another that a certain pessimism seems justified. Nevertheless they have from time to time hit upon a formula that has proved valuable and a lasting gain: the constitutional and parliamentary form of government appears a case in point. But even here there were some ironic developments. The Founding Fathers of the American Constitution thought they had found a blueprint for a pastoral small-sized sociey, free from the corruption of Europe's big cities. As it turned out, their Constitution became the legal framework for the biggest and most urbanized industrial state of all time. Not only did their handiwork misfire in this sense, but it was also in many ways the outcome of English history. The combined action of president and congress, upon which it is built, goes back to the medieval condominium of king and parliament, which shows that a modern economy can flourish in an old-fashioned Constitution.

Do people learn from the past or is the history of public law no more than a graveyard of deceased Constitutions, where we can only wonder aimlessly and shake our heads over so much misguided effort? Possibly, but even if people do not learn from the past, they are easily obsessed by it and remain its prisoners. At the time of the Second Vatican Council an interesting experiment was started to promulgate a Constitution for the Church, called 'Lex Ecclesiae Fundamentalis', with traditional elements from the modern Constitutions, including a chapter called 'de Christifidelibus et juribus eorum' ('on the faithful of Christ and their rights'). Nothing, however, came of these plans, inter alia, because the canon lawyers could find no material or terminology in the age-old tradition of ecclesiastical law, which had been too thoroughly dominated by Roman law, absolutism and centralization.[26] Whereas the past can weigh on the present, the bright future can also

---

[26] For texts and comments, see: El proyecto de ley fundamental de la iglesia. Texto bilingue y analysis critico (Navarra, 1971); H. Aymans et al., 'Lex ecclesiae fundamentalis. Bericht über die Arbeitsergebnisse eines kanonistischen symposions in München 1971', Archiv für katholisches Kirchenrecht 140 (1971), 407–506; W. J. Ladue, 'A written constitution for the Church', The Jurist 32 (1972), 1–13; R. Metz, 'Droits de l'homme ou droits du chrétien dans le projet de la lex fundamentalis? Quelques réflexions' in Festschrift für B. Panzram (Freiburg, 1971), 31–41; Legge e Vangelo. Discussione su una Legge fondamentale per la chiesa (Brescia, 1972); P. E. Bolte, Les droits de l'homme et la papauté contemporaine. Synthèse et textes (Montreal, 1975); P. Hebblethwaite, The runaway Church (London, 1976); R. Ris, Der Kirchliche Konstitutionalismus (Tübingen, 1988).

inspire political action. Messianic millenarianism and dreams of equality and eternal peace have played a role in certain of the experiments which we will encounter in the pages of this book. The most successful Constitutions seem to be those which combined a belief in progress with a healthy respect for tradition and the 'experience of the centuries'.

# CHAPTER 2

# Tribal kingship: from the fall of Rome to the end of the Merovingians

The dramatic disappearance of the Roman empire in the West left a great void: the political home in which millions of people had lived for centuries was no more. Finally it was unable to survive the twofold onslaught of the Germanic peoples in the north and the Arabs in the south. First the Pars Occidentis, with Rome herself, fell to the tribes from beyond the Rhine–Danube *limes*; afterwards much of the Pars Orientis, Byzantine 'new Rome', fell to Islam. From the storms that raged from the fifth to the seventh century three worlds emerged, three heirs of classical Antiquity. Greek Christendom in Byzantium was the direct, but much reduced continuation of the Roman empire in the east, ruled by a Roman emperor and living under Roman law. Latin Christendom lived under Germanic tribal kings, who had taken their religion from Rome, but little culture and even less law. The Arab world of Islam, stretching from Asia via northern Africa to Spain, had inherited not much law and even less religion from Antiquity, but a good deal of Greek science.

It is in the Latin Christian world of the early Middle Ages, from the fifth century onwards, that our narrative starts. The void which originated there was caused by the loss of some fundamental ideas and structures. The first victim was the centralized imperial state itself and with it the basic notion that its millions of multiracial inhabitants were subjected to one common domination, and that no other autonomous kernels of legitimate power existed beside it: all public authority had been vested in the emperor or descended from him. This emperor – called *dominus* since Diocletian (*d.* 316) – was absolute, i.e. not bound by the law, as he was himself its supreme source. He was not accountable to the people or their chosen representatives. The Roman senate was no more than an ornament of politics and a distant memory of its previous importance. The daily life of this enormous empire rested on two pillars, a severe fiscal regime and an extensive bureaucracy. Both were so oppressive that many citizens came to prefer the 'barbarians' to the 'blessings of civilization'. The Roman state was viewed as a magistrature. It was not the personal patrimony of the emperor or his lineage, but an abstract and eternal entity, the *res publica* or *res Romana*, administered by magistrates for the Roman people. The emperor was the highest magistrate and as such was in the service of the empire, which he was expected to govern, preserve and even extend according to his own insight. This state was Roman, Hellenistic, and oriental. It owed to Rome its legal and administrative genius, to Greece its cultural language, its arts and science, and from the Orient came the absolute power of the divine *dominus*. As the empire encompassed the whole civilized world, it was deemed universal. In the fourth century the empire came first to tolerate Christianity and then to promote it as the sole protected and privileged religion of the state; conversely the Christian churches were placed under the imperial protection and control. From this imposing construction only the Christian Church survived in the West after the fifth century, and it had special links with the new rulers, the tribal kings. The latter did not dominate the Church, but accepted its moral authority, as became those humble recent converts.

In this new world of the 'barbarians' the late-Roman elements were replaced by the following. The division of the old Pars Occidentis into numerous tribal kingdoms betrayed the fundamental dispersion of power. Even within each of those often minuscule kingdoms the idea of centralism was absent. To the new mentality public authority could be exerted autonomously by many individuals in several places and at different levels over several groups of people, without any need for it to be derived from one central ruler. There was a king, but it was his function to hold the other rulers together and to mobilize them for endeavours of the whole ethnic group. Kingship was tribal in origin, in other words it was linked to a group of people, wherever they might be living. It was only later that it became territorial, after the Germanic nations, which had been wandering far afield, had settled down and become sedentary.

In these circumstances there was no question of universalism. Each kingdom was self-sufficient within its own tribe and land, and did not look beyond these limits, except to embark on conquest and plunder. This could lead to mega-kingdoms (see the conquests of Clovis), but these could be quickly divided among the king's heirs. One victim of the loss of universalism was Roman law. The Germanic nations had their tribal laws, which had nothing in common with Roman law, put in writing. For their Romanic subjects compendiums of Roman law were written, which preserved some elements of the classical heritage, particularly in Mediterranean lands. Only private law was concerned, as in the new, tribal dispensation there was no room for Roman constitutional law. And it should be remembered that even in the Mediterranean zone Germanic kings – Visigoths, Ostrogoths and Lombards – held sway.

Initially the Germanic kings were temporary military leaders (*Heerkönige*) elected for the duration of a campaign. In normal times the ethnic group had no permanent ruler, and political decisions were taken in meetings of *nobiles*, or elders or even all freemen. These *Heerkönige* developed at the time of the great migrations into permanent rulers, which is not surprising as the tribes were continuously at war, either against the Romans or among themselves. The kings enjoyed, however, no absolute power. Although they sometimes appeared to eliminate all opposition by a combination of terror and success in war, the fundamental idea was that the king had to respect the rights of his subjects and to live himself under the ancient and sacred tribal customs. These he could only explain or supplement, and even so only with the consent of the people.

Fiscal oppression and ubiquitous bureaucracy had disappeared. The Roman land tax could not be maintained for lack of expert personnel. The old state tax was replaced by the primitive custom of *dona* ('gifts'), offered to the king by the notables, and the *fodrum*, an obligation on the local populace to provide the peripatetic kings with food, drink and shelter. Various ancient indirect taxes on the sale and transport of merchandise were maintained. The administration, however, collapsed. The registration of public and private charters diminished and finally disappeared altogether, at the central as well as the local level. Fewer people were capable of drafting documents – in decent Latin – and finally literacy among the laity was completely lost and became a clerical monopoly.

The abstract notion of the state and the magistrature was also gone and replaced by the patrimonial conception of the kingdom as family heirloom. The reigning dynasty disposed of the state as of a private estate. Public and private revenue and expenditure were not distinguished, hence the custom of dividing the realm among the sons upon the death of the king. This is the origin of a system which prevailed for many centuries: the kingdom, duchy or county was treated as a private estate and not only divided among the heirs, but pawned, parts of it given in dowry to a daughter or exchanged for other, more desirable bits of territory – all without the population being consulted.

That some elements from Antiquity survived in this strange new world was the work of the Church. The Germanic nations and their governments were all eventually converted to Catholicism and recognized the Church of Rome as their spiritual head. This led to close political links between kings and clergy, a situation which existed already in the late Roman empire, but the balance of power had changed in favour of the clergy. This was not unexpected, as the Church was in a much stronger position vis-à-vis the *reges barbarorum* than it ever dreamt of vis-à-vis the Roman emperor, the *dominus mundi*. It is in those early medieval times that the Church came to occupy a position which remained typical for many centuries, that of a great landowner, enjoying an enormous prestige as the teacher of the 'barbarians' and being the sole guardian of the Christian faith and classical culture. Hence the Church enjoyed many privileges, and was administered by its own government, lawgivers and judges. It was the starting point of centuries of collaboration, but also of some dramatic conflicts.

The interpretation of these early medieval times has varied. Admittedly in Italy, Gaul and Spain Antiquity did not disappear overnight, suddenly giving way to illiterate barbarians who had never heard of the splendour of the Mediterranean (as was the case with the Anglo-Saxon invaders of the Roman province of Brittany). Consequently even after the fifth century numerous elements of Roman times survived in Western Europe, which has led some historians to stress these witnesses of continuity and to place the beginning of the Middle Ages not, as tradition, in the fifth century (which witnessed a massive Germanic invasion and the deposition of the last Roman emperor in the West), but in the seventh, when the advance of Islam was reputed to have cut off Western Europe from its classical Mediterranean roots, or even in the eighth century, when Charlemagne is said to have founded the first truly medieval empire. It seems to me that not too much importance should be attached to isolated survivals or appearances: it is not because Clovis, the illiterate and recently converted war-lord of the Franks, put on the imperial diadem and purple cloak and received the minor title of

consul from the real emperor in Constantinople that the Roman
empire lived on in his person. The same can be said of the miserable
attempts of the Frankish kings of the Merovingian dynasty to
continue issuing imperial gold coins (*solidi*). Nor did Antiquity
survive because Isidore of Seville compiled for readers who knew no
Greek a small, elementary encyclopedia, salvaging some of the
achievements of Greeks and Romans. It is undeniable that a
fundamentally new situation was established in the fifth century,
when rapacious tribes from Central and Northern Europe occupied
the place of the old *caput mundi* ('head of the world'), imperial Rome.[1]

We shall now analyse the impact of these events on public law,
limiting our remarks to the realm of the Franks, who played the most
important role in the history of Western Europe. The question may,
however, be posed whether and to what extent we are justified in
speaking of public, as opposed to private law. For the Romans, as we
have seen, this distinction was evident, but in Frankish times things
were different, as will appear from the following considerations.

We shall look in vain for distinct chapters on constitutional law in
the laws of the Germanic nations. The Salic law, for example,
mentions the king only rarely and incidentally, nor do we find
chapters on the army or popular assemblies. Criminal law, which we
nowadays consider to be part of public law, was seen as concerned
primordially with private interests. Not only were the damages
(*faidus*) greater than the part of the fines that was paid into the royal
treasury (*fredus*), but criminal law consisted really of tariffs of
payments for damage suffered by private parties. If the latter failed to
agree on such payments, they were at liberty to end their conflicts
through private vendettas (*faida*). Also, criminal law was seen as
concerned with financial transactions, such punishments as execution
by fire for black magic being redeemable for money. The law courts,
moreover, were not manned by professional and bureaucratic judges,
as in the late Roman empire, but by notables and landowners who
had received no professional education and were elected by the
populace each time the *mallus* (local law court) met. Often they acted
as arbitrators rather than judges, and were expected to propose a
solution that pleased the public. Nor were their 'judgments' enforceable
unless the parties had consented to stand by them. The initiative of

---

[1] For a survey of this controversy, which centred round the 'Pirenne-thesis', so called after the
medievalist Henri Pirenne (*d.* 1936), see B. Lyon, *The origins of the Middle Ages. Pirenne's
challenge to Gibbon* (New York, 1972).

criminal prosecution was also normally left to the interested parties, which again calls the public character of the judicature into question. Legal terminology is most revealing here. Thus the term *publicus*, which used to refer to the commonwealth or the state, as in *res publica Romana* and *aerarium publicum* ('public treasury'), came simply to mean 'royal'. Similarly *fiscus* no longer referred to the finances of the imperial government, but to the personal treasure of the ruler or some particular royal manor (manorial revenue being the Frankish kings' main source of income). As the private moneys of the kings were not administered separately from the treasury of the state, there could hardly be a financial distinction between private and public law. The same applied to some extent to military organization. Military service admittedly was imposed on all freemen, and thus belonged to the domain of public law. However, kings and other lords also disposed of their *Gefolgschaften* (warrior-followers), who had entered their service through free agreements and were promised maintenance, military ventures and booty. These private militias, well known in Germanic Antiquity and adapted to the uncertainties of the early Middle Ages, operated outside the national armies.

Whatever the relevance of the 'public' and 'private' categories at that time, we shall now proceed to analyse some aspects of what in present-day parlance would be called the public law of the Merovingian era.

The territory was not yet the essential element of the state to which later centuries have attached so much importance. Although the Franks had ceased to be nomads and had settled in ancient Gaul and conquered lands of other Germanic tribes, the Merovingian king was still the king of a people – *rex Francorum* – and not of a country (*Francia* or *Gallia*, or whatever it might have been called). The personal link between the king and the members of his tribe (in ancient times his kinsmen) was still more important than the geographical criterion of the occupation of a precisely marked stretch of land.

The king was the permanent cornerstone of the political organization of the Franks. The monarchy was hereditary. The kings admittedly were traditionally elected, but the dynasty of the mythical King Meroveus had imposed itself to such an extent that the elective element was obscured, but not entirely eliminated, by the loyalty to the royal lineage, which was deemed to descend from Germanic deities: a dynasty that brought luck to the people deserved to be maintained. The Merovingian family was sacred, and its long hair was the primitive symbol of this halo. Consequently when the last Merovingian king, Childeric III, was deposed in 751 and shut up in an abbey, his long hair was cut off.

In legal terms the central element of royal authority was the *bannum*, the right to command and to prohibit, i.e. domination. This *bannum* was not purely personal or unlimited, as the consent of the *populus Francorum* had to be obtained. The people owed allegiance not to the state and its Constitution, but to the person of their ruler. This was the all important duty of *fidelitas*, and it meant that the most heinous crime was the *infidelitas*, personal disloyalty, leading to banishment and confiscation.

The king stood under the ancient customary law. It did not behove him to change it, as it was an eternal and fixed norm which no mortal could modify. The king was no real lawgiver, nor could he be. Nevertheless he played a role in the development of the law, as he assembled the *populus Francorum* in order to put the tribal laws in writing, and he was also empowered to clarify and supplement the nation's customs.

The king lived, as we have seen, mainly from the revenue of his manors, usually old Roman public land, obtained at the conquest of Gaul. This and the primitive, almost moneyless, economy of the period forced the king and his court to lead a peripatetic life, travelling from domain to domain and consuming the agricultural produce on the spot. This incidentally meant that there could be no real capital of the realm. One important attribute of the state that escaped from direct royal control was coinage. It became a private industry, in the hands of numerous entrepreneurs who turned it into a profitable business. The reliability of the coins rested no more in the imperial effigy, but in the name of the moneyer, the man who ran the mint. It was not until the Carolingians that coinage returned to royal hands.

The Franks lived in a class society, not only in the sense of social groups but in the sense of established categories with rights and duties recognized and imposed by law. The principal estates were the freemen (*ingenui*), the serfs (*servi*) and the *mancipia*, a description which is difficult to translate, as it concerned people who were unfree like the *servi*, but did not have their own farm. They were servants whose status resembled that of ancient slaves, although, unlike the latter, they enjoyed personal rights.

Most Germanic laws also mention *nobiles*, the estate of the nobility.

Tacitus refers to them in his *de Germania*, but it is noteworthy that the laws of the Franks, in contrast with the narrative sources, do not mention them. This creates a problem for the legal historian, particularly for the Merovingian era. It is on the one hand hard to believe that the Franks at that time would have been totally without nobles, but it is on the other hand very difficult to explain why their laws, foremost the Salic law, should completely ignore them. Some strange theories have been advanced to solve this dilemma, one being that the Merovingian kings liquidated their own old nobility (a notion that seems more familiar in our own time than in the so-called Dark Ages). This is not the place to enter into the details of this controversy, but it is a fact that a Carolingian nobility is documented as a warrior aristocracy which maintained that vast empire and whose descendants in post-Carolingian times provided numerous ruling families all over Western Europe. It is possible that this aristocracy of great landowners was to the Frankish mind endowed with leading functions, but not with such personal privileges that they formed a separate legal estate above the Frankish nation of free warriors. This might explain why they do not appear in the legal texts as a separate group.[2] An indication in this sense may be found in the fiction of the Frankish popular assembly. Even in Carolingian times the meeting of the magnates – abbots, bishops, dukes, counts and direct vassals of the king – was still referred to as the *conventus populi Francorum*, or even simply as the *populus Francorum*. However, what had in the past been a general meeting of all free warriors, equal in law, had developed into an assembly of the political top. Nevertheless it was still called the (meeting of the) people of the Franks, and not the assembly of the nobility. The aristocracy was replenished by the accession of new individuals, and the main lever of this upward nobility was personal service to the monarch, the entry into his *comitatus*, his circle of followers. That there was a top group of big landowners in Merovingian times appears, even though the term 'noble' is not used, from laws stipulating that the *comites* of the *pagi*, the royal officials who were at the head of the local districts, had to be recruited from the ranks of the local lords and landowners. This

[2] This is an old controversy, to which Paul Vinogradoff devoted an article entitled 'Wergeld und Stand' in 1902 (*Collected Papers*, II, Oxford, 1928, 84–152). For some recent assessments, see H. Grahn-Hoek, *Die Fränkische Oberschicht im 6. Jahrhundert. Studien zu ihrer rechtlichen und politischen Stellung* (Sigmaringen, 1976); J. Hannig, *Consensus Fidelium. Frühfeudale Interpretationen des Verhältnisses von Königtum und Adel am Beispiel des Frankenreiches* (Stuttgart, 1982); *Studien zu den germanischen Volksrechten. Gedächtnisschrift für Wilhelm Ebel* (Frankfurt, Berne, 1982).

incidentally indicates that the control of the monarchy over its own territorial agents was limited. They should in no way be seen as subjected creatures of the government, as they not only had to be local *potentes*, but also people who enjoyed a considerable measure of independence, based on their landed wealth and consequent economic independence.

Towards the end of this period, in the first half of the eighth century, Western Europe was in a bad way. In the British Isles Ireland and Wales were opposed to England, itself divided into several kingdoms. On the Continent Visigothic rule in Spain collapsed, leaving the largest part of the peninsula under Muslim rule. In northern Italy the kingdom of the Lombards was at daggers drawn with the papacy and the Franks, whereas some powerful Germanic tribes, such as the Saxons, were still heathen. The realm of the Franks, which was often divided in sub-kingdoms, not only lacked unity, but was 'ruled' by an outworn dynasty, which had lost the economic strength and moral influence it might ever have had. The Frankish Church also was in deep crisis. Many people in the West, such as Pope Gregory the Great (*d.* 604), had for a long time believed that the unnatural rule of the 'barbarians' would not last and the world would return to normalcy, which meant that the Eastern Roman emperor would restore his authority and the empire would again extend from Hadrian's Wall to the Persian frontier. Slowly people came to realize, especially after the catastrophic blows suffered by Byzantium at the hands of the Arabs, that the old order was gone forever. So the Latin West had to take its fate into its own hands. This was done through an alliance between the papacy, which finally turned its back on the Greeks, and the Carolingian house, which launched a vast attempt to unite the peoples of the West in one great state. In that way the Roman empire would be restored after all, not the whole ancient Mediterranean state, but a part of it, based politically on the north-west of the Continent and ideologically on the city of the 'heir of St Peter'. We shall now proceed to the presentation of the consequences of this development for public law.

# CHAPTER 3

# The First Europe: the Carolingian empire

## THE POLITICAL FRAMEWORK

In the second half of the eighth and the first half of the ninth century the Franks, under the Carolingian dynasty, founded an empire that united the greater part of western Christendom in one state. The Carolingians, a leading and wealthy family from the non-Romanized eastern part of the kingdom known as Austrasia, had played an important political and military role long before the middle of the eighth century, but it was through a coup d'état, supported by the papacy, that in 751 they acceded to the royal dignity in the person of Pippin III. This date traditionally marks the start of the Carolingian era, whose climax came under Charlemagne (d. 814) and the earlier years of his son Louis the Pious (d. 840). At that time the Carolingian empire contained, in present-day terms, France, western Germany, Belgium, the Netherlands, Luxembourg, Switzerland, north-east Spain (called the *Marca Hispanica*) and northern Italy (the old kingdom of the Lombards), to which could be added the protectorate over the papal state in central Italy. Within Latin Christendom only the British Isles remained outside. The establishment of this vast complex was realized through the strengthening of royal authority inside the old Frankish lands – which was not always an easy process, as the events in Aquitaine showed – and through conquest and expansion: the Saxons (those that is who had stayed behind on the Continent) were subjected and forcibly converted, and the *regnum Langobardorum* was conquered by Charlemagne, though it continued as a separate kingdom, united with the Frankish monarchy by a personal union. The disintegration of this empire – which had become an empire *stricto sensu* at the imperial coronation of Charlemagne – had already begun under Louis the Pious, and the quarrels among his sons led to the division of the Treaty of Verdun of 843 and eventually the rise of the kingdoms of France, Germany, Burgundy and Italy. Within the newly-established kingdom of France the political decomposition continued, and the country was divided into a number of 'territorial principalities' ruled by autonomous regional dynasties. French kingship survived, but the Carolingian dynasty was eliminated in the late tenth century; in Germany it had already disappeared three generations earlier.

<h2 style="text-align:center">FUNDAMENTAL CHARACTERISTICS</h2>

The Carolingian empire broke with the old tribal outlook of the Franks and built a vast supranational political home for the peoples of the Western-European Continent, which was not equalled until our own day. This 'First Europe' was for many centuries also the last; it is possible that the end of the twentieth century may see the rise of a United (Western) Europe that would be even larger than the realm of Charlemagne.

The Roman empire had disappeared in the West, but it was not forgotten. Learned circles continued to believe that empire was desirable and even natural for a large community of nations and it is in that light that the coronation of Charlemagne in Rome on Christmas Day 800 by Pope Leo III can best be understood. It meant the recognition of the supranational, even universal significance of the king of the Franks and the Lombards and the protector of the Latin Church, which had abandoned the Greeks and turned to the Franks. It expressed the feeling that the 'time of troubles' was over and the Latin West was the equal of the Greek East, where the continuity of the ancient empire was never lost. The Roman, or as we might more aptly call it, the neo-Roman empire of Charlemagne was in several respects different from its ancient model. Though it was Roman, it refused to be Byzantine, and Charlemagne had been displeased at the eastern ritual followed for his crowning. If his empire accepted to be Roman, it was because Rome was the holiest city in the West and her bishop the 'heir of St Peter'. The main source of inspiration for the new emperor was not the political traditions of the Roman empire or Roman law, but the Christian religion. Particularly the Old Testament and its anointed kings excited his imagination: it was no coincidence that in the inner circle of the court he was

known as David. A Christian, rather than a Roman empire, is
what he had in mind.[1]

## The monarchy

The monarchy was the cornerstone of the whole political edifice.
Kingship was hereditary, even though in times of crisis election had a
chance: Pippin III was 'chosen' as king by the Franks. The kings were
sacred: from Pippin III onwards the rulers of the Franks, and even the
crown princes, were anointed by the Church, which put them into a
direct relationship with God and above the ordinary laymen.[2] The
form of government was personal and the *bannum* 'from the king's own
mouth' was decisive. Important decisions were taken in consultation
with the *populus Francorum*, but this was no popular assembly or
parliament of elected representatives, as it contained only the leading
members of the clergy and laity. Whereas their consent was important,
it could hardly be withheld under leaders of Charlemagne's stature.
The personal character of the regime was underlined by the importance
of the oath of loyalty to the king, which was demanded from
everyone. This usage may have originated in the conspiracy against
Charlemagne in 785 and the king's desire to protect himself by this
universal obligation of the oath of fealty (a practice which had existed
in the past, but was abandoned in the seventh century). The
capitulary which introduced it and placed it under the supervision of
the royal envoys known as *missi dominici* is lost, but we know that its
stipulations were carried out in 789, and the wording of the oath is
preserved in a capitulary of that year. Two years after his imperial
coronation, in 802, Charlemagne again and for the last time imposed
the swearing of the oath. This oath of loyalty of the whole population
should be distinguished from the oath of fealty of a vassal to his feudal
lord: the royal vassals, who had sworn the vassalitic oath, were
required to swear the general oath as well.[3]

---

[1] Among recent overviews the reader may consult the following: E. James, *The origins of France: from Clovis to the Capetians* (London, 1982); R. McKitterick, *The Frankish kingdoms under the Carolingians* (London, 1983); P. Riché, *Les Carolingiens: une famille qui fit l'Europe* (Paris, 1983).

[2] The classic book on the wonder-working kings is by M. Bloch, *Les rois thaumaturges* (Strasbourg, 1924). See also the more recent study by an eminent specialist: R. Folz, *Les saints rois du moyen âge en Occident (VIe–XIIIe siècles)* (Brussels, 1984).

[3] F. L. Ganshof, 'Charlemagne's use of the oath' in F. L. Ganshof, *The Carolingians and the Frankish monarchy* (London, 1971), 111–24.

The religious inspiration of the Carolingian dynasty went much deeper than under its predecessor: the expansion of the Christian faith and the protection of the Roman Church occupied a central place. The kings of that house also considered themselves as rulers by God's grace and answerable to God. They attached importance to the protection of their weaker subjects, such as women, orphans and generally speaking all *pauperes*, the poor who were continually exposed to the pressure of the *potentes*, the powerful who threatened their land and their liberty.

In this light one also understands the Carolingian interest in legislation and the courts. Royal legislation was revived in the shape of the capitularies, which constituted a considerable body of laws and instructions on diverse temporal and spiritual topics. They became particularly abundant after Charlemagne's imperial coronation, but disappeared before the end of the ninth century in the successor states of the Frankish empire. Plans were made to put the laws of the Germanic nations in writing, to improve the existing texts and even to bring about legal unification, but were crowned with little success. The administration of justice received a good deal of attention. It was one of the tasks of the *missi dominici*, whom we have just mentioned. They were sent by the king to local judges and administrators in order to supervise in the king's name respect for the laws and to introduce and explain new instructions.

All these initiatives betray a heightened consciousness of the public role of the monarchy, a greater awareness of the role of public law in society. The introduction of royal coinage, after the private enterprise under the Merovingians, can also be seen in this light. The same can be said of attempts to improve the efficiency of the government, through the use of writing in administrative and judicial business. It was a difficult task in the prevailing primitive circumstances of massive illiteracy.

Also, only Latin and no Germanic or Romanic vernacular was used in writing, so that not only the barrier of the art of writing had to be conquered, but also of learning Latin. The use of writing made demonstrable progress under Charlemagne, particularly after the imperial coronation. Although he never learnt to write, he understood the importance of literacy. It will forever be impossible to quote statistical data on this subject, as written texts of a transient character, called *indiculi* (such as summonses, manorial accounts or mobilization orders), were not preserved, let alone copied on rolls or registers, as was the case with the charters containing title to land. Almost all these *indiculi* are understandably lost, and we know of their existence only through formularies containing model texts to be used in various circumstances. The extent to which the *indiculi* were used, as compared to verbal messages, must remain obscure. The very small number of officials employed in the royal writing office, where the official documents were drafted and sealed, is a warning not to overestimate the use of written documents.[4]

The finances of the monarchy were based on its landed wealth. As no distinction was made between public and private revenue and expenditure, and the treasury of the state coincided with the private purse of the king, court as well as government expenses were all covered by the income from the royal manors. These were vast, the Carolingian family being the greatest landowner in the country, and better run and controlled than those of the Merovingians. Fewer lands were irrevocably given away than under the preceding dynasty (who ended penniless), because the feudal system allowed the Carolingians to put land at the disposal of their vassals on a temporary basis and to retain ultimate control in their own hands. Nevertheless even the immense landed wealth of the Carolingians was dissipated in the course of the ninth century. Besides its manorial revenue the monarchy also drew income from fines, tolls, rents and booty, with occasional windfalls such as the treasure of the Avars who were conquered by Charlemagne in 795.[5]

## Church and state

The Carolingian monarchy had close links with the Church. The Franks supported the papacy against the Lombards, and in the winter of 800–1 Charlemagne supported Pope Leo III against various Roman factions. Also the conversion of the Saxons owed much to Frankish military intervention. Within the Frankish frontiers this collaboration was equally intense. The dynasty made the payment of ecclesiastical tithes compulsory, and Charlemagne made efforts for the diffusion and study of the standard text of the Bible, the

[4] See the survey in R. McKitterick, *The Carolingians and the written word* (Cambridge, 1989).
[5] Fifteen carts, each drawn by four oxen, were necessary to transport all the gold and silver and fine textiles to the West; one of the sources of the treasure of the Avars was the yearly tribute of between 80,000 and 100,000 gold *solidi* which Byzantium had been paying them for almost a century. See H. Fichtenau, *Das karolingische Imperium. Soziale und geistige problematik eines Grossreiches* (Zurich, 1949), 90.

Roman liturgy and the Roman canonical collections. His efforts to improve the knowledge of classical Latin, the language of the Church, can also be seen in this light, even though the name of 'Carolingian Renaissance', given to this movement, is somewhat optimistic. The Church on the other hand was tireless in its support of the regime. This was the case not only in the religious and magical sphere, where the monarchy was given a metaphysical aura, but also in the practical field: the royal chancery was from Carolingian times onwards manned exclusively by members of the clergy.[6]

## Feudalism

The Carolingian monarchy created the system of fiefs and vassals which stamped the medieval world for many centuries. Although separate elements that went into its making can be traced to ancient, Germanic or Merovingian sources, their combination into a system and the latter's introduction into the political constitution were realized under the Carolingians.

The starting point of feudalism was the vassalitic element, i.e. the personal bond between a lord (*dominus, senior*), who was a rich and leading personality, and a vassal (*vassus, homo*), a freeman of a more modest social standing. Their bond, entered into for life by a free contract, created mutual rights and obligations: the lord owed his man maintenance and protection, the man owed his lord loyal service, mainly military in character. Originally maintenance was provided by the lord by accepting his vassals into his hall, sheltering, clothing and feeding them, and providing them with booty. Subsequently the provision of the vassals' material needs was done through the grant by the lord of part of his landed property to his vassals for the duration of their contract. This was the fief, called *beneficium* in Carolingian times, which was held by the vassal from his lord and whose revenue (as the peasants went with the land) was destined for his maintenance.

This technique of binding free warriors to their service and to provide them with the necessary revenue from land was used by the Carolingians on a large scale. It allowed them to raise an army of

[6] See the following surveys or collections of articles. F. L. Ganshof, *Frankish institutions under Charlemagne* (Providence, R. I., 1968); W. Ullmann, *The Carolingian renaissance and the idea of kingship* (London, 1969); F. L. Ganshof, *The Carolingians and the Frankish monarchy* (London, 1971); J. L. Nelson, *Politics and ritual in early medieval Europe* (London, Ronceverte, 1986).

horsemen, without giving away royal manors irrevocably. It also made it possible to bind the leading figures throughout their vast multiracial country to the monarchy by taking them into the royal vassalage. The lay holders of office and, from Louis the Pious onwards, the prelates also became royal vassals, holding their offices in state and Church – and the land attached to them – in fief from the crown. The system was not elaborated through legislation, but by custom, and its later development was also due to changes in custom. Thus, originally fiefs were not heritable, and a lord who lost a vassal took his fief back and could, if he wanted, grant it to someone else of his choice. Although this was logical enough, the vassals, who wanted to ensure the position of their families, put so much pressure on the lords that fiefs became heritable. Similarly, vassals initially could only serve one lord and hold fiefs from him, but here again the land hunger of the feudal tenants led to a change, and a new custom – and customary law – arose, allowing men to become vassals of several lords and hold fiefs from them. The reader will look in vain for legislation or doctrinal works on this subject until well into the twelfth century; it all happened through custom and case law.

The spread of feudalism greatly affected the public law. It changed the constitutional position of the king, who came to assume a twofold, if not equivocal role. As king he was and remained a ruler by God's grace, the leader, legislator and highest judge of his people; as feudal overlord he had a contractual relationship with his men based on a mutual expression of free will and entailing mutual rights and duties. The king/feudal suzerain had duties towards his vassals, and the neglect of those duties gave them a right of resistance and disobedience.

Another important consequence was that worldly public offices became heritable because they had become fiefs, and the fiefs had become heritable. This could easily lead to greater independence for the local office holders: an official whose position is hereditary is naturally more independent than his appointed and dismissible colleagues. Thus feudalism, conceived to enhance cohesion, contained the seeds of a weaker state. As the crown had assumed an equivocal role, feudalism also appeared to be a double-edged sword.[7]

---

[7] The most recent edition of the classic work of F. L. Ganshof, *Qu'est-ce que la féodalité?*, is the fifth, and was published in Paris in 1982; the third edition of the English translation of the second French edition was published in London in 1964. See also the recent posthumous survey of a renowned specialist, W. Kienast, *Die fränkische Vasallität von den Hausmeiern bis zu Ludwig dem Kind und Karl dem Einfältigen*, ed. by P. Herde (Frankfurt, 1990).

### DECLINE OF THE FIRST EUROPE

In the eighth century the Frankish monarchy had attempted to weld together the old inhabitants of Roman descent and the Germanic newcomers into one large and stable state, but already in the ninth its reborn West Roman empire collapsed and gave way to new kingdoms and dynasties. One of those kingdoms carried the disintegration even further and fell apart into autonomous regional principalities. That Frankish unity was gone forever was not immediately evident, and both the French and the German kings went on for a long time calling themselves 'kings of the Franks'. Finally people came to accept the new reality of a divided Europe and all this entailed: endless wars between large and small states and, at least in the short run, a loss of security for the whole area, threatened by Vikings, Magyars and Saracens. All this led to a profound militarization of the West and the rise of the typical aristocracy of knights, who dominated and even terrorized the land around their castles and its inhabitants. From the late eleventh century onwards, this society geared to war and led by warriors went onto the offensive, to north, east and south, and eventually established western hegemony in large new areas. There was an interesting chain reaction here. Internal and external insecurity had led to a defensive militarization. The resulting society, geared to feudal warfare, produced a political–military complex that was ready for conquest in the following, offensive stage. Its military base was the castle and the mail-fisted knight, the economic foundation was the manor and the seigniory, and the feudal monarchy was its political expression. The model was exportable: the Normans introduced it in England, and the Crusaders in the Holy Land.

The failure of the Carolingian efforts had such far-reaching consequences that the question of its causes deserves to be posed. The geographical extension, although considerable, does not seem to offer an explanation. History has known other empires which lasted for many centuries in spite of vast areas and slow, primitive communications. The Latin Church is also an example, at least from the Gregorian Reform onwards, of a centralized organization which operated efficiently in spite of slow and dangerous travel and an area much larger than the Carolingian empire. Other, more fundamental factors must have played a role, among which the following could be mentioned. The ethnic diversity and the Frankish domination kept alive a strong regional or tribal consciousness. The problem was solved to some extent by the formula of personal union which, as we have seen, preserved the Lombard kingdom as such, or by the appointment of members of the royal house as viceroys in particular areas, as happened with Louis the Pious in Aquitaine. Another obstacle was the ingrained patrimonial way of thinking of the Franks and their kings, which viewed the realm not as a *res publica* administered by magistrates, but as the patrimony of the ruling family. This implied that the kingdom was divided among the sons of the deceased king, as any other estate and as had happened time and again under the Merovingians. Remarkably enough, Charlemagne followed the old paths, even after his imperial coronation. In his *divisio regnorum* ('division of the kingdoms') of 806 he indicated in advance which parts of his empire would eventually be inherited by which of his three legitimate sons, Charles, Pippin and Louis. Fate decided otherwise, as the two oldest sons died before their father, leaving Louis the Pious as the sole heir in 814, but the division of 806 remains a significant proof of the strength of the customary ways. It is ironic that, in 817, Louis decided to abandon the traditional path, and to maintain the unity of the empire. His *ordinatio imperii* of that year stipulated that at his death the empire would pass in its entirety to his oldest son Lothair, and instituted him as co-emperor with immediate effect. Here again events decided otherwise, for Louis' realm was in fact divided among his sons in 843, in spite of the *ordinatio* of 817. The latter document was not easily agreed upon, for there were two groups among the notables who had been specially summoned to Aachen. One pleaded for the continuation of the ancient practice of division, as this was the customary law of the Franks and had been recently confirmed by the example of Charlemagne himself. The other, where the clergy was most influential, pleaded for unity, as this was favourable for the imperial protection of the Church and also in unison with Roman imperial thinking, to which learned circles were more sensitive. In truly medieval fashion the decision on this difficult problem, where both sides meant well (as the document expressly states), was left to divine inspiration, which came after a triduum of fasting and prayer.[8] Other centrifugal factors were no doubt the intellectual climate and the economic situation. Agriculture was primitive, productivity being so low and monetary circulation so small that centralizing royal revenue and central

---

[8] See P. Classen, 'Karl der Grosse und die Thronfolge im Frankenreich', *Festschrift H. Heimpel*, III (Göttingen, 1972), 109–34.

payment of salaries were impossible. Also, political ideas stressed the role of the sacred figure of the king and personal loyalty rather than abstractions such as the state and civic duty.[9]

All this does not mean that the Carolingian empire, an underdeveloped country in twentieth-century parlance, could not have survived, as there are examples of other mega-states which lasted for centuries or even millennia in spite of backward agriculture and, to our mind, primitive political institutions. There is, in any case, no doubt that the hesitant and easily influenced personality of Louis the Pious, whom older French authors called 'Louis the Debonair', because he was as weak as his father was forceful, must have influenced the chances of survival of his state in a negative way.[10]

In spite of its undoubted failure the Carolingian experiment has left deep and lasting traces on the development of European public law. Anointed kingship has for centuries been the most important political institution on the Continent and, till this day, in Britain. Not only was kingship blessed with the enormous prestige of religion and towered above ordinary mortals, but the bonds between state and Church – the political and the ideological establishments – remained fundamental for many centuries. This osmosis of religion and politics, in a *do ut des* ('I give so that you shall give') relationship, is a phenomenon which outlasted the Middle Ages, for although its theory was questioned in the fourteenth century and it was to some extent discarded by the Calvinists, the first Constitution which rejected it on principle was, as will be discussed later, that of the United States of America.

The Holy Roman Empire was also a Carolingian legacy, even though it became a Germanic institution, as we shall see. Similarly, feudalism was a Carolingian system which outlasted its original breeding ground for many centuries and profoundly marked European public law. In later centuries one finds fiefs, feudal lords, vassals, homage, feudal castles and feudal courts in many countries, far from the Frankish heartland of their origin. Although the system often got out of control and went hand in hand with political division and discord, this was not linked to the system as such, which had been devised for the sake of cohesion. When feudalism 'went wrong', it was because the monarchy was so weakened that it could not control its

---

[9] See J. Fried, 'Der karolingische Herrschaftsverband im 9. Jahrhundert zwischen "Kirche" und "Königshaus"', *Historische Zeitschrift* 235 (1982), 1–43.

[10] P. Godman (ed.), *Charlemagne's heir. New perspectives on the reign of Louis the Pious (814–840)* (Oxford, 1990).

own vassalage. The case of post-1066 England shows that where kingship was strong, feudalism could be an element of cohesion.

The legend of Charlemagne should not be left unmentioned. The great emperor of the West, whom so many ruling houses claimed as their ancestor, has fired the imagination of countless generations. To the German monarchy he was the archetype of the universal Christian emperor and a great legislator; to French kings he was the model of the fighter for the true faith and a national symbol.[11]

[11] See the excellent survey by R. E. Sullivan, 'The Carolingian age: reflections on its place in the history of the Middle Ages', *Speculum* 64 (1989), 267–306.

# CHAPTER 4

# Europe divided: the post-Carolingian era

## THE DISINTEGRATION OF THE FRANKISH EMPIRE

The life of the first united Europe was significant but short. Decomposition started under Louis the Pious, whose quarrelling sons imposed the division of the Treaty of Verdun of 843. The disintegration of the empire of the Franks took place in two phases. There was, to begin with, the division into France (the western Franks), Germany (the eastern Franks) and Lotharingia, Lothair's long, drawn-out middle kingdom, which eventually became part of Germany. So the old Frankish mother country gave birth to two great kingdoms, France and Germany. For a long time they both considered themselves as Frankish, and it is hard to decide when they finally realized that they were Franks no more, but French and German, and that the realm of Charlemagne belonged to the past. The *regnum Italiae*, the old kingdom of the Lombards, enjoyed a phase of independence, but already under King Otto I (*d.* 973) it came under German hegemony. The process of disintegration, started under Louis the Pious, did not, however, stop there. Even within the frontiers of the new kingdoms the weakening of unity continued, though not everywhere to the same extent. The German kings had to accept that several regions, where old ethnic feeling remained lively, achieved a good deal of autonomy under powerful ducal dynasties, the *Stammesherzogtümer*, or ethnic dukedoms. What happened in France went even further. Here royal authority came to be ignored altogether, because of the rise of separate states, which started in the late ninth century and led to the so-called *principautés territoriales*, the territorial principalities. They were large areas where local noble dynasties took over the reins of government, even, because of the weakness of the monarchy, assuming responsibility for external security. In some cases, in the duchy of Burgundy, for example, old tribal loyalties going back to the Burgundians of the time of the Germanic invasions can have played a

54

role. In others, like the county of Flanders, this was clearly not the case. There had never been a tribe of that name in Germanic Antiquity and the bilingual principality was created because of the threat of the Vikings, its eccentric position in France and the leadership of an exceptional line of counts, who followed each other in direct succession from the ninth till the twelfth century. The kings, although in theory still the national rulers of the whole of France, were in fact reduced to the level of territorial leaders of the Isle de France. In the course of the tenth century that area, surrounding Paris, witnessed a power struggle between scions of the old Carolingian family and a new lineage of dukes of '*Francia*', the Robertinians, who finally overcame their rivals and occupied the throne of France at the election of Hugh Capet at Senlis in 987. The disappearance of the Carolingians led to the total break between northern and southern France and inaugurated an era where the Midi, i.e. southern France, completely ignored the national monarchy. The accession of the Capetians did not stop the process of division. On the contrary, within some principalities a second wave of disintegration took place which finally left public authority in the hands of owners of land and castles who dominated their local areas without any checks and were supported by groups of knightly vassals; some of these areas were not larger than 5 km around the lords' strongholds. Thus legitimate power had passed into the hands of local leaders of gangs of armed men, the ultimate consequence of the demise of state power.

Where this situation arose, for example in the counties of Poitou and Mâcon (but not in the duchy of Normandy or the county of Flanders), one can speak without exaggeration of the disappearance of the state, a remarkable situation which every public lawyer will find interesting to analyse in some detail. Power was exercised by landowners who led a military life. They were leaders of small groups of warriors and recognized no higher authority, not even of the regional count, let alone the king in Paris. Public authority on such a small scale caused insecurity and was hardly compatible with even a minimum of public order. These local potentates managed to keep order within their own mini-territories and to impose their discipline on the peasantry, but there was no one to force them to respect each other's possessions or those of inhabitants or travellers. Invasions, attacks, acts of robbery and local wars were an everyday matter; warfare was a way of life for the dominant class. This iron age was the European equivalent of the Japanese samurai era and could in terms of public law best be described as a time of quasi-anarchy.[1] It was clear that society could not forever live in a state of permanent alarm and insecurity, but it was unclear how the situation could be overcome. Eventually the monarchy was to re-establish public law and order (as we will see later on), but for the contemporaries of the weak French kings Henry I (*d.* 1060) and Philip I (*d.* 1108) this was hard to foresee. They had therefore tried other ways and experimented with some strange creations of public law in order to protect goods and persons and to install a minimum of security. One such initiative was the proclamation of the Truce and the Peace of God, popular movements inspired by the Church which tended to fill the vacuum left by the state. They consisted in mass meetings directed by the clergy, where people swore to abstain from violence towards certain particularly vulnerable persons and goods and on specified holy days and liturgical periods. The sanctions were ecclesiastical (what else was there?), mainly excommunication. Religious sentiment, awareness of the invisible world and the fear of hell-fire to some extent made excommunication an adequate deterrent. Sculptures of this period have survived which, with obvious relish, depict wicked knights being carted off to hell by horrible demons.[2]

## FEUDALISM

The post-Carolingian era is the period of classic feudalism and therefore deserves some detailed analysis. This will be all the more useful since such phrases as 'feudal disintegration' and 'feudal dislocation' could easily create the impression that feudalism was responsible for political separatism. We shall concentrate our attention on three themes, the legal development of feudal institutions, the feudalization of public life and the relation between feudalism and monarchy.

The rules of the feudal game, i.e. the norms that regulated the relations between lords and vassals and the legal nature of the fiefs, had changed since Carolingian times, even though the fundamental elements remained the same. The accents, however, were placed differently, for whereas initially the personal, vassalitic element was

---

[1] See M. Garaud, *Les châtelains de Poitou de l'avènement du régime féodal aux XIe et XIIe siècles* (Poitiers, 1964); E. Bournazel, *Le gouvernement capétien au XIIe siècle 1108–1180. Structures sociales et mutations institutionnelles* (Paris, 1975); J. P. Poly, *La Provence et la société féodale. Contribution à l'étude des structures dites féodales dans le Midi* (Paris, 1976).

[2] H. Hoffmann, *Gottesfriede und Treuga Dei* (Stuttgart, 1964).

predominant, in later times the material aspect, the fief, came to occupy the forefront. Whereas at the start the fief had been the means, in the end it became the aim: previously one received a fief because one was a vassal, afterwards one became a vassal in order to obtain a fief. The following developments will serve to illustrate our point.

Fiefs eventually became hereditary. Initially the lord had taken back the fief upon the death of his vassal in order, if he wanted, to grant it to someone else of his choice. In the course of time the vassals' ambition to safeguard their fiefs for their descendants prevailed, allowing them to preserve the material foundation of their lineage. But the inheritance was transmitted undivided, usually going to the first-born son. This rule of primogeniture was to the advantage of the feudal lord, as only a complete fief could support his vassal and secure the desired service from the latter's heir, but it was also advantageous for the vassal, as only an undivided fief was a sufficient material base for the desirable social and economic position of a noble or knightly family. The principle of inheritance itself was, however, the object of a long tug of war between lords and vassals, the former detesting and the latter desiring it. The story of the eventual victory of the vassals is long and complicated. We already find a recognition of the heredity of fiefs in a capitulary of Charles the Bald of AD 877, but two centuries later it was still a bone of contention in Anglo-Norman England. And after it was finally recognized there in the twelfth century, lords and vassals went on quarrelling about the amount of the relief. This was a tax payable by the new vassal to the lord upon receiving the inherited fief from his hands. That eventually women also, who did not take part in warfare in medieval times, could become vassals was another indication that the original idea was getting lost and the desire to keep the fiefs within the family, even when male heirs were temporarily missing, was paramount.

The multiplicity of fiefs is another aspect of this 'realization' of the feudal relationship. Originally the bond between lord and man was exclusive, and the vassal could only serve one master and therefore hold fiefs from him alone. Subsequently the hunger for fiefs led to vassals offering their loyal services to several lords and receiving tenures from all of them. The situation was scandalous in the theological sense of the term, as it could easily lead to perjury if the lords of one vassal quarrelled, and all demanded his loyal service. The practice nevertheless became widespread and examples are known of important people who were vassals of several kings, counts and bishops, thus accumulating a considerable feudal patrimony. It may be imagined what happened in those circumstances to their oaths of fealty. The land hunger of the aristocracy went so far that even kings of France did not deem it beneath their dignity to become vassals of their own vassals in order to get hold of fiefs and castles situated at strategic points; in the twelfth century, however, the rule was accepted that in such cases the kings were not supposed to do homage. What became in all that of the initial feudal concept of personal service and loyalty? It was degraded to a burden upon the fief: possession of feudal land entailed performing specific services – mainly military and judicial – to certain lords, a charge which did not rest on allodial land that was possessed in full, independent ownership.

The feudalization of public life made enormous progress during this period. Defence, the administration of justice, fiscal organization and to some extent even ecclesiastical administration were all stamped by feudalism. We may limit ourselves to some examples.

The nerve centre of political life was the *curia regis*, the king's feudal court. It was composed by the king and feudal overlord and his direct vassals, the tenants in chief, who were great clerical and lay landowners holding their lands and positions directly from him and owing him *consilium et auxilium* ('counsel and support'). The court dealt with all kinds of topics of public interest – military, dynastic, feudal, judicial, political or fiscal – without division of labour or specialization. It had no fixed abode and travelled with the king. As the kingdoms had their king's court, so the principalities had their duke's court or their count's court. Indeed, every lord on whom a number of vassals depended held a court, where topics of common interest were discussed, according to the feudal principle that the lord had to go about his business in consultation with his vassals instead of deciding autocratically. The ultimate logic was that if a feudal lord was in conflict with one of his men, the case was brought before his court and freely decided there – the judgment of the vassals possibly going against their own lord.

The feudalization of military service was a striking phenomenon. In Frankish times there had been an army of free peasants, who fought on foot during short campaigns in spring and summer, as everyone had to be back home in time for the harvest: defence was a general obligation. The feudal armies looked very different, as military duty was founded on the contract between lord and vassal. The former summoned the latter to the military service he owed: vassals in any case received their fiefs in order to enable them to fight as professional warriors. The political implications were far reaching. As the old peasant armies disappeared – in some areas the free peasantry itself disappeared and was reduced to serfdom – the knights became the absolute leaders of society.

The administration of justice was also profoundly affected. Charlemagne had instituted the *scabini* in the ordinary district courts; they were judgment finders appointed for life. They did not disappear in subsequent centuries, but witnessed the rise of a novel type, the feudal courts, composed of the vassals of the presiding lord and empowered to give judgment in conflicts between them. These new courts gave judgment on the legal character of fiefs and their possession and inheritance, but also on personal conflicts involving the disloyalty of a vassal or the illegal behaviour of a lord. As more lands and offices became feudal, these courts gained importance. Sometimes they were even given jurisdiction over non-feudal criminal cases, because the ruler found them more suitable.

Administration became feudalized in the sense that numerous offices were held in fief by particular families: as tenures became hereditary, so did feudally-held offices. This took place in the royal households, with their hereditary dignitaries, and also on the regional level. Thus the Flemish castellans, who headed the castellanies into which the county was subdivided, held their offices and the lands that went with them in fief from the count.

Public revenue was also affected by the impact of feudalism. The lord who was obliged to provide for his vassals could himself appeal to them if he needed their aid (*auxilium*). This feudal request for financial assistance was the starting point of the late medieval demands for grants addressed by kings and other princes to towns or rural districts and to the assemblies of estates or parliaments. What aid a lord could reasonably ask for and on what occasions he could do so – for his ransom, for the knighting of a son or the marriage of a daughter – was a hotly debated question, which often led to arrangements put in writing.

Feudalism was so all-pervading and so deeply affected kingship itself that historians speak of 'the feudal monarchy'.[3] The term is appropriate as the monarchical form of government was maintained, but the latter was transformed by the feudal way of life, which turned the king into a Janus-faced figure. On the one hand he was and

[3] The classic work is by C. Petit-Dutaillis, *La monarchie féodale en France et en Angleterre* (2nd edn, Paris, 1971).

remained the ruler of his subjects, which created one-way traffic from the top to the base; on the other hand he was the feudal overlord of his vassals and sub-vassals, and this relationship was based on a contract involving both parties in mutual rights and duties; this created a two-way traffic, so that the king's followers could call him to account and even defy him by renouncing their allegiance (*défi féodal*) if he continued treating them badly.

It is striking what an adaptable, multi-purpose institution feudalism was, being adequate for the most diverse situations. Feudal relations were used for small-scale business such as holding a few acres of village land from a local lord (a transaction of private law in modern parlance). But feudal notions were also used for international relations – clearly a public-law concern. Thus ties between an autonomous duchy like Normandy or an autonomous county like Flanders and the French monarchy were feudal in nature – dukes and counts holding in fief from their royal lord. Nevertheless a legal category that was used both for the tenure of a few acres of agricultural land and the holding of a principality with hundreds of thousands of inhabitants which was called a *regnum* in the texts of the time had become an empty shell. Formally it was used in a similar way for legal relations which hardly had anything substantial in common.[4]

Feudalism was a European phenomenon and few countries managed to avoid it altogether, even though in Friesland and Scandinavia its impact was minimal. The geography and chronology of its spread are still insufficiently studied. Maps for successive periods would be useful, but the main lines are discernible. The origins of classic feudalism are to be found in the Frankish heartland between the Loire and the Rhine. From there it spread to southern France and northern Italy, where the Franks had held sway. From southern France it entered the Christian kingdoms of Spain, developing some interesting characteristics of its own. It reached Germany early on, and was used as an element of cohesion by the Ottonian kings and emperors; it was not used in a systematic way before the Hohenstaufen emperors, particularly Frederick I Barbarossa, who introduced the *Heerschildordnung*, a formal feudal hierarchy. In the eleventh century the Western European feudal model was adopted wholesale in the papal state, where the popes used knightly vassals for supporting their authority as temporal rulers. Around the same time the Normans, who became acquainted with

[4] J. R. Strayer, 'The two levels of feudalism' in J. R. Strayer, *Medieval statecraft and the perspectives of history* (Princeton, 1971), 63–76.

Frankish feudalism after they settled on the Lower Seine, exported fiefs and vassals to their two main conquests, southern Italy and England. From England feudalism entered Scotland. It entered Central and Eastern Europe in the wake of German cultural and political influence. Finally the system was implanted in the crusader states of the Near East, where its military element suited the situation in those Christian outposts in Muslim surroundings.[5]

## THE SEIGNIORY

The seigniory or manorial lordship (*seigneurie, Grundherrschaft*) was the public-law framework which controlled the everyday life of millions of peasants in the Middle Ages and Modern Times. The seigniory could cover a village or parish, but some seigniories contained several villages, whereas others covered only a fraction of a parish. The seigniory normally coincided with a manor or agricultural domain, but the manorial is not identical with the seigniorial system. The manor was a way of organizing agriculture and the lives of the peasants in a collective exploitation under the supervision of the landowner. Such a large domain, with its demesne land, its farms and its commons, was a social and economic unit. However, when the landlord also exercised the rights of *bannum*, which we associate with public law, such as justice, police and taxation, the manor acquired a different character: it became a mini-state and the landowner became a lord or ruler, who governed the peasants, free and unfree, living on his land, to the exclusion of the normal bearers of public authority, kings, dukes and counts. In post-Carolingian times the seigniory became widespread, both in the sense that ever more peasants were drawn into its net and that the rights of the lords became greater.[6] The rise of modern states and their growing

---

[5] P. Toubert, *Les structures du Latium médiéval. Le Latium méridional et la Sabine du IXe siècle à la fin du XIIe siècle* (Rome, 1973); R. C. van Caenegem, 'Government, law and society' in J. H. Burns (ed.), *The Cambridge history of medieval political thought c. 350–1450* (Cambridge, 1988), 174–210; G. Giordanengo, *Le droit féodal dans les pays de droit écrit. L'exemple de la Provence et du Dauphiné, XIIe–début XIVe siècle* (Rome, 1988); J. P. Poly and E. Bournazel, *La mutation féodale, Xe–XIIe siècle* (2nd edn, Paris, 1991).

[6] The system goes back to the immunity, the exemption from the authority of royal officials, which was granted by the Carolingians to some landowners. See F. L. Ganshof, 'L'immunité dans la monarchie franque' in: *Recueils de la Société Jean Bodin, I: Les liens de vassalité et les immunités* (2nd edn, Brussels, 1958), 171–216. See also A. Verhulst (ed.), *Le grand domaine aux époques mérovingienne et carolingienne. Die Grundherrschaft im frühen Mittelalter. Actes . . . Colloque . . . 1983* (Ghent, 1985).

centralization reduced the role of the seigniories, and national governments curtailed the power of the manorial lords, without altogether abolishing it (which only occurred at the end of the Ancient Regime). The seigniory was well established in feudalized areas, where knights normally headed seigniories held in fief from their suzerains; also their authority over a submissive peasantry must have seemed natural in a society dominated by a class of landowners and warriors, who were hardly kept in check by the remote and weak kings of the period. This does not mean, however, that the manorial regime and feudalism were identical and went necessarily hand in hand. Indeed, one can easily conceive a society where dependent peasants lived on large domains under the public authority of knights and lords who did not hold their land in fief from anyone else. The best proof that the two categories – fiefs and seigniories – are conceptually distinct can be found in the Old English kingdom before the Norman Conquest. The latter introduced feudalism into England, but manors and lords exercising public authority over the peasantry – mainly on the authority of royal grants of jurisdiction – had been widespread there for a long time.[7]

The small scale of public life during this period appeals to modern man. We are nowadays, more than in the nineteenth century, appreciative of a world where local affairs were dealt with by local lords and their staffs, and discussed by the whole village community in manorial and other minor courts, without interference from bureaucrats in some far away megalopolis. On the other hand those agrarian mini-states were incapable of securing the external safety of the inhabitants, who were also inadequately protected against arbitrary and rapacious lords who did not know when to stop imposing new burdens in the form of payments in kind or money or labour services. These were the *malae consuetudines* ('bad customs') from which the peasants could only escape through flight to the towns, which offered personal freedom, or to new lands in Eastern Europe or in Spain, where favourable conditions were offered to attract new settlers. They 'protested with their feet', like some people in our own time who flee their country in order to escape intolerable fiscal oppression. It seems obvious that this peasant discontent was a support for the reassertion of the monarchy as against the feudal barons in the twelfth century.[8]

[7] B. Lyon, *A constitutional and legal history of medieval England* (2nd edn, New York, 1980), 86–8.
[8] See R. Boutruche, *Seigneurie et féodalité* (2 vols., Paris, 1968–70); *Handwörterbuch zur deutschen*

## THE EMPIRE

Under Charlemagne all Latin Christendom except the British Isles formed one West Roman empire, as Greek Christendom was politically united under one East Roman emperor. The Byzantine state survived for many centuries, but the Frankish–Roman empire was short-lived. As early as the ninth century the imperial title fell into the hands of nonentities, and in the early tenth it vanished altogether. However, the memory of Charlemagne survived, and many people felt that the West ought to have the Roman empire as its political superstructure. Consequently it was reborn for the second time, when the German king Otto I was crowned emperor. He was the most powerful ruler in Europe, and his victory over the Magyars, who had penetrated deep into Western Europe, gave him the prestige of the saviour of the Continent. Following in Charlemagne's footsteps he had in 951 obtained, after the German crown, that of Italy as well[9] and was finally crowned emperor by the pope in Rome in 962. This was the beginning of the most brilliant period of the German Middle Ages, known as the *Kaiserzeit* ('the time of the emperors'). Germany then played a leading role in Europe, well outside its national frontiers, and this lasted until the decline of the House of Hohenstaufen (Frederick II died in 1250). Thereafter the Roman empire, which became known as the Holy Roman Empire of the German Nation, led a shadowy life, until its final extinction in 1806, at the hands of Napoleon. This Roman–German empire belongs to the oddest creations public law has produced in the course of the centuries. It deserves a brief analysis.

The dignity of Roman emperor was linked to that of German king. From Otto I onwards the German king was entitled to his papal coronation as Roman emperor, which was, until the sixteenth century, performed in Italy and gave him the right to bear the title of Roman emperor. During the period between his election as German king and his imperial coronation he carried the transitional title of king of the Romans.[10] The German–Roman medieval empire was an

*Rechtsgeschichte*, I (Berlin, 1971), 1824–42; G. Fourquin, *Seigneurie et féodalité au moyen âge* (2nd edn, Paris, 1977); W. Rösener (ed.), *Strukturen der Grundherrschaft im Mittelalter* (Göttingen, 1989).

[9] See on the political scene in Italy under the Ottonians R. Pauler, *Das Regnum Italiae in ottonischer Zeit. Markgrafen, Grafen und Bischöfe als politische Kräfte* (Tübingen, 1982).

[10] R. Buchner, 'Der Titel rex Romanorum in deutschen Königsurkunden des 11. Jahrhunderts', *Deutsches Archiv* 19 (1963), 327–38; H. Beumann, *Der deutsche König als Romanorum Rex*, (Frankfurt, 1981).

artificial construction, a doomed attempt to resurrect – once again – a vanished universal state. The whole strange contraption can only be understood in light of the conviction of medieval man that his own epoch was a weak copy of the brilliance of Antiquity. This same sentiment inspired his awe for the great authoritative texts of the past, the Bible, the Church Fathers, Roman law and Aristotle: giants on whose shoulders the medieval dwarfs were sitting. Everything about this medio-Roman empire was unreal. There was no Roman nation, although there were Latin Christians full of veneration for the Holy City of Rome; there was no Roman country, and no Roman citizenship: people felt they were the subjects of their respective kings, dukes and counts. Even in Italy they did not consider themselves Roman citizens any more, but the subjects of the king in the north, the pope in the centre, and various Arab, Byzantine and later Norman rulers in the south. It is obvious that, in the absence of a Roman state, there was no question of a Roman administration carrying out imperial policy throughout Western Europe, nor of imperial legislation enforced throughout the West (only a few edicts of the medieval Roman emperors were incorporated into the *Corpus Iuris*). A supreme imperial court of law for the whole of Europe was equally lacking, as was a neo-Roman senate, with representatives from various countries sitting with the emperor. Nor, finally, was there any trace of a separate imperial treasury or taxation: the revenues from the kingdoms of Germany and Italy had to pay for the imperial policies of the Saxon, Salic and Hohenstaufen rulers. The modern historian should see through all the nostalgic titles and rituals and not be carried away by letters as pompous as the one sent by Conrad III in 1142 to his Byzantine fellow-emperor John II Comnenos, pretending that all Europe, including France, Spain, England and Denmark, had made its submission to him and that the whole of Italy was impatiently expecting his arrival (to be crowned).[11] The truth of the matter is that the national monarchies did not feel inferior and never showed any trace of submission to the German–Roman emperors. On the eastern flank of Germany there were, however, countries which did recognize to some extent imperial suzerainty: Bohemia, Poland and Hungary, Bohemia even becoming a kingdom within the empire and its king one of the German Electors. Elsewhere, and particularly in the kingdom of France, German ideas of hegemony were categorically

[11] H. Keller, *Zwischen regionaler Begrenzung und universalem Horizont. Deutschland im Imperium der Salier und Staufer 1024–1250* (Berlin, 1986).

rejected.[12] The most the emperor could hope for there was a vague ceremonial precedence and the recognition of the title of imperial notary – a very modest achievement.[13]

What was the significance of the Roman empire at its heyday? It was, I believe, in the first place a sublimation of the German monarchy, which from the tenth to the thirteenth century headed a multinational complex of states without parallel in Europe. The empire was therefore condemned to follow the ups and downs of German kingship: the latter's failure in urbanized northern Italy and its concessions to the ambitious German princes, spiritual and temporal, at home, had weakened it so much that in the end even the illusion of a universal empire could not survive. So, by the end of the Middle Ages the Roman empire had become German and events had come full circle; having passed through a zenith as universal rulers, the German kings had returned to their national starting point. With hindsight it seems doubtful whether the northern Italians could ever have greeted the German kings as their 'natural lords of the land': there are eloquent indications that the Italian population, particularly the urban, non-feudal segment, saw its German rulers, who descended from the Alps upon Italy with their knights and foot soldiers for the imperial coronation, as a foreign occupation which they came to fight in numerous battles.

There was another dimension to the empire which could have provided a solid foundation for a universal monarchy, i.e. the imperial protectorate of the Roman Church. As the papacy was universally recognized, so its protector could have participated in that esteem: one universal pope and one universal emperor, both appointed by God to lead Western Christianity. This configuration made a deep impression on the faithful until well into the eleventh century, witness the ceremony in 1027 when Conrad II was crowned emperor by Pope John XIX in the basilica of St Peter and walked to his throne surrounded by two kings, Canute of Denmark and England and Rodolph III of Burgundy, under the acclamation of the

---

[12] John of Salisbury, a known critic of the empire, asked in 1160: 'who appointed the Germans to be the judges of the nations?' and he described Barbarossa as 'the German tyrant': see R. L. Benson, 'Political *renovatio*: two models from Roman antiquity' in R. L. Benson and G. Constable (eds.), *Renaissance and renewal in the twelfth century* (Oxford, 1982), 379.

[13] K. F. Werner, 'Das hochmittelalterliche Imperium im politischen Bewusstsein Frankreichs (10.–12. Jahrhundert)', *Historische Zeitschrift* 200/1 (1965), 1–60; W. Kienast, *Deutschland und Frankreich in der Kaiserzeit (900–1270)* (Stuttgart, 1974–5); K. J. Leyser, *Medieval Germany and its neighbours 900–1250* (London, 1983); K. F. Werner, *Vom Frankenreich zur Entfaltung Deutschlands und Frankreichs* (Sigmaringen, 1984).

Romans. However, the Gregorian Reform and the Investiture Struggle put an end to this illusion: pope and emperor, the only two leaders with a universal appeal, were involved in a power struggle which cost the German monarchy dear. After the death of Frederick II the German kingdom itself went through a deep crisis – its Italian policies were in ruins – but two generations later the papacy, under Boniface VIII, also suffered a severe humiliation at the hands of the French. In the end neither of the two universal leaders was victorious and their exhausting conflict had prepared the way for the sovereign nation states.

It seems apt to conclude these pages on the medieval empire with the question as to what modern historiography has made of this puzzling phenomenon. The traditional view, which took shape in the nineteenth century, sees the imperial ambitions and the whole Italian policy of the German monarchy as a hopeless and chimerical endeavour. And as if this were not bad enough, the whole undertaking was blamed for the distintegration of the medieval German state: the kings not only wasted the energy they should have spent on building a strong and centralized Germany in chasing after cosmopolitan illusions, but they even made unacceptable concessions to the ecclesiastical and lay princes in Germany in order to have a free hand in Italy. As a result they ended up empty-handed and Germany entered upon a long period of internal division and external weakness (which led, for example, to loss of territory to the French monarchy at the time of Philip IV). There is a good deal of truth in that theory, but we should remember that nineteenth-century historiography was nationally inspired and believed that the unitary sovereign nation state was the ultimate achievement of European history. At present, however, we tend to see things differently: we do not accept the nation state unquestionably, and the supranational European dimension holds a greater appeal. Seen in this light, the attempts of medieval emperors and popes to create a public law that would encompass all European nations seem less utopian. There is no reason why the nation state should be the absolute yardstick with which to judge the statesmen of the past. Besides, what is utopian? Would we until recently not have dubbed utopian any speculation on the peaceful reunification of Germany or on the collapse of the Soviet Union and its one-party regime? Nevertheless, our greater sympathy for the medieval empire does not change the fact that its chances of success were hazardous, to say the least.

## THE CHURCH

In the ninth century papal prestige was undisputed and, as the popes supported the Carolingians, so the Frankish kings and emperors added to the eminence of the papal office. The two leading figures supported each other in their respective spheres. It is therefore not surprising that the crisis of the Carolingian empire had serious consequences for the papacy: the absence of a common political leader in the West led to the decline of the pope's spiritual leadership. Political and religious disintegration went hand in hand: in the late ninth century the flow of papal decretals dried up, and in the tenth the papacy went through its most disreputable phase ever. The *cathedra beati Petri* was occupied by insignificant and even worthless individuals, appointed through local cabals and without any contact with the mainstream of society. The other churches – provinces, bishoprics and abbeys – went their separate ways and fell into the hands of national or regional rulers and lords. Finally the papacy itself came under the control of the Roman emperors, just as other prelates were controlled by their own rulers. It was the great era of the proprietary churches, which were run by lay rulers and lords who owned the buildings and appointed the clerics. The system worked at the local level, where landowners built churches on their domains for their peasants, and administered church income and expenditure – many abbeys also were the proprietary monasteries of leading lineages. At the regional and national level it meant that counts, dukes and kings controlled the bishoprics in their lands, appointing bishops, enfeoffing them with their dioceses, installing them in their ecclesiastical offices ('investiture') and including them in the circle of their vassals by accepting their feudal homage.

The practice was most systematically applied in Germany, where the kings went a step further. They not only controlled their own churches, but went so far as to entrust the temporal government of large areas of Germany to the local bishops and abbots. This at first occasional practice became a real system, and is known as the *Reichskirche* ('Imperial Church'). It meant that the prince-bishops or prince-abbots combined two different offices, one ecclesiastical, i.e. the *cura animarum* of their diocese or the guidance of a community of monks, the other a worldly, political task, i.e. the exercise, in the name of the emperor, of the administrative, police, judicial, military and fiscal responsibilities of government. The system was started under Otto I and extended to Italy; even the bishops of Rome were, until well into the eleventh century, appointed by the German kings/Roman emperors, who treated the Holy See as if it were part of the *Reichskirche*. The practice went back to a distant past, as the Christian emperors in late Antiquity had not only protected but even dominated the Church (as the Byzantine emperors continued to do) and Louis the Pious had begun investing Frankish bishops with their office. The advantages of the system were substantial, as the prince-bishops were selected from the only learned or even literate section of the population, the clergy, were recruited from the personnel of the royal chancery and, being unmarried, could not found regional, separatist dynasties. The device worked flawlessly until the Gregorian Reform, but even afterwards it was essentially maintained, even though it was adapted in various points. Right up to the end of the Ancient Regime numerous German principalities were governed by a bishop and his cathedral chapter or by an abbot. One of numerous examples is the prince-bishopric of Liège in present-day Belgium, which existed for some eight centuries as a prosperous regional state headed by the bishop of Liège and enjoyed great autonomy within the kingdom of Germany[14] until its abolition and annexation by the French republic. Many splendid episcopal palaces in the old empire – in Würzburg and Salzburg for example – remind the visitor of their occupants, who were not only prelates but rulers as well.

There was, however, one essential condition for the good functioning of the system: the undivided loyalty of the prince-bishops to their king and feudal lord, the highest leader in the country's political and religious affairs. This element of cohesion was bound to become a factor of disruption as soon as the hierarchy of the Church decided to go its own way, independent from and, if need be, against the political establishment. As long as the papacy enjoyed a pre-eminent position in the West, was integrated in the Imperial Church and accepted the situation, all went well, but as soon as the popes freed themselves from imperial tutelage to follow a policy of their own – even against the emperor if need be – the German clergy was torn between two opposing loyalties. As heads of German provinces and royal vassals the bishops owed service to their king, the 'anointed of the Lord', but as churchmen they owed obedience to their spiritual leader, who

---

[14] See the fundamental study by J.-L. Kupper, *Liège et l'Eglise Impériale XIe–XIIe siècles* (Paris, 1981).

occupied the See of St Peter and whose name was 'unique in the world' (as the *Dictatus Papae* of 1075 put it). If that ever happened, conflict was unavoidable, for the German king could not possibly give up his control of the bishops and abbots of the Imperial Church, as they belonged to the political leadership of the country and administered large parts of it. Similarly the pope could not renounce his religious guidance of all the churches in Latin Christendom: nobody could reasonably expect him to let the German bishoprics escape the spiritual authority to which all others were submitted. This conflict, known as the Investiture Struggle, arose as a consequence of a religious movement of emancipation, the Gregorian Reform (so called after its main leader, Pope Gregory VII), and its consequences for public law were far reaching. The Reformers attacked some inveterate customs which, according to them, had shackled the Church to worldly institutions, preventing it from carrying out its own religious mission with the necessary degree of independence. The conflict went very deep and pitted the national state against supranational ideology – a situation with which our own century has been well acquainted. The action of the Reformers was directed against the following abuses (as they saw them).

Clerical marriage, which was widespread among parish priests but exceptional among the bishops (the monks were all celibate), was considered too much of an involvement with secular life and condemned; compulsory celibacy was imposed in the course of the twelfth century and was the normal situation by the thirteenth. Many Church lands and tithes had passed into secular hands through violence, usurpation or illegal transactions concluded by bishops and abbots. This state of affairs was condemned and measures taken to remedy it. As a consequence the system of proprietary churches declined markedly, particularly in the twelfth century, and numerous tithes were transferred to religious owners. Simony was an abuse that was practised frequently and unashamedly. In this sense it is, for example, comparable to the control exerted by political parties over appointment to public office which exists in some countries in our own time: everybody deplores the abuse, but nobody has the courage to change it. Simony was the name given, after a personage in the New Testament, to the commercialization of spiritual goods and values, particularly the sale by kings and prelates of ecclesiastical offices; kings sold bishoprics to the highest bidders and the new bishops, who had borrowed money to pay for them, at once proceeded to sell the lower diocesan offices of dean, archdeacon, etc. The aim of the Reform was to eradicate this practice and to replace it with the election of the most competent candidate by an ecclesiastical body and without the corrupting influence of money. Possibly the most visually striking sign of the submission of prelates to the government was the ecclesiastical investiture performed by kings and other rulers, from whose hands the bishops received ring and staff, the symbols of their being wedded to their church and offering protection to their flock. This abuse was found to go against ancient canons and successfully condemned. Feudal homage, however, another sign of the dependence of the prelates on the crown, was maintained. The new practice which resulted – no investiture from royal hands, but homage to the king – was worked out in the early twelfth century. It was a compromise based on the distinction between *spiritualia* and *temporalia* in the function of the bishops, who were indeed spiritual leaders, but also played a temporal, political role. The distinction was applied for the first time in a governmental act at the London Concordat of 1107, concluded between King Henry I and Archbishop Anselm of Canterbury, and again in the Concordat of Worms of 1122, between Emperor Henry V and Pope Calixtus II: henceforth the bishops would no more receive the ecclesiastical investiture from the hands of the emperor and would be elected by clerical bodies, but the emperor was allowed to influence the elections and to accept feudal homage from the bishops. The concordat of 1122 was no more than a lull in the power struggle between the two universal leaders of the time. The conflict was resumed with great violence under the Hohenstaufen emperors, Frederick I Barbarossa and Frederick II.

The outcome of the European Investiture Struggle, by no means a peculiarly German problem, was advantageous to the Church. The hold of the state on the Church was weakened, and so was the stature of the emperor in Italy and eventually in Germany itself. Papal authority consequently reached its zenith and the Roman curia intervened constantly in the political affairs, national as well as international, of the crowned heads; the pope even became feudal overlord of several kingdoms and principalities. In the long run this ecclesiastical emancipation has had some unforeseen consequences for the states. By forbidding the kings to perform the clerical investiture because they were laymen, a process of secularization was inaugurated and the road opened for a clear conceptual distinction between the organs and aims of secular society and those of the

Church. Authors such as Marsilius of Padua in the fourteenth century stressed the autonomy and legitimacy of the state as the organization responsible for the temporal well-being of its citizens, and not for some religious objective. The exclusive reservation of religious affairs to the organs of the Church restricted the state to its own specifically political mission.[15]

---

[15] Among important recent publications see the following, R. Schieffer, *Die Entstehung des päpstlichen Investiturverbots für den deutschen König* (Stuttgart, 1981); *La cristianità dei secoli XI e XII in Occidente* . . . *Atti* . . . *Settimana* . . . *Mendola* (Milan, 1983); K. Pennington, *Pope and bishops. The papal monarchy in the twelfth and thirteenth centuries* (Philadelphia, 1984); B. Szabó-Bechstein, *Libertas ecclesiae: ein Schlüsselbegriff des Investiturstreites und seine Vorgeschichte, 4.–12. Jahrhundert* (Rome, 1985); H. Fuhrmann, '"Der wahre Kaiser ist der Papst". Von der irdischen Gewalt im Mittelalter' in *Das antike Rom in Europa* 12 (Regensburg, 1986), 99–121; B. Tierney, *The crisis of Church and state 1050–1300* (Toronto, 1988); C. Morris, *The papal monarchy. The Western Church from 1050 to 1250* (Oxford, 1989); *La riforma Gregoriana e l'Europa. Congresso* . . . *Salerno* . . . *1985*, I: *Relazioni* (Rome, 1989); I. S. Robinson, *The papacy 1073–1198. Continuity and innovation* (Cambridge, 1990). It is well known that a fundamental importance is attached to the Gregorian Reform in the renowned work of H. J. Berman, *Law and revolution. The formation of the western legal tradition* (Cambridge, Mass., 1983).

CHAPTER 5

# The foundation of the modern state

## GENERAL OUTLINE

The period from the twelfth to the fifteenth century, sometimes called the Second Middle Ages, witnessed the foundation of the political structures of modern Europe. In those years a new model originated in which we can easily recognize the nation state of our own time. Some elements of the older public law naturally survived, in the first place the monarchy itself, even though its character was transformed. Thus the period saw the end of the deeply religious rulers of the type of Louis the Pious (*d.* 840), who was constantly swayed by the clergy, Edward the Confessor (*d.* 1066), whose main concerns were his collection of saints' relics and the construction of his beloved Westminster Abbey, or Henry II of Germany (*d.* 1024), who systematically pursued the organization of the Imperial Church and conceived his policy entirely in a clerical and even monastic perspective. The new kings by contrast found inspiration in Roman law rather than the Bible; they were hard, secular and realistic leaders such as Frederick II in Germany and Italy (*d.* 1250) or Philip IV the Fair in France (*d.* 1314). Not only the monarchy, but the state itself changed in character. Whereas previously public life was dominated by the opinionated knights, administration now passed into the hands of centrally appointed functionaries. The old undifferentiated feudal councils, which used to conduct the affairs of state in an amateurish fashion, gave way to established professionals, appointed to look after the financial, judicial and legislative tasks of the monarchy.

The geographical borders within which this structural transition took place differed widely and depended on the vagaries of politics, which need not detain us here in detail: a general outline should suffice.

In the most straightforward case there was a unitary kingdom where the authority of the one national monarchy was generally recognized and effective. The kingdoms of England, Hungary and Denmark come to mind, where the modernization of political organization took place from the start within the national framework.

The French situation was more complicated, as the monarchy had lost effective control of the largest part of the realm and only began to regain the lost territory in the twelfth century, the start of a process of reunification that was completed at the end of the Middle Ages. Here the structural transformations initially took place within the borders of the territorial principalities, followed later on by the royal *domaine direct*. The principalities, which gradually came under Parisian rule, had embarked upon their modernization before the crown took them over and replaced the dukes and counts by royal bailiffs and seneschals.

In Spain also the internal transformation had started on the regional level and only reached the national dimension after the kingdom of Spain was established at the end of the fifteenth century. This was only natural, as there was in Spain, in contradistinction to France, not one single embryo of a national monarchy, which could have gradually absorbed all the provinces. Indeed, the national monarchy of Visigothic times had disappeared from Spanish history and been replaced by a number of minor, independent kingdoms, which, while they modernized their internal organization, gradually coalesced into one nation state.

The German situation was different again. Initially there was a national monarchy which avoided the sort of disintegration which France underwent, even though the dukedoms achieved a larger degree of autonomy than the English earldoms, for example, ever obtained. But in the thirteenth century, when the administrative transformation went ahead, the political situation had changed to such an extent that it was not in the nation state, but in the German princedoms, that the modern structures were being erected. This was also true of the Low Countries, which to a very large extent were situated in the kingdom of Germany, and which, before the nineteenth century, never constituted one kingdom themselves.

In Italy things were different again. In the south the Norman conquerors began in the eleventh century to erect a state which under the kings of the Houses of Hohenstaufen and Anjou grew into one of the most modern of the time. In the centre of Italy the papal state witnessed a rather slow administrative development, which is remarkable as the papal government of the Latin Church was at the forefront of the modernization of public law in Europe. In the north, the situation of the old *regnum Langobardorum*, which had become the *regnum Italiae*, was legally unequivocal. The kingdom was indissolubly linked to the German monarchy, which exercised its legitimate authority there. It was supported by local officials, first of the feudal and later of the modern–official type (*podestà*). Reality, however, began to look rather different from the late eleventh century onwards, and the main cities, united in leagues, managed to gain so much autonomy that they eventually were turned into independent city-states or urban republics. The constitutional consequence was obvious, particularly after the failure of attempts by the emperors to introduce a centralized state run by their officials (Frederick II being the last to make strenuous efforts in that sense). So the cities developed their own municipal Constitutions, in the midst of frequent struggles between oligarchy and democracy, resulting in most cases in the establishment of the monocracy of some leading urban family (so aptly described in Machiavelli's *Il Principe*). The triumph of the personal rule of these princes has led some observers to the depressing conclusion that democracy is doomed to end in failure and to lead to the rise of popular dictators.[1] In all the cases we outlined the size of the national or regional states held the middle ground between the very large scale of the Roman empire and the very small scale of the seigniories and mini-counties of feudal times.

### THE NEW STRUCTURES

Centralization was the most striking phenomenon, as public law developed from the Germanic dispersion of the centres of power to the Roman concentration of all authority in one hand, that of the ruler assisted by his council. Previously local authorities even when acting

---

[1] Among recent works on the Italian city-states we mention the following. W. B. Bowsky, *A medieval Italian commune. Siena under the Nine 1287–1355* (Berkeley, 1981); J. N. Stephens, *The fall of the Florentine Republic 1512–1530* (Oxford, 1983); D. Ciampoli, *Il capitano del popolo a Siena nel primo Trecento* (Siena, 1984); T. Dean, *Land and power in late medieval Ferrara. The rule of the Este 1350–1450* (Cambridge, 1987); H. Maurer (ed.), *Kommunale Bündnisse Oberitaliens und Oberdeutschlands im Vergleich* (Sigmaringen, 1987); D. Waley, *The Italian city-republics* (3rd edn, London, 1988); J. H. Mundy, 'In praise of Italy: the Italian republics', *Speculum* 64 (1989), 815–34; *Milano e il suo territorio in età comunale ( XI–XII secolo)*. Atti dell' XI congresso internazionale di studi sull'alto medioevo . . . 1987 (2 vols., Spoleto, 1989); G. Tabacco, *The struggle for power in medieval Italy. Structures of political rule, 400–1400* (Cambridge, 1990); C. Lansing, *The Florentine magnates. Lineage and faction in a medieval commune* (Princeton, 1991); A. Rutigliano, *Lorenzetti's Golden Mean. The Riformatori of Siena, 1368–1385* (New York, Berne, 1991). See the chapter on 'The mixed constitution and Italian republicanism' in J. M. Blythe, *Ideal government and the mixed constitution in the Middle Ages* (Princeton, 1992), 278–300.

as royal representatives enjoyed a high degree of independence. Their office was not only for life, it was even hereditary; also, they belonged to the nobility and enjoyed the status and influence of big landowners. From the twelfth century onwards they were replaced by a new type of official, who was no member of the nobility (often a knight and modest landowner), but a salaried appointee of the ruler, to whom he owed his whole position. Many of those modern-style bailiffs, seneschals, justiciars and provosts came from inconspicuous families and owed their role in society to their previous expert service in the administration of the royal manors. As agents of the central government in their respective areas they were responsible for judicial, fiscal and military tasks. In some countries, such as Flanders, an entirely new type of official was created, the comital bailiff, who in the twelfth century came to replace the old-style feudal castellan. In England, in the same century, the kings first tried to replace the traditional sheriff (*shire gerefa*, *vicecomes*) by an official of a new type, the local justiciar, but this was a passing experiment, and the sheriff remained the local representative of the central government. The old office was, however, modernized through the appointment of people from less exalted origins and the imposition of stricter controls.

The central organs of state were themselves transformed. The feudal king's court was split into specialized departments manned by full-time officials, who followed routine procedures. The oldest were the 'chambers of accounts' – in England called the Exchequer – where the accounts of the agents of the crown were kept and scrutinized and fiscal litigation settled. They were followed by central courts of law, such as the Court of Common Pleas at Westminster and the Parlement of Paris. Their professionalism led to bureaucratic methods, as the role of writing gained in importance and most decisions were taken by groups of councillors who bore no political responsibility but proceeded according to fixed norms and precedents, without personal intervention by the monarch. These officials and judges had been thoroughly trained, either – as in England – in practice or – as often on the Continent – through the study of Roman law in the universities. The social origins of this, to present-day standards, very small group of people could be found mostly among the gentry and prosperous townspeople; they were united by their expertise and loyalty to the crown. The cost of these state services was covered by the traditional income from crown lands and increasingly by grants from towns and parliaments. The Church was also made to contribute, as many royal officials and judges, particularly in the earliest phase, were clerics who lived on prebends and in fact worked for the state while being paid by the Church. Careers in the service of the state opened new perspectives for the turbulent knighthood, but at the same time tended to tame it: its military way of life and its traditional dominant position were harnessed by the crown. Also, many knights found in the service of the state a solution for their financial problems, as they were caught between the pincers of rising costs (caused by inflation and conspicuous consumption) and unchanged revenue from ancient rents. One should, however, not imagine that the old feudal order was completely bureaucratized: as soon as a political crisis at home or abroad offered it a chance of showing its prowess on the battlefield and gaining booty and mercenary pay, it grasped it with enthusiasm – whether it was in the Hundred Years War between France and England or in the English Wars of the Roses.

A last striking shift in the politics of the period concerns the basis itself of the monarchy. For centuries this had consisted of a group of people, rather than a fixed territory. The transformation which took place in this respect is most clearly expressed by the official titles of the rulers. Whereas they used to call themselves 'kings of the Franks' (or later, of the French) or of the English, or 'counts of the Flemings', around AD1200 the new style 'king of France', 'king of England', or 'count of Flanders' was introduced. This showed that the state had become a territorial instead of a personal unit, and within the fixed boundaries of this territory the crown constituted henceforth the sole government. Even where the direct organs and officials of the crown had to leave some room for the older institutions, such as feudal and manorial courts, the latter's jurisdiction was reduced: they lost the *causae majores* ('major cases') and what was left was placed under central control through the procedure of appeal (at least in civil matters).

## HALF-WAY BETWEEN FEUDALISM AND THE MODERN STATE

The late medieval state was clearly positioned half-way between the old feudal constitution and the absolute monarchy of Modern Times. It clearly bore the marks of the previous phase and suffered various limitations, which were not discarded until the era of absolutism. The following elements deserve our attention.

The state was semi-feudal, in so far as the tenants in chief and main landholders still had ambitions to play a role in the national government, beside and sometimes against the royal entourage. The baronial revolts under the English king Henry III (*d.* 1272) illustrated the seriousness of this threat. Consequently the state was only semi-bureaucratic. The role of the learned officialdom was limited to routine tasks in administration and law: decision making was outside its field and bureaucratic ambitions led to clashes with the nobles, who firmly believed that the business of government ought to be left to them. To illustrate our point we can refer to the resistance offered by the Peers of France to the jurisdiction of the learned unaristocratic Parlement of Paris and their contention that they ought to appear exclusively before their fellow tenants in chief, i.e. in the *cour des pairs*, as in the days of the old *curia regis*. Also, it is well known that in the Netherlands in the sixteenth century the objections of aristocratic members in the Council of State against the bureaucratic government of Philip II were instrumental in unleashing the Revolt of the Low Countries.

The distinction between the areas of public and private law was also still imperfect and the ancient patrimonial approach was still strong. Princes thought very much in dynastic terms and considered their countries as estates which had to be preserved and passed on to their descendants intact and, if possible, augmented. Admittedly the division of kingdoms among the heirs had disappeared, but there was no lack of obvious relics of the old attitudes. One example was the assignation of apanages, a system used to compensate the younger sons for the fact that the oldest inherited the whole kingdom, by appointing them at the head of certain provinces: the duchy of Burgundy, which was the starting point of the Burgundian Netherlands, was such an apanage, created in 1363 by the French king John the Good for his fourth son, Philip the Bold (*d.* 1404). Some rulers were still prepared to give away part of their principality if this could improve their daughter's chances of marrying royalty. This sort of deal annoyed the inhabitants, who were attached to their country and did not want it to be carved up. This is clear, for example, from the *Joyeuse Entrée*, a charter granted by Joan and Wenceslas upon their accession to the duchy of Brabant in 1356, in which the promise was made that Joan's younger sisters would be suitably compensated, but without severing any part from the duchy. The force of the ancient patrimonial approach also appeared from the continuing confusion between the public and the private finances of the princes. Expenditure for the maintenance of the royal family and its court was treated on an equal footing with that for the internal and external activities of the state and the revenue from the crown lands was not distinguished from the yields of tolls, fines and grants. It is only in Modern Times that the separation of these financial spheres was carried out, when the civil list was established and what was left of the old crown domain was liquidated. Nevertheless the late Middle Ages had gone some way in that direction. Thus in England the royal receipts *in camera* and for the wardrobe were distinguished from those paid into the treasury by the sheriffs and accounted for in the Pipe Rolls at the Exchequer.

Late medieval monarchy was not yet absolute, because it was subjected to certain internal and external restrictions. This is an aspect which deserves a detailed analysis.

### THE LEGAL LIMITATIONS OF THE LATE MEDIEVAL MONARCHY

The limitations which restricted the monarchy were, as we have already indicated, both of an internal and an external nature. The internal ones were caused by urban autonomy, constitutionalism and parliamentarianism; the external ones were caused by the supernational role of the empire and the papacy. The movement for autonomy in larger cities was an important political factor in the constitutional development of numerous kingdoms and principalities: some crowned heads were obliged to share power with the towns or even to abandon it to them altogether. The situation varied from country to country and was, of course, linked to the balance of power prevailing in each one of them. The main factors were the degree of urbanization and the strength of the monarchy. It is obvious that the problem did not arise in backward, purely agricultural areas which contained only small towns with a modest market or garrison or offering minor administrative services. The situation was quite different in countries with powerful towns: here everything depended on the political evolution. In England, ruled by an ancient and forceful monarchy, towns never achieved political autonomy. This situation appears normal today, when mighty agglomerations like London and New York are subjected to the national government and only carry such political responsibility as the central authorities leave them. But the situation in northern Italy was the exact opposite. It was the most urbanized part of Western Europe, with large cities of 100,000 inhabitants, and it had an enfeebled royal government. Consequently the towns freed themselves from the crown and founded urban republics which followed their own policies, not infrequently entering into conflict with each other.

In Germany the decline of the monarchy allowed some cities to achieve political autonomy, the *Reichsstädte* or imperial cities, but others, situated in principalities with a strong government, remained subjected to the territorial state.

In France the communal movement followed the evolution of the monarchy. Initially the towns, which were numerous and important, achieved considerable freedom, as could be expected because of the weakness of the crown. But as the latter re-established itself and extended its power, thanks *inter alia* to the support of urban militias, the towns lost many of the privileges they had gained in a different political climate, and their autonomy was greatly restricted. The failed Parisian revolt under the leadership of Etienne Marcel (*d.* 1358) was a last reminder of their erstwhile political ambitions, but it had been evident since about 1300 that urban liberties were eroded by the state, and the urban magistrates reduced to the status of local cogs of the national machinery of government.

Flanders witnessed a specific development, because it combined exceptional urban growth with early modernization of the administration of the state. The chances of an Italian-style evolution were considerable, and under the captain of Ghent, James van Artevelde (*d.* 1345), it looked for a moment as if the county would be divided into three city-states, Ghent, Bruges and Ypres. However, the rulers of the House of Burgundy saved the monarchic principle and restored central government, even though the resistance of Ghent, after abortive revolts against Duke Philip the Good and Emperor Charles V, was not finally broken until the city capitulated to the armies of Philip II of Spain in 1584.

Late medieval constitutionalism was an important European creation, whose impact on public law is most notable in our own day: there is a direct continuity between the fundamental laws of the later Middle Ages and the Constitutions and Bills of Rights of our own world, especially as far as human rights and citizens' freedoms are concerned. The word 'constitution' has several meanings. It can be applied to persons, who are said to have a weak or robust constitution. It can be applied to states, in the sense of the way they happen to be constituted, established, organized and ruled, or in the more restricted sense of a particular written document in which the fundamental principles governing the exercise of political authority are laid down.[2] Consequently 'constitutionalism' refers to a legal tradition based on the idea that the exercise of political power ought to be restricted by a fundamental pact between the governors and the governed, safeguarding the rights of the latter and defining the tasks and powers of the former.

The historic starting point of European constitutionalism was the increased impact of royal power on the persons and possessions of their subjects. As the latter resisted the threat of arbitrary rule, and political strife broke out, solemn charters were granted in which the rulers promised to eliminate specifically named abuses, and to treat their subjects according to the law. These types of texts, which were seen as basic pacts between the prince and his people and as guarantees of personal freedom and the rule of law, were widely known throughout Europe. The earliest appeared in northern Spain in the late twelfth century, but the most famous is the English Magna Carta of King John, issued in 1215. It deserves our special attention, not only as it is typical of the genre, but also because it played an important role in later centuries, influencing the constitutional development in England, the United States of America and the entire modern world.

King John's tyranny caused a revolt, led by the feudal barons and supported by the city of London and the Church. The king and his agents were accused of treating the subjects arbitrarily and illegally and causing damage to their persons and goods. The *Magna Carta Libertatum* ('Great Charter of Liberties') was granted and sealed by the king under the military pressure of the insurgents. It contained a number of precisely-worded royal promises that various recent abuses would in the future be avoided. They naturally concerned the feudal practice of the time and are therefore irrelevant in the modern world: most of them were abolished by the nineteenth-century Repeal Acts. The lasting message of the document is, however, as significant today as it was in 1215, i.e. the principle that governments are bound to operate under the law and that the subjects (in 1215 the 'freemen') are protected by the law in their persons and their goods. In other words it contains the famous common-law notion that 'nobody is

---

[2] See the considerations in P. Bastid, *L'idée de constitution* (Paris, 1985).

above the law, be he ever so high' (with the exception, of course, of Parliament, which is not bound by any laws). It may be interesting to have a look at a few concerns of the Charter. There was, for example, an article on the feudal relief, a sort of death duty paid by the heir of a fief to the lord upon becoming his vassal and receiving the land from his hands: the Charter put an end to the arbitrary and exorbitant sums King John used to demand, and ordered the return to the traditional tariff. Other articles were aimed at arbitrary and ruinous fines and the forced remarriage – at the king's behest – of widows, who were sought after for their wealth and used to be 'sold' to the highest bidder. It is, however, Article 39 (of the 1215 version) that carried the greatest weight as one of the earliest milestones on the road to the rule of law, for it said that no free person could be punished (with imprisonment, loss of goods, banishment and so on) except by a lawful judgment of his equals or according to the law of the land: every free person was entitled to what later came to be called due process of law.[3]

The great medieval charters of liberties were not always respected and were often merely the passing fruit of a truce in the conflict between government and opposition. Many were forgotten in the age of absolutism or regarded as medieval curiosities. This was, however, not invariably the case. Joan and Wenceslas' *Joyeuse Entrée* was never forgotten in Brabant and when Joseph II annulled it in 1789, the result was a revolt known as the Brabantine Revolution.[4] Moreover, the English Magna Carta was a precious source of inspiration for the parliamentary opposition against Stuart absolutism in the seventeenth century.

The rise of parliaments was roughly contemporaneous with that of Constitutions and was equally important. In general terms parliamentarianism can be defined as a form of government whereby the ruler acted in consultation with representatives of the country – some of whom at least were elected. Parliament has become a universal paradigm and very few governments operate nowadays without some contact with representatives of the people. However, if this fundamental model is universal, the variations in its actual operation are infinite.

[3] See the recent authoritative survey in J. C. Holt, *Magna Carta* (2nd edn, Cambridge, 1992). See also J. C. Holt, *Magna Carta and medieval government* (London, Ronceverte, 1985) and A. Pallister, *Magna Carta. The heritage of liberty* (Oxford, 1981).
[4] See the considerations in B. Lyon, 'Fact and fiction in English and Belgian constitutional law', *Medievalia et Humanistica* 10 (1956), 82–101.

They veer between two extremes which could be defined as the watch-dog and lap-dog type. The former takes its task as freely elected representation of the people seriously and is independent and critical of the government. Members ask detailed and often annoying questions and may even withhold their confidence from a government supported by their own party, if they believe fundamental interests or rights are threatened ('backbench revolt'). The prime minister and other members of the cabinet will be questioned, and budgets ('appropriations') may be refused, thus forcing the government to give up unpopular policies. The lap-dog parliament, at the other end of the spectrum, is a sham and exists only to applaud a dictatorial government. It contains hand-picked members from the single party that is allowed. Meetings of these parliaments are few and far between and the proceedings are stage-managed, so that the question may be asked what all the fuss is about. It is nevertheless significant that the two main totalitarian regimes of the twentieth century, the Soviet Union and Nazi Germany, found it necessary to keep alive the semblance of a popular representation, respectively in the Supreme Soviet and the Reichstag. In between the two extreme types of parliament one can find various shades of subservience or independence. Even in western democracies there are parliamentary majorities which seem content to let the government get its way in all things and to pass all the laws it wants, even if they are of dubious legality and have been branded as such by courts of law. If the lists of candidates for the elections are drawn up by party headquarters, the danger is real that the resulting parliament will be largely composed of party hacks who will form a very imperfect expression of the will of the people.

The historic origins of present-day parliaments are to be found in the second half of the Middle Ages, when the old baronial *curia regis* was enlarged to include elected representatives of local – rural or urban – communities. These late medieval parliaments – also called estates, *cortes*, diet, Reichstag or *stamento* – were not only the direct precursors of the representative institutions of the present, in a few cases there exists an (almost) uninterrupted continuity between the Middle Ages and the present: the English (now British) Parliament goes directly back to the thirteenth century and the States General of the present kingdom of the Netherlands go back to the mid-fifteenth century, when Philip the Good assembled the representatives of the Burgundian Low Countries for the first time in Bruges in 1464. The matrix of those parliaments is to be found in the king's court of feudal times (hence *cortes* for parliament in Spain), where the king and feudal overlord consulted his top vassals, who owed him their *consilium*, on matters of state. Whereas these restricted meetings of the aristocracy may have been adequate and acceptable in feudal and agrarian Europe, this was no more the case when the revival of the towns and the economy in general had changed society: the *curia regis* was enlarged to include representatives of the landed gentry and the urban bourgeoisie. This extended representation was certainly not elected by the whole population – the peasant masses were almost invariably left out – but it spoke for a much broader social spectrum than the old tenants in chief. On the Continent the parliaments usually met in three chambers, the estates of the clergy, the nobility and the townspeople (third estate). In England the bicameral system prevailed. The House of Lords was the continuation of the old feudal *curia*, where the temporal and spiritual barons met, the lay and ecclesiastical great landowners. It was essentially a hereditary chamber of aristocrats, as the lay lords or peers were more numerous than the bishops and abbots. The other house was the House of Commons, where elected representatives of the gentry, i.e. the smaller landowners, and of the urban bourgeoisie sat together. There were other variations in various parts of Europe. In some countries there was a fourth estate, where representatives of the peasantry assembled. And the county of Flanders was so dominated by the main towns that the so-called Members of Flanders, containing representatives of Ghent, Bruges and Ypres (to which the Liberty of Bruges, i.e. the countryside round the town, came to be added), totally eclipsed the Estates of Flanders, who should have been the real representatives of the land.

The earliest medieval parliaments met in northern Spain in the late twelfth century, when the *curia regis* was extended to include urban representatives. All through the Middle Ages Spanish parliaments played an important role, so much so that fifteenth-century Spain was famous for the strength of its parliamentary institutions. The victory of absolutism in the sixteenth century has tended to obscure this fact and to create the false image of Spain as an essentially autocratic country. The English Parliament, which also went through an eclipse in the sixteenth century but reasserted itself in the seventeenth, goes back, as we have seen, to the middle of the thirteenth century. The first assembly of the French Estates General took place in 1302 in Paris.

Parliaments became a common European phenomenon, even

though there was some terminological confusion. Thus the same Latin root *parliamentum* produced the English word of parliament, referring essentially to a political meeting of representatives of the country, whereas in French it produced *parlement*, which referred to a higher court, composed of learned judges. The activity of the parliaments was supported by the authority of Roman law, as far as the legal theory of representation and full powers given to attorneys is concerned. Medieval lawyers had no hesitation in quoting from the *Corpus Iuris Civilis* out of context. A famous example is afforded by the line from the Code (*C*. 5, 59, 5, 3) *'Quod omnes tangit, ab omnibus approbetur'* ('what concerns all should be approved by all'). The phrase seems to offer good Roman-law authority for democracy, which believes indeed that what concerns all the citizens should be approved by all of them, or at least by their spokesmen. However, upon closer inspection the passage from the Code appears not to refer to the organization of the state at all, but to tutelage, an institution of private law, and merely says that for certain acts of administration of the property of minors the consent of all the tutors is required.[5]

The fate suffered by the medieval parliaments at the hands of absolute kings has varied. We have already seen what happened in Spain. In England the power of Parliament reached a provisional peak in the fifteenth century, when national legislation, for example, was in the hands of both king and Parliament. The latter continued to sit and play its old role in the sixteenth century, at least formally, but its independence and impact on political life were much reduced, as one docile parliament after another voted in laws demanded by the overpowering Tudors. Under the Stuarts it ended its relative impotence and entered into a victorious power struggle against royal absolutism. In France, by contrast, the Estates General played an important role throughout the fifteenth and particularly the sixteenth century, but quickly lost their power in the early seventeenth, when the monarchy asserted itself as soon as the Wars of Religion were over: they never met between 1614 and 1789. In the Republic of the United Provinces the Estates General remained an organ of the state of real importance, even though power and sovereignty resided in principle with the

---

[5] See on the coupling of this Roman-law maxim with the novel conception of the community of the realm of England: E. Hall, 'King Henry III and the English reception of the Roman law maxim *quod omnes tangit*', *Studia Gregoriana* 15 (1972) 125–45. See among the more recent literature: A. Gouron, 'Aux origines médiévales de la maxime *quod omnes tangit*', in *Mélanges J. Imbert* (Paris, 1989), 277–86.

provincial Estates. In the southern Netherlands, which remained under Habsburg rule, the Estates General disappeared in the first half of the seventeenth century. In Poland the diet, dominated by the nobility, not only continued to meet, but came to dominate the monarchy to such an extent that modern Poland is sometimes referred to as an aristocratic republic.

The tasks of these ancient parliaments varied greatly. One should never forget that they were created by the crown as sounding boards and providers of funds. Their primary function was to listen to royal policy declarations, to agree to them and provide the required financial means. Slowly the parliaments broke out of this passive role and produced legal desiderata of their own, which led to their participation in legislation. They also had a judicial competence, relics of which can be detected in the judicial activity of the present House of Lords and the impeachment procedure in the Congress of the United States. It is through their control over the use of the grants they made that parliaments became actively engaged in political affairs: they discussed internal and external policies (even though kings for a long time believed that the latter were far above the understanding of the Commons and should be left to the government). They also took a lively interest in monetary problems, as these greatly affected trade. Nevertheless there was as yet no question of the modern dependence of governments on a parliamentary majority: ruling the country was the God-given task of the king, who reigned personally, and not of politicians whose authority was based on the popular will.[6]

As was pointed out, the late medieval monarchy was also subjected to external limitations: it was not only not absolute, it was not sovereign either, as it recognized, at least in principle, an *auctoritas superior* ('a higher authority'), which existed in the twofold shape of the empire and the papacy. National sovereignty became such a significant issue that it deserves more detailed scrutiny.

The western monarchies have never recognized the medieval empire as an effective supernational authority: to the French the Roman emperor was a German monarch and a neighbour whom they regarded with caution, and it was essential not to let him use his imperial title in order to interfere in France's internal politics. Nobody denied that the imperial crown ranked above the royal, but

---

[6] I will suffice here with two short and useful surveys by well-known authorities: A. Marongiu, *Medieval parliaments. A comparative study* (London, 1968) and A. R. Myers. *Parliaments and estates in Europe to 1789* (London, 1975).

the legal fiction that 'the king was an emperor in his own kingdom'[7] effectively took the wind out of the imperial sails and prevented any patronizing attitude from the east. In northern Italy the situation was different, as the emperor was king of the *regnum Italiae*. His power there was admittedly to such an extent eroded by the towns that it became theoretical, but there was nevertheless a pro-imperial Ghibelline party and thinkers such as Dante in his *de Monarchia* defended the universal monarchy. Also, the modern Italian principalities, which issued from the medieval urban republics, were held by their dukes and counts as imperial fiefs. It is in Central Europe that the empire has really enjoyed political authority even outside Germany's frontiers. Poland at times recognized German suzerainty and the kingdom of Bohemia not only became part of the empire, but its king was even one of the seven German Electors.

Papal claims to universal leadership were taken more seriously. The bishop of Rome and 'heir of St Peter' was the undisputed head of Latin Christendom. As a widely accepted and supernational authority in the Catholic world, he was, in an age of religious fervour, the obvious figure-head to satisfy the desire for western unity. This became particularly manifest after the Gregorian papacy had freed itself from imperial control and Pope Gregory VII had shown his supernational ambition by condemning and deposing Emperor Henry IV. The rise of papal theocracy from Gregory VII (*d.* 1085) to Boniface VIII (*d.* 1303) shows how close the Roman curia has been to the establishment of a European government above all governments. Popes launched and co-ordinated international military expeditions and called for crusades against the infidel; they acted as arbiters between the Christian kingdoms, but occasionally called one ruler to war against another who had displeased the Holy See. They also intervened in the internal politics of European nations, as when Innocent III annulled King John's Magna Carta as having been granted under duress. Several princes went so far as to transfer their countries to the Holy See and to receive them back as papal fiefs, thus becoming papal vassals. This universal leadership was based, among other things, on the theory of the two swords, which held that God had given a temporal sword, involving physical constraint, to

---

[7]  Similarly the English Act in Restraint of Appeals of 1533 contained the striking phrase 'This Realm of England is an Empire'. See on *rex imperator in regno suo* and its uses in various centuries and countries: W. Ullmann, '"This Realm of England is an Empire"', *Journal of Ecclesiastical History* 30 (1979), 175–203.

emperors and kings, and a spiritual sword to the pope: as the heavenly sphere was higher than the earthly, so ecclesiastical was superior to worldly authority, whose mission it was to use the lay arm in order to enforce spiritual values.

The vision of a Christendom guided by the Roman curia and of crowned heads listening to the Holy Father as obedient sons was ruined in the early fourteenth century. It stranded on the growing national pride of European nations, first among them France, which was at the time of Philip IV by far the mightiest kingdom. King Philip, who rejected the universal claims of Emperor Henry VII (crowned in 1312 after an imperial vacancy of sixty years) by referring to France's special position, had previously rejected similar pretensions by Pope Boniface VIII, whom he even ordered to be arrested and against whom he prepared an indictment for heresy. If a united Europe was to be established, it had to be under French leadership and with Paris, not Rome, as its capital. King Philip radically rejected the thesis which Henry VII had defended in a circular letter addressed to the kings and rulers of the world, that all kingdoms and provinces were subjected to the Roman emperor and monarch, as in religious matters they owed obedience to God's representative on earth. Philip IV had already incurred the pope's wrath by emphasizing French sovereignty in the face of imperial claims, and provoked the pope into condemning the *superbia Gallicana* ('French pride'), which 'pretended to recognize no higher authority'.[8] French hegemony found its expression in the humiliation of Boniface VIII and the so-called 'Babylonian captivity', when the popes left Rome and resided in Avignon, then on the French border and under French influence (1309–76).[9] In England also national feeling became more pronounced in the late Middle Ages, resulting in the rejection of the influence of the Roman curia, which was felt to constitute foreign interference and was of course finally eliminated by Henry VIII. Just as in Gregory VII's day the Church had freed itself from the state the same now happened in the other direction. The emancipation of the nation states received ideological support from the writings of authors such as Marsilius of Padua (*d.* 1343), who stressed the legitimacy of the temporal order and maintained that the

[8] Quotation from a speech made by Boniface VIII to a consistory in 1303: see C. N. S. Woolf, *Bartolus of Saxoferrato: his position in the history of medieval political thought* (Cambridge, 1913), 333–5.
[9] See the authoritative works by J. Favier, *Philippe le Bel* (Paris, 1978) and J. Strayer, *The Reign of Philip the Fair* (Princeton, 1980).

state ought to decide freely what its aims were and how society was to be organized, without being subjected to religious considerations, which belonged to another order.[10]

All this, however, did not change the fact that the late medieval monarchy was still deeply attached to religion. It considered the protection of the true faith as an important responsibility and never forgot the unique position anointing conferred on crowned heads. It still on the whole respected the ancient judicial and fiscal privileges of the clergy, as bishops and other clerics were still conspicuous in the councils of state.

### AN OPPRESSIVE OR A DEMOCRATIC STATE?

Has late medieval public law produced a friendly state, governments with a human face, or tyrannical regimes which oppressed the subjects and weighed heavily upon them? It is clear in our own century that some regimes can be described as internally oppressive and externally imperialistic, whereas others are welfare-oriented and democratic on the internal level and living in peace with their neighbours. They can be described as democratic because they exist for the people and belong to them and they are dedicated to the principle of the *Rechtsstaat*, because their governments are under the law. Although this dichotomy may look Manichean to some readers, it is real enough and goes back a long way in European history. In fact its origin can be detected in the period under review.

Under King Philip IV of France, for example, the state showed its ugly face. Its oppressive and iniquitous character revealed itself by the prosecution – or rather persecution – of the Templars, the confiscation of their estates and the judicial murder of their leaders, who were, in a style all too familiar from certain 'purges' in our own century, accused of a grotesque series of religious and sexual crimes and subjected to torture. The aggressive nature of King Philip's regime was demonstrated by his invasion of the county of Flanders, the annexation of German provinces and the brutal treatment of Pope Boniface VIII. Its basic idea was that of an almighty autocracy, 'not bound by the laws'. This famous expression occurs in Justinian's *Corpus Iuris*: 'princeps legibus solutus est' ('the prince is not bound by the laws') (Dig. 1, 3, 31). It justified the tyranny that would later

---

[10]  See the survey by J. J. Wilks, *The problem of sovereignty in the later Middle Ages* (Cambridge, 1963).

invoke the *raison d'état*. It meant that the government was not accountable to the people and was responsible to God alone. The ancient Christian idea that the state was a repressive organization unfortunately necessitated by human wickedness strengthened this attitude and accentuated its negative image, and the inhuman criminal law of the period, with its torture and horrible executions, could only worsen it. And yet, there existed in the same broad period a monarchy with a human face: that of Louis IX of France, for example, who administered justice to ordinary people under the legendary oak tree of Vincennes and, establishing an unusual truce in an age-old chain of French– English strife, reached a peaceful modus vivendi with King Henry III at the Treaty of Paris of 1259.

Leading jurists of the common law, such as Henry de Bracton (*d.* 1268), expressly placed the king '*sub Deo et sub lege*' ('under God and the law'). Accursius (*d.* 1263), a leading glossator of the *Corpus Iuris Civilis*, clearly had strong reservations about the *legibus solutus* idea and suggested that the emperor was indeed obliged to obey the law, even though there was in the ancient Roman empire no person or institution empowered to sanction imperial misbehaviour. Furthermore, feudal law was based on a free contract between lord and vassal which created mutual rights and duties. This meant that every feudal overlord, even of royal rank, had to fulfil his duties, that in cases of conflict the king's claim was submitted to a feudal court and if he went on neglecting his duties and injuring his tenants, the latter were free to denounce their allegiance. The notion that the ruler stood under the law and the jurisdiction of the courts and that he was accountable to his subjects is, for example, clearly expressed in the twelfth-century county of Flanders. Thus, Article 1 of the borough charter of Saint-Omer, granted in 1127 by Count William Clito, stipulated that the count would see to it that the judgments of the municipal law court were enforced against all men, including the count himself.[11] And the diary of Galbert of Bruges, containing the narrative of the dramatic events caused by the murder in 1127 of Count Charles the Good, extensively reports a speech made in Ghent in 1128 by Iwain of Aalst, one of the leaders of the opposition against Count William. The speaker reproached the count for treating his subjects illegally and tyrannically and suggested that he should appear before a court of law, composed of

[11] R. C. van Caenegem, 'The borough charter of Saint-Omer of 1127 granted by William Clito, Count of Flanders' in R. C. van Caenegem, *Legal history: a European perspective* (London, Rio Grande, 1991), 61–70.

the Peers of Flanders and responsible members of the clergy and the people, to hear their judgment; if it should appear that Count William had acted illegally, he would be deprived of his office and the people would look for a suitable successor. The idea of popular sovereignty, i.e. that the government exists for the people and not the other way round, is unmistakable.[12] Two centuries later scholars like the aforementioned Marsilius of Padua would, with a considerable display of learning and references to Aristotle, expound the doctrine of popular sovereignty, and of royal government as the organ of the nation.

Late medieval constitutionalism shows that people had grasped the fundamental idea of the rule of law, and the same applies to the notion of democracy, at least in its indirect, parliamentary form. A word should be added about direct democracy, a typically urban fruit, and about the related notion of the urban rule of law. It is indeed within the walls of his cities and boroughs that medieval man became acquainted with direct political democracy. In the fourteenth and fifteenth centuries in particular many decisions were left to – often unruly – mass meetings instead of urban magistrates. These popular masses were often structured, in guilds and crafts for example, and were led, in Italy, by the latter's priors and the *capitani del popolo*. The self-ruling communes had at an early date grasped the principle that everything in public life, including acts of administration, had to follow the law, so that we could call them 'cities of law' by analogy with the 'state of law'. An early expression of this awareness can be found in the borough charter of the aforementioned town of Saint-Omer, granted by Count Thierry of Alsace in 1128, and whose Article 25 specified that, in the context of the feudal right of resistance, the Flemish barons had sworn that, if the count infringed the town customs and damaged the burghers, disregarding the judgment of their court, they would break with him and side with the townspeople until the count restored the law and accepted the pronouncement of the aldermen. The message was clear: in the town the law had to be respected even by the government of the land, and in case of conflict it was for the aldermen's court to decide, even if their judgment went against the count, whose aldermen they were.[13]

---

[12]  R. C. van Caenegem. 'Galbert of Bruges on serfdom, prosecution of crime, and constitutionalism (1127–28)' in B. S. Bachrach and D. Nicholas (eds.), *Law, custom, and the social fabric in medieval Europe. Essays in honor of Bryce Lyon* (Kalamazoo, 1990), 102–7.

[13]  Text in G. Espinas, *Recueil de documents relatifs à l'histoire du droit municipal en France des origines à la Révolution. Artois*, III (Paris, 1943), no. 623, p. 306.

# CHAPTER 6

# The classic absolutism of the Ancient Regime

## GENERAL CHARACTERISTICS

In the sixteenth century Europe entered the era of classic absolutism, which for most countries lasted until the second half of the eighteenth century. The *Fürstenstaat* ('state of the prince') of the Ancient Regime, which lasted for three centuries, was characterized by the unbridled rule of kings who were not bound by national laws, and by the sovereignty of the nation states, which were not subjected to any supranational jurisdiction. These liberated states, which chose their political course arbitrarily and in function of their own interest, became more and more menacing as their economic and military strength grew. In the twentieth century the European and world wars caused by this unfettered behaviour led at long last to the realization that unlimited sovereignty was a recipe for disaster.

On the internal level royal absolutism meant that the will of the monarch was law: he could not be bound by laws, as otherwise he would bind himself. The Roman expression *princeps legibus solutus* or *absolutus*, which we have already encountered, is the etymological origin of the term 'absolutism'. This basic principle of autocracy (from the Greek *autos*, self, and *kratein*, to dominate) was widely recognized in the sixteenth century and was supported by Roman public law and the writings of Roman-inspired political thinkers such as Jean Bodin, author of the *Six livres de la république* (1576). Here *république* did not stand for the republican form of government, but for the state, and the book was in fact an apology for strong monarchy.[1]

That absolute monocracy gained the upper hand depended, however, not on the influence of scholars but on vast political changes, which temporarily eliminated its competitors or kept them

---

[1] See J. H. Franklin, *Jean Bodin and the sixteenth century revolution in the methodology of law and history* (New York, 1963); J. H. Ford, *Jean Bodin and the rise of absolutist theory* (Cambridge, 1973).

at bay. The medieval parliaments lost much of their power, if they did not disappear altogether. Under the Tudors the English Parliament underwent a twofold development. On the one hand it became less of a court of law (in spite of the description of the king's 'High Court of Parliament') and more of a vigorous legislative body, wielding (always, in collaboration with the crown) a sovereign and omnicompetent authority. On the other hand its political position vis-à-vis royal power became weaker than in medieval times. This was made particularly clear in ecclesiastical matters where Parliament was submissive and passed in quick succession contradictory acts according to the will of the monarch. The French Estates General met, as we have seen, for the last time before the Great Revolution, in 1614.[2] In Germany most parliaments stayed in business and in the sixteenth century even played a political role of some importance, but afterwards they sank to the level of mere administrative organs carrying out various tasks, fiscal and otherwise, with which the monarchy entrusted them.

Medieval constitutionalism was the next victim. Grants of the Magna Carta type were now classed as privileges, and the new political ideology had never heard of rulers who were fettered by other people's privileges: if the king could grant charters, he could also retract them. Acquired rights or vested interests were considered relics of the past and unacceptable obstacles on the road to the modern state.

The same could be said of urban autonomy, which was anyhow itself based largely on royal grants. Henceforth all subjects were to obey the will of the central government, and no exceptions could be made for people who were entrenched behind medieval walls (which were no match for guns and gunpowder) and invoked the authority of some old parchment against the majesty of the state. The old burgesses, who had been so full of local pride and so parochially selfish, were no match for princes who spoke for the country at large. One is reminded of the European Commission of our own day acting for the whole of the European Community, and the rearguard actions of the old 'sovereign' states and parliaments. In most countries the proud medieval cities were reduced to obedience, often enough by the use of force, as happened under Charles V in Florence and Ghent, and in Spain at the time of the *comuneros*.[3] It was not until two

[2] J. M. Hayden, *France and the Estates General of 1614* (Cambridge, 1974).
[3] S. Haliczer, *The comuneros of Castile. The forging of a revolution, 1475–1521* (Madison, London, 1981); J. N. Stephens, *The fall of the Florentine republic, 1512–1530* (Oxford, 1983).

centuries later that another bourgeoisie, with a national outlook and consciousness, would again take up the struggle against the monarchy and cause its downfall.

The nobility, with which the monarchs had been obliged to share power for many centuries and whose endless revolts had filled the chronicles of the Middle Ages, was finally tamed. While it continued to enjoy a considerable social and economic eminence in the countryside, it was eliminated from the process of political decision making at the national level. As a sop, the nobles could amuse themselves in Versailles and other palaces, warmed by the sun of a munificent monarch. As the hour of the nobility was gone, that of the bourgeoisie had not yet arrived, and the temporary void was filled by the autocrats: for one group it was too late, for the other too early, but for the monarchy the time was just ripe.

The national Churches also, with their wealthy and influential regular and secular clergy, had to accept the yoke of the autocrats. This was very much the case in England, where the Church was nationalized by the Act of Supremacy of 1534. But it was not otherwise in Lutheran lands, where the ruler became the protector and father of the *Landeskirche*. And even in countries that remained Roman Catholic the papacy and the national clergy had to accept a reduced status and agree to a much greater royal impact on, for example, the appointment of bishops, while a royal *placet* was needed before papal bulls obtained force of law in the country.

As the internal obstacles to the state were thus overcome, the last external limits on the sovereignty of the nation states were also removed. The role of the emperor as supranational arbiter, let alone universal ruler, belonged to the distant past. But the papacy had acted as arbiter of nations right up to the end of the Middle Ages: in 1493 Pope Alexander VI had arbitrated between Portugal and Spain and granted to the latter country all American territories west of the meridian situated one hundred miles to the west of the Azores and Cape Verde, territories to the east being assigned to Portugal (which is why till this day Portuguese is spoken in Brazil, and Spanish in the rest of Latin America). In Modern Times no such supranational authority existed to act as judge or arbiter of the nations of Europe.

That the absolute monarchy was in principle above the law should not blind us to the real situation. Indeed, legal aspirations and theoretical pronouncements had to be taken with a large pinch of salt. It is not any different in our own age, when the discrepancy between political reality and constitutional theory – or fiction – can be hallucinating. The autocracy of the Ancient Regime suffered from a number of weaknesses which a realistic analysis should not leave unmentioned.

Inadequate finance was probably the basic flaw: the treasury was constantly short of cash, and in a few extreme cases the state was declared bankrupt. There were several causes for this state of affairs. There is no doubt that the conspicuous consumption of the courts was to blame, as were the dynastic wars which the crowned heads loved to indulge in. The inefficient fiscal administration was also at fault; the collection of taxes was farmed out to private financiers, who pocketed a considerable slice of the revenue. Finally there was the resistance of the propertied classes, who defended their fiscal privileges and repeatedly thwarted governmental attempts at modernization. It was, for example, typical that the immediate cause of the French Revolution was the resistance against Louis XVI's more democratic taxation scheme, whose failure left the government no other choice than the convocation of the Estates General, if bankruptcy was to be avoided. The considerable, although not absolute, respect for ancient class privileges meant that the less well-off bore the brunt of the fiscal charges, but they were too poor to provide the state with an adequate revenue.

Just as the so-called absolute monarchy failed to overcome the fiscal hurdle, so it failed in many countries to overcome the barriers of old engrained regionalism. Even in Spain and France, which entered the modern era as unitary kingdoms, many provinces remained proud of their own identity, which was never overcome by the central government. Thus, after the battle of Almansa in 1707 the Spanish king Philip V punished the rebellious provinces of Aragon and Valencia by decreeing the abolition of their own laws, customs and privileges. On that occasion the king declared that one of his principal offices was that of lawgiver, which included 'both the prerogative of creating new laws and rescinding old ones', so that he was empowered 'to alter the statutes of the realm as circumstances altered'. And France was divided into three sorts of provinces, called the *pays d'élection, pays d'états* and *pays conquis*, whose status depended on when they had come under the control of Paris (the latest acquisitions, the 'conquered lands', being worst of); they were also separated by internal toll barriers.

The freedom of action of the 'absolute' monarchy was furthermore in varying degrees thwarted by the judges, who took it upon themselves to defend traditional liberties and privileges, and acted as self-appointed keepers of the fundamental laws of the land and protectors of the people. Determined to break the resistance of the courts, Philip II of Spain had recalcitrant judges executed. In France, in 1771, the government resorted to the arrestation and internal banishment of councillors of the Parlement of Paris, who resisted the modernizing plans of Chancellor Maupeou. In the eighteenth century the noble councillors in the French parlements, who had bought their offices and were irremovable, systematically thwarted governmental attempts at innovation of public law.[4]

In the long run we may presume that religious intolerance was another factor of weakness, even though at the time public opinion did not see it that way. Indeed, the principle of religious homogeneity was widely accepted, and the metaphysical foundation of the monarchy was such an essential element of the Constitution that people failed to see how one king could appeal to different denominations as the supernatural bases of his authority. Our own century has seen so many regimes built on a single ideology that we easily comprehend the situation in the old monarchies. Many people were prepared to pay the price of intolerance if it freed them from the horrors of civil and international wars of religion. Rejection or even criticism of the king's religion was viewed as disloyalty and treason. It is against this background that one should see measures such as the revocation by Louis XIV in 1685 of the toleration edict of Nantes, which in 1598 had given French Protestants a recognized position in society. Nevertheless intolerance must have weakened the state, as we have already suggested. This is obvious in the economic field, as numerous capable entrepreneurs and craftsmen left France for such countries as England, Holland and Prussia, which were made attractive by ideological tolerance (a similar brain drain had happened previously in Spain and the southern Netherlands). But in political terms also intolerance in the end turned against the monarchy, as it

---

[4] J. H. Shennan, *The Parlement of Paris* (London, 1968); A. N. Hamscher, *The Parlement of Paris after the Fronde 1653–1673* (London, 1976); J. P. Royer, *La société judiciaire depuis le XVIIIe siècle* (Paris, 1979); H. Coing, 'Der Fall Loisel' in J. A. Ankum, J. E. Spruit and F. B. J. Wubbe (eds.), *Satura Roberto Feenstra* (Fribourg, 1985), 649–58; A. N. Hamscher, *The conseil privé and the parlements in the age of Louis XIV: a study in French absolutism* (Philadelphia, 1987).

reduced the level of spontaneous acceptance, always a factor of stability for a regime.

The liberal tradition naturally condemns absolutism, even in its enlightened form (about which more in chapter 7). The essential reproach is the tyrannical and unpredictable nature of personal government and its blatant flouting of the rule of law. A notorious case from sixteenth-century France may illustrate what this meant in practice. On 13 January 1527 a well-to-do businessman called Jacques de Beaune, baron de Semblançay, was arrested and thrown into the Bastille, his goods being seized. The object of the exercise was quite simply to rid King Francis I of a tiresome creditor. Semblançay's trial took place the same year, the indictment amounting to lese-majesty, i.e. high treason (*laesio majestatis* was a crime borrowed from imperial Rome). His somewhat unorthodox bookkeeping was indicative of sixteenth-century habits rather than fraud and was a consequence of the complexities of existing fiscal practices. The trial of Semblançay, who was both a banker and a minister (*contrôleur général des finances*), was a travesty, impartial judges being dismissed and replaced by creatures of the government or personal enemies of the accused. After the latter's condemnation to death the case came before the king himself, who confirmed the sentence and ordered the execution to proceed. Semblançay was hanged on 11 August 1527. His widow and son appealed against the sentence, only to be condemned in their turn, the widow's goods being confiscated and the fugitive son being condemned to death (he was later pardoned).[5] It is clear that business could hardly flourish in such precarious circumstances: it is well known that in our time one of M. Gorbachev's basic ideas was that the establishment of the rule of law formed a precondition for the economic recovery of his country. Some readers may well point out that in Semblançay's case a judicial procedure was, formally speaking, followed; the king did not simply order the businessman's killing, but resorted to a trial in the law courts. However, what is the use of judges if they can be made to comply with the government's unlawful pursuits? How wide is the margin between judicial murder and murder outright?

---

[5] See the chapter 'The fall of Semblançay (1527)' in R. J. Knecht, *Francis I* (Cambridge, 1982), 195–9. See on arbitrary punishment in late medieval and modern France: B. Schnapper, 'Les peines arbitraires du XIIIe au XVIIIe siècle (doctrines savantes et usages français)', *Revue d'Histoire du Droit* 41 (1973), 237–77, 42 (1974), 81–112; A. Lebigre, *La justice du roi. La vie judiciaire dans l'ancienne France* (Paris, 1988).

Other readers may argue, and rightly so, that the Semblançay case was exceptional and that judges and juries often resisted governmental pressure, but it remains difficult to maintain that a law-based state existed when the royal government could pervert the course of justice as happened in France in 1527.

All this makes all the more pregnant the question how this sort of regime has prevailed for so long in so many parts of Europe: the historian tries to explain, which does not mean to excuse. It must have been that these strong regimes had a lot to offer. Indeed, a government paralysed by class privilege and without the strength to break the 'crust of custom' in order to modernize the law was incapable of ensuring the constitutional transition from medieval to modern Europe, at a time when enormous cultural and economic changes were taking place. This entailed the reduction or elimination of various vested interests of towns, corporations and estates, which could only be brought about by a forceful central government, capable of curbing the notables and breaking the power of privilege. It was also clear to many observers that the nations which were harassed by external enemies and by internal religious dissension saw in a strong government their only hope for peace and salvation. Thus Tudor absolutism owed its undeniable popularity to people's relief at being freed at last from the aristocratic anarchy of the Wars of the Roses. And when Henry VIII succeeded in depriving not only the medieval nobility, but the Church as well, of their ancient positions of power (by nationalizing the secular clergy and dissolving the monasteries), his policy was widely acclaimed. Not even the king's wanton cruelty was held against him, although his treatment of the London Carthusians in 1535, for example, was so fiendish that it shocks even the conscience of our own age, blunted as it is by unparalleled atrocities.[6] In France the success of Louis XIV's absolutism can best be understood if one realizes that it came after decades of unrest caused by religious wars and aristocratic Frondes. Public opinion also realized that government by a central bureaucracy manned by graduates (in law) was more orderly and efficient than the rule of unguided aristocrats and landowners. Modern top officials were more interested in conscious mercantilist policies, such as the protection of national industry and the foundation of state manufactures. That a strong national government offered solid advantages was

---

[6] L. Stone, *The past and present revisited* (2nd edn, London, 1987), 146.

evident. The question was whether personal, arbitrary rule entailing uncertainty for persons and property was not too high a price to pay, and whether it was possible to organize an efficient and solid central government without the drawbacks of absolutism, i.e. a government bound by the law and working in consultation with the nation, or at least its politically active part.

The parliamentary and constitutional monarchy which, as we shall see, took shape in England gave a satisfactory solution to this apparent dilemma. It provided a solid central government, which protected the national interest, but was nevertheless bound to operate within the parameters of the law, *inter alia*, because of the impact of an influential and independent judicature. It had moreover to respect individual rights and to govern with the support of a majority in Parliament, which – at least in the Commons – was elected by inhabitants of all parts of the country. It was a practical middle way between utter subjection and complete anarchy and looked like the answer to Tacitus' famous observation about 'men who can bear neither total servitude nor total liberty' (a remark allegedly made by the emperor Galba to his adoptive son and designated successor Piso).[7]

### ANALYSIS OF THE PUBLIC LAW IN TWO COUNTRIES

#### *France*

France can be considered the model *par excellence* of modern absolutism, which found its classic expression in the long reign of Louis XIV. It inspired numerous kings, dukes and counts throughout Europe, who all wanted to have their own Versailles; similarly, the fall of French absolutism sounded the knell of the Ancient Regime in the rest of the Continent. French public law revolved around the personal rule of the king. At a moment when the regime was contested Louis XV reminded his subjects of this fundamental principle in no uncertain terms: 'It is in my sole person that sovereign authority resides, it is to me alone that legislative power belongs . . . ; the entire public order emanates from me'. The basic idea was the concentration of all the powers of the state in one hand – the exact opposite of the

---

[7] See the following general surveys: P. Anderson, *Lineages of the absolutist state* (London, 1974); N. Henshall, *The myth of absolutism. Change and continuity in early modern European monarchy* (London, 1992); R. Mousnier, *La monarchie absolue en Europe du Ve siècle à nos jours* (Paris, 1982).

eighteenth-century theory of the *séparation des pouvoirs* ('separation of powers'). The king was the supreme legislator and issued 'ordinances', 'edicts' and 'declarations', in which he was only exceptionally assisted by the Estates General. He exercised the executive power and decided personally on all matters of national and international policy, including war and peace and the appointment of top officials. He was assisted by a Council over which he himself presided and whose members he appointed, and also by secretaries of state who had to execute his political decisions. Ever since the late Middle Ages the king of France had ceased to be dependent on the Estates General for the levying of taxes. He was also the supreme judge of the land, for although the courts and parlements normally exercised their jurisdiction without direct royal interference, their judgments could always be revoked by the *Conseil du Roi*, because of the principle of the royal *justice retenue* (the final jurisdiction which the king had retained in his own hand and not transferred to his judges). Also, as is well known, the king could bypass the ordinary judicial circuit and imprison individuals by means of royal *lettres de cachet*, whenever he thought this to be justified or politically expedient.

For a long time the monarchy was nevertheless not considered as simply arbitrary and tyrannical. It was, on the contrary, deemed to be a 'tempered monarchy' and the king was regarded as the supreme defender of the 'Constitution' or the 'fundamental laws of the realm', which he was expected to follow. This Constitution was an unwritten and very vague body of norms and usages which were considered inviolable. It contained rules of public law concerning the hereditary and Catholic nature of the monarchy and the inalienability of royal authority in all its component parts. It also contained elements of private law, concerning the respect for the person and the property of the citizens, called the *honnête liberté des Français*. A distinction was made between *lois ordinaires*, which expressed the will of the king, and the *lois fondamentales*, which were binding upon him. If the king acted against the latter, his action was deemed arbitrary: they had to be obeyed during that monarch's reign, but after his death they were abrogated.[8] It is possible that the annulment by the young Louis XVI of the aforementioned severe measures of Louis XV against the Parlement of Paris was based on this conception. At certain junctures there were official pronouncements by which the king recognized that

[8] M.-B. Bruguière, H. Gilles and G. Sicard, *Introduction à l'histoire des institutions françaises des origines à 1792* (Toulouse, 1983), 165–90.

it was 'fortunately impossible' for him to 'change the fundamental laws' (for example, in September 1715 and July 1717).[9]

The Catholic nature of the French monarchy, expressly stated at the accession of the Protestant King Henry IV who had converted to Catholicism, contributed to the accentuation of the monolithical character of the country and to the persecution of dissenters (after the aforementioned revocation of the Edict of Nantes), creating a 'closed society', in Karl Popper's terms. Religious intolerance, embodied in state censorship of the press, found its political corollary in the prohibition of political parties: the king and no one else was responsible for the affairs of state. Only two institutions come to mind which might have put a brake on the king's personal rule, the Estates General and the Parlements, particularly that of Paris. They deserve our attention now.

The Estates General met infrequently, and only in times of unrest or crisis. Louis XI assembled them only once, in 1468, when he needed their assistance against yet another baronial revolt. The Estates General which met in Tours in the year of his death, 1483, published declarations against authoritarian methods and wanted to put an end to royal taxation without their consent. However, as soon as those troubled times were passed, the Estates General were again left at home, as neither Louis XII (*d.* 1515), Francis I (*d.* 1547) nor Henry II (*d.* 1559) convoked them. It was the religious wars that again led to their being consulted, but their impact on public affairs was modest, and after they receded, in 1614, in disorder and with a feeling of futility, they did not meet again until 1789, when the Third Estate proclaimed itself the National Assembly and took in hand the task of the total reorganization of the state and the shaping of a new system of public law.

The principal twofold role of the Estates General consisted in agreeing to grants of money requested by the government and in formulating *doléances* ('grievances'). They were moreover expected to advise the crown – the ancient feudal *consilium* – and to put the seal of their consent on possible changes in the fundamental pact between the monarchy and the nation – a notion that turned out to be purely theoretical. There were other representative assemblies besides the Estates General. The *Assemblées des Notables* were a sort of surrogate,

---

[9] S. Rials, 'Aux origines du constitutionalisme écrit. Réflexions en marge d'un projet constitutionnel de la Ligue (1588)', *Revue d'histoire des facultés de droit et de la science juridique* 8 (1989), 181–268.

which could be convoked and manipulated more easily than the Estates General; they led a long shadowy existence and only came to life in the final phase of the regime, in 1787. There were moreover Provincial Estates. In the Middle Ages their role diminished, and in the heartland of the monarchy, the area between the Seine and the Loire, they disappeared or were greatly weakened, even before the time of Richelieu (*d.* 1642). Elsewhere they remained important until the revolution, not only in such large provinces as Languedoc, Brittany and Burgundy, but also in smaller regions such as Artois and French Flanders. These Estates were emanations of the local oligarchies and mainly competent for raising taxes – a task which they kept out of the hands of the central government – and for conducting negotiations with Paris in order to obtain advantages for their respective provinces. The towns were subjected to the tutelage of royal government: an edict of 1683 contained a detailed regulation of this control, stipulating, for example, that the municipal budget had to be submitted to the *intendant*, the main local representative of the crown in France, or to the King's Council; communal borrowing and taxes were subjected to similar restrictions. The towns were ruled by oligarchies, *inter alia*, because the urban offices were sold, as were so many others in the country. An interesting attempt at the democratization of town government was undertaken in 1764 and 1765, involving the abolition of the sale of offices and the introduction or re-introduction of elections. This modest step in the direction of democracy was already undone in 1771, for the simple reason that the national treasury could not do without the revenue from the sale of those offices.

The parlements were the other potential centres of opposition. They were higher law courts and their leader was the Parlement of Paris, which was founded in the mid-thirteenth century (it was followed by provincial parlements, created to relieve its workload). The councillors of the parlements, as we have seen, saw themselves as the defenders of the fundamental principles of the law and distrusted new enactments which might threaten the established order or acquired rights and privileges. They enjoyed great prestige and belonged to rich and noble circles, and had bought or inherited their offices after studying law at a university where the demands upon the students were light. The legal technique they used to influence royal legislation was the *droit de remontrance*, the right of remonstrance or protestation. In the late Middle Ages the usage had arisen for new royal ordinances to be sent to the Parlement of Paris in order to be registered and thus considered officially published and binding. In this context the custom had grown for the councillors to formulate critical remarks and to 'remonstrate' with the government on legal grounds. The criticized ordinance was sent back to the government which could either take account of the remarks and emend the text, or reject them and ordain registration by royal authority. Eighteenth-century parlements frequently used their right of remonstrance to sabotage reform plans, and the government usually gave in; Maupeou's reforming zeal in 1771, to which we have already referred, was exceptional.

Although the Parlement of Paris was a law court, it was deeply involved in politics – a predicament not unknown to the constitutional courts of our day. Numerous royal decrees which posed legal problems were checked by their court to make sure they agreed to the hallowed traditions and fundamental laws of the realm. This applied to political and constitutional issues as well as to changes in private law. Thus, for example, the Parlement throughout the centuries firmly defended the liberties of the Gallican Church, a highly emotional question in French ecclesiastical politics.

It was the duty of the Parlement to preserve both the law and the monarchy, which was based on it. It therefore held the balance between the rights of the king, admittedly the sole source of the law and the state's chief judge, and those of the subjects which he was obliged to respect. The monarch was expected to act through legal channels, and it was never considered that kingship might be arbitrary and uncontrolled. However, the boundary between sovereignty and despotism was not always easy to establish and not every king refrained from crossing it. For although royal ordinances were subjected to judicial review, the Parlement had no absolute right to refuse registration. It is not surprising therefore that the most illustrious of absolute kings, Louis XIV, found the Parlement's interference intolerable, and it was typical that, in 1673, he ordained that its remonstrances against royal enactments sent to the court could henceforth only be made after registration (which made the protest politically futile). Consequently no more remonstrances were made by the Parlement of Paris during the remainder of his reign. It was equally typical, however, that as soon as he had died, the regent, the duke of Orleans, restored the court's ancient right of remonstrance to the form in which it had existed before 1673.

At the end of its long life the Parlement of Paris unwittingly provoked the French Revolution by rejecting the fiscal modernization planned by the government and by referring the crown to the Estates General for the desperately needed fresh revenue. The plight the government found itself in was partly caused by the opposition of the Parlement to the introduction of tax equality, an onslaught on privilege which the councillors would not countenance. *Parlementaire* hostility to new taxes was a familiar feature in French politics. The Parlement fought the capitation tax (imposed in 1695, suppressed in 1698, re-established in 1701) and opposed new taxes in 1749, 1756 and 1759. It opposed Turgot's fiscal measures, including a tax on all landowners, which were registered after a *lit de justice* in 1776. In 1786 Calonne wanted to introduce a new tax, the *subvention territoriale*, based on legal equality and levied on all property owners, but in 1787 the Parlement firmly rejected his plan. Again a *lit de justice* was required to obtain registration of the new tax, whereupon the councillors declared this authoritarian registration null: the *subvention territoriale* was repealed. The solution was left to the Estates General: the tapping of the financial market could go no further, and about half of the total expenditure of the state was spent on servicing the debt; in 1788 the government was forced to stop all public payments. The Parlement, which had also caused the convocation of the Estates General by maintaining on the basis of the precedent of 1614 that all voting in the Estates General was to be held per estate and not per head, provoked the Third Estate into proclaiming itself the National Assembly.[10]

### England

Royal absolutism was a European phenomenon typical for the transition from the Middle Ages to Modern Times. The reign of King Philip II not only affected Spain, but also the Low Countries, lands marked by local, regional and social privilege, where his attempt to impose a new-style autocracy caused the famous Revolt of the Netherlands. His father, Emperor Charles V (also King Charles I of Spain) had shown the way by quelling the revolt of the Spanish *comuneros*. And every reader of Machiavelli's *Il Principe* knows that the Italian principalities had also discovered the possibilities offered by absolute rule.

[10] Recently the lectures on this theme by an eminent legal historian who taught in the Law Faculty of Paris in the period 1921–51 were gathered and published: F. Olivier-Martin, *L'absolutisme français* (Paris, 1988).

It is not always understood that England also in many ways followed this European fashion. This is because in the seventeenth century that country produced a very different Constitution, which came to inspire liberal movements in many lands. However, the outcome of the conflicts in the Stuart period was not written in the stars and should not blind us to the fact that the Tudors ruled England in a forceful fashion, even though they shunned a formal doctrine of absolutism and preferred to work through existing procedures and institutions. Recent research has combated both the older view that the seeds of the English civil war were sown in the Tudor age and the idea of a Tudor 'lower house marching steadily onwards and upwards to the constitutional confrontation of 1640' (Graves). Historians now stress the importance of the sixteenth century as a period with its own physiognomy.

The personal decisions of Henry VIII and his two daughters, the Catholic Mary and the Protestant Elizabeth, determined England's religious course, which was the most burning issue of the age. Henry VIII wanted and carried out the nationalization of the Church, the break with Rome, the dissolution of the monasteries and confiscation of their landed wealth. Non-compliance with his policy frequently meant death, and even the expression of politically incorrect opinions was a capital offence. Thus, in 1533, his marriage to Catherine of Aragon was declared void and that to Anne Boleyn valid: slandering the latter marriage constituted treason, but in 1536 another statute annulled Anne's marriage and this time anyone who judged that marriage valid was declared guilty of treason. Similarly, various statutes under Henry VIII declared statements against the king's anti-Roman policy to be treasonable, but not long afterwards, under his Catholic daughter Mary, an Act of 1555 made it treason to speak against the restored Roman connection. As attachment to the old Church led Thomas More to the scaffold in 1535, under Henry VIII, so Protestant beliefs led Thomas Cranmer to the stake in 1556, under Queen Mary. Elizabeth I imposed her own *via media*, an English middle course between the Scylla of Roman Catholicism and the Charybdis of the Geneva-style Calvinism followed by English Puritans. Catholicism was equated with treason, and the pope was considered a foreign head of state who hoped to topple the legitimate queen of England. International politics were in any case the domain of the monarch, in which Parliament was not supposed to dabble. It was Elizabeth who imposed on the Commons the distinction, of dubious constitutionality, between commonwealth matters, on which they could speak freely, and matters of state, to be debated only with her permission. Similarly, her father had in 1532 explained to the members of Parliament that the question of his intended divorce was not a matter for them to consider and discuss.

The most solemn laws, the Acts of Parliament, were still, as in the later Middle Ages, formally the work of king and Parliament, but the latter was kept under constant royal pressure, not only, as we have seen, on sensitive religious issues, but also in ordinary civil affairs. Under Henry VIII Parliament carried out a massive law reform, concerning such diverse matters as wills, debt, the limitation of prescription, the protection of lessees, wrongful disseisins, joint tenancies and marriage, but it appears that many or even most of these Acts were officially inspired.[11]

Besides Acts of Parliament Royal Proclamations were also issued, a less solemn form of legislation, bypassing the Houses at Westminster, but given force of law by an Act of Parliament of 1539. The judiciary did not escape the impact of royal absolutism. The traditional common-law courts continued to operate with a remarkable degree of independence and followed the traditional rules of evidence (even though Henry VIII did not hesitate to browbeat the judges to secure a favourable outcome in a test case over the validity of uses in 1533). But they suffered the competition of the prerogative courts, exceptional tribunals created by the crown in order to attack more efficiently certain social evils or recalcitrant powerful individuals. The Star Chamber, for example, which developed into a full and proper court under Cardinal Wolsey's guidance, was not bound by common-law procedure and frequently resorted to unusual punishments. Torture was not applied in the courts of common law or the Star Chamber, but in criminal cases with political overtones the rack was used to secure confessions in the king's Privy Council, the supreme governmental organ, and by the security services of the Tudor state.[12]

The bill of attainder, which had begun during the Wars of the Roses, took on a new and more sinister life in the sixteenth century, and particularly under Henry VIII, when it was used to bring people to the scaffold who had displeased the crown (among them Thomas

---

[11] G. R. Elton, *English law in the sixteenth century: reform in an age of change* (London, 1978), 17.
[12] See the chapter on 'England. The century of torture 1540–1640' in J. L. Langbein, *Torture and the law of proof. Europe and England in the Ancien Régime* (Chicago, London, 1977), 73–143.

Cromwell, who had used it himself as an instrument of tyranny). It broke every rule of natural justice and led to the execution of political enemies, convicted of treason on the basis of mere accusations, without the hearing of witnesses or a chance of presenting a fair defence: in the procedure of the bill of attainder Parliament might dispense at its pleasure with ordinary rules and forms of law and use so-called evidence inadmissible in the ordinary courts.

Just like in France and Spain, the English 'new monarchy' employed a novel style bureaucracy of royal secretaries of state, who were neither mere executive agents, nor politicians responsible to Parliament. The first in this line was Henry VIII's aforementioned secretary, Thomas Cromwell; the most famous were father William and son Robert Cecil, who served Queen Elizabeth I.

The question may be asked as to what caused this comparative weakening of Parliament in relation to the crown. In the fifteenth century the strength of the national representation had to some extent resulted from the crisis of the divided monarchy, and after the 'anarchy' of the Wars of the Roses the country welcomed the strong regime of the Tudors as its best chance of stability and order. In England as elsewhere in Europe the power of the old warrior nobility was on the wane and posed no threat to the crown any more, whereas the bourgeoisie and the gentry were still far from powerful enough to try to seize power on a national level. Not until the seventeenth century would their political ambitions lead them to question royal absolutism and to use Parliament as their warhorse.

Financial matters, which became so important under the Stuarts, did not worry the Tudors overmuch. Only twice did the House of Commons offer less money than they requested, and at no time did it refuse a grant outright. Moreover Henry VII was so parsimonious that he could usually manage with the revenue from the crown lands and seldom had to assemble Parliament and ask for grants (something the population was thankful for). Henry VIII confiscated the wealth of the regular clergy (a boon that was unfortunately not repeatable). Elizabeth I kept her head above water without giving in too much to her infrequent Parliaments (of which she was not fond) by successfully speculating in colonial enterprises and liquidating large chunks of royal demesne land. Also, the nationalistic policy of the Tudors was widely acclaimed by the patriotic and king-worshipping English people, as it freed the country from its age-old involvement with the Continent, secured external safety, even vis-à-vis Spain, the leading superpower of the day, and laid the foundations for a great maritime future.

Whereas Tudor England resolutely and successfully espoused the modern state model, it nevertheless retained several important medieval institutions, even when their impact was reduced. Two pillars of late medieval England come to mind, the common law and Parliament. Both survived the storm of strong personal rule, and so were ready to resume their ancient roles in the next century and to push back the tide of modernism.[13] The common law remained the cornerstone of the legal system, in spite of the competition of statutes, Roman law and non-common-law tribunals. Parliament proved indispensable, even though it almost invariably granted what the crown requested and was usually prepared to follow the government's legislative initiatives. The Tudors never thought of ruling without Parliament and the monarchy saw itself as operating under the law. But the Tudor Parliament was no rubber stamp assembly, where bills introduced by the royal Council were always unanimously acclaimed. There were opposing views and negative votes. Thus at the start of Mary Tudor's reign when the Commons debated the repeal of the Edwardian, Protestant Reformation, no less than 80 of the 359 members present voted against the government, and, in the same House, the Queen's Bill to return first fruits and tenths to the papacy passed by only 193 votes to 126. Also numerous bills inspired by specific concerns in counties, towns or corporations were successfully introduced by private members: even though only a fraction reached the statute book, they reflect the vigour of the old institution, and particularly of its Lower House.

[13] G. R. Elton, *England under the Tudors* (London, 1955); G. R. Elton, *Studies in Tudor and Stuart politics and government. Papers and reviews 1946–1972* (2 vols., Cambridge, 1974); G. R. Elton (ed.), *The Tudor Constitution. Documents and commentary* (2nd ed., Cambridge, 1982); M. A. R. Graves, *The Tudor Parliaments. Crown, Lords and Commons, 1485–1603* (London, 1985).

CHAPTER 7

# *The absolute state no lasting model*

GENERAL CONSIDERATIONS

The classic absolute regime as described in the previous chapter, also known as high absolutism (*Hochabsolutismus*), was no more than a passing phase in the development of public law. Unfettered personal rule was eventually contested everywhere, but with varying results. In some cases the monarchy itself disappeared and was replaced by a republican regime, in others it was preserved but underwent a profound transformation: sooner or later perestroika – to use the parlance of our own time – arrived everywhere. In constitutional and parliamentary kingdoms the monarchy formally continued, but assumed a role that was rather symbolic, abandoning political decisions to parliaments and to governments supported by parliamentary majorities. In the lands of enlightened absolutism the monarch kept the reins of power firmly in his own hand, without being accountable to the nation or parliament, but instead of acting in his dynastic interests or the defence of the Church he wanted to implement the ideas of the Enlightenment, promote the happiness of his subjects and establish a humane society. The following pages will be devoted to three models of modern constitutional law.

In the first the monarchy was maintained, but divested of its autocratic aspects. England is the classic example, at least after the dramatic events of the seventeenth century put an end to Stuart absolutism and a constitutional and parliamentary regime was established: here an oligarchy of nobility, gentry and affluent bourgeoisie captained the ship of state and created the appropriate legal framework for a flourishing market economy. Another, but very different example was the Polish so-called aristocratic republic, which, although a kingdom, was in fact totally dominated by a parliament run by the nobility (which wielded the *liberum veto* in order to paralyse any royal attempt at effective government).

In the second model the absolute monarchy was conserved, but placed itself at the service of the general welfare and carried out a policy of rationalization, inspired by modern natural law or *Vernunftrecht* ('the law of reason') and the philosophy of the Enlightenment. This was the 'caring state' which did 'everything for the people', but left the 'caring' to the wise ruler and not to some noble or bourgeois oligarchy, let alone to the lower ranks. The reigns of Frederick the Great of Prussia and Emperor Joseph II of Austria provide examples of such 'enlightened monarchy'.

In the third model kingship was abolished and replaced by a republic. England, as is well known, went through a short republican phase under Oliver Cromwell, Switzerland consisted of a loose confederation of urban and peasant republics, and Venice remained an illustrious urban republic for many centuries. But the most famous examples of success with this form of government were the Republic of the United Provinces and the United States of America, two countries with federal Constitutions. The American republic was younger than the Dutch and also more advanced. The hereditary, quasi-monarchical element represented in the Dutch republic by the stadholders of the House of Orange was entirely absent in America, where executive power was in the hands of a president elected for a limited period. Also the special relationship between the Dutch state and the Reformed religion was absent in the United States, where the separation of Church and state was provided by the Constitution.

Although France finally joined the republican camp, it hesitated between various regimes for almost a century. The Ancient Regime was replaced in 1791 by a constitutional monarchy, which soon gave way to the First Republic, which itself ended in the military dictatorship of Napoleon and his First Empire. This was followed by the restoration of the monarchy, which lasted until 1848. After the brief interlude of the Second Republic there followed another restoration, not of kingship but of the empire: Napoleon III's Second Empire lasted from 1852 till 1870. After its fall, in the wake of the disastrous Franco-Prussian war, there was a period of hesitation between royalists and republicans until, in 1875, the republic finally won the day.

## THE TRANSFORMATION OF ENGLISH KINGSHIP

In 1603 the Stuarts came to the throne of England in the person of King James I. As Queen Elizabeth's 'Scottish nephew' had already been king of Scotland as James VI for many years, his new kingship resulted in a personal union between the two kingdoms. As king of England he was the head of the established Church and as a convinced absolutist he defended personal rule by God's grace in learned treatises and in eloquent speeches. Addressing Parliament in 1609 he explained that 'the kings are not only God's lieutenants upon earth, and sit upon God's throne, but even by God himself they are called Gods'. As outspoken protagonists of the established Church and absolute kingship, the Stuarts collided with two powerful currents in public opinion. One was politically inspired and wanted to defend Parliament, the common law and the ancient Constitution of England against the growing menace of Stuart autocracy.[1] The other was religiously inspired. Its followers were known as Puritans (a term of abuse that appeared in the 1560s), but called themselves 'the godly'. They objected to the medieval, 'popish' rituals, doctrine, sacraments and episcopal organization of the Church of England, as it was established in the early years of Queen Elizabeth I, and wanted to purify it. A radical branch of this movement, known as separatists, repudiated the state-Church altogether and formed congregations of their own. Puritanism was an extreme form of Calvinism and much of its inspiration came from Geneva: its followers believed in a disciplined Church run by elected 'elders' and they distrusted the royal court, whose luxurious manner offended their own sober life style and whose drift towards France and Catholicism caused them great alarm. At the Hampton Court meeting in 1604, shortly after the accession of James I, the moderate Puritans had been disappointed in their hope that the new king would change the episcopal organization of the English Church.[2] It was the combination of the parliamentary and the 'godly' opposition – expressed in the claim of Parliament in 1642 to act for the liberty of the subject and for true religion – which led to the civil war and the downfall of Charles I.

---

[1] See J. G. A. Pocock, *The ancient constitution and the feudal law* (2nd edn, Cambridge, 1987); M. I. Finley, *The ancestral constitution* (Cambridge, 1971); R. J. Smith, *The Gothic bequest. Medieval institutions in British thought, 1688–1863* (Cambridge, 1987); G. Burgess, *The politics of the ancient constitution. An introduction to English political thought, 1603–1642* (London, 1992). For the sixteenth-century Parliament see the recent survey by J. Loach, *Parliament under the Tudors* (Oxford, 1991).

[2] C. Hill, *Society and Puritanism in pre-revolutionary England* (Oxford, 1961); C. Hill, *Change and continuity in seventeenth century England* (London, 1975); J. P. Sommerville, *Politics and ideology in England 1603–1640* (London, 1986); R. Ashton, *The English Civil War. Conservatism and revolution 1603–1649* (2nd edn, London, 1989); C. Russell, *The causes of the English Civil War* (Oxford, 1990). On the anti-absolutist scholar John Selden, see the recent work by D. Berkowitz, *John Selden's formative years. Politics and society in early seventeenth-century England* (London, 1988).

Some readers will be struck by the parallel with the fate of King William I of the Netherlands in the period 1815–30. He too encountered, in the south of his kingdom, i.e. present-day Belgium, a twofold opposition, one of religious (the Catholic hierarchy) and the other of political inspiration (the Liberal politicians) and he also lost his throne, in the south at least, after these two currents had concluded an alliance which triumphed in the revolution of 1830.

It may be useful to recall the main events in England before passing on to the analysis of the leading constitutional texts of the period. Under James I's son Charles I, who ruled from 1625 to 1649, the conflict became sharp and even violent. His father had, in spite of ringing ideological claims, maintained a stable consensual system, which now came to an end. More and more people, in Parliament and elsewhere, came to believe that the king eroded the ancient Constitution and that the common law might fail to protect their persons and their properties against the incursions of the absolute prerogative. Parliamentary control of taxation became an important issue, serving both to protect property owners and to put pressure on the royal government. In English law whenever the king could not cover his (public and private) expenditure with the revenue from crown land, he had to ask the country for a grant, to which Parliament alone could consent (there was no automatic royal taxation as in France). This legal situation was of particular importance as the Stuarts had inherited a financial system that was close to breakdown. Since every request for a grant was only consented to by Parliament with reluctance and in exchange for the acceptance of various demands and criticisms, kings tried to rule without this cumbersome relic of the medieval past. In normal circumstances the crown could just about manage, thanks to the use of techniques that were not strictly legal, such as 'benevolences', forced loans and compulsory billeting of soldiers, which naturally caused discontent. Mounting opposition was countered with mounting repression, exercised by courts of special jurisdiction and through arbitrary imprisonment 'by the king's special command'. Many people were alarmed, in 1627, by the *Five Knights' case,* also known, by the name of one of them, as *Darnel's case.* The five knights were imprisoned by order of the Privy Council for refusing to pay a forced loan. The court of King's Bench required that a cause for their detention be given if they were to be refused bail, whereupon the Privy Council answered that 'his majesty's special commandment' was the cause. Thereupon the judges, by a 'rule of court', disallowed bail, pending further procedures. Although this was no real judgment and no precedent in favour of the thesis of the government, it caused great disquiet, not least because of the argument used by the Attorney-General that the king's absolute power could be employed in proceedings at common law and by his reference to *arcana Dei* and *arcana imperii* (the secrets of God and the state) as justification for imprisoning men who refused to pay what amounted to a tax not sanctioned by Parliament.[3] Determined to manage on his own, Charles I ruled quite successfully without grants from Parliament from 1629 to 1640. But in 1639 a Scottish revolt broke out, provoked by the king's high-handed religious policy which threatened the national identity of the northern kingdom. It led to a Scottish invasion of England and a war that could not be financed except through taxation. The king was compelled to assemble Parliament, which used its position of strength to put pressure on the government and redress the traditional balance of power which had shifted in the previous eleven years in the direction of royal absolutism. In 1641 King Charles' opponents gained a financial stranglehold on him, a situation which he refused to accept. When, in 1642, it appeared that neither the royalists nor the parliamentarians would given in, civil war broke out, involving not only England, but Scotland and Ireland as well. Both parties claimed to uphold tradition and charged the other with innovating. Parliament, the Constitution and the common law were doubtless ancient and venerable pillars of English society, but so was anointed kingship, but whereas divine-right monarchy and constitutionalism had previously lived and worked together, they were now in opposition to each other, placing many people before an impossible choice and dividing social groups and even families. To a neutral contemporary observer it must have seemed that the monarchy was the dynamic progressive force, while the defenders of the ancient Constitution were traditionalists, out of touch with the modern world and defending sectional interests. It is ironic that later generations reversed this judgment and saw absolutism as a spent force and Parliament and the Constitution as the harbingers of a new era.

The royalist party, whose support came mainly from the north and west, fought the parliamentarian forces from the economically advanced south and east of the country, including the city of London,

---

[3] J. A. Guy, 'The origins of the Petition of Right reconsidered', *The Historical Journal* 25 (1982), 267–88.

led by Oliver Cromwell whose New Model Army finally won the day. The king was tried by a special tribunal, appointed by radical elements in a Parliament purged of its moderates by the army. He was sentenced to death and executed in 1649: the first public execution of a king by his subjects in modern Europe. As the country had lived for eleven years without Parliament, it now lived for eleven years, from 1649 to 1660, without a king. It was the era of the 'godly' republic under Oliver Cromwell and, very briefly, his son Richard. In 1660 kingship was restored under Charles II, son of the king executed in 1649, but although the monarchy was restored, and under the same dynasty, it was not the same monarchy. The new ruler did not attempt to reintroduce the absolutism of his ancestors, and ruled in harmony with the country, where his crown was respected. Things went wrong, however, under his younger brother, James II, when feelings flared up again, not only because the king ruled without Parliament, but because he was a Catholic and favoured Catholics. In 1688 a revolt broke out, led by a group of aristocrats, and after William of Orange, a leading Protestant on the European scene and husband of James II's Protestant daughter Mary, had invaded England at their instigation, the king lost his nerve and fled to France and Louis XIV, who had subsidized him.[4] He was succeeded by his daughter and her husband, who became king of England as William III. The Stuart era ended in 1714 upon the death of Queen Anne, a younger daughter of James II. She was succeeded by George I of the House of Hanover.

The Stuart era resulted in constitutional limits being imposed on the monarchy, and supreme power passing into the hands of Parliament; thus the celebrated model of constitutional and parliamentary government, which was to be influential throughout Europe and beyond, took shape. The gist of this momentous development was embedded in a few famous constitutional texts, written elements of an otherwise unwritten Constitution.

The Petition of Right of 1628 was the fruit of Charles I's third Parliament, where an agreement was worked out granting the king the money he requested, on the understanding that he would accept the promulgation of a number of inviolable rights of his subjects, i.e. the limitation of his royal prerogative. The document belonged to the tradition of the medieval charters of liberties and refers expressly to

[4] J. Carswell, *The descent on England. A study of the English revolution of 1688 and its European background* (London, 1969).

the Magna Carta of King John. The Petition of Right was the fruit of a temporary truce between the crown and the opposition, as had been the case in 1215, and Charles I hoped to free himself from its constraints as soon as the balance of power changed. The name of the document is, in contrast to the Bill of Rights of 1689, not self evident, as it was not really a petition but a law; it started as a petition, addressed to the king, but became law by his words of consent: 'soit droit fait comme est désiré' ('let it become law, as requested'). The petition of right was an old procedural device used for claims against the crown. As it seemed unacceptable for royal judges to give sentence against the king, plaintiffs had no other option but to 'ask' him to give them their due – a request which the crown, being the fountain of justice, would naturally grant.[5] Formally speaking the Petition of 1628 belonged to that tradition, but its substance was, of course, quite different. The following stipulations are among the most important.

Article 1 minces no words and concerns taxation, as could be expected. It states expressly that the king's subjects 'have inherited this freedom, that they should not be compelled to contribute to any tax, tallage, aid, or other like charge not set by common consent, in Parliament'. That free people were not taxable without their consent distinguished them from medieval serfs who were *taillables à merci*, i.e. could be made to pay tallage at their lord's will. Article 3 repeats the principle in Magna Carta, which we analysed in chapter 5, that free people can only be punished on the basis of a fair trial. Article 4 elaborates on this point and uses the famous phrase of 'due process of law'. Article 5 condemns imprisonment 'by the king's special command' as an unacceptable abuse.

Some fifty years later, in the reign of Charles II, the protection of the citizen against imprisonment without judgment again appeared in a text of great constitutional importance, the Act of Habeas Corpus of 1679, which contained some detailed regulations on the use of the writ of habeas corpus. The Act is important because it is considered in England till this day as the ultimate bulwark against arbitrary imprisonment, i.e. imprisonment not imposed by a court of law. To understand this it is necessary to know the role and character of the writ of habeas corpus, which is a written royal mandate addressed to an official, ordering the transfer of a prisoner in his power to a specific court to stand trial. *Habeas corpus* means 'have the body' (of the

---

[5] The rule that no claims could be made against the crown was in principle abolished in 1947; until then plaintiffs had to rely on ex gratia payments consequent to a petition of right.

prisoner), and the writ with which the Act of 1679 was concerned was the writ *ad subjiciendum*, i.e. to subject (the prisoner to a judicial process and judgment); it was issued by the chancellor in favour of the prisoner who had requested it or on whose behalf a request had been made. The writ was of medieval origin and had served various purposes in the course of the centuries. Initially a purely administrative routine document, which merely served to indicate which court was to deal with which case, it became in the seventeenth century a weapon against arbitrary arrest, imprisonment and remand in custody. As the government and other authorities had sometimes sabotaged the use of the writ by various chicaneries, the details of its application were fixed by law in 1679, and sanctions imposed against abuse. That habeas corpus remains important till this day in common-law countries does not mean that long and exaggerated remand is unknown there. In England as in many other countries detention on remand, awaiting trial, can last for a long time – cases of one year not being unknown (Scotland has a statutory maximum of 110 days). Nor should it be forgotten that the protection against detention without judgment, offered on principle by habeas corpus, can always be suspended by the British Parliament for particular areas or periods of time, as was the case with the Northern Ireland (Emergency Provisions) Act of 1973.[6]

The most famous constitutional text from the agitated seventeenth century is the Bill of Rights of 1689. This solemn proclamation of various fundamental freedoms was made at the accession of William III and Mary. The flight of James II in 1688 had created a constitutional vacuum. To fill it, Parliament assembled early in 1689 and deposed him; it also declared that no Catholic monarch would ever be acceptable in England. The vacant throne was accepted by James II's daughter Mary, and since her husband, William of Orange, declined to accept the position of a prince consort, he was recognized as king of England. The new king and queen agreed to the solemn proclamation of the inviolable rights and liberties of their

---

[6] R. J. Sharpe, *The law of habeas corpus* (Oxford, 1977). See for the European context the report *Waiting for justice*, published by the Quaker Council for European Affairs in 1987. The duration of remand varies greatly, from an average of eighty-three days in Denmark to an exceptional six years in Italy. Even the European Court of Human Rights in Strasbourg had to admit that it could not say what constitutes a 'reasonable length of time', but Belgium and Austria were in 1991 condemned there for having imposed custodies of respectively more than three and more than two years, deemed 'unreasonable'. See also some remarks in P. Stein and J. Shand, *Legal values in western society* (Edinburgh, 1974), 153–5.

subjects. This Bill is an important link in the long chain leading from the medieval Magna Carta to the modern Declarations of Human Rights. We mention the following articles, some of which contain fundamental principles of the rule of law.

Articles 1 and 2 declare that the 'pretended power of suspending of laws, or the execution of laws, by regal authority, without consent of parliament, is illegal', and the same applies to the 'pretended power of dispensing with laws'. The message is clear: no government is above the law, and no head of state can invoke his 'prerogative' (President Nixon, at the time of the Watergate Affair, in 1974, called it 'executive privilege') to dispense with the law. Article 4 returns to taxation, and aims at safeguarding property against the wanton rapacity of royal government. It declares that 'levying money for or to the use of the crown, by pretence of prerogative, without grant of parliament, for longer time or in other manner than the same is or shall be granted, is illegal'. Article 6 excludes a standing army in England in peacetime except by consent of Parliament. Article 7 guarantees the right of Protestant subjects to carry arms for self defence, a stipulation which was taken over, as we shall see, by the American Constitution (but without the element of religious discrimination). Articles 8 and 9 guarantee the free election of the members of Parliament and the freedom of speech and debate within its walls, as they 'ought not to be impeached or questioned in any court or place out of Parliament'.[7] Article 10 contains the famous prohibition of 'cruel and unusual punishments', i.e. of arbitrary criminal justice. This article was also taken over by the American Constitution and, as we shall see, recently led to a lively debate, involving the Supreme Court, on the question whether the death penalty was a cruel and unusual punishment and therefore unconstitutional.

The outward form of the Bill of Rights deserves our attention. It presents itself as a declaration of ancient rights and liberties drafted by the Lords and the Commons, speaking as a 'full and free representation of this nation'; the declaration became law through the acceptance by the king and queen of these 'true, ancient and indubitable rights and liberties of the people of this kingdom' which were to be 'firmly and strictly holden and observed'.[8]

---

[7] This was an old issue: see W. N. Bryant, 'Commons' immunity from arrest: the earliest known case (1340)', *Bull. Instit. Histor. Research* 43 (1970), 214–15.

[8] L. G. Schwoerer, *The Declaration of Rights, 1689* (Baltimore, London, 1981). The question of the king's prerogative was much debated and one of the leading lawyers of the time devoted a

As the Bill of Rights aimed at ensuring greater political freedom, other steps taken around the same time were to lead to a similar result in the intellectual field. The Toleration Act of 1689 did not contain a proclamation of religious toleration on principle, but introduced a limited exemption from existing restrictions in favour of Protestant dissenters (i.e. non-Anglicans) – Roman Catholics, Unitarians, Jews and unbelievers being expressly excluded.[9] The Test Act of 1673 which provided that all magistrates must receive communion according to the rites of the Church of England remained in force, and so did an Act of 1685 imposing like conditions on the holders of all public offices (these restrictions were not abolished until 1828). The spirit of the Toleration Act was hardly compatible with state censorship in favour of one official creed, and in 1695 England abolished censorship before publication by not renewing the Licensing Act. Criminal prosecution of seditious, obscene, blasphemous or slanderous material after publication was maintained: what had disappeared was the legal obligation to submit writings to a censor before printing.

The last years of the reign of the Stuarts also produced the Act of Settlement, a constitutional text of 1701, which basically concerned the succession to the throne (the occasion being the death in 1700 of the last surviving child of the future Queen Anne). The Act excluded James II and his son James the Old Pretender, and laid down that after the deaths of William III and Anne the throne would pass to the Electress Sophia of Hanover or her descendants. The aim was to ensure that England would not be ruled by a Roman Catholic monarch, and the Act said in so many words that the successor to the throne had to be a member of the Church of England (the rule is valid to this day). The Act also concerned the independence and more specifically the irremovability of the judicature – a highly important aspect of the rule of law – and laid down that the judges could not be deposed by the government (as had happened in the past), the two Houses of Parliament alone being empowered to remove judges (a step that was never taken, although in a few, very rare cases the

treatise to it; see D. E. C. Yale, *Sir Matthew Hale's The Prerogatives of the King* (London, 1976). In 1974 the US Supreme Court, in *US* v. *Richard M. Nixon, President of the US*, decided that executive privilege could not stand up to the judicature: see J. Beauté, *Un grand juriste anglais: Sir Edward Coke 1552–1634. Ses idées politiques et constitutionnelles, ou aux origines de la démocratie moderne* (Paris, 1975), 10. For the international repercussions of the events of 1688–9, see J. I. Israel (ed.), *The Anglo-Dutch moment. Essays on the Glorious Revolution and its world impact* (Cambridge, 1991).

[9] The dissenters, although small in numbers, played a considerable role in social development. See M. R. Watts, *The dissenters. From the Reformation to the French Revolution* (Oxford, 1978).

procedure was set in motion). It should be made clear, however, that this impressive degree of independence of the Bench only extends to its highest ranks, where the essential development of the law takes place, i.e. the judges in the High Court and the Court of Appeal, and the Law Lords (fewer than 150 individuals altogether), whereas the others are under the (disciplinary) authority of the lord chancellor, who is a member of the government.

Oliver Cromwell and his Puritans had bold and far reaching plans for the modernization of the law, private as well as public. They by no means carried them all out, and what they realized was often undone at the Restoration, which explains why legal historians have tended to neglect their legal endeavours. This seems unjustified, for our attention should not only be absorbed by successful enterprises: selective 'winners' history' deforms the reality of the past. The Puritan episode produced some highly interesting initiatives in various fields of law, procedure, the courts and the Constitution of the kingdom. The Puritans' basic aim was democratization and the reorganization of the state in accordance with their religious beliefs.

The Puritans were deeply interested in the law and the courts, and they proceeded to a radical 'clean up'. The prerogative courts, considered products and symbols of autocracy, were abolished. The Star Chamber, which had been severe on Puritans, disappeared forever; the Court of Chancery, being not a common-law court, was another victim, but not for good. The Puritans also wanted to bring the courts into closer contact with the people, which led to initiatives such as the decentralization of the judicial system (the most highly centralized in Europe), the introduction of the English language to replace the medieval, esoteric Law French (which was incomprehensible to all but a few hundred members of the profession) and the codification of the law – all measures which got no further than discussions in commissions, or were revoked at the Restoration.

The Constitution underwent drastic changes. Kingship was abolished, as was the House of Lords, the ancient aristocratic chamber. England became a republic, called Commonwealth or Free State. The year of Charles I's execution and the beginning of the republic was named officially the 'first year of freedom by God's blessing restored' (anticipating the rhetoric of the French Revolution). The established Anglican Church and the episcopal hierarchy were abolished, as were the old feudal, military tenures (the one lasting measure in this series). England remained a parliamentary regime for the time being, although based on a different conception. The Rump Parliament (1648–53), what was left of the Long Parliament (1640–53), remained in office, but real power rested in the hands of the military, and when the Rump Parliament showed insufficient submissiveness, it was driven out by the army. Its place was taken by a parliament composed in a novel way, not through elections, but through appointments by Cromwell's Council from ecclesiastical lists of 'saints'. It is known as Barebones Parliament, and looked more like a religious meeting (of a sort of Christian ayatollah's) than a political assembly. It was utterly useless and generally derided, and soon disappeared. The army seized power overtly in 1653 and proclaimed Cromwell Lord Protector (a regime which replaced that of the Commonwealth and lasted till 1659). In this same year of 1653 a new Constitution was proclaimed, the Instrument of Government, which can be considered the first written Constitution in European history, not in the sense of a constitutional declaration of rights and liberties, but as a fundamental and permanent law describing the main organs of the state and their respective roles. A few more parliaments met, failures all of them, and finally, with the dissolution of the 1658 Parliament, the ancient institution itself disappeared. This was a remarkable outcome if one realizes that the struggle for Parliament had been one of the main aims of the opposition to the Stuarts, and the paradoxical result was that the restoration of the monarchy in 1660 brought about the restoration of Parliament as well: two victims of the Puritan Revolution were reborn together. The military take-over had been legalized by the establishment in 1655 of the regime of the Major Generals and the division of the country into eleven military districts.[10] The Puritan Revolution had run an unforeseen course, which seems to be the lot of most revolutions. And the abolition of Parliament and the introduction of a military regime were, as so many other aspects of the English revolution, to be repeated closely in France a century and a half later.

In the wake of Cromwell's political revolution there arose, again as would happen later in France, a radical current for social and

[10] G. B. Nourse, 'Law reform under the commonwealth and protectorate', *Law Quarterly Review* 75 (1959), 519–29; S. E. Prall, *The agitation for law reform during the Puritan Revolution 1640–1660* (The Hague, 1966); M. Cotterell, 'Interregnum law reform: the Hale Commission of 1652', *Engl. Histor. Rev.* 83 (1968), 689–704; J. Brewer and J. Styles (eds.), *An ungovernable people? The English and their law in the seventeenth and eighteenth centuries* (London, 1980); B. Shapiro, 'Sir Francis Bacon and the mid-seventeenth century movement for law reform', *American Journal of Legal History* 24 (1980), 331–62.

economic reform. Its inspiration was derived from the Bible and it was prompted by oppositional groups which in some ways resembled present-day 'green' parties, advocating, for example, the return to nature and country life, where everybody would dig his own field (hence the name of 'diggers'). The main aspiration was for more democracy, including general franchise and economic equality (hence the name 'levellers'). The agitation of these radical groups led to serious conflict in the Puritan camp, and Cromwell personally intervened against the general suffrage demanded by the extreme democratic wing, alleging that it was irresponsible to give the vote to have-nots with no other stake in the nation than the air they breathed (the existing system reserved the vote to owners of property yielding at least 40 shillings a year).[11] Tension rose and tempers flared to the point that the conservatives eliminated the radicals *manu militari* – an operation involving the Council of State and executions. The revolt, the work of 'turbulent spirits' supported by 'simple manual workers who were inclined to tumult', was summarily dealt with and it was not until the following century that this sort of plebeian agitation showed its menacing head again.

Ever since the Glorious Revolution of 1688 and the Bill of Rights of the following year it was clear in what direction the Constitution of England and Britain would develop (in 1707 England and Scotland turned their personal union into a real one by the establishment of the United Kingdom of Great Britain). The monarchy was to be conserved, but restricted by constitutional bonds, and the oligarchic Parliament, consisting of an hereditary House of Lords and an assembly elected according to a restricted, property-based franchise, would take political power into its own hands. How these principles, developed through custom and not written in a Constitution, would be worked out in daily life remained for the time being an open question. The answer was given under the dynasty of Hanover, which in Britain came to the throne in 1714 in the person of King George I (creating a personal union between Britain and Hanover which would last till the accession, in 1837, of Queen Victoria, excluded from the succession in Hanover as a female).

The executive, which used to be in the hands of the king and his secretaries, passed to the cabinet of ministers, who were politicians carrying their own responsibility and headed by the prime minister,

---

[11] D. Hirst, *The representatives of the people? Voters and voting in England under the early Stuarts* (Cambridge, 1976).

the effective political leader of the nation. The name of prime minister was of French origin, where Richelieu, for example, had been known as the *premier* or *principal ministre*. This government was expected to implement the will of Parliament, and particularly of the House of Commons, which voted the necessary budget laws. The budget was established annually, which made governments chronically dependent on Parliament and more specifically on the Lower House. Since the early eighteenth century the custom had arisen that budget laws voted by the Commons were not held up by the Lords, and a grave constitutional crisis arose at the beginning of the twentieth century when the Lords suddenly wanted to go against this rule, arguing that it had never been declared law. The financial dependence meant that the Hanoverian cabinet had to manage – or even manipulate – Parliament, which could only be done by able political leaders, so that government accountability indirectly strengthened the crown.

The rise of the cabinet was the logical result of the momentous changes in the balance of power between crown and Parliament witnessed in the previous century. It was, however, also encouraged by fortuitous circumstances such as George I's ignorance of English and his and his son's lack of interest in English politics, German affairs being closer to their hearts. They declined to preside over cabinet meetings or even to attend them, a habit which became an unwritten constitutional rule and remains so till this day. In these circumstances it was only natural that the king's personal preference had to give way to the will of the majority in Parliament so that he could be forced to accept a government whose policy he disapproved of. King George III tried to regain some of the lost territory and in 1807 even dismissed the government – for the last time in British history – but that was no more than an idle gesture.

The cabinet was not just a meeting place for independent secretaries, each with his own separate and autonomous competence, but a firm team of ministers who governed together and carried out a single collective policy. It was rightly called a 'ministerial government with collective responsibility to the House of Commons'.

We have seen that the cabinet reflected the will of Parliament, or at least the majority of its members. It could not be reasonably expected that these hundreds of people would reach a unanimous judgment on all questions, and there was a serious risk of quarrelling fractions – or factions or cabals – paralysing the leadership. This did not take place, because of the rise of a stable two-party system, of the Whigs, who were in the ascendant until about 1760, and the Tories, who took over from that date.

Whigs and Tories (nicknames that became party names) were the precursors of the Liberal and Conservative Parties. Initially they were unlike the organizations we know today, with a central office, elaborate directives, party discipline and a sharp ideological profile. They resembled rather political families, linked to different social and economic strata and interests, and ideas on Church and state. Their origin goes back to the last phase in the struggle over the Stuarts.[12] The Tories tended to favour the monarchy and even tried to keep the Hanoverians away from the throne in favour of the Stuarts. They were close to the landowning classes and the Anglican Church. The Whigs were the great winners of the Glorious Revolution and adversaries of (Stuart) absolutism. They counted many dissenters in their ranks and were closer to urban mercantile interests than those of the gentry and agriculture. In fact eighteenth-century politics was often a question of compromises and deals between a few leading families and their clientele, without much attention to ideological issues; there was also a small but important group of members who stayed outside the party game. Consequently politics and the Church were dominated by about seventy great families. One does not see, moreover, what ideological strife there could have been as there were no differences of opinion within the leading classes about the foundations of public life, i.e. oligarchic rule and freedom of enterprise and thought.[13]

One factor of strength for the House of Commons was the fact that it contained the gentry as well as the urban bourgeoisie, in contrast to the Continent where nobility and bourgeoisie met and voted in separate chambers. Another strong point was the principle formulated in the eighteenth century that the members were not sitting in order to defend local interests – which meant that local 'instructions' were condemned – and were expected to act only in the national interest, being 'the attorneys of the people of England', as a ministerial declaration in Parliament put it in 1745. This explains why till this day a member of Parliament does not necessarily have local roots.

---

[12] B. W. Hill, *The growth of parliamentary parties 1689–1742* (London, 1976); F. O'Gorman, *The emergence of the British two-party system* (London, 1982).

[13] See the classic work by L. B. Namier, *The structure of politics at the accession of George III* (London, 1929). See also the recent survey, placed in a European context, by H. Eichler, *Verfassungswandel in England. Ein Beitrag zur europäischen Rechtsgeschichte des 17. und 18. Jahrhunderts* (Berlin, Munich, 1988).

Many, of course, do, and represent the same constituency for many years, but sometimes politicians whom the central party office wants to get into Parliament are sent, only weeks before an election, to a 'safe seat' where they have never been in their lives.

The aspect of the British Constitution which most impressed continental observers was the separation of powers, so eloquently described by Montesquieu in his *Esprit des lois* of 1748, and such an important point for the American and French revolutionaries. However, not even in Britain were the three powers – legislative, executive and judicial – completely separate. Nor is this easily conceivable in practice, as even in the United States, where it is a fundamental constitutional tenet, the three powers overlap and influence each other all the time. Impeachment, for example, is a weapon in the hands of the legislature against members of the executive and the judiciary. Judicial review of the constitutionality of the laws is an example of the impact of the judges on the legislators, and the presidential veto interferes with the work of Congress. In Britain the higher judges are indeed independent from the government, but not from Parliament; legislative power rests in fact with Parliament but formally Acts of Parliament are the work of both the king and the two Houses at Westminster. Parliament is, of course, a legislative body, but nevertheless the House of Lords was and is also the highest law court in the land. Many continental lawyers visiting London must have observed with amazement the changing roles of some famous lord chancellor in the Upper House, where at one moment he presided over the meeting of a legislative chamber, at another acted as a member of the government, and on yet another occasion took part as a law lord in a judicial decision. All these observations do not, however, detract from Montesquieu's perception, that there was in Great Britain a measure of separation of powers much greater than in his own fatherland, where the unity and concentration of powers in the king's hand was the leading principle. In Britain the judicial function was indeed separate and independent from the king and his ministers. Legislation in reality was the province of Parliament, and the laws it passed were and always are signed by the monarch: the last to veto such an Act was Queen Anne (1702–14). On the other hand it was not Parliament's task to run the government on a day to day basis: it contented itself with the main direction and important decisions, leaving the executive to do its own job. The contrast, incidentally, is great with the regime of the *Convention Nationale* (which we will present later), where outside the legislative assembly there was no separate government or even a head of state, executive decisions being in the hands of committees of the Convention.

The constitutional liberties gained in the seventeenth century were not put in jeopardy under the Hanoverians, but they should be appreciated at their true value. Censorship was not reintroduced, but that did not mean that one could publish anything unpunished. Criticism of Parliament or even reporting its debates was a breach of privilege and an offence, and criticism of the crown could land a journalist in gaol, as the popular John Wilkes found out. In 1762 he published in his newspaper an attack on George III, was arrested and condemned by Parliament, of which he was a member, for treason and sedition. Mass demonstrations were the result, with cries of 'Wilkes and liberty'. The journalist fled to the Continent, was re-elected by his supporters, but disqualified by Parliament, only to be elected again. Demonstrations in his favour got out of hand and people were killed.

When at the end of the eighteenth century social and political radicalism was stirring again, notably under the influence of events in France, the government was alarmed and Parliament suspended habeas corpus, temporarily eliminating the constitutional safeguard against arbitrary imprisonment on the government's orders. The ruling oligarchy, which dominated the country via Parliament, acted harshly against radical clubs, strikes and workers' revolts, by means, *inter alia*, of Treason and Sedition Acts.[14] It was the time of the rise of industrial capitalism. Private enterprise developed in a favourable legal framework. The country formed one common market and the central government managed on the whole to protect law and order and to assure external safety and colonial expansion. This powerful state was, however, content to leave business alone and gave entrepreneurs a large measure of freedom. The absence of arbitrary government created institutional and legal security welcomed by business. The affluent members of Parliament were not going to make life difficult for the city of London and the captains of industry: the franchise was restricted and the law limited access to the Commons to the rich, whereas the House of Lords was by definition composed of the wealthier element. In matters of taxation there was no fundamental inequality in law. The medieval taxes of the tallage type, which were

---

[14]  J. V. Orth, *Combination and conspiracy. A legal history of trade unionism 1721–1906* (Oxford, 1991).

class-bound, had long gone, and so had the ancient fiscal privileges. The clergy decided on its own taxes in its convocations. The main taxes, levied without class distinction or privilege, were the parliamentary 'subsidies' (*inter alia* on movables), the land tax (based on old and rather fictitious estimates), the window tax and excise duties and customs.

During the period under review a modern solution was devised for the problem of the finances of the crown. The ancient practice for the king to cover his private and public expenditure with the revenue of crown land – royal finance and state finance being inextricably linked – had in course of time turned into a fiction: the huge landed wealth of the crown had gradually whittled down and His Majesty's government had come to live on grants from the Commons. Legal thought rejected the impure confusion of public and private categories. So finally a formal distinction was made between the annual Civil List, destined for the king and his family and court, and the treasury of the state. What was left of the old crown lands went to the state, and Parliament granted the king an annual sum. It was furthermore accepted that the king could own private wealth and personally administer it. Until 1688, as long as the king's government was truly his own, the ancient link had continued, but afterwards, because of mounting war expenditure, control of military spending was taken over by the Commons, and from 1697 King William III was paid an annual sum by Parliament to cover both his personal expenses and the expenditure of the government for civilian purposes (hence 'Civil List'). Under George III these civilian expenses were also taken over by Parliament, so that, by 1830, the much-reduced Civil List was allotted purely for 'the personal dignity' of the king and queen. In 1800 the Crown Private Estate Act had given the king private financial status, allowing him, *inter alia*, to own land as an individual.[15]

## ENLIGHTENED ABSOLUTISM

### General considerations

Whereas the traditional authors speak of 'enlightened despotism', there is nowadays a tendency to speak of 'enlightened absolutism'. The terms 'despot' and 'despotism' are indeed associated with rulers who have no respect for the persons or the properties of their subjects,

[15] P. Hall, *Royal fortune: tax, money and the monarchy* (London, 1992).

interfere in the administration of justice and treat the citizens in a cruel and arbitrary way. The enlightened kings of the eighteenth century in no way fitted that image. On the contrary, they wished to operate within the law – at least in their own country – and genuinely desired happiness for their subjects in the light of the rational philosophy of their time. The name 'enlightened absolutism' describes their regime exactly, although they did not themselves use it: *despotisme éclairé* or *despotisme légal* were popular terms in the eighteenth century, being used by the physiocrats in the sixties. The philosopher Diderot used the expression in his correspondence, and it appeared for the first time in a published work by G. Raynal, who wrote in a book of 1770 that the happiest government would be that of a 'just and enlightened despot' (he was no doubt inspired by Plato's 'philosopher king'). In ancient Greek *despotes* had no pejorative sense and simply meant lord of the house, governor or ruler, and so it was still with the French *despote* in the eighteenth century. Afterwards the negative meaning of 'tyrant, oppressor' began to dominate (and is now well established) and as a consequence the term enlightened absolutism made progress. W. Rocher introduced the expression *aufgeklärter Absolutismus* in 1847 in an article on the various forms of absolutism (while *aufgeklärter Despotismus* also continued to be used, after the eighteenth-century fashion).

Terminological discussions apart, enlightened absolutism was no less absolutist than the older species: the ruler did not need the consent of the people or the social classes (or their representatives in provincial or national estates) and, although he had to respect the legal order on principle, there was no political or judicial body that could sit in judgment on him and force him to obey the Constitution. This form of government was merely the last phase of the classic European absolutism, whose origins went back to the Middle Ages. It accepted unequivocally the Roman principle of the concentration of power in one pair of hands, and had abandoned the ancient Germanic idea of the diffusion of legitimate authority over numerous individuals and bodies. The enlightened absolute kings also believed in unlimited national sovereignty and the pre-eminence of the *raison d'état*, which served to justify everything. Thus Frederick the Great of Prussia had no qualms about invading and conquering Silesia without any legal grounds: lawyers could be found to think up some argument to justify his attack, as they had done for Louis XIV's wars of conquest. Legal doctrine had elevated the *raison d'état* to a distinct category and explained that *arcana dominationis* and *ius dominationis* ('the secrets and the law of domination') took precedence over the *ius commune seu ordinarium* ('the common or ordinary law'), with the *bonum commune* in view.[16]

Enlightened absolutism is distinguished from the older, unenlightened variant by a new vision and a new aim. It reminds the present-day reader of M. Gorbachev's attempt to modernize Soviet society, while maintaining the old controlling position of the Communist Party. The enlightened rulers of the eighteenth century believed in the ideas of the *Aufklärung* ('enlightenment') which gained wide support in Europe. In the legal field this meant the success of natural law and the decline of the authority of Roman law. One can find a remarkable expression of the new ideas in Christian Wolff's *Vernünftige Gedanken vom gesellschaftlichen Leben der Menschen* of 1721 ('rational thoughts on man's life in society'). The work is mainly concerned with the individual and his 'human rights', the state being founded on a contract between free people in order to achieve the 'Beförderung der gemeinen Wohlfart und Sicherheit' ('advancement of the general welfare and security'). In this line of thought several authors expressed the feeling that man was not yet emancipated enough to see his own good and had to be forced to a higher stage of consciousness. G. F. Lamprecht, for example, a professor at the University of Halle, said in his *Versuch eines vollständigen Systems der Staatslehre* of 1784 that it is the task of the state 'to make the citizens in all respects more moral, healthier, more enlightened, prosperous and secure, and to provide them with the commodities and comforts of life'. T. Kretschmann went even further and visualized the state as a highly disciplined school whose task it was to educate people to a 'higher degree of development': he advocated a police- and nanny-state. It is significant that the Constitution of the United Kingdom of the Netherlands of 1815 contained a provision on the role of the state as educator, and King William I (*d.* 1843), who stood in the tradition of enlightened absolutism, took this to heart and gave a great impulse to education, from primary schools to universities (in the southern Netherlands he founded universities in Ghent, Liège and Leuven). All this stood in sharp contrast to other countries, where education was left to private initiative, and where the *laissez-faire* philosophy rejected the idea of governments being responsible for people's welfare and education –

---

[16] See for the use of these terms, A. Clapmarius (*d.* 1604) in his posthumous *De arcanis rerum publicarum libri sex* (Bremen, 1605; 2nd edn, Jena, 1665).

forced or not – to 'higher stages of perfection'. It is obvious that enlightened absolutism did not aim at the personal or dynastic advancement of the ruler, but at the well-being of the people, material as well as intellectual. Hence education in a rational spirit, struggle against ancient superstitions and a policy favouring intellectual freedom: the state became a welfare state.

The new philosophy also meant the end of the monarchy's old patrimonial approach. The country was no more the patrimony of the dynasty; the prince had become the 'first servant of the state'. The old crown lands became state property, and the ruler received a revenue from the state. The enlightened monarchs justified their position no more by an appeal to God. They did not rule by God's grace, nor were they surrounded by the metaphysical halo of the 'anointed of the Lord'. Henceforth they believed in the utility principle: a well-ordered society needed leadership and the kings were predestined for their task by their illustrious origins and education, and had to carry it out for the general good. Because of his training and exalted position the 'father of the land' saw further than his subjects and was above their regional outlook and occupational and sectional interests and prejudices. The king was capable and obliged to advance the general welfare according to his own judgment and without giving in to pressure groups. The emperor Joseph II, for example, scorned the trappings of majesty and behaved and looked more like a general manager than a Holy Roman emperor. Not everyone was enchanted by this transformation. The people of the Austrian Netherlands were disappointed when Joseph II, dressed soberly, visited their country, wearing no imperial regalia and clearly more interested in details of administration and industry than in pomp and circumstance. The renunciation of religious prestige led, in the spirit of the Enlightenment, to the secularization of the state, with such measures as the dissolution of 'useless' monasteries (i.e. not engaged in education or sick relief), the foundation of state schools, tolerance of denominations other than the established Church, ending the exclusive ecclesiastical jurisdiction over marriage, and generally abandoning the old idea that it was the ruler's prime task to protect and support the national Church. The enlightened rulers were proud of their modernity. They not only rejected superstition and other relics from the Dark Ages, but campaigned against the inhumanity of criminal law and procedure. Their respect for the law and belief in its emancipatory role inspired their legislation. Modern codes were drafted, introducing a *gemeinverständlich* ('commonly understandable') system based on the 'law of reason', and although no formal Constitutions were proclaimed, these codes contained norms which were binding even for the government and were a step in the direction of a constitutional state. These governments, whose regime could be described as 'absolutism with a human face', were more than cosmetic attempts to save the authoritarian Ancient Regime.

Enlightened absolutism was a continental phenomenon, unknown in Great Britain, which had rejected autocracy before the Enlightenment took hold of Europe. On the Continent it was widespread, not only in Central Europe (we shall analyse the development in Prussia and Austria in more detail), but also in Italy, Portugal and Russia. France, which played a leading role in the propagation of the philosophy of the *Encyclopédie*, took paradoxically no part in the constitutional experiment which it produced. Both Louis XV, who ruled from 1715 to 1774, and Louis XVI, who ruled from 1774 to 1793, remained loyal to the old fashioned high absolutism of their predecessors, notwithstanding some late measures in connection with the abolition of torture and serfdom.

### Prussia and Austria

Frederick II's Prussia and Joseph II's Austria are classic examples of enlightened absolutism, to which we shall now turn our attention. But first it is necessary to say something about the political history of these two countries and their relations with the German empire, to which most Prussian and most Habsburg lands belonged.

In the history of public law the Holy Roman Empire of the German Nation – briefly the German empire, or even the empire (*das Reich*) – occupies an anomalous position, so much so that it is very hard to define the nature of its Constitution using the traditional terminology: Pufendorf (*d.* 1694), in his *De statu imperii Germanici*, aptly called it '*irregulare aliquod corpus et monstro simile*' ('some irregular body and similar to a monster'). German history alone can explain how this 'monster' came about.

While in most kingdoms centralized and unitary nation states were established, rising above regional and social particular interests, Germany after the fall of the Hohenstaufen in the mid-thirteenth century took the opposite road. The power of the spiritual and temporal principalities and the main towns expanded, while kingship was degraded to a mere symbol of German nationhood, without effective control. The empire as such had neither an army, nor finance, nor an administration of its own; the effective might of which the German king disposed came from his own territory. His position was comparable to that of the kings of France in the eleventh and twelfth centuries. There also we found a kingdom divided into autonomous provincial states, which in theory all lived under royal authority, although the monarch in fact only ruled over his own *domaine direct*. Since the mid-fifteenth century the German kings belonged almost invariably to the House of Habsburg, which originally came from Swabia and Switzerland, to which was added the *Ostmark* (Austria) with some neighbouring territories and, through the marriage of Maximilian of Austria to Mary of Burgundy, also the Burgundian Netherlands.

From the tenth century onwards, as we have seen, German kingship and Roman empire were linked and, until Frederick II, the German kings/Roman emperors played an active role in Italian politics, and even after his reign went on being crowned Roman emperors in Italy, the last being Charles V in Bologna in 1530. This supranational, strictly speaking even 'universal' empire had become more and more fictional, mainly because of Italian and papal resistance, so that the German nature of the imperial monarchy became ever more conspicuous. Hence, since the fifteenth century, the name of Holy Roman Empire of the German Nation was used and finally, after Charles V's coronation, the Italian crowning was omitted. The loss of various French-speaking provinces of the medieval empire to France accentuated the German national character of the *Reich*, even though non-German speaking regions, such as Bohemia and part of Wallonia, remained German.

The enormous area in the centre of Europe, which older French authors used to call *les Allemagnes*, had a very weak structure and could be described as a confederation of independent states, with an emperor and a Reichstag as expressions of nationhood, but disposing of little jurisdiction over principalities and towns. A forceful attempt was twice made to turn this large and heterogeneous Germany into a national monarchy after the French or English model, but each time the enterprise failed, *inter alia*, because religious dissension came on top of all the older elements of disunity. The first was made by the emperor Maximilian at the Reichstag of Worms in 1495 and was widely supported by the humanist movement. The second was the work of the authoritarian Emperor Ferdinand II (1619–37) who, for religious and other reasons, dismissed the Count Palatine in 1621 and transferred the dignity of Elector to Maximilian of Bavaria. Ferdinand's policy was a product of the Counter-Reformation, but its result was the opposite of what he aimed at: the Thirty Years War, unleashed by his illegal attempt, resulted in the Treaties of Westphalia of 1648, which not only contained international dispositions, but also concerned the internal structure of Germany, one element being the express recognition of the sovereignty of the German territories. These newly sovereign states, Prussia and Austria, for example, nevertheless continued to be part of the German empire, even when, as in Maria Theresa's and Frederick the Great's time, they were at war with each other. During the Seven Years War the German empire as such was a belligerent, allied to Austria and against Prussia, which meant that one of the princes of the empire was not only at war with another, but with the empire itself.

It was clear that the Reich had become a fiction, and only a few principalities in the south and west still seemed to take it seriously, because they were too small to have a policy of their own and to safeguard their security. Yet even these mini-states could not really keep the empire, a relic of the feudal past, alive. The Reichstag, which had turned into a sort of meeting place for the German states, only became a permanent institution, called the *immerwährender Reichstag*, because at its meeting at Regensburg in 1663 it did not succeed in reaching any decision and determined to reside there indefinitely (not that it ever realized anything of political importance).

The Reichskammergericht ('Imperial Chamber of Justice') turned in fact into an international court of law and underwent a constant erosion of its jurisdiction through the grant of numerous territorial privileges *de non evocando* and *de non appellando*, ensuring that cases did not leave the privileged principalities. The anomaly of their Constitution was puzzling even to the Germans. They realized very well that their country was different from the run of the mill nation states. But what was it? Some lawyers simply called the Reich a construction *sui generis*, which could not be described with the terminology and categories applicable elsewhere in Europe. An emperor without a government, army or finance of his own could hardly be considered a national monarch: the Austrian administration, army and revenue belonged not to the empire but to one of its component parts. Nor could Germany be considered an oligarchy or 'aristocracy', as some French authors, notably Jean Bodin, maintained, for although real power was in the hands of a limited group of princes (since the Treaties of Westphalia some 300 to 320 sovereign territories depending directly on the empire, and some 1,400 territories depending on the first category and therefore only indirectly on the empire),[17] it was difficult to ignore altogether the role of the emperor, the universal ruler par excellence, and for the same reason it was impossible to call Germany a republic. Nevertheless calling the country a 'republic of princes', as Poland was called a 'republic of the nobility', would not be totally amiss. After all, under Napoleon the first German empire underwent a fate that is comparable to that of Poland, i.e. disappearance in terms of public law and partition at the hands of the conqueror. Could Germany be considered a confederacy, an alliance of states? Not really, for if each of the members had a sovereign head of state, what was the position of the emperor? Nor was Germany a federal state, as it lacked the fundamental division between federal and state affairs and the assignment of the former – defence, currency, foreign relations – to specific federal agencies. The best one can do is to conclude that the Constitution of the German empire had been overtaken by events to such an extent that it became meaningless and only survived because no one had abolished it; conceivably nobody even knew who would have been competent to do so. The Holy Roman Empire of the German Nation finally disappeared under pressure by Napoleon in 1806, when the states of the League of the Rhine, which could still be considered part of the Reich, left it, and the emperor Francis II laid down his Roman crown, although he continued as emperor of Austria, which he had become in 1804.

The German empire may have seemed a monster to lawyers trained in Roman and natural law, but it is not the only monster on the constitutional scene. What, for example, are we to make of the European Community? It presents oddities as baffling to us as those of Ancient-Regime Germany were to Pufendorf.[18] Is the Community, which began as an economic and is developing into a political organization, a confederation, i.e. a political association of sovereign states, or is it – or is it on the point of becoming – one federal or

---

[17] These *c.* 1400 *reichsmittelbar* territories enjoyed no sovereignty and had no seats in the Reichstag, but had nevertheless a good measure of judicial and administrative autonomy.

[18] A. Randelzhofer, *Völkerrechtliche Aspekte des heiligen Römischen Reiches nach 1648* (Berlin, 1967) carefully analyses the Constitution of the old Reich and suggests that it may contain useful indications for the problems of international public law in our time; he devotes a chapter, pp. 271–96, to a comparison of the old empire with the United Nations Organization.

composite state? The suggestion that the latter might be the case sent tremors through the British political establishment in 1991 at the time of the signing of the Treaty of Maastricht, and a controversy arose about the true meaning of the word 'federal': did it refer to a centralized superstate or to the opposite?[19] So what is the legal nature of the European Community? The normal organs of state – head, government, parliament – are not clearly visible or, in the case of the head of state, completely absent. The European Commission often looks and acts as a government and certainly runs the daily business of the Community, but its members are more like civil servants than politicians, they are not elected but appointed for a four-year term by the member states and do not depend on a majority in the European Parliament, which has no say in their nomination. The Commission proposes lines of action to the Council of Ministers and executes the latter's policy decisions with the help of some 15,000 employees; in doing so the Commission can even impose sanctions, which is somewhat anomalous for a bureaucratic body. Is the Council of Ministers, often described as the political organ par excellence of the Community, the real European government? Not quite, as it does not carry the daily burden of the affairs of state, only meets occasionally and is composed not of a body of European ministers, but of cabinet ministers from the various nation states, delegated by them to meet from time to time and become European for a while, before going back home to real life in their respective countries. The Council is also the true lawgiver of the Community, although the European Parliament wishes to share the power to enact legislation with the Council. The Parliament is directly elected by the people, but its legislative powers are limited, as we have seen, and so is its hold on the Community's finances, since it only has the last word on the non-compulsory expenditure (i.e. which is not the inevitable consequence of Community legislation). Parliament, however, has the right to reject the budget as a whole, as happened in December 1979 when it threw out the draft budget for 1980 placed before it by the Council (the present tendency is clearly towards greater parliamentary influence on the budget). Parliament can also influence European policy by its often used right to pose questions to the Commission or the Council, but this does in no way make the Council accountable to it. One drastic means for the

---

[19] R. C. van Caenegem, 'Historical and modern confrontations between continental and English law' in B. de Witte and C. Forder (eds.), *The common law of Europe and the future of legal education* (Deventer, 1992), 621–38.

people's representatives to assert themselves exists on paper: they can by a motion of censure force the whole Commission to resign, but this has never happened so far. The fact is that the European Parliament has basically only a consultative role, even though it embodies elective democratic legitimacy, so that there is no real democratic control of the legislative and executive powers in the Community. Only the European Court of Justice is simply what its name suggests, a court of law manned by professional judges. Small wonder that two learned authors have said about the European Community that its 'constitutional structure remains still in the sphere of speculation'.[20]

Out of the chaos of the German *Kleinstaaterei* two territories stepped forward to join the ranks of the Great Powers, Prussia and Austria. The latter was as it were predestined to play a leading role, as the Habsburgs had been a supranational force for a long time and in the sixteenth century had become the most powerful dynasty in Europe. By contrast nothing seemed to indicate that the dynasty of Hohenzollern would ever become a major force. Both Brandenburg and Prussia were eccentric provinces – Prussia did not even belong to the German empire, as it was a Polish fief – and the only striking thing about them for a long time was their poverty in natural resources. It was the forceful and unashamed militarism of the Hohenzollerns which put Prussia on the road to influence – a striking example of the triumph of politics over economic conditions. The kingdom of Prussia was a political conglomerate among many others and was, as the Burgundian Netherlands three centuries before, brought together by a common lineage of rulers which united a multitude of older mini-states and free cities. Its origins are to be found in the duchy of Brandenburg, to which were joined several territories in the west, such as Cleve, in the east, particularly Prussia which became a kingdom in the eighteenth century, and in the south-east, i.e. Silesia, conquered from Austria. These territories were united into one large unit by Frederick William the Great Elector (1640–88), whose son King Frederick I (1688–1713) and the latter's son King Frederick William I, the 'king corporal' (1713–40), ruled alone, according to the absolutist model of the day. This entailed the demotion of the assemblies of estates, permanent taxation and a remarkably large standing army, which had nothing in common any more with medieval urban militias or feudal hosts. The country was one great garrison, divided into cantons of about

---

[20] D. Lasok and J. W. Bridge, *Law and institutions of the European Communities* (5th edn, London, 1992), 29.

5,000 hearths, each regiment being attached to a canton for finding the necessary recruits. This is the state over which Frederick II the Great (1740–86) came to rule but, in contrast to his father, in the spirit of the Enlightenment. His regime can be described as follows.

The king acted as an absolute monarch; he was not bound by a written Constitution and did not depend on a parliament for the necessary financial means. His ministers were accountable to him alone and he himself to God. He knew what was best for the people and acted accordingly. Frederick the Great was a man of letters and expressed his ideas as follows in his *Essai sur les formes de gouvernement et sur les devoirs des souverains* of 1781: 'The prince is to the society which he governs what the head is to the body; he must see, think and act for the whole community, in order to provide it with all the advantages which it can expect'.

The regime was enlightened, as Frederick was a follower of the *Aufklärung* and in sustained contact with the leading *philosophes* of his day. He broke, in the same rationalist spirit, with the religious dimension of the monarchy and created a neutral state whose mission was not to protect the Church, let alone to be in its service, but to create an institutional framework where various denominations could flourish. As he put it: 'in my kingdom everyone can be saved in his own way'. His belief in progress and his desire to stimulate popular advancement led to an ambitious educational policy, particularly regarding primary schooling, which in most of Europe was still in the hands of amateurs who found a meagre extra income by teaching the children or rather 'keeping them out of mischief' during the winter months, when they could be missed on the farm.[21]

Frederick also had an enlightened attitude towards the law. He believed in it, and was convinced that it behoved him to respect it. He could only act freely within the limits of the legal system and it was his express policy not to interfere with the normal activity of the courts. As he put it in his political testament in 1752: 'I am resolved never to interfere with the course of a judicial process, for in the courts the laws should speak and the sovereign keep silent'. It was a policy which he adhered to, at least in civil cases, for in criminal affairs he sometimes took matters into his own hands, even dismissing or punishing judges, who were considered servants of the king. The practice for the king and his closest advisers to pronounce judgments out of his plenitude of

---

[21] J. Van Horn Melton, *Absolutism and the eighteenth-century origins of compulsory schooling in Prussia and Austria* (London, 1988).

power (*Machtsprüche*), bypassing the ordinary judicial channels, known as *Kabinettsjustiz*, fell into disuse in civil cases.[22] His enlightened philosophy led him to legislate and to codify the law according to modern ideas inspired by natural law. The codes were to ensure cognoscibility, accessibility and security. It is in this line of thought that early in the nineteenth century the Germans, as we have seen, began to mention the *Rechtsstaat*, as opposed to the *Obrigkeitsstaat*, as a monarchy bound by the law, but without falling into the extreme republicanism of the French model: the German *Sonderweg* ('special path') between the extremes of arbitrary kingship and a radical republic. The spirit of this monarchic *Rechtsstaat* is clearly expressed in Frederick's *Allgemeines Gesetzbuch für die preussischen Staaten*, where the rule of law was to be guaranteed by the prohibition of the royal *Machtspruch* and by legislation that was binding for everyone. To ensure authoritative interpretation of the laws a *Gesetzkommission* ('legislative commission') was instituted. According to the senior officials who created the *Allgemeines Gesetzbuch*, J. H. C. Carmer (*d.* 1801) and C. G. Svarez (*d.* 1798), its norms played the role of a written Constitution for Prussia.[23]

Some scholars are of the opinion that the Reich's only real importance lay in the judicial field, and they point at the activity of the Reichskammergericht, which retained some jurisdiction even over principalities which enjoyed the aforementioned *privilegium de non appellando*. This was notably the case when private plaintiffs acted against their own princes: the territorial courts were useless, as they could not give judgment against their own rulers, but the empire could. Unfortunately this often turned out to be mere theory, because many dukes and counts managed to slow down the judicial process and even to prevent the execution of the judgments. Nevertheless Ancient-Regime lawyers believed in principle that privately acquired rights were protected by the courts, even against the government. The only exception was made for affairs of state (*Polizei* in the etymological sense of the Greek word for politics), for if judges had been able to decide on them, they and not the prince, from whom they

---

[22] J. Regge, *Kabinettsjustiz in Brandenburg-Preussen. Eine Studie zur Geschichte des landesherrlichen Bestätigungsrechts in der Strafrechtspflege des 17. und 18. Jahrhunderts* (Berlin, 1977); D. Merten, *Der Katte-Prozess* (Berlin, 1980); M. Diesselhorst, *Die Prozesse des Müllers Arnold und das Eingreifen Friedrichs des Grossen* (Göttingen, 1984).

[23] D. Merten, 'Friedrich der Grosse und Montesquieu. Zu den Anfängen des Rechtsstaats im 18. Jahrhundert' in *Verwaltung im Rechtsstaat. Festschrift für Carl Hermann Ule* (Berlin, 1987), 187–208.

held their jurisdiction, would have been sovereign. The principle that every act of administration is subject to judicial review still belonged to the future, but the citizens were not entirely defenceless in the face of arbitrary government, as legal doctrine maintained that if the monarch violated private interests involving his *dominium eminens*, he had to show *idoneae rationes* ('sufficient reasons') when challenged in the courts of the empire.

Another aspect of Frederick's enlightenment was his vision of royalty as being in the service of the state. He abandoned the old patrimonial attitude and believed that the state ought not to serve the dynasty but the other way round. Consequently the crown revenue consisted only of 'certain incomes and uses', the old crown lands having become state property. Moreover, waste on Versailles-type luxury being condemned, these revenues had to be used sparingly and efficiently. As Frederick put it in his aforementioned *Essai*: 'The citizens have accorded precedence to one of their equals only with an eye to the services they expect from him . . . Princes, sovereigns and kings have not been invested with the highest authority in order to wallow unpunished in debauchery and luxury'.

However modern, the Prussian regime still conserved certain ties with the past. Thus the nobles, although submissive to the crown, went on ruling over their serfs on their large estates in medieval fashion. Prussia remained an unashamedly class society and the powerless bourgeoisie carried no weight in the councils of state, whereas the famous Junkers were the powerful lords of manors and large estates, especially east of the Oder. In the nineteenth century the modernization of the state, desired by the monarchy and the civil service, was sabotaged by the aristocracy, but the alliance between crown and Prussian nobility was of such military importance that the government often had to kowtow to the wishes and interests of the Junkers.

The other German dynasty which became a major power and strove for hegemony was the House of Habsburg. The Danube monarchy ruled over a conglomerate that was even more heterogeneous than the Prussian, as it contained Austria, Bohemia, Hungary (which itself had an important Slav minority, the Slovaks), northern Italy and the southern Netherlands. What held this political multinational together was loyalty to the ruling family and, to a large extent, Roman Catholicism, as the Habsburgs loved seeing themselves as the defenders of the true faith against Turks and Protestants. Here also the Enlightenment led absolutism onto new paths. It began under the empress Maria Theresa (1740–80), and her enlightened civil servants, like Wenzel Anton von Kaunitz (*d.* 1794), and led, *inter alia*, to a reduction in the use of torture, the drafting of modern codes and the rationalization and some measure of homogenization of the administration in various parts of the empress's large domains. The full impact of the new ideas on public law was felt under Joseph II who reigned as emperor from 1780 to 1790 but had ruled with his mother, Maria Theresa, as associate emperor from 1765 onwards. The rule of this revolutionary emperor – or shall we call him an imperial revolutionary – bears the stamp of his unflinching sense of purpose. His aim was to break with the dark past and its unsystematic growth, and to introduce new structures according to a rational plan and for the greater happiness of the people. He was the Gorbachev of his time. His new structures were the fruits of his rational mind and disregarded archaic notions and attitudes, feelings of local patriotism, useless traditions and the vested rights of the notables, whose feelings and interests he hurt. His reign, as impetuous as it was enlightened, led to the following developments.

The links with the Catholic Church were loosened, and the religious sphere surrounding the monarchy was replaced by a more secular approach. Joseph II, who omitted the traditional ceremony of the coronation in his Hungarian and Bohemian kingdoms, behaved more like a calculating businessman than the miracle-working anointed of the Lord. He was far from anti-religious and deemed religion useful for the people, if only it was freed from superstition, useful and embedded in the life of the nation: hence the abolition of contemplative orders. Already during his mother's life he had founded state schools to replace the colleges of the Jesuit order, abolished by the pope in 1773, and the *Allgemeine Schulordnung* of 1774 introduced compulsory schooling for the six- to twelve-year-olds – a measure with far reaching consequences, even though its practical implementation was less than perfect. Around that time also the universities lost their medieval status of free corporations and became state institutions. The government also, in 1783, took upon itself the supervision of the training of the clergy, which henceforth was to take place along modern lines, on a high intellectual level and in state seminaries: an enlightened state needed an enlightened clergy. The Patent of Toleration of 1781 was a measure in favour of denominations other than the Catholic Church and was based on the idea of the

*Schädlichkeit allen Gewissenszwanges* ('the obnoxiousness of all constraint on conscience'). In the same line measures were taken to abolish ecclesiastical monopoly in matters of marriage: civil marriage and divorce were introduced and population registers were to be kept by parish priests, who were treated in this respect as civil servants.

The desire to break with the past and its organic growth and bewildering diversity led to a new administrative division of the realm according to a uniform and rational scheme, conceived and carried out from the centre. The state was divided into thirteen uniform and nameless districts, subdivided into circles (*Kreise*) placed under the command of captains; all this was done with disregard for ancient regional feelings. Urban autonomy, or what was left of it, was abolished and the municipal authorities appointed by the government. Whereas his mother had assembled the estates with the traditional ceremonial display and obtained what she wanted, Joseph II found them a waste of time and left them at home. Worse was to come, as the central government, in order to strengthen the one and indivisible Habsburg empire, deplored the linguistic diversity and saw it as an obstacle on the road to centralization and efficiency: German was to become the universal language of government. This excited the ire of the Hungarians, who revolted, in spite of the fact that in 1687 they had abandoned their feudal *ius resistendi*, and they forced the emperor to retract his measures. Joseph II reminds one of the Stuarts, who accompanied their new policy in England with programmatic declarations, whereas their predecessors had – like Maria Theresa in Austria – preserved a semblance of continuity and conservation.

The emperor was interested in the law and the courts. Here, as in so many fields, the existing situation was the muddled result of centuries of haphazard development, and the citizens were caught in a maze of courts, secular and ecclesiastical, public and private, allodial and feudal, manorial and urban, or belonging to corporations such as the universities. Jurisdiction was often an appendage of landed property and not exercised or appreciated for its own sake but because it provided social prestige. For a long time the notables in town and countryside had enjoyed being the local bosses, unhindered by the 'big boss' in far away Vienna, but this was to change. For here also the emperor wanted to introduce unity, clarity and planning. His judicial initiatives in the Austrian Netherlands are a famous example of this policy and its consequences, for they provoked a revolt, led by the notables, and known as the Brabantine Revolution (1789–90). His reorganization entailed the replacement of the maze of existing tribunals by a uniform system of sixty-three courts of first instance, two courts of appeal – in Brussels and Luxembourg – and a sovereign council of justice in Brussels. The administration was expected to operate within the law, so that here also an early form of the *Rechtsstaat* may be discerned, even though here as in Prussia state business (*Polizeisachen*) was still to a large extent exempt from the normal impact of the law and the courts.[24]

The Enlightenment, with its belief in equality and humane values, inspired such measures as the abolition of torture, of serfdom and of the *Religionskommission*, which used to prosecute heretics. It is not surprising that the radical reformer and idealist Joseph II showered his subjects with new laws and ordinances: during the ten years of his reign he issued some 6,000 of them.

The practical implementation of imperial policy was in the hands of university-trained top civil servants, mainly lawyers, who owed their positions only to the confidence of the monarch and not to some popular mandate. The role of these learned officials was, of course, much older and had begun with the medieval legists, but the civil servants of the *Aufklärung* differed from their predecessors by their enlightened convictions and their preference for natural law, as against the *Corpus Iuris* and its medieval doctors. We are here confronted with the continental bureaucratic model, which contrasted sharply with the situation on the other side of the Channel. In Britain civil servants with university degrees and state salaries were very few, as innumerable administrative and judicial functions were carried out by unpaid gentlemen, who seldom had university degrees (and had certainly never studied 'cameralism'),[25] but were destined to play a role in public affairs because of their birth and landed wealth. Their most typical representatives were the justices of the peace, judicial officers as well as local administrators, who ruled the countryside for

---

[24] K. Kroeschell, 'Justizsachen und Polizeisachen' in K. Kroeschell (ed.), *Gerichtslauben-Vorträge. Freiburger Festkolloquium zum fünfundsiebzigsten Geburtstag von Hans Thieme* (Sigmaringen, 1983), 57–72.

[25] *Kameralismus* was, particularly in German universities in the eighteenth and nineteenth centuries, a popular course in administration taken by future civil servants. It concerned economic statistics and the mercantilist philosophy, but also natural law and the *Aufklärung* in general. Frederick William I introduced it in 1727 as a recognized discipline in the Prussian universities of Halle and Frankfurt a.d. Oder. It may be considered the social and economic as well as administrative theory of enlightened absolutism, with Joseph von Sonnenfels (*d.* 1817) as its most famous representative. See A. Tautscher, *Staatswirtschaftslehre des Kameralismus* (Berne, 1947).

many centuries. The civil servants of Joseph II and Frederick II were appointed for life, on the basis of merit, neither having purchased their offices (as in France), or received them through political protection (the British 'patronage' system). In the eighteenth century the enlightened monarchs also began to use officials of their own for the direct collection of taxes, instead of farming it out to private financiers or being dependent on local authorities.[26]

## Final considerations

It is not easy to assess the significance of enlightened absolutism. To begin with, it seems wise to make a distinction between its impact in the short and in the long run. Joseph II's reforms were so radical and attempted to reverse age-old ideas and Constitutions in so short a time and hurt so many vested interests that violent reactions could be expected. In Hungary and the Austrian Netherlands, geographically and psychologically more remote from Vienna than Austria, there were full-blooded revolts, and Joseph II had to give in. Shortly afterwards the gale of the French Revolution blew over Europe and – except for Russia – left no throne unaffected: old-fashioned absolutism had had its day. This did not mean, however, that republicanism was victorious. On the contrary, everywhere the monarchy was restored, even in France, and in the Netherlands it replaced the old Republic of the United Provinces under the sceptre of King William I.

This new-style monarchy was not as modern as in Britain (with ministerial accountability to Parliament), but it was not absolute any more, without Constitution or parliament. In most of the new monarchies the spirit of enlightened absolutism was still strong – the kingdom of the Netherlands under William I being a good illustration. It may be said that in Prussia, even after the shocks of 1848, and later in the German empire of the Bismarck era many ideas, institutions and measures were influenced by the enlightened absolutism of the previous century. We mention, to illustrate our point, the extensive powers of the emperor and the chancellor, who was accountable to him. We also believe that Bismarck's paternalistic social security

---

[26] R. Schnur (ed.), *Die Rolle der Juristen bei der Entstehung des modernen Staates* (Berlin, 1986). See also the important survey of Constitution, society and intellectual currents in eighteenth- and nineteenth-century Germany in R. Vierhaus, *Deutschland im 18. Jahrhundert* (Göttingen, 1987). See also the interesting collection of studies in K. O. von Aretin (ed.), *Der Aufgeklärte Absolutismus* (Cologne, 1974).

policy went back to the Prussian tradition of the 'caring state'. It is possible to go even further and find in the socialist one-party states of the recent past a fundamental idea from the age of Enlightenment, favouring a strong state which is supposed to educate the population willy-nilly to a higher material and intellectual level.

A few remarks as to the Prussian–German relationship may be appropriate here. Even after the loss *de jure* of the Republic of the United Netherlands and the Swiss Confederation at the Treaties of Westphalia, and after the French conquest of several territories and cities in the west of the old Reich, Germany was still a very large and potentially mighty land, which had merely turned into a playground for its warring neighbours because of its own division and consequent weakness. If ever a unification of all German lands came about, there was bound to arise a giant which would change the European situation fundamentally. The old Reich was not capable of bringing about this unification, which in the light of European history could be considered normal: it was not even a state any more and so was incapable of building up a centralized unitary form of government. Instead of a unification around the ancient imperial core of the Reich, two mighty territorial states arose which could have united the German lands (and even some outside Germany's historic frontiers). Both became empires, Austria in 1804, while the Prussian monarchy reached imperial rank in 1871 (no Prussian, but a German empire). In spite of some exalted hopes, a Great-German unification, i.e of all Hohenzollern and Habsburg lands, did not come about, *inter alia*, because of the numerous non-German nationalities under the Austrian crown; so the German empire proclaimed at Versailles in January 1871 realized only a Little-German unification. Not until Adolf Hitler was a Great-German unification – briefly – carried through. His Reich collapsed in 1945. Austria still exists as a small, independent republic, but Prussia was abolished as a political formation by law no. 46 issued by the Allied Commission of Control on 27 February 1947.

## THE REPUBLIC OF THE UNITED NETHERLANDS

The Constitution of the Dutch Republic, a Great Power which lasted from the late sixteenth till the late eighteenth century, deserves our special attention, for it belongs to the most interesting legal experiments of the Old European era and through its influence on the Constitution of the United States of America played a significant role in world history.

The republic never knew a written Constitution as the term is understood today, but some of its basic principles can be found in the famous Treaty of the Union of Utrecht of 1579, a defensive alliance concluded between several provinces and towns in the northern and southern Netherlands against the armies of King Philip II of Spain. They included the sovereignty of each of the provinces (a principle that was never abandoned), the freedom of conscience, to which William the Silent personally attached great importance and which made the republic a more tolerant land than many in Europe even though the reformed religion occupied a privileged position, and respect of the medieval charters of liberties and privileges of regions, towns and corporations. The absence of a modern Constitution, with a description of the organs of the state and their competence, was partly responsible for the somewhat confused character of the public law of the republic. The republican form of government is a first indication of a certain lack of clarity, for whereas the Seven Provinces clearly constituted a republic and no monarchy, the House of Orange, the descendants of William the Silent, played a quasi-monarchical role, as it was from their ranks that the stadholders were normally (in a later phase exclusively) recruited. The role of the hereditary stadholderate again indicates that all was not clear-cut in the workings of the United Provinces for, whereas the stadholders during certain phases looked like a *de facto* monarchy, in other times, the so-called stadholderless periods (1650–72, 1702–47), there were no stadholders at all. Initially the stadholder was a provincial lieutenant of the Burgundian and Habsburg princes, who usually lived abroad; William the Silent, for example, was stadholder of Holland and Zealand. In the republic the stadholder became, after sovereignty had passed from Philip II to the provinces, a functionary in the latter's service. Strictly speaking each of the Seven Provinces – Holland, Zealand, Utrecht, Gelderland, Overijssel, Friesland and City and Province of Groningen – could have its own stadholder and there was no obligation to take him from the House of Orange, but finally, in 1747, the point was reached where there was one stadholder for the whole republic and the office (together with those of captain-general and admiral-general of the Union) belonged hereditarily to the House of Orange.[27]

Another obscure point concerns the very nature of the republic:

[27] H. H. Rowen, *The princes of Orange. The stadholders in the Dutch Republic* (Cambridge, 1988).

was it a federal state or a confederation of states? Many scholars believe the latter to be the case, because the Treaty of Utrecht was a defensive league between sovereign allied states against an alien foe. As against this point of view, it must be said that this so-called federation of sovereign states disposed of a number of central, common institutions with such an important impact on internal and external affairs that the impression of a federal state is very strong. Whatever the merits of this discussion, the main political organs of the republic can be described as follows.

The States General, also called the Generality, were an assembly of deputies of the provincial states, which themselves were the representative bodies of the social components of each of the Seven Provinces. The number of the members of the States General was undetermined, but each of the Seven Provinces disposed of one vote. Whereas the Union of Utrecht had prescribed unanimity only for questions of war and peace and for the introduction of new taxes, in practice by the eighteenth century unanimity was required for all decisions of some importance. In contrast with the British Parliament, the members of the Generality were spokesmen of their respective provinces, bound by instructions from home and compelled to communicate with their mandate givers. The States General were constantly in session, year in year out, and were generally responsible for the politics of the republic, including defence. They were the permanent principal organ and represented the Union vis-à-vis foreign countries. They were, however, only competent for common – say federal – affairs (including the administration of the Generality Lands)[28] and were not supposed to meddle in the internal business of the provinces.

The Council of State was conceived as an executive organ for home affairs. It was also composed of regional representatives and only had delegated powers, which could always be withdrawn by the States General. The Council of State operated in the shadow of the States General and, mainly for that reason, never achieved the political standing for which it seemed to be destined. Thus it initially

[28] This is the name given to a complex set of eccentric territories and towns in the south and east of the republic which did not initially belong to it but were reconquered from the Spaniards in the early decades of the seventeenth century. They belonged mainly to the duchy of Brabant and the county of Flanders and constituted a glacis, keeping the enemy away from the great river line of Rhine and Maas, the main defence of the Dutch. The Generality Lands stood under the direct authority of the States General and lacked the autonomy guaranteed to the other provinces by the Union of Utrecht. Their requests to be admitted to the Union as the eighth province with full membership were repeatedly rejected, *inter alia*, out of fear that their Catholic population would affect the Protestant orientation of the republic.

developed a legislative activity, issuing ordinances for the Generality Lands, but this led to a collision with the States General, to whom legislation was in the end abandoned (not that it ever amounted to very much). The Council had a secretary and used the services of the treasurer-general of the Union as financial expert and adviser. Some high ranking government officials, namely the grand pensionary of Holland, the registrar of the States General, the secretary of the Council of State and the treasurer-general, bore the title of minister. In contrast to the quick turnover of the deputies, these officials formed a stable and lasting element in the life of the republic and were less tied to local interests. The republic never had many civil servants, but their role was all the more important.

The General Chamber of Accounts and the Monetary Chamber of the Generality exercised central control over the finances of the republic and over the coinage. The latter was, however, not unitary, as the Generality ran no mint of its own and left coinage to the provinces, as an expression of their sovereignty. The financial resources of the republic consisted mainly of the yearly aids requested by the States General and granted by the provinces in proportion to their very different wealth, Holland alone contributing more than the six other provinces together. The yearly budget, produced by the Council of State, was called the General Petition and was accompanied by an exposé of the state of the Union.

The five Admiralties dealt with the navy, most important both for the security of maritime trade and for colonial expansion, the twin pillars of Dutch prosperity. The grand pensionary was the president of the states of Holland and permanently attached to the States General. Although he was, according to present-day parlance, a paid civil servant and not an elected politician, the grand pensionary was the cardinal figure in the politics of the republic, even in international affairs. The reasons are to be found in the permanent character of his office (attached to the main central body of the republic), in the fact that he was the voice of Holland, by far the most important province, and in the exceptional personal qualities of several bearers of the office. We mention the 'land's advocate' John van Oldenbarnevelt (*d.* 1619), a jurist and humanist and the main architect of the young state,[29] John de Witt (*d.* 1672), who was the undisputed leader of the republic during the first stadholderless era,[30] and Anthonie Heinsius

[29] J. den Tex, *Oldenbarnevelt*, transl. by R. B. Powell (2 vols., Cambridge, 1973).
[30] H. H. Rowen, *John de Witt, grand pensionary of Holland, 1625–1672* (Princeton, 1978).

(*d.* 1720), William III's collaborator who played a great role in European politics.

There was no supreme court for the whole republic, although there was a court of appeal for Holland and Zealand, called the High Council of Holland and Zealand. The void caused by the disappearance of the Great Council of Mechelen, which sat in the southern, reconquered Netherlands, was not filled. It would have been logical to create a replacement in the republic for appeals from the northern Netherlands which used to be lodged at Mechelen, but this did not happen: another sign of the weakness of the central, federal element and the strength of provincial feeling. There was no national university, the institutions of higher education being regional or local.

Constitutions fix the framework and the rule for the political power game, and normally reflect the dominant forces in a given society. The Seven Provinces were no exception, as their institutions mirror their bourgeois, oligarchic and mercantile character. The republic was dominated by Holland, and the states of Holland were dominated by the towns: in Holland, as in Zealand, only one member of the nobility sat in the provincial states, all the others being urban representatives. The towns themselves were dominated by the 'regents', a merchant aristocracy, reminiscent of the oligarchy at the helm of the Venetian republic, which replenished itself through co-optation and formed the backbone of public life. It assumed the role played elsewhere in Europe by the nobility and the civil servants of the monarchy. Outside Holland and Zealand the states were not so markedly urban, and in some rural areas the nobility was still prominent; there was, in any case, no question of democracy, direct or indirect. The one popular, plebeian element in the republic's political life was paradoxically provided by the role and prestige of the stadholders of the House of Orange, who, as we said before, formed a quasi-monarchic focus which alone could possibly check the grip of the notables. For that reason, the stadholders often stirred the enthusiasm of the little man, who was unorganized and kept under the tutelage of the 'regents': *Oranje boven* ('up with Orange') was his anti-oligarchic war-cry.

To the legal historian the public law of the republic appears as a strange mixture of old and new, of medieval and modern elements; contemporary observers also viewed its institutions as a mixture, but they thought in terms of the well-known triad of monarchy (the stadholders), the oligarchy (the nobles in the states) and democracy (the burghers). The survivals from the Middle Ages were conspicuous: the provincial and general states were of medieval origin, and so were the provincialism, the ingrained respect for acquired rights and for the privileges of social groups, towns and corporations, the grants system, the role of the urban oligarchy, the anti-authoritarian cockiness of Amsterdam (rather like medieval Ghent in the county of Flanders) and the legal parochialism. On the other hand there were elements of striking modernity: the abolition of monarchy, the considerable degree of religious tolerance, the disappearance of the clergy as a privileged estate and the federal form of government.

It is those modern elements that assure the constitutional experiment of the republic a special place. Its rise and development went completely against the grain of the time. While the European trend was towards unitary states and strong and even absolutist monarchies, where the bourgeoisie enjoyed little social prestige and the nobility all the more, there rose in the northern Netherlands a state that was federal, republican and unashamedly bourgeois. Its chances of survival were initially deemed slim, as the whole adventure looked rather absurd and far-fetched. Queen Elizabeth I expressed the general feeling when she declared that ordinary people were not fit to rule, and in seventeenth-century Leiden professors taught that monarchy was the form of government par excellence. In spite of these forebodings the republic became a great success, and it was made manifest that people who were neither of royal nor of aristocratic blood were quite capable of running the state, and that a non-unitary, non-centralized republic could become rich and powerful and win the loyalty of its people. Clearly, a small nation – the republic counted a mere 1.5 million inhabitants – was able to free itself from an oppressive and unjust regime, send the old monarchy packing and go its own way. The lesson was not lost on the Americans, and influenced their Constitution. The federal organization of the Dutch republic was its model, but also a warning, for in the balancing of federal and state competence America, learning from the Dutch experience, made the central, federal government stronger than it had been in the Netherlands. This is obvious from such American decisions as the creation of a Supreme Court for all the states, the preference for one federal currency and the establishment of a House of Representatives that was elected by the American people instead of consisting of deputies of provincial parliaments.

The starting-point of the republican Constitution was not to be found in some doctrinal preference, but in the political circumstances of the last quarter of the sixteenth century. The revolt of the Netherlands against Philip II's absolutism and intolerance created discord among the population, as some – particularly in the agrarian areas – feared the big towns and their Calvinists even more than King Philip, and sought a *rapprochement* with the crown. After the failure of the Pacification of Ghent of 1576, caused largely by Calvinist intransigence in that city, two alliances arose in the Netherlands. The Union of Arras of 6 January 1579 grouped a number of French-speaking provinces and towns that were loyal to the Spanish crown (Artois, Hainaut, Douai) and were reconciled with King Philip, whereas the Union of Utrecht of 23 January 1579 brought together various provinces and towns which were determined to continue the resistance to Spain (Holland, Zealand, the province of Groningen, Utrecht, Zutphen and Gelderland, gradually joined by Overijssel, Friesland, Drenthe, Ghent, Ypres, Antwerp, Bruges, Lier, Breda, Venlo and Mechelen). The Habsburg general Farnese reconquered the two most powerful southern provinces, the county of Flanders and the duchy of Brabant, but the north – the Seven Provinces – escaped and remained free. In 1581 they declared that Philip II, who was still recognized as monarch in 1579, had forfeited the throne, because he had broken his contract with the people and behaved like a tyrant. Forsaking Philip did not mean forsaking the monarchy as such, which was hardly conceivable at the time. On the contrary, the Act of Abjuration of 1581[31] made it clear that Philip was to be replaced by another prince, and the rebellious provinces went searching for a suitable candidate. In fact the search had already started before 1581, as negotiations had been under way since 1576 for a transfer of the sovereignty over Holland and Zealand to the duke of Anjou (*d.* 1584), and afterwards people toyed with the idea of proclaiming William the Silent count of Holland and Zealand. After he was murdered, in 1584, the idea was mooted of offering sovereignty to Queen Elizabeth of England, who in 1585 sent Robert Dudley, earl of Leicester (*d.* 1588) as governor-general of the Netherlands, and it was only after all these attempts failed that the States General in 1587 decided to give up the search, go ahead without a monarch and accept the republican form of government. One is reminded of what happened in France after the fall of the Second Empire in 1870, when there was a majority

---

[31]  This is the traditional rendering in English of *Akte van Verlatinge*, which literally means Act of Abandonment or Forsaking Act.

for the restoration of the monarchy, but the endless quarrelling between the two pretenders led the country, in 1875, to adopt a republican Constitution. The eminent jurist Hugo Grotius gave legitimacy to the momentous decision of 1587 in his *De antiquitate reipublicae batavicae* of 1610, where the thesis was defended that the Dutch republic was the continuation of the primeval traditions of the free Batavians, Franks, Frisians and Saxons, who had been temporarily suppressed by tyrannical usurpers – an interpretation comparable to the Norman Yoke Theory in seventeenth-century England. Grotius, who was a humanist and knew his Roman history, also referred to examples from Antiquity in order to extol the republican form of government. There were, of course, famous precursors nearer home, the Calvinist Republic of Ghent (1578–84), for example, which had itself consciously imitated the Swiss model.

Whereas the immediate starting points of the Seven Provinces were the Union of Utrecht and the Act of Abjuration, other roots went back to the medieval Netherlands. The opposition between the urban, bourgeois forces and the world of the nobility and the monarchy was older than the sixteenth century, and the separation of the Low Countries meant that the former element was victorious in the north, and the latter in the south – until they were combined again in the nineteenth century, when the north reintroduced the monarchy and the south adopted the bourgeois Constitution of 1831.

The fall of the Dutch Republic, like its rise, was the result of external political events. Admittedly the eighteenth century witnessed the growth of an internal democratic opposition, which demanded a 'popular government by representation', but the fall of the republic was not its doing. It was the French revolutionaries who fatally wounded the existing regime when they overran the country in 1795 and, with the help of French-oriented progressive activists, founded the Batavian Republic, a French vassal state. This ephemeral construction gave way to the satellite kingdom of the Netherlands under one of Napoleon's brothers, King Louis, which soon disappeared in its turn, when the kingdom was annexed by the French empire.

It is amazing that the Republic of the United Provinces not only managed for two centuries to lead an independent life, but even to become one of the Great Powers and, under William III, the pivot of European resistance to the ambitions of Louis XIV, all this in spite of a manifest inequality between its human and material resources and those of England, France and Germany. That the republic had no chance against a resolute invader overland was demonstrated in 1672 when France easily overran it and in 1787, when Prussia did the same. And that the Union could not stand up to Britain on the high seas became abundantly clear at the debacle of the Fourth English War of 1780–4. That, in spite of some brief interludes, the republic managed for two centuries to maintain its territory and even to extend it (with the Generality Lands in the south), and on top of that to found a world-wide colonial empire, was due to the dynamism of the people and to their free Constitution, but was also explained by the – at least temporary – weakness of its neighbours. Germany was so divided that it could harm no one and even, in 1648, accepted the sovereignty of the Dutch Republic, which was a historical part of the German empire. The immediate neighbour in the south, the Habsburg Netherlands, was a Spanish or Austrian appendage with no policy of its own and a buffer zone between the republic and France. The latter country suffered for a long time from internal dissension and when, under Louis XIV, it was united and mighty again and launched itself into expansionist adventures, it produced a European reaction that saved Holland. England was happy to see the estuaries of the great rivers, Scheldt, Maas and Rhine, not under the control of a major continental power, but of a small republic, with which her relations were friendly, except when Dutch shipping became too much of a nuisance. Moreover Dutch external policy usually towed the British line and even the national life of the republic underwent a strong British influence. The small scale of the institutions of the republic is attractive to many modern observers, as it enabled direct contact between government and citizens, but it also led to dissension and weakness in the face of external threats. In the age of unbridled national sovereignty not even the successful republic was able to protect its frontiers (nor was the kingdom, as appeared in 1940).

## THE UNITED STATES OF AMERICA

### Introductory remarks

The American Constitution is of exceptional importance, both because of its bold innovations and its universal impact. American constitutional law is the result of the dramatic events known as the American War of Independence or the American Revolution. Both names are correct. The United States were established at the cost of a war of liberation waged by the thirteen British colonies on America's east coast against the mother country, from which they declared their independence in 1776. The name American Revolution is also justified, as the new state not only ended its dependence on the British crown, but at the same time created a political regime which broke with so many traditional principles that it can certainly be called revolutionary. Although this radical change took place in America, it occupies a special place in European legal history, not only because it was brought about by European immigrants or their direct descendants,[32] but also because it took place within a legal system – the English common law – and a philosophical current – the Enlightenment – which were of European origin. Moreover the American development has, from very early on, influenced the public law of the old Continent. In order to realize how revolutionary the American Revolution was one has only to recall the fundamental institutions and ancient pillars of western civilization which were then thrown overboard: the unitary nation state, the nobility, the ties between Church and state, and class society. All this disappeared to give way to a presidential and federal republic and legal equality.

### Historical circumstances

The establishment of this new form of government and social order became possible when the colonial population decided to take its political fate in its own hands and to throw off the tutelage of the British Parliament and government. The main episodes of the crisis were the following. Until shortly after the Seven Years War (1756–63) the inhabitants of the thirteen colonies had accepted their colonial status, because colonies by definition carry out what the mother country decides. London had the last word in all important questions and the colonies were administered by English governors, usually appointed by the crown. The colonials were treated as second-class Englishmen, fit to produce raw materials and buy the finished products from the mother country, without control over their own foreign trade. On top of that the British Parliament, after the Treaty of Paris of 1763 and the transfer of Canada from France to Britain, decided to make the Americans contribute to their own defence costs, and by the Stamp Act of 1765 introduced a stamp tax on newsprint,

---

[32] Around 1800 some 90 per cent of the *c.* 2.5 million inhabitants of the United States were of British (80 per cent of English), and about 6 per cent of German descent.

conveyancing documents, ships' papers, insurance policies and even playing cards. The Americans felt it was an onslaught on their traditional rights. They naturally had paid taxes before, but these were destined to cover their own expenses and were passed by their own colonial representative institutions. In the case of the Stamp Act there was taxation without representation for, as there were no representatives of George III's American subjects in the Parliament at Westminster which imposed the stamp tax (at the time, a current tax in Britain and on the Continent), the principle 'no taxation without representation' was disregarded. American reaction was violent, a trade boycott was organized and vociferous pressure groups, like the Sons of Liberty, sprang up.

A meeting of representatives of nine of the thirteen colonies was called in New York, known as the Stamp Act Congress, and a resolution was passed denying the British Parliament the right to tax the colonies without their consent. Westminster retreated and, in 1766, abolished the Stamp Act, but insisted on a Declaratory Act containing the principle that the colonies were and ought to remain under the ultimate authority of the mother country. New British laws followed which caused tempers to flare and led to a demonstration in Boston which was violently suppressed by soldiers, the 'Boston Massacre' of 1770. In 1773 the Tea Act allowed the East India Company, which was in financial trouble, to dump its enormous tea reserves on the American market, causing great harm to traders there. The reaction was the Boston Tea Party, when this cheap tea was thrown overboard into the sea in the harbour of Boston, always the leader in the anti-British agitation. London was not willing to tolerate this sort of unruliness and sent troops to restore order. The escalation went on and led to the first armed encounter between British troops and American insurgents at Lexington in 1775. In the meantime things had been moving on the political level as well. In 1774 at Philadelphia the First Continental Congress met.[33] The Second, in 1775 in the same town, appointed George Washington as leader of the revolutionary army. In 1776 the Declaration of Independence, drafted by Thomas Jefferson (*d.* 1826), one of the most famous products of modern political thought and written in a most elegant style, was published.

With French help General Washington fought the British right up

[33] J. G. Marston, *King and Congress. The transfer of political legitimacy, 1774–1776* (Princeton, 1987).

to their surrender at Yorktown, in 1781. The political settlement followed at the Treaty of Versailles in 1783, when Great Britain recognized the independence of the thirteen ex-colonies. The Declaration of Independence of 1776 had enumerated, after a fashion familiar in European history, the abuses committed by Britain, and had therefore declared the king forfeit – this also harked back to European precedents, in the Netherlands in 1581 and in England in 1688, for example. A new element was the appeal to the rights of all men, 'created as equals and entitled to inalienable rights, such as life, liberty and happiness'.

The causes of the American success were manifold: the enormous distance from Britain (three months for the return journey), the disappearance of the French threat in Canada, the toughness of the colonial population, hardened by the struggle against nature and the natives, and the belief in the American way of life, rural and unspoiled by the luxury and corruption of Old World entrepreneurs and politicians. It is clear that America was ripe for emancipation from the colonial yoke. This does not mean that no solution other than total independence, or no other way of reconciling conflicting political and commercial interests, was thinkable. An American representation in Westminster, although difficult because of the long distances (according to the Stamp Act Congress even impossible), was conceivable, and was proposed. After all, the English Parliament had welcomed Scottish members after the United Kingdom was created (and a generation after American independence the same happened with the Irish members). Also, before the revolution there were permanent American agents in London who lobbied Parliament and government. At one moment the Americans proposed that, if Great Britain gave up taxation, the colonies would accept British authority over their trade or, if they were given free trade, would contribute to the expenses of the British empire (if the British contributed no less themselves). London rejected the proposal. There were also suggestions that America should become a sort of dominion, and at one point the British Parliament was even prepared to give in on all points, except complete sovereignty: some link with the crown had to subsist (which reminds us of discussions in present-day Australia about the role of the queen). Some recognition of the monarchy would have been acceptable to many Americans (and welcomed by the loyalists) if George III had not had the ambition to play a personal role, adopting an anti-American stance. This was one of the reasons for the success of Thomas Paine's attacks on the king and the monarchy, in his *Common sense*, published in 1776.

## The Constitution

The Constitution of the United States of America is the oldest working written Constitution in the world. The American Constitution consists of two panels. The first, called the Constitution, dates from 1787 and concerns the organization of the state, the second, dating from 1791, concerns the liberties of the citizens and consists of the first ten Amendments, also known as the Bill of Rights. This Constitution is, as we said, still valid and has been little changed in the course of its more than two hundred years of existence. Such changes as were made concerned mainly the franchise, the position of the president and the rights of the citizens; they were introduced in the form of new Amendments.

The main elements of the first panel are the following. The United States is a federal state. Initially the Articles of Confederation of 1776, ratified in all the states by 1781, instituted a loose confederation with a weak central organ, called Congress, resembling a meeting of ambassadors from independent countries. In 1787, however, the idea prevailed that a 'more perfect union' was required, particularly in view of external security; there was no question of a unitary republic, because the states were too different and attached to their own institutions, traditions and interests.

Some federal regimes can be called centripetal, because they create common, federal institutions above previously independent components, others are centrifugal, because they divide previously unitary states, while keeping some common elements; the United States is an example of the former, and the Austro-Hungarian *Ausgleich* ('Compromise') of 1867 and the present federalization of Belgium are examples of the latter variety. Determined to create this 'more perfect union' the Convention of Philadelphia met and in a few months hammered out the American Constitution, in a spacious room which still attracts numerous tourists. Some of the leading figures were George Washington, Benjamin Franklin, Alexander Hamilton and James Madison. The principle of the Constitution was that every state with its own organs – popular representation, government headed by an elected governor, and judiciary – was competent for all aspects of public life (i.e. government, constitutional and ordinary legislation, administration of justice and taxation) except those expressly reserved for the federal authorities. These common, 'federal' matters were foreign affairs, currency, defence, the respect of civil liberties and general welfare, and they belonged to the competence of the federal legislature, executive and judiciary; federal taxes were voted by Congress. Thus every citizen came to live on two levels, that of his own state and that of the Union.

Congress in Washington is the legislative assembly of the United States. It consists of two Houses, which are differently composed because of America's federal structure and in order to avoid less populated states being overpowered by the others. In the House of Representatives the number of members is proportional to the population of the states, but the Senate contains two members per state, independent of size or population. Nowadays both Representatives and Senators are elected by the people, but until the Constitution was changed in 1913 the Senators were elected by the state legislatures.[34]

Whereas Europeans find it normal that initiatives for new legislation are taken by the government (so that the majority of new Acts are introduced by the government and not as private members' bills), this is seldom the case in the United States, governmental initiative being limited on principle to the yearly presidential Address on the State of the Union held in Congress. But it would be wrong to conclude that the separation between the executive and the legislature is almost complete, as the president's signature is needed for federal laws, and in contrast to some other regimes, the president is in no way obliged to follow the lawgivers. On the contrary, a presidential veto is a frequent and very interesting phenomenon, because it leads to a stalemate between two federal powers, both elected by the people and therefore both enjoying a perfect democratic legitimacy. Someone has to give in, and the Constitution ordains that it is the president, whose veto can be overruled by Congress, but only with a two-thirds majority in both Houses.

The president is head of state and head of the government, and is elected by the people in such a way that in every state electors are chosen and these electoral colleges choose the president; since time

[34] The old article spoke of 'two senators from each State, chosen by the Legislature thereof', which the new article changed to 'elected by the people thereof'. We shall see later that in the Third Republic in France the constitutional laws of 1875 also provided for a senate elected by the departmental councils and not by the people.

immemorial this election runs on the two-party system, as does the election of the members of Congress.

Although the president plays the representative role befitting a head of state, he is in no way limited to a symbolic function. On the contrary, he is an active party politician, even the party leader, and the head of the government. He chooses his own ministers, called secretaries, albeit in consultation with the Senate,[35] and they are expected to carry out his policy in their respective departments. This is notably different from the practice in some other countries where, although the Constitution stipulates that the king freely chooses his ministers, in fact this choice is mainly in the hands of party offices. The role of the president can therefore be summarized as follows. He is head of state, leads the government and the federal administration (with *c.* 3 million employees), is the supreme commander of the armed forces (Congress having the right to declare war) and is responsible for foreign affairs.

The federal judiciary consists of a network of federal law courts throughout the country, headed by the illustrious Supreme Court in Washington, the new capital built in the early nineteenth century, which also contains Congress and the president's official residence, the White House. The task of the nine judges of the Supreme Court is threefold, the maintenance of the constitutional order, including conflicts of competence between state and federal bodies, the uniform interpretation of federal laws and the settling of inter-state disputes. One of its most conspicuous tasks is the control over the constitutional character of federal and state legislation. The judges in the Supreme Court are appointed by the president of the United States, in consultation with the Senate – which again shows that the separation of powers is far from absolute. The effectiveness of the Senate's intervention has varied greatly, as periods when its consent was more or less a formality have alternated with others – such as our own day – when the Senate takes its role very seriously, subjects the president's nominees to a detailed scrutiny and not infrequently rejects them. The separation between the executive and the judiciary is, however, complete in a number of states, where the judges are elected by the people for a limited term, with possibility of re-election. The election of judges, known briefly in France at the time of the revolution, is

---

[35] Rejection by the Senate of a nominee of the president is very rare, as only eight cases are recorded in some two hundred years where the Senate refused a president his choice for a Cabinet post.

constantly under debate in America. For roughly the first three-quarters of their existence the United States were mainly in favour of appointed magistrates, which was followed by half a century when the tide went the other way and election was on the increase, but this in its turn led to a reaction in favour of appointment: at present nine states, among them Texas, have elected judges. Both the advantages and disadvantages of an elected Bench are obvious. Election by the people is by definition democratic, as it makes the judges accountable to their fellow citizens, especially when they seek re-election. It also avoids the danger of a judicial caste, alienated from public opinion, a not imaginary peril with appointment and even more with co-optation. Election also fits in with American democracy as described by Alexis de Tocqueville in his *De la démocratie en Amérique* (1835–40). The negative aspect relates to the link with the political parties whose support the candidate has to seek and the high cost of the election campaign. This may well amount to a million dollars and may be funded by large companies that might later appear in court before their own candidates. There is also the consideration that a judge without tenure is more likely to be exposed to various forms of pressure.[36]

American democratic and anti-aristocratic attitudes go back a long way. The immigrants in the thirteen colonies came mostly from social strata which had fled the rule of the landowners and the friends of the official Church, in order to find more freedom and equality in a new land. Such aristocracy as there was in America consisted mainly of Englishmen who had been appointed through court intrigue and, like Roman proconsuls in Antiquity, returned home after they had enriched themselves. Also most of the loyalists, opponents of the revolution, had belonged to the better classes, another cause for popular mistrust. The Constitution consequently abolished the nobility, which automatically put an end to the Ancient-Regime privileges it had enjoyed.

The American Revolution was directed against the tyranny of the colonizing mother country and against the king who had betrayed his

---

[36] As in Texas there are no limits on campaign gifts by companies to would-be judges, the appearance can be created that justice might be for sale, so it is not surprising that in 1988 there was talk of a drive to abolish the elective process in that state. See M. L. Volcansek and J. L. Lafon, *Judicial selection. The cross-evolution of French and American practices* (New York, 1988); P. A. Freund, 'Appointment of justices: some historical perspectives', *Harvard Law Review* 101 (1988), 1146–84 (concerns the Supreme Court, from the early nineteenth century to the present).

role of 'father' and cheated his 'loyal children'. The rule of the tyrannical, unfaithful father was to be replaced by that of reliable and uncapricious law, put in writing and binding for everyone, above all for those in authority. This is the basic idea of the rule of law and it was essential to the fathers of the American Constitution, among whom lawyers were conspicuous. Although the drafting of the Constitution was a collective effort, one writer stood out among his peers, the 'Father of the Constitution', James Madison (*d.* 1836). He later became the fourth president of the United States, from 1809 to 1817.[37] Two institutions deserve our special attention here, judicial review of the constitutionality of federal and state legislation, and impeachment.

Judicial review[38] can theoretically be exercised by every court, but in fact belongs to the Supreme Court. It is an undisputed element of American constitutional practice, although it is not expressly mentioned in the Constitution. It was widely advocated in the early years of the republic and some people thought it was implicit in the Constitution, as flowing from the separation of powers. The basic idea is the belief that the lawgiver must also respect the norms of the Constitution – what is otherwise the meaning of a fundamental, overriding text? – and that judges and not legislators are best qualified to decide what is constitutional and what not, since this is, after all, a legal problem. Judicial review entered American legal history in 1803, with the judgment given by the Supreme Court in *Marbury* v. *Madison*. This precedent was created under the impulse of John Marshall (*d.* 1835). It was he who wrote that 'certainly all those who have framed written constitutions contemplate them as forming the fundamental and paramount law of the nation and consequently the theory of every such government must be that an act of the legislature repugnant to the constitution is void'. Article VI(2) of the Constitution of 1787 had laid down: 'This Constitution . . . shall be the supreme Law of the Land; and the judges in every state shall be bound thereby', and Marshall thought that this stipulation justified his

---

[37] Madison was in favour of a strong federal power and played an important role in the drafting of the Bill of Rights of 1791. See R. J. Morgan, *James Madison on the Constitution and the Bill of Rights* (Westport, Conn., 1988).

[38] 'Judicial review' *lato sensu* is every control, check or revision by judges of another judgment or legislative or administrative act. In English law the term is currently used for judicial review of acts of administration (what in some continental countries is the task of the *conseil d'état*). Elsewhere it is mostly used for judicial control of the constitutional character of legislation, and we shall use the term here in that sense.

approach.[39] Although criticized, this case law was definitely confirmed by the *Dred Scott case* of 1857 and has remained till this day a fixed element in the American legal landscape.[40] The American example has, especially after the Second World War, been imitated in Europe, *inter alia*, through the creation of constitutional courts.[41] But the American innovation has had no success in Britain, where the sovereignty of Parliament is a sacred dogma and the judiciary expressly declared itself incompetent to examine the compatibility of Acts of Parliament with the Constitution or the fundamental principles of the common law.[42] Ironically England had in earlier times defended the thesis that laws had to be in agreement with the principles of the common law and that it was the task of the judges to decide whether this was the case. The theory was enunciated and embedded in a judgment by the most learned jurist of the time, the

[39] *Marbury* v. *Madison* was the first decision in which the Supreme Court declared void an Act of Congress on the ground that it was contrary to the Constitution. The case was complex and concerned William Marbury, plaintiff, who had been appointed justice of the peace but been refused his commission by James Madison, then Secretary of State. Judgment was given in favour of the plaintiff, and a relevant section of the Judiciary Act of 1789 declared unconstitutional. In the political background lurked the fear of the radical democracy of an elected assembly. See especially the profound analysis in G. L. Haskins and H. A. Johnson, *Foundations of power: John Marshall 1801–15* (New York, 1981), 182–204, and the source material in C. F. Hobson et al. (eds.), *The papers of John Marshall*, vi: *Correspondence, papers and selected judicial opinions, November 1800–March 1807* (Chapel Hill, N.C., 1990). See also G. E. White (with G. Gunther), *The Marshall Court and cultural change, 1815–35* (New York, 1988), the older work by R. K.Carr, *The Supreme Court and judicial review* (New York, 1942) and J. H. Choper, *Judicial review and the national political process. A functional reconsideration of the role of the Supreme Court* (Chicago, 1980); D. P. Currie, 'The Constitution in the Supreme Court: the New Deal 1931–1940', *University of Chicago Law Review* 54 (1987), 504–55; W. Brugger, *Grundrechte und Verfassungsgerichtsbarkeit in den Vereinigten Staaten von Amrika* (Tübingen, 1987); C. Egerer, 'Verfassungsrechtsprechung des Supreme Court der USA. Die Wurzeln des Prinzips des "judicial review" in Marbury v. Madison', *Zeitschrift für vergleichende Rechtswissenschaft* 88 (1989), 416–32. For a stimulating comparison between America and Europe, see K. Lenaerts, *Le juge et la constitution aux Etats-Unis d'Amérique et dans l'ordre juridique européen* (Brussels, 1989).
[40] C. M. Wilson, *The Dred Scott Decision* (Philadelphia, 1973); D. E. Fehrenbacher, *The Dred Scott Case. Its significance in American law and politics* (New York, 1978); W. Ehrlich, *They have no rights: Dred Scott's struggle for freedom* (Westport, Conn., 1979).
[41] Professor Cappelletti has been a pioneer in the comparative-historical study of judicial review. See, among his numerous publications on the subject: M. Cappelletti, *El control judicial de la constitucionalidad de las leyes en el derecho comparado* (Mexico, 1966); M.Cappelletti, *Judicial review in the contemporary world* (Indianapolis, 1971); M. Cappelletti, 'Repudiating Montesquieu? The expansion and legitimacy of constitutional justice', *Catholic University Law Review* 35 (1985), 1–32; M. Cappelletti, *The judicial process in comparative perspective* (Oxford, 1989). See also K. C. Wheare, *Modern constitutions* (2nd edn, Oxford, 1966), 100–20.
[42] H. W. R. Wade, 'The basis of legal sovereignty', *Cambridge Law Journal* 14(1955), 172–96; T. R. S. Allan, 'Legislative supremacy and the rule of law: democracy and constitutionalism', *Cambridge Law Journal* 44 (1985), 111–43; A. W. Bradley, 'The sovereignty of parliament – in perpetuity?' in J. Jowell and D. Oliver (eds.), *The changing constitution* (Oxford, 1985), 23–47.

Chief Justice of the Common Pleas, Sir Edward Coke, in *Bonham's case* of 1610, and for nearly a century afterwards the idea seemed attractive.[43]

In the eighteenth century doctrine changed and the leading jurist of the age, Sir William Blackstone (*d.* 1780), maintained that Parliament was sovereign and no judge could declare an Act of Parliament void, because he would be usurping the legislative function. The Americans, however, who distrusted the Parliament at Westminster (where Blackstone sat), found Coke's approach attractive, because it constituted a barrier against new laws passed by capricious parliamentary majorities, manoeuvred by pressure groups and party deals.

It is noteworthy how different the American and Belgian developments have been in the nineteenth century, against a background of similar fundamental data; neither Constitution, the American of 1787 or the Belgian of 1831, mentions judicial review, and both were based on the separation of powers. In both countries it was left to the highest court of law to decide what to do about possibly unconstitutional laws. We have already seen what happened in 1803 in America. In Belgium in 1849 the Court of Cassation chose exactly the opposite way, rejecting judicial review and leaving to parliament responsibility for the constitutionality of the laws. It was hoped that a parliament that flouted the fundamental covenant of the nation would not be re-elected. Neither in America nor in Belgium could purely legal arguments be found that were decisive, because of the silence of the constitutional texts, hence the possibility of two opposed solutions in the Supreme Court and the Court of Cassation. In the last analysis the decision was political, as it concerned the question as to who ought to have the last word, the elected parliament or the professional judges. If it was the latter, power might pass into the hands of the judicature and a *gouvernement des juges*, to quote the title of a famous book,[44] could be the result.[45]

It is undeniable that the American Supreme Court has been called

---

[43] T. F. T. Plucknett, 'Bonham's case and judicial review', *Harvard Law Review* 40 (1926), 35–45; S. E. Thorne, 'Dr Bonham's case: statutory construction for constitutional theory', *University of Pennsylvania Law Review* 117 (1969), 521–45.

[44] E. Lambert, *Le gouvernement des juges et la lutte contre la législation sociale aux Etats-Unis* (Paris, 1921).

[45] For the Belgian doctrine, see M. Barzin, 'Du contrôle de la constitutionnalité des lois', *Académie royale de Belgique. Bulletin de la Classe des Lettres*, 5th ser. 52 (1966), 335–50; F. Dumon, 'Le contrôle de la constitutionnalité des lois. Réforme constitutionnelle de 1988', *Journal des Tribunaux*, 2 July 1988, 449–50. Recently Belgium moved towards judicial review by the creation of a Court of Arbitration: see F. Dumon, 'La Cour d' Arbitrage. Ses compétences, étendue et limites', *Journal des Tribunaux*, 6–13 April 1985, 229–35.

upon more and more, especially in the past decades, to decide on some of the most burning issues of our time by testing the constitutionality of controversial laws. Theoretically the lawgiver has the last word, because he can always change the Constitution, but in fact this is a cumbersome and rare procedure, because of the very nature of the Constitution and the high special majorities required (two-thirds in both Houses of Congress, and three-quarters of the state legislatures). Thus the Supreme Court has been made the highest arbiter in three issues that have agitated public opinion, race relations, abortion and the death penalty.

Segregation, including separate schooling for whites and African Americans, was introduced by law in many southern states and validated in 1896 by the Supreme Court as not unconstitutional, on condition that equal chances were offered to all. In 1954 the Supreme Court reversed its earlier stance and, judging that segregation fatally led to unequal chances, declared it unconstitutional, using the phrase 'the Constitution is colour blind' (the plaintiff was a Mr Brown whose eight-year-old daughter was barred from a nearby school for racial reasons). This put an end to segregation in schools and buses: several enactments in the sixties put federal penalties on segregation and, in Little Rock in 1957, it was even necessary to deploy federal troops to enforce the new orientation.

In the past abortion was a criminal offence and generally condemned. More recently voices were raised in favour of women's liberty to decide whether or not to have an abortion, and the old laws were said to violate the personal freedom guaranteed by the Constitution. This meant that the issue would one day end up before the Supreme Court. That day came in 1973, in *Roe* v. *Wade*, a Texan case, when the Court, in a landmark ruling, granted a judgment that met the liberal point of view and declared the Texan anti-abortion law unconstitutional. The Court held that during the first three months of pregnancy a woman's right to abortion was absolute, that during the three following months termination of pregnancy could only be carried out in approved settings, and that during the last three months it could be forbidden without going against constitutional liberties. Public opinion interpreted the ruling as granting abortion on demand. Afterwards, however, the Supreme Court, manned gradually by nominees of conservative presidents, retreated from the liberal position of 1973, *inter alia*, in a judgment of July 1989 concerning an anti-abortion law from Missouri. However, the Missouri theory that life begins at conception was rejected as being a 'religious doctrine' and contravening the First Amendment (see further). *Roe* v. *Wade* was never overturned, but is being eroded as greater freedom is granted to the state legislatures to restrict abortion by issuing various specifications, most recently by a judgment of June 1992 on a Pennsylvanian law. All this is happening amidst agitation by pro-life and pro-choice forces, battling respectively for the sanctity of life and the sanctity of personal freedom.

From time immemorial the death penalty has been used as the ultimate deterrent in the world at large, and also in the United States of America. Recently voices were raised to impugn the constitutionality of laws providing the death penalty. It was claimed that executions were cruel and unusual punishments, which are forbidden by the Eighth Amendment, and consequently unconstitutional. This was again a divisive and much debated issue which ended up before the Court in Washington, but this time the liberal tendency, which had won some striking civil rights rulings, could claim no victory. After 1967, while the decision of the Supreme Court was awaited, executions were stayed throughout the United States, and after the Court's rejection of the liberal thesis, in 1976, capital punishment was again legal and applied in numerous states, mainly in the south. The Supreme Court, however, imposed in 1976 certain guidelines, concerning procedure and the proportionality between crime and punishment and the absence of arbitrariness, whose disregard would make the death penalty cruel and unusual. Also, in 1988 the Supreme Court decided that it was unconstitutional to apply the death penalty to offenders under the age of sixteen. In other words, while the death penalty is not intrinsically a cruel and unusual punishment and is therefore not per se unconstitutional, certain circumstances can make it so. In the past some states had abolished the death penalty, but that had been done through legislative reform. The choice before the Supreme Court was agonizing, not only in human terms but also because the fundamental issue of judicial activism was at stake. How far can the judges go in their interpretation of the sacred texts, and are they bound by the intention of the lawgiver? If they are, the anti-capital punishment campaign has no leg to stand on, for it is clear from the Fifth Amendment that the constitutional lawgiver had no objection to capital punishment. The Amendment states indeed that nobody 'shall . . . be deprived of life, liberty, or property, without due process of law' (the Fourteenth Amendment similarly provides:

'nor shall any State deprive any person of life, liberty, or property, without due process of law'). To jurists who feel compelled to respect the intention of the lawgiver this is conclusive, but not to judicial activists who believe that the interpretation of a text should take into account 'evolving standards of decency' and insights of present-day society. Thus whether a punishment is cruel and unusual should not depend on what lawgivers thought two hundred years ago, but on 'contemporary societal values'. The debate is, of course, open and there are good arguments on both sides, but if the judicature could set aside an age-old practice and the clear intention of the lawgiver, the risk would be great that the judges would assume the role of the lawgiver.[46]

The executive and the judicature must abide by the Constitution in the same way as the lawgiver, otherwise they risk being impeached by him. Impeachment exists not only at the highest level, where Congress can depose federal judges and administrators, not excluding the president (admittedly an extremely rare procedure), but also at state level, where it is from time to time used by state legislatures against governors and judges (in 1988 the governor of Arizona was deposed by the state's senate, the first US governor to be deposed in fifty-nine years). Impeachment is an old common-law form of process, which fell into disuse in England around the beginning of the nineteenth century, but survived in America. It makes possible the enforcement of the rule of law. As we have pointed out already, Roman law taught that the emperor was expected to abide by the law, but could not be compelled to do so by any of the existing bodies known in the empire. It is this defect that was made good by impeachment: not only must even the highest holder of office, the President of the United States of America, obey the law but there is an institution, Congress, sitting as a court of law, that can judge and depose him. The procedure consists of two phases, indictment by the House of Representatives, helped by the House Judiciary Committee

[46] See the eloquent plea in favour of judicial activism by one of the leading liberals (until his retirement in 1990) in the Supreme Court, W. J. Brennan, 'Constitutional adjudication and the death penalty: a view from the court', *Harvard Law Review* 100 (1986), 313–31 (The 1986 Oliver Wendell Holmes, Jr Lecture). See also M. Meltsner, *Cruel and unusual. The Supreme Court and capital punishment* (Cambridge, Mass., 1973); *United States of America. The death penalty* (Amnesty International, London, 1987); D. P. Currie, *The Constitution in the Supreme Court: the second century 1888–1986* (Chicago, 1990). An echo of the sometimes agonizing discussions among the judges of the Supreme Court can be caught in the following book which does not contain a legal analysis, but rather sketches of the way the Court operates on a day to day basis: B. Woodward and S. Armstrong, *The brethren. Inside the Supreme Court* (New York, 1979).

(with specialists of constitutional law from both parties), and judgment by the Senate, where a two-thirds majority is required for a condemnation. A famous example of the impeachment of a president occurred in 1868, when Andrew Johnson avoided condemnation by one vote. In recent years the presidential impeachment has been the object of a good deal of attention after President Richard Nixon resigned in 1974 rather than face impeachment for the Watergate affair.[47]

The second panel of the American Constitution consists, as we have seen, of a series of Amendments. The first ten, known as the American Bill of Rights, were proclaimed together in 1791, after arduous negotiations and protests because the civil liberties had not been defined straight away in the Constitution of 1787. The Bill of Rights guarantees the traditional individual freedoms and the safety of persons and property: 'the rights of the people'. The link with the English chain of texts, from Magna Carta to the Petition of Right of 1628 and the Bill of Rights of 1689, is easily discernible. The prohibition of cruel and unusual punishments, for example, was borrowed from the Bill of 1689; and so was the freedom of the citizens to carry arms (both of which we have mentioned before). The Bill of Rights of 1791 contains the freedoms of speech, peaceable assembly and the press, the inviolability of persons and homes, and the right to due process of law, including the jury. Here also, again from the English past, we find habeas corpus, the well-known remedy against imprisonment without trial. And, in the First Amendment, the twofold principle of religious liberty and the separation of Church and state is proclaimed: 'Congress shall make no law respecting an establishment of religion, or prohibiting the free exercise thereof'. It was a tremendous break with the European past, where politics and religion had been intertwined since time immemorial, and it still contrasts today with the world of Islam, where society as a whole and in all its activities is subject to one divine law and one religious revelation. On this point the American Revolution has broken radically with European practice, not only as far as the ties between government and Church are concerned, but also the privileges of the clergy and the preferential treatment of certain denominations (if not the total exclusion of all others). The First Amendment has in fact been interpreted and adhered to in the strictest

---

[47] M. L. Benedict, *The impeachment and trial of Andrew Johnson* (New York, 1973); R. Berger, *Impeachment: the constitutional problems* (Cambridge, Mass., 1973); C. L. Black, *Impeachment: a handbook* (New Haven, 1975).

way. It is carefully observed and leads to litigation on such questions as the legality of a nativity scene in a town hall or school prayers. The separation not only excludes an established Church or salaries from public funds for clerics, but also official subsidies to schools and hospitals run by religious orders.

The First Amendment was in no way an expression of anti-religious feelings, which are not widespread in America, but the consequence of particular historic circumstances. The Anglican Church could, of course, not count on the sympathy of the early settlers, as it was part and parcel of the regime against which they had revolted and numerous early emigrants had left England precisely in order to escape pressure and even persecution by the official Church: the very idea of a state Church filled them and their descendants with horror. Many would have liked to found their own strict God-fearing society, led by the 'saints', but this radical Puritan position weakened in course of time. Nor were there only Protestants in the colonies: Maryland was predominantly Catholic, William Penn (*d.* 1718), the founder of Pennsylvania, was a Quaker, and there were other denominations as well, including the episcopalians, who remained loyal to the Anglican Church. It was therefore hardly possible or indeed desirable to elevate one of them to the position of the one official Church. Granting complete religious freedom and avoiding all official involvement with religious life seemed the most reasonable, even though radical solution. And, no doubt, the religious tolerance favoured by the Enlightenment, with which the American leaders were familiar, also tended in the same direction.

The original Ten Amendments to the Constitution have been expanded in the course of the years to a total, by 1970, of twenty-six (Article 5 of the Constitution had laid down the procedure, as we explained before). Some momentous Amendments dealt with race relations: the Thirteenth, of 1865, had abolished slavery at the end of the War of Secession, and the Fourteenth, of 1868, guaranteed the rights of African Americans; others concerned the franchise and the re-election of the president. How difficult a change in the Constitution is and how averse public opinion is towards meddling with it appeared in 1983, when an Amendment against sex discrimination was proposed and vigorously defended by women's groups, but narrowly failed being passed by three-quarters of the states (it was three short of the required thirty-eight), although it had taken the hurdle of the two-thirds majority in Congress.

The proclamation of the American Bill of Rights of 1791 was preceded by several declarations of human rights and promulgations of constitutions in separate states. Some of these texts, notably the Bill of Rights of Virginia of 1776, are famous in the history of public law, *inter alia*, because of their direct influence on the French Declaration of Human Rights of 1789. Thus one could read in the Constitution of Virginia, which contained two panels, a bill of rights and a description of the organization of the state, that 'all men are by nature equally free and independent and have certain inherent rights . . . namely the enjoyment of life and liberty, with the means of acquiring and possessing property and pursuing and obtaining happiness and safety'. The text goes on to say that 'all power is vested in and consequently derived from the people' and that 'magistrates are their trustees and servants and at all times amenable to them'. It was moreover said that bad governments could be reformed, altered or abolished by a majority of the community, that the legislative and executive powers of the state ought to be separate and distinct from the judiciary, and that 'the freedom of the press is one of the great bulwarks of liberty and can never be restrained but by despotic governments'. The last section declares that religion 'can be directed only by reason and conviction, not by force and violence and therefore all men are equally entitled to the free exercise of religion, according to the dictates of conscience'. It is remarkable – and it illustrates the modernity of the American way – that three generations after this principle was written into a constitutional text the papacy was still, in the *Syllabus errorum* ('list of errors') attached to Pope Pius IX's encyclical *Quanta cura* of 1864, condemning religious freedom as one of the wrong-headed liberties of the modern world. This policy was reversed at the time of the Second Vatican Council (1962–5) and the principle of freedom of conscience officially recognized by the Catholic Church.

### Interpretation

The importance of the events across the Atlantic was such that an analysis of their background is called for. Not everything was new in the American Constitution, however revolutionary it was. The rich colonial life of the seventeenth and eighteenth centuries had taught the Americans how to govern themselves, even though far away Britain had the last say, and American self-government was schooled in the democratic forms of government of numerous religious denominations, in town meetings, where direct democracy prevailed, and in regional parliaments, where elected representatives from various colonies sat and deliberated. They had, amongst other things, a considerable fiscal competence and were a check on the governor and his council, who constituted the local government. The great majority of the colonials were, as we have seen, of English origin and had English law in their bones; they were familiar with the great jurists of the mother country, especially Coke and Blackstone. It is therefore interesting to analyse which elements of the English heritage the Americans preserved, and which they rejected.

The following features were abandoned. Hereditary anointed kingship, possibly the most ancient and most sacred institution of the English people, class society and the natural leadership of the nobility, whose ancient aristocratic bulwark, the House of Lords, was still the most prestigious body in England at the time of the revolution, were all given up: in America all legal privileges were abolished, together with some feudal relics like primogeniture, and legal equality was established. The ties between Church and state, another millenary institution which, although vigorously contested, was anchored deeply in the English tradition, had to go. The sovereignty of Parliament, an English principle that became undisputed in the eighteenth century and was described by the great authority of the age, William Blackstone (and given its classical expression in the following century, in A. V. Dicey's *Law of the Constitution*, as we shall see) was rejected by the Americans, who placed even their Congress under the Constitution and the supervision of the judges. They also granted a far greater role in the process of law giving to their head of state than was the case in Britain. Unitarism was another thing to go. England was amongst the oldest unified kingdoms in Europe. It knew no autonomous duchies and counties or independent regional assemblies of estates: there was one king, one parliament and one common law for the whole of England. Wales was absorbed in the sixteenth century, and in 1707 the Scottish government and parliament gave way to the one British seat of power in London, even though Scots law and ecclesiastical organization were preserved. This marked unitarism, which remains strong till this day, was in America replaced by the federal form of government.

In spite of these momentous breaks with the past a good deal of continuity can be observed. The following elements may be mentioned.

The tradition of civil rights and limited state power, going back to Magna Carta, and the more recent acceptance of ideological and religious pluralism were conserved from the English past. The belief in the separation of powers (although never absolute) and a healthy distrust of the concentration of too much authority in the hands of one person or one body were also maintained. The obsessive fear of tyranny led to the well-known system of 'checks and balances', where the diffusion of public authority created several centres of power which restrained each other. It is possibly in their attitude to the authority of the state that the Americans differ most markedly from many Europeans. In its most extreme form, the state to an American is 'a bunch of people', politicians and their officials whom he watches with critical and even distrustful eyes; he sees the state as a powerful instrument that belongs to and is operated by groups of people for their own ends. At the other extreme one finds in Europe the adoration of the state as something majestic, transcendent and even divine (in the tradition of the 'divine' emperors of Rome). Nobody expressed this feeling better than the famous philosopher Hegel, who was professor at the Prussian University of Berlin from 1818 to 1831 and wrote: 'The march of God in the world, that is what the state is. In considering the Idea of the State we must not have our eyes on particular states . . . Instead we must consider the Idea, this actual God, by itself'.[48]

The rule of law and the right to 'due process of law', i.e. the rejection of the *princeps legibus solutus* idea, was another element the Americans preserved from the English heritage, as was its corollary, the absence of the dichotomy between public and private law (at least in its continental European severity) and of the notion that special standards apply to the sphere of public law, stacked in favour of the state and against the subjects. The English common law has remained, in spite of some early hesitation and appeals in favour of codification, the basic element of American law. This English orientation was, we have seen, sometimes so pronounced that the Americans preserved common-law institutions which the mother country had already abandoned or was abandoning, such as judicial review and impeachment.

No one should conclude from this analysis that the Americans did

---

[48] Quoted from the *Philosophy of right* (transl. T. M. Knox) in Lord Lloyd of Hampstead, *Introduction to jurisprudence* (3rd edn, London, 1972), 654. The contrast with Lord Acton's saying that 'power corrupts, and absolute power corrupts absolutely' is striking.

nothing else but keep or reject existing English materials. On the contrary, they also innovated in a very radical and creative way. Besides federalism, the essential innovation was the far reaching and consistent democratization of political institutions. We mention a few examples.

The election of the president by the people is by its very nature democratic, and so is the election of the governors of the states. It is also democratic, in the sense of direct democracy, that the elected president is head of the government and chooses his team of ministers without depending on a majority in Congress, but solely to carry out the programme on which he is elected. European democracy is much more parliamentary and indirect. The difference between the president of the United States and the prime minister of the United Kingdom, for example, is instructive. The latter is constantly in Parliament; he himself and almost all cabinet ministers are members of Parliament. In America 'question time' does not exist and the president rarely appears in Congress, and only when invited (his yearly State of the Union message is a notable event); ministers appear in Congress when they are summoned to be interrogated by some critical commission. To Europeans, accustomed as they are to governments that stand or fall with the changing majorities in parliament, this is a remarkable state of affairs: how can the government govern if it has no majority in parliament willing to vote the necessary budgets? In America it often happens that the president belongs to a party without a majority in Congress. Nevertheless he can govern, because he was elected by the people to head the government, and Congress must respect this fact, so that he and his ministers cannot be toppled as a cabinet in a European parliament. The legitimacy of both the Congress and the president rests on the will of the people. Consequently what is required is constant negotiation between them both till solutions acceptable to both sides are found for their divergent views. Paradoxically the nearest precedent can be detected in the medieval kingdoms, where negotiations between crown and parliament were the bread and butter of politics, as each side needed the other and both enjoyed full legitimacy, the one being chosen by God to rule, the other representing the country. The election of judges in several states is another democratic element, to which we have already drawn attention.

We believe, finally, that the decision to issue a written Constitution was also inspired by democratic considerations. A fundamental law, where the citizens can read which are the powers in the state, how they are organized and what is their function and competence, offers guarantees of cognoscibility and certainty, as does the definition of the inviolable rights of the people. A fixed and clearly drafted Constitution, with the civil rights precisely put down in writing, is more democratic than an opaque tangle of old and new customs and traditions (or so-called traditions) which are nowhere to be found in writing. The American preference for a written Constitution was logically followed by the decision to entrust the control of its observance to a college of independent, professional judges, with tenure for life, rather than to the politicians in Congress and their changing majorities.[49]

### Factors

Every great revolt which, between the sixteenth and the twentieth century, led the way to the modern world had its typical sources of inspiration, conditioned by the *Zeitgeist*, the philosophical current of the time. The Revolt of the Netherlands against Philip II as well as the Puritan resistance to Charles I were inspired by the *jus resistendi*,[50] the attachment to ancient rights and privileges, anti-absolutism and calvinism. The American Revolution shared many of these roots but, as a child of its century, owed much to the Enlightenment, natural law and the belief in progress. The French Revolution was marked even more deeply by the *philosophes* and the *Encyclopédie*, and the Russian October Revolution swore by the youthful ideology of Marxism. It was also marked by anti-legalism, because to Marxists the law was an oppressive weapon in the hands of the bourgeoisie, which would become superfluous in an ideal, classless society – a notable difference with the American and French Revolutions, where faith in the law and particularly constitutional law, was lively and the role of the lawyers considerable and even predominant. For a long time this aversion to the law was official Bolshevik Party policy and it was only in the last years of the ex-Soviet Union that the climate

---

[49] Whether one trusts a parliament more than a law court or prefers politicians to judges is a political choice depending on one's ideological orientation and value judgment. Also the choice may not be so clear cut as is sometimes thought, since not even the judges can escape the conflict of the great political curents, as the tug of war around the appointments in the Supreme Court has shown.

[50] D. Böttcher, *Ungehorsam oder Widerstand? Zum Fortleben des mittelalterlichen Widerstandsrechtes in der Reformationszeit (1529–1530)* (Berlin, 1991).

began to change and the law was viewed in a more positive light and lawyers began to play a greater – though still modest – role in the councils of the party and the state.[51]

There is a good deal of discussion among historians of the American Constitution whether its principal source of inspiration was the English common law or the Enlightenment. Both, of course, have been influential – and we refer to Locke, Montesquieu and Rousseau for the philosophical impact – but the recent tendency underlines the contribution of the English tradition and points out that the rebellious Americans constantly appealed to English law for arguments to support their claims. We have already seen, for example, that they shared Coke's views on the sovereignty of Parliament (or rather the lack of it). The Americans were often closer to the views of the English anti-Stuart opposition than to the English doctrine of their own time. American fear of tyranny was closely related to the English oppositionist movement of the seventeenth century, but this was irrelevant in Hanoverian England. What the American lawyer James Otis (*d.* 1783) wrote, namely that 'an Act against the Constitution is void' was in line with Sir Edward Coke's doctrine, but not with that of Blackstone and Lord North.[52] The Republic of the United Netherlands was also a model and source of inspiration to the American state builders, who were familiar with its history and institutions.[53]

The difference between the American and the French Revolutions is considerable, in spite of their proximity in time and the shared influence of the Enlightenment. The French Revolution was, as we shall see, less radical in its initial phase and remained closer to the British model: no republic, but a constitutional monarchy. Later on, however, it became much more extreme, waging war on Christianity (which had not happened in America) and producing the Terror, whose bloodbaths were much worse than the harassment and confiscations suffered by the loyalists on the other side of the Atlantic. Later constitutional developments in France and America were also

---

[51] See the prophetic book by an eminent specialist, J. N. Hazard, *Managing change in the USSR. The politico-legal role of the Soviet-jurist* (Cambridge, 1983).

[52] See the discussion in H. Hartog (ed.), *Law in the American Revolution and the revolution in the law* (New York, 1981).

[53] A translation of the Act of Abjuration was found among the papers of Lord Somers, a statesman of King William III's time, and was published in vol. XIV of *Somers' tracts* (16 vols., London, 1748–51). See on the Dutch influence, J. W. Schulte Nordholt, 'The example of the Dutch Republic for American federalism', *Bijdragen en Mededelingen voor de Geschiedenis der Nederlanden* 94 (1979), 437–49; J. P. A. Coopmans, 'Het Plakkaat van Verlatinge (1581) en de Declaration of Independence (1776)', ibid. 98 (1983), 540–67.

strikingly different, as one country went through a succession of different regimes and Constitutions, and the other's fundamental law remained basically unchanged for more than two centuries.[54]

The struggle for the Constitution is not only waged between conflicting ideologies, but also between opposing material interests. It was not different in America, as appears from quarrels around British taxes and grumbling about prejudice to American trade and colonial exploitation. Independence gave the ex-British subjects freedom to exploit their immense natural resources for themselves, even using the weapon of protectionism. To what extent self-interest could be at cross-purposes with political credo appeared from the phrases about equality and the inalienable right to freedom used by authors who were themselves slave owners and, with few exceptions, never thought of freeing their human capital. They had no qualms about invoking the equality of men on their own behalf against a tyrannical king, and at the same time denying that equality to the slaves on their plantations. Similarly they saw no contradiction between the proclamation of the citizens' equality and the imposition of a restricted franchise (although this led to a less drastic limitation of the vote in America than in Europe, because of more widespread landowning). This is one example among many others of the exalted phraseology beloved by revolutionaries which too easily misleads the public and historians. Magna Carta was more honest, for it stated unambiguously that its liberties were only guaranteed to 'free people', making it clear that serfs were left out. Not until 1865 was slavery abolished by law in the United States, turning the ideal of equality into a legal reality. The leaders of the American Revolution abhorred a tyrannical, even a strong state. They wanted freedom for themselves, but not for their inferiors, whose lot was legal dependence for the slaves and political dependence for the poor whites who had no vote. All this changed with the abolition of slavery and the introduction of the general franchise. Nevertheless the United States remains a land of great social inequality, which bothers government and Congress less than in Europe: a weak or absent state naturally gives free rein to the rich and influential.

Political revolutions often lead to social radicalism: the levellers under Cromwell, the sansculottes and *enragés* under Robespierre, the Bolsheviks after the bourgeois February Revolution of March 1917

---

[54] See the interesting historico-comparative observations in L. Cohen-Tanugi, *Le droit sans l'Etat. Sur la démocratie en France et en Amérique* (Paris, 1985).

come to mind. It is noteworthy that the American Revolution has produced nothing of the sort: political radicals have kept social radicals under control, and there was no large-scale redistribution of wealth, as happened in France in the wake of the revolution.

Two final remarks may be appropriate here. Although the political institutions framed by the American Revolution have proved perfectly adequate for the huge expansion of capitalist industry in the nineteenth and twentieth centuries and the rise of the country to a leading position in the world, this had never been the aim of their creators. Late eighteenth-century America had nothing to do with big industry and was still untouched by the machine age, which was only beginning then in England, and her leaders belonged to the pre-industrial 'unspoilt' agrarian world. Their ideal was an unsophisticated, pastoral and small-scale environment and they themselves lived in a small-scale, rural society, whose 'giant cities', Philadelphia and New York, counted respectively 45,000 and 33,000 inhabitants and where 97 per cent of the population lived in the countryside. As Jefferson put it in 1787: 'I think our governments will remain virtuous for many centuries as long as they are chiefly agricultural . . .; when they get piled upon one another in large cities, as in Europe, they will become corrupt as in Europe'. It is therefore remarkable that the constitutional foundations they laid proved so suitable for the modern industrial giant and world power of today.

Equally remarkable is the fact that so many elements in the American Constitution are so strikingly medieval in origin. In the later Middle Ages, as we have seen, politics was a power game between the king, whose legitimacy was based on God's grace, and parliaments or estates, whose legitimacy was based on the idea of national representation. Kings seldom managed to govern without grants from parliament, but parliament was not at liberty to make it impossible for the anointed of the Lord to govern his people: hence conflict, tempered by collaboration, negotiation and consent. This basic configuration is at the heart of the American Constitution, but with a president whose legitimacy, following enlightened philosophy, depends on election by the people instead of inheritance and ecclesiastical blessing.

We have already remarked on the medieval antecedents of the Bill of Rights of 1791: impeachment, judicial review (whose medieval precedents Coke systematically traced in the court rolls) and habeas corpus. All this demonstrates that certain political procedures and ideas can obtain a usefulness and value which transcend the contingencies of changing economic circumstances and cultural fashions. Some historians are reductionists, others autonomists. The former see law and science as surface-phenomena, reflecting all-important social and economic trends and forces, the latter believe that political and cultural developments lead a life of their own and follow an internal logic. The history of the American Constitution provides food for thought in this debate.[55]

## THE FRENCH REVOLUTION AND THE NAPOLEONIC REGIME

### *The political development*

The evolution of public law in general and constitutional law in particular is closely linked to political development. In some cases the adaptation of constitutional law to political change follows a gradual pattern and is hardly visible, because the words of the Constitution remain unchanged while practice and usage go their own way: thus Article 65 of the Belgian Constitution still says, as it did in 1831, that 'the king appoints and dismisses his ministers', which nowadays in no way reflects the real situation. In other cases the very foundations of the constitutional order are suddenly subverted in short, dynamic periods of violent political change that brutally and openly demolish the existing framework and – which usually proves more difficult – erect a new constitutional construction. The transformation of French fundamental law which we will presently analyse belongs to the latter type, as in one generation, i.e. some twenty-five years, France went at breakneck speed through a succession of changes and experiments which left no stone of the old building unturned. Declarations, Constitutions and a flood of laws which carried out this 'fresh valuation of all values' were, of course, closely linked to political events, which deserve to be briefly outlined.

The first phase of the period under review ran from 1789 to 10 August 1792 and witnessed the liquidation of the Ancient Regime and the creation of a bourgeois *Rechtsstaat*, with a constitutional and parliamentary monarchy. The direct cause of the revolution was the

---

[55] The classic work of C. A. Beard, *An economic interpretation of the Constitution of the United States* (New York, 1935) stresses the economic factor, as the title indicates. For a recent rejection of this approach which is said to 'lead to an impasse, as do all attempts to explain the profound movements of history by the economic factor', see J. Baechler, *Démocraties* (Paris, 1985), 609.

financial crisis of the kingdom. As bankruptcy was looming and the privileged classes, supported by the Parlement of Paris, rejected the general land tax proposed by the government, King Louis XVI saw no other solution than the convocation of the Estates General. This ancient assembly of the three estates of the realm, which could, *inter alia*, grant aids, had not met since 1614, and its disappearance had been one of the factors that made royal absolutism possible. Its convocation, in 1788, was greeted with enthusiasm in the whole of France, not only, as could be expected, by the Third Estate, which was keen to play at long last the political role to which it felt entitled, but also by the lower clergy, where a strong democratic current was at work (the bishops belonged to the nobility), and even, strangely enough, by some noblemen, who hoped to gain from the abolition of royal absolutism. Elections were organized per estate and the suffrage was notably democratic for the time. The resulting Estates General contained numerous members of the lower clergy who were prepared to throw in their lot with the Third Estate, which was almost exclusively composed of the bourgeoisie, including some four hundred lawyers. On government initiative the elections were accompanied by a popular consultation in the age-old form of the drafting of *cahiers de doléances*. These 'lists of grievances' reflected the complaints of the people about inequality and lack of freedom, demanded the abolition of privilege and of arbitrary rule, and requested a Constitution and frequent meetings of the Estates General. The monarchy was not questioned and foreign observers agreed that there was in Europe no other country as loyal to the crown as France. As soon as the newly elected Estates met at Versailles in 1789 the problem of how they were going to vote was posed.

Traditional doctrine held that in these assemblies voting had to proceed per estate, and there was a ruling of the Parlement of Paris in this sense, which referred to the precedent of 1614. This meant that the Third Estate would be outvoted by the other two, in other words that the representatives of the vast majority of the French people could be neutralized by the old dominant minority. This block of the ambitious and self-confident majority was unacceptable, and on 17 June 1789 the Third Estate, outraged by governmental procrastination, proclaimed itself as the National Assembly of France and, on the following 9 July, as the National Constituent Assembly empowered to draft a Constitution. Henceforth the old Third Estate considered itself the sole representative of the nation, speaking not for a single social class, but for the country as a whole. The step taken on 17 June was revolutionary, and was in fact the first truly revolutionary action of the year, as it went against all ancient rules and concepts. It was nevertheless accepted by the king, albeit after some hesitation, and thus legalized. Consequently France had a legitimate national parliament, which could go about its task of putting the finances of the state in order and also, and more importantly to many people, providing France with modern laws, including a Constitution.

The financial problem was solved in the short run, not by introducing new taxes (not a way of making the revolution popular), but by confiscating the wealth of the Church and issuing bonds, the assignats, so called because they represented land 'assigned' to the bond holder. The assignats came to be used as currency, so that they were in fact paper money with the *biens nationaux*, i.e. Church and crown land, as security (to which later was added the landed property of the *émigrés*, noblemen who had fled the country).[56] The great sell-out of land started in 1790, the royal domain coming first, followed by that of the Church. The sale was carried out in big lots, so that only rich buyers could compete. What the Constituent Assembly wanted was a solution to the financial crisis, not a redistribution of land inspired by social considerations. In 1792 the privatization of the ancient village commons was decreed. The legislative work of the Assembly underwent important external impulses. A commune was founded in Paris, followed by communal movements in other towns, and in the countryside big landowners were attacked and their castles and churches plundered. The communal movement, which harked back to old precedents and traditions of urban autonomy, deposed the existing oligarchies and replaced them by more representative organs, based on the electorate of the Estates General of 1789. Urban

---

[56] 'Assignat' was an old customary-law term, referring to the allocation of property to serve as security for the payment of a debt, especially a money-rent; this debt burdened, or 'was assigned', to a particular property. After the Assembly had in principle decided to alienate the *biens nationaux* in December 1789, it did not put them all on the market at once, but issued bonds on the security of them and thus immediately raised the cash it needed. These bonds were deemed to represent the value of the old crown and Church lands. This paper money consisted chiefly of notes for 100 francs and the first issue, in 1790, brought in 400 million francs. This facile plan of providing government income was constantly extended, until 45,578 million francs' worth of assignats were issued. Their purchasing power declined as they were issued in ever greater quantities, so that by 1793 severe measures had to be taken to compel their acceptance at their nominal value, and maximum food prices were fixed by the government. At last their value sank to almost nil and in March 1796 they were withdrawn. The only people who had not suffered from this devaluation were the purchasers of public lands, who had paid with assignats.

militias were also organized, those in Paris being mobilized against threatening troop movements. In this atmosphere the people of Paris on 14 July 1789 stormed the Bastille, a medieval royal bastion built to keep the capital under control. By 1789 the fortress had lost all usefulness, but to the popular imagination it was a dark and threatening symbol of the past and of arbitrary rule; it contained only a few prisoners of no political importance, but also a store of weapons which fell into the hands of the revolutionary masses who were mainly artisans and lower middle class people. Much impressed by the dramatic events in Paris and elsewhere, the Assembly passed a number of decrees with far reaching consequences, such as the celebrated abolition of 'feudalism' on 4 August 1789, and a whole series of other measures which changed French society so drastically that after a short while it was unrecognizable. The legal aspects of this revolution will be analysed later; all we need to say here is that the Ancient Regime, with its basic ideas and fundamental institutions, was buried. Following the British example, a unitary constitutional monarchy was introduced, but with a unicameral national parliament, called *Assemblée Nationale* and, later, *Assemblée Législative*.

However radical, the political upheaval had avoided certain extremes and preserved a number of traditional, bourgeois ele-ments.Thus the monarchy was maintained and the new regime was conservative in the social and economic field, witness the restricted franchise and respect for the sanctity of property. In 1791 Joseph Barnave, a notable orator of the Assembly who was guillotined in 1793, had warned, discussing the progress of legal equality: 'un pas de plus dans la ligne de l'égalité, c'est la destruction de la propriété' ('one step further towards equality means the destruction of property rights'). Extreme radicalism was postponed, but not forever: it came in the second phase of the revolution, which started with the coup d'état of 10 August 1792 and was the work of the Parisian clubs of Jacobins. During this phase the National Convention reigned supreme. It was an assembly elected by a minority of extremists and composed of radical revolutionaries, almost all of them members of the bourgeoisie and deeply marked by ideological considerations (about one-third were lawyers). The monarchy was abolished, the republic proclaimed, a series of European wars 'against the tyrants', which lasted with short intervals until 1815, launched, and revolutionary frenzy reached a peak under the Terror. In Paris and the country at large some 40,000 victims fell among the real or presumed counterrevolutionaries, some of whom were killed in prison ('September massacres'). The dictatorship of the radical clubs and the sansculottes led not only to political, but also to ideological extremism – in the form of the persecution of Christianity[57] – and social radicalism – in the form of economic regimentation, heavy direct taxation and redistribution of wealth by, for example, the sale of land of *émigrés* to the less well-off who were allowed to pay in instalments ('no patriot ought to be without property'). All this was aimed at installing not only legal, but also social and economic equality.

This phase ended with the fall of Robespierre on 9 Thermidor of the Year II of the republican calendar (27 July 1794),[58] an event that was joyfully celebrated by the survivors, and was followed by the Directory. This form of government maintained itself for a few years, but with great difficulty and through a series of irregularities which were in reality as many coups d'état, staving off its enemies on the left – the social radicals – and on the right – the clergy and the royalists. Against the latter the *Cinq Cents* (see the section on the Constitution under the Directory) in 1799 passed a law authorizing the imprisonment of relatives of *émigrés*, reviving memories of the worst excesses of the Terror.[59] The Directory tampered with election results in order to stay in power and became ever more corrupt, until it saw no other way out of the dramatic financial situation than war, conquest and plunder on a massive scale. Italy in particular was unashamedly pillaged, and General Napoleon's letters from that country proudly told the government in Paris how many more millions the ransomed cities there had paid or were expected to pay in money, jewels and other valuables. In 1796 it was estimated that the Italian plunder had already produced 46 million francs in money and 12 million in art treasures as 'legitimate spoils of war'. These military adventures played into the hands of the generals until one of them, Napoleon Bonaparte, finally toppled the Directory and founded his own personal rule.

His seizure of power, on 18 Brumaire of the Year VIII (9

---

[57] See the recent study by W. Schmale, *Entchristianisierung, Revolution und Verfassung. Zur Mentalitätsgeschichte der Verfassung in Frankreich, 1715–1794* (Berlin, Munich, 1989).

[58] G. Walther, *La conjuration du Neuf Thermidor* (Paris, 1975).

[59] Striking at 'evil blood' by punishing relatives who had committed no offence is a familiar phenomenon in the history of criminal law. The medievalist will remember the traitor Ganelon, from the epic literature on Charlemagne, whose relations were hanged with him, and the historians of the twentieth century will be reminded of the *Sippenhaftung* in the last phase of the Nazi era.

November 1799), led to profound legal and constitutional changes (see the section on the Napoleonic Constitution). Napoleon put an end to the rule of the assemblies and committees of lawyers and professional politicians, and introduced a strong executive, which he led in a dictatorial fashion and to which the legislature was utterly subjected. His regime was popular, as appears from several plebiscites which yielded huge majorities and from the massive enthusiasm which greeted his return from Elba in March 1815. Napoleon's popularity had several grounds. France had had enough of the long years of instability and internal strife, and had reached the limit of what was bearable. The new ruler promised peace and order – of the military sort – and posed as the national conciliator who could put an end to ten years of permanent revolution. On the one hand he kept various innovations of the revolution and acted as a republican, but on the other he reached an agreement with the pope, restored the Catholic religion and welcomed into the meritocracy of his adminis- tration talented people from various political backgrounds. Only the incorrigible leftist Jacobins had no place in his society, based as it was on respect for property, personal rule and the patriarchal family. His regime was unfriendly to the workers, as appears from the discipline of the *livret d'ouvrier* (a sort of internal passport that workers had to carry, with specifications of their employment) and from the law of 1803 which punished workers' 'coalitions' with two to five years' imprisonment. In spite of all this, his military expansionism and glorification of the *grande nation* were acclaimed in wide circles of the population, at least until his luck on the battle-field ran out and ever more conscripts were sacrificed on the altar of Mars. The enthusiasm which greeted Napoleon in March 1815 in spite of everything can be explained to a large extent by deep republican fears of the restoration of the monarchy and the return to power of the old privileged classes. The end of the Napoleonic adventure was caused by his ultimate failure on the battle-fields of Europe: the empire with its plebeian Caesarism was so much made to his measure that it could not survive him.[60]

The political balance sheet of the agitated quarter of a century under review looks as follows. Although in 1814–15 the monarchy

---

[60] What becomes of a *Führerstaat* after the *Führer*, i.e. what happens to the uncharismatic successors of a charismatic leader, is a question to which Max Weber devoted some attention. See R. C. van Caenegem, 'Max Weber: historian and sociologist' in R. C. van Caenegem, *Legal history: a European perspective* (London, Rio Grande, 1991), 201–22.

returned and the 'Restoration period' began, Ancient-Regime France was gone forever: feudalism, privileged estates, corporatism, the Gallican Church and royal absolutism all belonged irrevocably to the past. Much of what the revolution had achieved was preserved; the unitary state, the Constitution, a national parliament, a good deal of liberty, equality in law, a centrally directed and highly qualified bureaucracy[61] and one codified law for the whole country. Nevertheless quite a few extreme policies and forms of government of the previous years were reversed, such as the republic, the dominant position of assemblies and committees, general suffrage, Caesarism, permanent warfare, democracy (political as well as social and economic), anti-Christian agitation and the new rationalist forms of worship. The Catholic religion was restored and went hand in hand with the monarchy, but the Church had lost its old landed wealth irremediably, as the Concordat concluded in 1801 between Napoleon and Pope Pius VII had not reopened this question. The huge transfer of land caused by the revolution and the speculative profits made by commercial and industrial entrepreneurs led to economic openings at the expense of the previous owners, especially the clergy. They were, however, not to the advantage of the poorer groups, and communist conspiracies arose, which were already repressed before Napoleon's rule. We refer to the failed coup of François-Noël, known as Gracchus Babeuf, the first communist in French history, who initially played a modest role in Jacobin ranks and fought the moderate party of the Girondins and the Directory following the fall of Robespierre. After imprisonment in 1795 he launched a movement for social and economic equality, based on the idea that people were not only legally equal but also in their needs, and that private property was the fruit of usurpation. The movement formed a secret anti-Directory and published the *Manifeste des Egaux* ('Manifesto of the Equals'). It was suppressed by the government as being conspiratorial, anarchist and a danger to the state, and in 1797 its leader, Babeuf, was executed.[62]

The constitutional monarchy of bourgeois France (with its restricted

---

[61] P. Legendre, *Histoire de l'administration de 1750 à nos jours* (Paris, 1968); P. Legendre, *L'administration du XVIIIe siècle à nos jours* (Paris, 1969); P. Legendre, 'La royauté du droit administratif. Recherches sur les fondements traditionnels de l'Etat centraliste en France', *Revue historique de droit français et étranger*, 4th s., 52 (1974), 696–732; E. N.Suleiman, *Politics, power, and bureaucracy in France. The administrative elite* (Princeton, 1974); G. Thuillier, *Bureaucratie et bureaucrates en France au XIXe siècle* (Geneva, 1980); J.-L. Mestre, *Introduction historique au droit administratif français* (Paris, 1985) (Middle Ages to end of the Ancient Regime); F. Burdeau, *Histoire de l'administration française du 18e au 20e siècle* (Paris, 1989).

[62] R. B. Rose, *Gracchus Babeuf, the first revolutionary communist of modern time* (London, 1978).

franchise), which existed after 1815, corresponded largely to what the Constituent Assembly of 1789 had in mind, and what it might have realized if the 'second revolution' of August 1792 had not spoiled its plans for a modernized France, with a Constitution and parliament after the British model, wary of ideological or social extremism and favourable to the enterprising Third Estate.

### Public law under the Constituent and the Legislative Assemblies (1789–92)

The legislation, constitutional and otherwise, of the Constituent Assembly (1789–91) and of the Legislative Assembly (1791–2) aimed at achieving legal equality and freedom.[63] This implied the following.

The absolute, arbitrary rule, i.e. the personal and irresponsible power of the king over the persons and possessions of his subjects, was abolished. The rule of law where even the state and its organs must act in accordance with the law and under the supervision of independent judges was founded and popular participation in political decision making was introduced: no one could be deemed a free citizen who exerted no political influence at all; only where at least some dignitaries were elected could freedom flourish. Personal liberty was guaranteed in so far as serfdom was abolished, which used to subject peasants to their lords and tie them to the lords' land. Economic freedom was made possible through the abolition of the closed and hereditary corporations and the sale of offices, which had made careers inaccessible to talented people who happened to be born into the wrong family or could not afford the entrance fee to a guild or craft.

All this legislative activity was inspired by the belief in a better future. Faith in progress, as is well known, became a most popular tenet in the later eighteenth and nineteenth centuries, but previously this had not been so. Indeed, until the seventeenth century, revolutionaries, including the Puritan movement, referred to the past and aimed at the restoration of the good old days and the good old laws, which had been perverted by recent abuse: old law was good law and innovation was bad (*revolvere* and *revolutio* meant to turn the wheel back to pristine goodness). The American revolutionaries partly adopted the old and partly the new attitude, for while they looked to the future and were inspired by the modern Enlightenment,

---

[63]  G. van den Heuvel, *Der Freiheitsbegriff der Französischen Revolution. Studien zur Revolutionsideologie* (Göttingen, Zürich, 1988).

they still attached great importance to their ancient English common law. The French revolutionaries never did this sort of looking back; the past held no attraction for them, as belief in progress and the will to innovate dominated everything.

The main laws passed to achieve their aims were the following. The *Déclaration des droits de l'homme et du citoyen* of 26 August 1789 was a declaration of human rights in the line of the great English texts, natural law and the Enlightenment. It was inspired more specifically by the Bill of Rights of Virginia, which is understandable as some influential Frenchmen, such as de La Fayette (*d.* 1834), who proposed the text, had played a role in the American Revolution and influenced the events in France. The Declaration of 26 August contained seventeen articles, devoted to such matters as the legal equality of all men, their right to liberty, security and resistance to oppression, guarantees of lawful criminal justice and freedom of thought, religion and communication; it also proclaimed the separation of powers ('without which there could be no Constitution') and the sovereignty of the people.[64] The French Declaration of 1789 has inspired many others throughout the world, such as the Universal Declaration of Human Rights of 1948, proclaimed by the United Nations, and the European Convention on the Protection of Human Rights and Fundamental Freedoms (Rome, 1950).

Already on 4 August 1789, while the Assembly resolved to proclaim the aforementioned Declaration, it had abolished *la féodalité*. The decision to do away with 'feudalism' referred to all the privileges of the Ancient Regime and liquidated with one stroke of the pen innumerable age-old foundations of society: feudal law, ecclesiastical tithes, manorial courts, serfdom and the charters and privileges of towns and corporations. All these institutions were dubbed 'feudal', although many of them had nothing to do with feudalism as such, but in the imagination of the people they were all condemned as one set of legal instruments of oppression and exploitation.

In order to introduce a rational and unified administration and to underline the irreversible break with the past, a new division of the kingdom was carried through. The old duchies and counties and

---

[64] G. Del Vecchio, *La Déclaration des droits de l'homme et du citoyen dans la révolution française* (Paris, 1968); C. Fauré (ed.), *Les déclarations des droits de l'homme de 1789* (Paris, 1988) (texts and commentary); J. Imbert, 'Les déclarations des droits de l'homme pendant la révolution française', *Bulletin de l'Académie des Sciences et Lettres de Montpellier*, n.s., 20 (1989), 169–78.

other historic regions were abolished, as were all internal borders. France was to be strictly unitary and, in January 1790, was subdivided into eighty-three departments of more or less similar size, called after rivers and other topographical elements, so that even the ancient names of principalities and provinces were obliterated. This system was later applied to conquered and annexed territories, such as the Austrian Netherlands and the prince-bishopric of Liège, where historic names such as Flanders, Brabant and Liège had to give way to the 'department of the Scheldt' or 'of the Forests' (after the end of French rule the old names came back, but the borders of the departments remained unchanged).

The Constituent Assembly could not ignore the problem of the relations between state and Church. The link between the monarchy and the Gallican Church had been so close and so fundamental an element of the defunct regime that profound changes were unavoidable. The Church was also the largest of all the old privileged corporations, with a patrimony of its own, its own law and law courts, and the pretension to control intellectual life, while freedom of thought was one of the main goals of the revolution. Change, as we said, was inevitable; the only question was what course the reform would take. Generally speaking the Assembly adopted two lines of action. It respected religion and recognized that France was a Catholic country, so that the doctrinal primacy of the pope was left untouched, but this was not the case with the French Church as an institution, for it was subjected by the Constituent Assembly to a drastic administrative reform, without consultation of any Church council or the Roman curia. To begin with, Church property had, already in the autumn of 1789, been confiscated and, as we have seen, used as security for the assignats. The landed wealth of the Church was immense, some of it going back to the early Middle Ages, when people were scarce and land plentiful and of little value; afterwards demographic expansion and higher productivity had made Church property much more valuable, while canon law forbade its alienation. In 1790 the clergy were granted a salary from the treasury in compensation for their expropriation. In light of the notion of the unalterable right to individual liberty the regular clergy were freed from their vows and the religious orders dissolved by decrees of February and March 1790. The status of the secular clergy was the object of a sort of organic law, somewhat surprisingly called a Constitution, and passed on 12

July 1790 under the name of *Constitution civile du clergé*. It integrated the Church into the new French state and made it more democratic. The old bishoprics and ecclesiastical provinces disappeared and were replaced by a division which followed the new administrative borders in the realm, with one bishopric per department and one parish per commune. Religion was a public service and underwent the same administrative law as the others. Bishops and parish priests were to be chosen by the electors of the department or district, including the non-Catholics (which underlined the character of the new clergy as public servants). Although the election of bishops *a clero et populo* had not been unknown in canon law, that of parish priests was a complete innovation, and even the election of the bishops 'by the clergy and the people' had already given way in the later Middle Ages to appointment by pope or king. The bishops and priests, turned officials of the state, were required to express their allegiance to the new regime by an oath of loyalty to the nation, the law and the king.

The nationalization of the Church went further than the most ardent defenders of the Gallican Church had ever imagined; the abolition of the old ecclesiastical borders and the confiscation of the land of the secular clergy went further than what Henry VIII had done in England, but the Assembly did not follow his extreme example of cutting all religious links with the papacy. The French clergy was initially hesitant and divided, as the democratization appealed to many, and the law of 1790 carried some tendencies of the Gallican Church, which had always been very close to the national state, to their logical conclusion. Later developments, particularly the condemnation of the *Constitution civile du clergé* by Pope Pius VI in March 1791, led to an estrangement between the Church and the revolution and caused a rift among the faithful and among the priests, some of whom swore the required oath (*assermentés*), while others refused (*insermentés*). It was the beginning in traditional Catholic circles of the dislike of the republic and all its works, which remained a political factor of importance – and a support for royalist opinion – for many years.

That France would receive a written Constitution was never in doubt, and it had been one of the express desiderata of the *cahiers de doléances*. It nevertheless took two years before the text was ready to be proclaimed on 3 September 1791 by the Constituent Assembly. It was the first written Constitution on the European Continent (with the exception of the short-lived Polish Constitution of 3 May of that year).[65] It repeated the Declaration of Human Rights of 1789 and fixed the main principles of political organization, based on the separation of powers. France remained a monarchy, but of course a constitutional one. The executive was in the hands of the king, who chose his ministers, but they needed the support of the Legislative Assembly. Possibly inspired by the American 'checks and balances', the Constitution gave the king a veto over new laws, whose proclamation he could prevent or at least delay: when three successive assemblies passed the same act, which could take from four to six years, the royal veto was overruled. The king was declared 'inviolable and sacred', an echo of the anointed monarchy of the Ancient Regime which did not save King Louis XVI's head in January 1793. The Constituent Assembly saw the legislature, the representation of the nation, as the highest authority in the land. Legislative power was entrusted to a one-chamber parliament, called *Assemblée Législative*, whose members were elected via a restricted franchise, whose tax-paying limitation was less democratic than in 1789. It created two categories of citizens, called 'active' and 'passive', according to whether they paid a given minimum amount in direct taxes. The number of 'active citizens' – 4.25 million – is known, as we have the electoral lists with their names, the 'passive citizens' are estimated at some 3 million. In order to be eligible for the Assembly one was required to own a *propriété foncière* ('landed property'). The judicature was declared independent and was reorganized, the judges being elected for a six-year term.[66]

Three months before the Constitution was ready, on 14 June 1791, the law Le Chapelier was passed, prohibiting associations of workers: they were not allowed to appoint their own executives, or even to discuss affairs of common interest or pass resolutions on them. This violation of the right of association had a twofold goal, preventing the rebirth of the abolished corporations of the Ancient Regime and, after associations of employers had been prohibited, making organizations of workers suffer the same fate. Freedom of labour, enterprise and commerce was considered more important than freedom of association,

---

[65] The Polish Constitution, drafted in very liberal terms by the king, was issued on 3 May 1791, but already in 1792 a Russian invasion took place, leading to the second partition of Poland, followed in 1795 by the disappearance of the old kingdom. The Polish Constitution of 1791 adopted the separation of powers, abolished the *liberum veto* which had paralysed the old state, created modern ministries, preserved the monarchy and proclaimed religious equality; it did not, however, free the peasants.

[66] P. Dawson, *Provincial magistrates and revolutionary politics in France, 1789–1795* (Cambridge, Mass., 1972).

and the free-market economy had to prevail at all costs. The law Le Chapelier added nothing to the principle of the dissolution of the old guilds and corporations decreed on 4 August 1789, but it led in fact to the suppression of the associations of workers (*compagnonnages*), which so far had been left in peace. The application of the law was later extended to the countryside, where landowners as well as tenants, servants and labourers were forbidden to associate and prevent the free formation of prices and wages. The direct cause of the law Le Chapelier was a series of workers' revolts and strikes which the Assembly considered counter-revolutionary. The authorities wanted to combat more specifically a coalition of Parisian cabinet-makers, who had demanded higher wages in April 1791: the conflict came before the Assembly, which settled it by passing the said law. It even forbade workers to organize mutual assistance during strike or illness, because this was deemed a camouflage for illicit workers' associations. Workers' petitions and assemblies aimed at fixing prices or wages were equally forbidden, and violence used to endanger the freedom of work, i.e. the organization of strikes, was made a criminal offence. The law met no resistance from the left wing of the Assembly, as everyone interpreted it as the logical outcome of economic liberalism, which replaced the corporatist restrictions of the past (until well into the nineteenth century the law Le Chapelier remained an important legal factor in the rise of capitalist enterprise). In the same liberal light the *gabelle* (duty on salt) and town-dues were abolished as obstacles to free trade, as were many other indirect taxes: already in August–September 1789 the free circulation of goods inside the kingdom and the free determination of the price of grain were decreed.

### *The Constitution under the regime of the National Convention and the Directory (1792–9)*

The reign of the Legislative Assembly, instituted by the Constitution of 1791, lasted only one year.[67] It was succeeded by that of the National Convention, created after Robespierre's coup d'état of 10 August 1792, which assembled for the first time on 21 September of that year. The following day the monarchy was abolished and France became acquainted for the first time with the republican form of

---

[67] Some authors argue that already by the time the Constituent Assembly was dissolved, in the autumn of 1791, France was heading for the Terror. See N. Hampson, *Prelude to terror. The Constituent Assembly and the failure of consensus 1789–1791* (Oxford, 1988).

government. King Louis XVI was condemned by the Convention and executed on 21 January 1793. The National Convention imposed a radical and dictatorial rule, mainly through a number of committees, the most notorious being the Jacobin Committee of Public Safety. All power was so exclusively concentrated in the hands of the elected legislature and its organs that there existed no other real executive. Nor was there a president of the republic to replace the king, the result being a country without a head of state and even, after the six ministers had been abolished in April 1794, without a government. All power belonged to the Convention and its committees: this meant in reality Robespierre and, after his downfall, the Directory, instituted in 1795. The principal texts of those years are the Constitution of the Year I (the first year of the new regime which introduced the republican calendar) and the Constitution of the Year III, both of which we shall briefly present.

The Constitution of the Year I (1793) was the most democratic of the French Revolution. It contained a Declaration of Human Rights, which was no mere copy of that of 1789; the innovation concerned mainly social relations. Thus the line, 'all citizens are equal before the law' was significantly shortened to 'all citizens are equal', while Article 118 spoke of the 'pledge of care and recognition between the working man and his employer'. The Constitution also contained the rare express recognition of the right to work and of the right of resistance or rebellion against tyrannical authority, which could be interpreted as the right to strike. France was a unitary republic, as appeared straight away from Article 1, which said: 'La République Française est une et indivisible'. The three powers were maintained, but democratized by the use of elections. The legislature belonged to a *corps législatif*, elected by universal suffrage – but by men only.[68] The laws agreed upon by that body had to be approved by referendum. The executive was in the hands of the *Conseil exécutif*, elected by the *Corps législatif* from a list submitted by the electorate, every department proposing one candidate. All judges were elected by the people. The

---

[68] The revolution was not interested in votes for women, even though they were sporadically allowed to take part in certain districts in the referendum on the Constitution of the Year I. Female suffrage was not introduced in France until 1944. Public opinion was apparently still under the impression of the apodictic statement in Jean Bodin's *Six livres de la république* (VI, 5) that 'the rule of women flagrantly violates the laws of nature, which gave to men strength, prudence, weapons and domination, excluding women'. See V. Azimi, 'L'"exhérédation politique" de la femme par la révolution', *Revue historique de droit français et étranger* 69 (1991), 177–216.

Constitution of the Year I could be called a phantom Constitution, as it was never applied, although it had been proclaimed and, in the course of a civil festival on 10 August 1793, solemnly placed in a beautiful casket of cedar wood. But once the ceremony was over the Convention decided not to implement it, even though it had been adopted by referendum (out of 7 million electors, 1.8 million had voted yes, 15,000 no, and the rest stayed at home). The Constitution of the Year I is nevertheless of some interest, as it throws light on certain views on the left of the political spectrum. It was also the prototype of a certain sort of Constitution that was not so much a legal document as a political manifesto and an exercise in rhetoric and propaganda.

The Constitution of the Year III was of a different character and was in fact applied. It was the second Constitution of the Convention and introduced the Directory. Its basic aim was to end the exaggerated concentration of power which had made Robespierre's dictatorship possible. This was to be achieved by the separation of powers and by the introduction of a bicameral parliament. Legislative power was to be exercised by two chambers which would, it was hoped, guarantee more moderate and sober-minded policies. The two chambers were, however, not very different from each other – unlike the British Parliament – as they were both elected by the people and with a restricted tax-based suffrage. The differences concerned the age of the members and their role in the legislative process. The *Conseil des Cinq Cents* ('Council of the Five Hundred') consisted of young parliamentarians, at least 25 years old, and had the right to introduce (bold) bills. The *Conseil des Anciens* ('Council of the Elders') contained men at least 40 years old and married or widowers, and supposed to be old and wise enough to decide which bills deserved to become law: their role was limited to accepting or rejecting the proposals from the other chamber. The executive belonged to a body of five Directors. This Directory was no cabinet headed by a prime minister and with separate departments, each headed by its own minister, but one collective government with one general and common competence. The Directory worked through so-called 'ministers', who were public servants without political autonomy or responsibility. The members of the Directory were appointed by the legislature, one of the five being replaced every year, which was the only impact the legislature had on the government. All the judges were elected by the people; they were neither professionals, nor necessarily trained lawyers.

In several respects those Constitutions differed widely between appearance and reality. They belonged to various degrees to the paper Constitutions, which have not been unknown in the twentieth century: incredibly democratic and full of praiseworthy freedoms which were in fact flagrantly violated – democratic façades for oppressive regimes (the worst example of this species was probably the Stalinskaia of 1936, which we shall study in chapter 9). The new general franchise, introduced by the Convention on 11 August 1792, was, for example, the most democratic imaginable (except that it did not include women, as we have seen), but in reality the elections for the Convention were rigged and not democratic at all, and their result did not reflect the mood of the country as a whole. Through incomprehension, ignorance, indifference, epuration of the electoral rolls, annulment of 'royalist' votes and especially intimidation (voting taking place in public) only one out of ten people entitled to vote took part in the election. Thus the Convention represented a minority of radical activists and not the nation at large. Under the Constitution of the Year III the franchise was restricted by a tax-paying limitation, although the regime still proclaimed itself democratic. In fact the freedom of the people was severely curtailed, as the Convention had cynically ordained that two-thirds of the new Council of Five Hundred and Council of Elders had to be elected obligatorily among the members of the outgoing Convention. When this shameless attempt by the existing political class to retain power was torpedoed by the electorate, the elections, deemed politically incorrect, were annulled. The Directory also witnessed several coups d'état aimed at frustrating public opinion, which was veering towards the right, and at appointing only the devoted followers of the regime: the coup d'état of Brumaire was only the last in the series.

Respect for the constitutional freedoms was equally illusory. Official terror violated the liberties and human rights of innumerable citizens by, for example, expressly declaring suspects guilty (the *Loi des suspects* of September 1793 caused some 800,000 Frenchmen to be declared 'suspect') or quite simply by abolishing the rights of the defence (law of 10 June 1794). All priests, even the *assermentés*, were subjected to a special regime and, if any of them were denounced by six citizens as *inciviques*, were punished with banishment. 'Suspects' who were to be automatically arrested were not only the *ci-devant nobles*, but also their 'spouses, parents, children, brothers, sisters and agents who had failed permanently to show their zeal for the revolution' (law of 17 September 1793). The Constitution of the Year I guaranteed the *liberté indéfinie de la presse*, but the men in power at once made it clear that this 'unlimited freedom' did not extend to their (royalist) opponents, and publications that did not conform were suppressed. The freedom of the press which existed only for the government and its friends was a caricature, which was nevertheless defended as being the 'dictatorship of freedom'. Numerous journalists paid with their lives for their temerity, having been exposed as *empoisonneurs de l'opinion publique* ('poisoners of public opinion'). Another noteworthy contradiction concerned the position of the civil service. The Declaration of Human Rights stipulated in Article 15 that on principle 'society has the right to call every public agent to account concerning his administration', but a decree of 14 December 1789, confirmed by a law of 7–14 October 1790 and by Article 75 of the Constitution of the Year VIII, ruled that it was forbidden for the law courts to take cognizance, without previous permission of the administration, of alleged malpractices committed by a public servant in the exercise of his duties. This brings us back to the thorny distinction between public and private law, which we discussed in the first pages of the book.

### The Napoleonic Constitution, 1799–1815

The pendulum, which under the Directory began to swing from the legislature to the executive, reached its opposite extreme under Napoleon. His personal rule received a legal base from the Constitution of the Year VIII (1800) and the subsequent *senatus consulta*, which expressed the fundamental idea that the true representative of the nation was the government and not the assemblies and their egotistic pressure groups (an anti-parliamentarian attitude shared by many Frenchmen at the time).

The Constitution of the Year VIII organized the Decennial Consulate. All power was concentrated in the hands of the executive, which consisted of three consuls, one of whom, Napoleon Bonaparte, was in control, while the other two played an advisory role. The First Consul, who was, of course, Napoleon himself, initially received a mandate for ten years; this was turned into a mandate for life by a *senatus consultum* of 1802, and made an hereditary empire by a *senatus consultum* of 1804. The concentration of power gave the First Consul an extensive legislative as well as executive capacity: he introduced bills, which the legislative chambers could accept or reject, he could suspend or withdraw bills and could issue decrees to implement or replace laws (the decrees became more numerous as his rule advanced). He was assisted in his legislative work by a Council of State, whose members he appointed and who drafted most of his bills and decrees. In the exercise of his governmental work he was assisted by 'ministers', who were executive agents and not personalities with a political responsibility of their own.

The legislature consisted of the following three bodies. The Senate, composed by co-optation, checked the constitutionality of the laws, and also appointed most civil servants. The Tribunate consisted of 100 members appointed by the Senate; it discussed the legislative proposals of the Council of State and recommended their acceptance or rejection. It was the most republican and revolutionary body and, as it sometimes dared go against Napoleon's wishes, it was abolished in 1807. The Legislative Corps, whose 300 members were also appointed by the Senate, was expected to reject or accept without further discussion the legislative proposals, after hearing the opinions of the Tribunate and the Council of State. All bills originated with the executive.

The judicature was drastically reformed, as the 'people's judges' were replaced by professionals appointed by the First Consul. The main outline of the judicial organization has remained unchanged to this day, and consists of a network of justices of the peace, courts of first instance, courts of appeal and, at the top of the pyramid, the Court of Cassation. The Constitution of the Year VIII contained no declaration of human rights, but mentioned the inviolability of the home and guaranteed personal liberty. No freedom of the press was mentioned, which was only honest, as the press was immediately put under supervision, and censorship formally instituted in 1810. The number of newspapers was limited in 1811 to four in Paris and one per department in the provinces (with the authorization of the prefect), and each paper was directed by a censor and a chief editor, who were appointed by the state. In Napoleon's view the papers ought to restrict themselves to official communiqués and news about cultural life and local events.

This did not mean, however, that cultural life escaped the state's attention. The opposite was true, as appears from the educational policy which led, in 1806, to the creation of a sort of Ministry of Education, the Imperial University, headed by a Grand Master. The state enjoyed the monopoly of education, which was directed from Paris. The *Université Impériale* encompassed all levels of instruction and in 1809 even the priests' seminaries were placed under its authority. This was not the only Napoleonic feature that brings to mind the rule of the enlightened kings: the government even made a single imperial catechism compulsory for the whole of France. All this supported Napoleon's remark that 'the people need religion, but it must be in the government's hands'. Higher education was provided in special 'schools', organized along military lines, which trained the engineers, doctors and lawyers the empire needed, but where talkative 'ideologues' were excluded. The regime took interest in the training of the cadres, but neglected primary schools, so that it comes as no surprise that in the empire 46 per cent of men and 56 per cent of women were illiterate.

Napoleon's Caesarism was not devoid of democratic features. The regime organized, for example, frequent plebiscites, and always with success. The new Constitution was submitted to a referendum, which could be construed as the legitimation of the coup d'état of Brumaire. The success was overwhelming, as there were over 3 million yes- and only 1,562 no-votes. Admittedly the procedure was rather peculiar, as two registers were opened in each commune, one for the yes- and one for the no-votes, which the electors were expected to sign in public. It is clear that many people saw the army as the saviour of France (the plebiscite on the proclamation of the empire in 1804 also yielded a massive approval). Another democratic feature, called a *façade démocratique* by many observers, was presented by the elections. They were also rather special, as the intention was not to let the people elect the dignitaries, but only to compile lists of notables, the so-called confidence lists, from which the government could make a selection for its appointments. Via a series of communal, departmental and national elections (with general suffrage) an ultimate list was drawn up of some 5,000 'notables', i.e. important tax payers, in whom the country seemed to have confidence and among whom the government made its choice for various posts and functions. The system can best be described as a blatant and officially organized plutocracy. Its philosophy was pushed to extremes when property requirements were imposed even for the clergy: the organic articles of the Concordat of 1801 required property yielding an income of at least 300 francs.

Napoleon's seizure of power came about through a mixture of

violence and legality that is remarkable and found some notable imitators in the twentieth century. Brumaire clearly was a military coup, as at the crucial moment the Jacobin members of the Council of Five Hundred, who resisted and shouted 'la constitution ou la mort', were thrown out by a posse of grenadiers to whom Murat, the future marshal and brother-in-law of Napoleon, had given the crisp order: 'Foutez-moi tout ce monde dehors' ('throw all this mob out'). Nevertheless Napoleon went to great lengths to secure the appearance of legality, taking the trouble, for example, to obtain a vote of confidence from the competent bodies. His friends managed, in comical circumstances, to assemble some 100 members of the Council of Five Hundred, who quickly appointed a *commission consulaire exécutive*, consisting of Sieyès, Ducos and Bonaparte, 'who were to be called the consuls of the republic'. Various procedural niceties were fastidiously observed: a study-group was appointed, and a report submitted and discussed (though no one opposed). The comedy took only a few hours and was, in the middle of the night, confirmed, again according to the rules, by the Council of Elders, who had spent the day of Brumaire dithering, asking for clarification and discussing points of legal detail.

The desire to preserve the republican regime under the empire, or at least not to disavow it completely, was expressed in the quaint preamble of the *senatus consultum* of the Year XII (1804), which declared: 'the government of the republic is entrusted to an emperor', adding that the emperor carried his title 'by the grace of God and the Constitutions of the republic'.

# CHAPTER 8

# The bourgeois nation state

## GENERAL OUTLINE

Nineteenth-century constitutional law reflects the political situation. In the age of Gladstone and Thiers the bourgeoisie, which had been locally powerful since the Middle Ages, gained access to the national centres of command.

The existing kingdoms of Britain and France were created not by the middle classes but by the monarchy, so that in those countries the Third Estate could simply pick the nation state as a ripe fruit and even, most notably in France, strengthen its unitary centralism. Elsewhere, in Germany and Italy, the nation itself only came into being in the nineteenth century. It was founded by the royal houses of Prussia and Piedmont-Savoy and their great ministers, Bismarck and Cavour, but with the collaboration and the stimulus of the bourgeoisie, which was interested in the abolition of internal economic barriers and the creation of a national common market. The middle classes understood that they could not play a global role with the old mini-states as bases and that capital and entrepreneurial initiative required wide and, if need be, protected markets.

The constitutional ambitions of the bourgeoisie were expressed in two key words, constitutionalism and parliamentarianism. The former excluded absolute, arbitrary rule and demanded a government operating under the law; it created the *Rechtsstaat*, where the citizens were no more dominated by individuals, but by laws to which everyone had to submit. The latter keyword signified a regime where the government and the legislature derived their authority from and were accountable to the nation, represented by an elected parliament. This excluded direct democracy and even, because of the restricted franchise, democracy itself. The parliaments of the nineteenth century were often blatantly oligarchic; in Britain until the early twentieth century the House of Lords, the assembly of the hereditary aristocracy, controlled legislation, and in Belgium the celebrated Constitution of 1831 gave the vote in parliamentary elections to about 1 per cent of the population.

The rise of this form of government came about via different paths in different countries. In Britain the nation state, the constitutional monarchy and the sovereignty of Parliament had been achieved in the past, so the nineteenth-century Constitution continued along the established pattern. The principal changes – the reshaping of the constituencies and the widening of the franchise – could be seen as adaptations of the existing order. In nineteenth-century France not the sovereign nation state but the choice of form of government was the problem. This was illustrated by the numerous and often violent changes ranging from the restoration of the old- and an experiment with a new-style monarchy to the short-lived Second Republic and the not so short Second Empire, and finally leading to the Third Republic, where the Constitution and parliament were triumphant. In Germany things were different again. The bourgeoisie admittedly obtained the national unification it wanted, and played a conspicuous role in parliament and in society at large, but it was hemmed in by the monarchy and the latter's ally, the army. No radical parliamentarianism therefore and no radical unification followed: even after 1871 the old kingdoms and principalities and their ruling dynasties remained in place, though they did not prevent the creation of the common market or the introduction of a common civil code.

Political liberalism, based on parliament and a Constitution, went hand in hand with a free-market economy which favoured capitalists and entrepreneurs and degraded labour to the status of merchandise, the price of which was determined by supply and demand. As the nineteenth century witnessed a spectacular demographic expansion and consequently a growing supply of labour, the position of the working class was both politically and economically weak. True democracy was in those circumstances excluded. Nor should the rise of the bourgeoisie, which was real enough, blind us to the fact that the landowning nobility still played an important role in society at large and in the House of Lords, the Herrenhaus or the Senate in particular.

As could be expected, the labouring and subjected masses eventually rose against the political and economic oligarchy. The earliest revolts were failures, because the bourgeoisie not only disposed of the machinery of the state, but was self-confident enough to use its position of strength to the full – witness the failure of chartism in Britain between 1830 and 1850 and the suppression of the Parisian revolts in 1848 and 1871. In the late nineteenth century workers' parties began to agitate for a change in the regime via parliamentary legislation, but they did not enter the government until the First World War.

GREAT BRITAIN

In Britain, as we have seen, the fundamental transformation had come about before the nineteenth century, and the nation state, the constitutional monarchy and the supremacy of Parliament were achievements of the past and not really questioned. The main change – or adaptation – in nineteenth-century Britain was the extension of the franchise, and the concomitant gradual democratization of Parliament, or rather of the House of Commons: the other House preserved its ancient composition and power until the early twentieth century.[1]

The modernization of the Commons was achieved by the Reform Act of 1832 and subsequent extensions of the franchise, each of which was accompanied by assurances that it was the last. The Act of 1832 redrew the boundaries of the constituencies, which reflected past vicissitudes and were hopelessly out of date. Some parts of the country were obviously overrepresented in the Commons, whereas others, especially in recently industrialized areas, were hardly represented at all. In this way the enterprising bourgeoisie of large parts of the kingdom was deprived of political influence, as if there had been no Industrial Revolution and rural England was still intact. In numerous insignificant countryside districts and the notorious 'rotten boroughs' the landowner simply nominated the local member of Parliament of his choice, which again advantaged the landed interest as against the new social and economic groups and their political ambitions. The old map of the constituencies was redrawn and to a large extent adapted to the demographic and economic reality, which automatically led to the decline of the old classes and the entry of *homines novi* into the Commons. The Act of 1832 went even further and granted suffrage to

---

[1]  This reflected certain economic realities, for it appeared from the 'new Doomsday' of Lord Derby (*d.* 1893) that four-fifths of the kingdom was in the hands of only 7,000 people, and that of the sixteen topping £100,000 a year in rentals, all but two were peers. See D. Sutherland, *The landowners* (London, 1968).

a new layer of voters from the middle class: the tax-paying qualification was lowered and the electorate grew by about 50 per cent so that about one Englishman out of five had the vote. In 1867 another step forward followed, as the second Reform Act extended the franchise so as to include a considerable section of the working class. This 'jump in the dark', which gave the vote and therefore power to millions of low income earners, had caused considerable alarm but, although it doubled the size of the electorate, did not result in any fundamental change, let alone the universal plunder of the propertied class. The Act of 1867, which had favoured town dwellers, was followed in 1884 by a comparable measure for rural workers, the third Reform Act, which was itself followed by new revisions of the constituencies in 1885 and 1888. Universal suffrage for men and women at last arrived in 1918.

These changes produced no sudden political cataclysm because the working class at first was no more than a pressure group inside the Liberal Party and only resolved to form a modern party of its own and to act independently in the House of Commons at the beginning of the twentieth century. In 1911 the Parliament Act severely reduced the legislative impact of the House of Lords, which could no longer hold up indefinitely laws passed by the Commons, but only delay them. It remains nevertheless till this day an important part of the legislature, where debate is carried on by people of experience and independence of mind, particularly the law lords and the life peers (members of the House of Lords who were not born into the aristocracy but made peers by the crown).

The modernization of Parliament was no doubt the main change in the British Constitution. But in its wake some other adaptations were carried out. In 1835 elected municipal councils were introduced to supplant the old closed patriciate. In 1888 elected county councils put an end to the patriarchal justices of the peace, who had dominated the countryside for centuries, not only as judges but as administrators as well, with, for example, the power of fixing prices and wages. In the same century the medieval common law and its courts were reformed, *inter alia*, by the Judicature Acts of 1873 and 1875. But nothing changed Britain's unitary, centralized structure: in the past decades plans for devolution in Scotland – with a Scottish parliament – failed to materialize.

Although quite a few elements of the Constitution had thus been emended, its peculiar character remained unchanged: it was based on custom and an unwritten and therefore flexible Constitution. This means that it consists of rules which are considered fundamental, but can nevertheless be changed at any moment by Parliament without any special procedural precautions (such as a declaration of the intent to change the Constitution before the election of a Constituent Parliament, the requirement of special majorities in Parliament or a referendum).[2] If one understands by a Constitution a rigid fundamental law, different from ordinary laws and binding even for the legislature, then it can be said that Britain has no Constitution at all: its Parliament is sovereign and can make or unmake any law it chooses, without being hindered by a Constitution, let alone judicial control.[3] The absence of a Constitution means that there is no written Bill of Rights, no textual anchor, where the fundamental freedoms of the citizens are written down.[4] This state of affairs, which has been accepted for a long time as dogma, is nowadays questioned and subjected to a lively debate.

The sovereignty of Parliament, i.e. its freedom to legislate being neither restricted by existing laws, the general principles of the common law or natural justice, nor subject to judicial review, was well established by the eighteenth century.[5] It was expounded most authoritatively by the Oxford professor A. V. Dicey, in his *Introduction to the study of the law of the Constitution* of 1885.[6] The basic idea is that

---

[2] For the distinction between rigid and flexible Constitutions see K. C. Wheare, *Modern constitutions* (2nd edn., Oxford, 1966), 15–18.

[3] There are some famous nineteenth-century pronouncements by judges on their submission to the lawgiver. Among more recent declarations in the same sense we quote Lord Morris in 1974 in *Pickin* v. *British Railways Board*: 'it is the function of the courts to administer the laws which Parliament has enacted' and Lord Reid, who in 1969 in *Madzimbamuto* v. *Lardner-Burke* maintained that moral and other considerations could make a law 'highly improper' in the eyes of many people, but that none would lead the courts to holding an Act of Parliament invalid (see A. W. Bradley, 'The sovereignty of Parliament in perpetuity?' in J. Jowell and D. Oliver (eds.), *The changing constitution* (Oxford, 1985), 26).

[4] See the discussion in J. W. Gough, *Fundamental law in English constitutional history* (Oxford, 1955).

[5] Blackstone, for example, wrote about Parliament: 'it hath sovereign and uncontrollable authority in the making . . . of laws, concerning matters of all possible denominations . . . this being the place where the absolute despotic power, which must in all governements . . . reside somewhere, is entrusted by the constitution of this kingdom' (quoted by D. Lieberman, *The province of legislation determined. Legal theory in eighteenth-century Britain* (Cambridge, 1989), 50. See also C. K. Allen, *Law in the making* (7th edn, Oxford, 1964), 450–66.

[6] This classic, which went through numerous editions, was criticized by W. I. Jennings, *The law and the constitution* (London, 1933) and more recently by P. P. Craig, *Public law and democracy in the United Kingdom and the United States of America* (Oxford, 1990), 13–55. See also the remarks in J. Jowell and D. Oliver (eds.), *The changing constitution* (Oxford, 1985); Lord Denning, *The closing chapter* (London, 1983), 115–39; and J. F. McEldowney, 'Dicey in historical perspective – a review essay' in M. McAuslan and J. F. McEldowney (eds.), *Legitimacy and the constitution* (London, 1985), 39–61.

nothing can go against the will of the people, that the will of the people is to be done, and that therefore the will of Parliament, which represents the people, is supreme. This unlimited, dictatorial power of a single assembly nowadays upsets many observers, who distrust absolute authority and fail to see why a parliament, once elected, should not be obliged to respect certain well-defined individual rights.[7] The critics of the existing situation argue that there ought to be a written and rigid Constitution, or at least a Bill of Rights, to protect the public from 'elective despotism'.[8] We find this view expressed both by academics and by members of the public.[9]

The Oxford professor P.S. Atiyah has supported the idea that there should be some fundamental rights which are not at the mercy of the government and its majority in Parliament.[10] Other scholars have voiced their unease at the existing state of affairs, i.e. 'the absence of any common core of guaranteed individual rights'.[11] On the other hand, some academics fail to see how the sovereignty of Parliament could be overcome, because of the principle that no parliament is bound by its predecessors or can bind by its successors. If no parliament can pass laws that are binding for a later parliament, how can a fundamental law, binding Parliament, ever be passed?[12] There is a risk of a *petitio principii* here, as the argument seems to be that we cannot have a Bill of Rights because no parliament can bind another,

[7] We are, of course, talking here about the British legal system, without reference to the possibility for British subjects to go to the European Court of Human Rights at Strasbourg with complaints about violations of human rights.

[8] The expression was used by Jefferson, who wrote: 'The concentration of these [the executive, legislative and judicial powers] in the same hands is precisely the definition of despotic government. It will be no alleviation that these powers will be exercised by a plurality of hands, and not by a single one: 173 despots would surely be as oppressive as one … An elective despotism was not the government we fought for' (quoted in M. L. Volcansek and J. C. Lafon, *Judicial selection. The cross-evolution of French and American practices* (New York, 1988), 24).

[9] It comes as no surprise that Jeremy Bentham was an advocate of a constitutional code. His *First principles preparatory to a constitutional code*, edited by P. Schofield (Oxford, 1989), contains the germs of Bentham's *Constitutional code*, which was published by the Clarendon Press in 1982. See also D. Lyons, *In the interest of the governed. A study in Bentham's philosophy of utility and law* (Oxford, 1974).

[10] P. S. Atiyah, *Law and modern society* (Oxford, 1983), 108.

[11] A. Lester, 'The constitution's decline and renewal' in J. Jowell and D. Oliver (eds.), *The changing constitution* (Oxford, 1985), 345. The author stresses the importance of the European Convention for the Protection of Human Rights and concludes: 'We find ourselves isolated from our neighbours in Europe in our lack of a written constitution. The hope must be that our adherence to the European system will bring about a new constitutional settlement'.

[12] H. W. R. Wade, 'The basis of legal sovereignty', *Cambridge Law Journal* 14 (1955), 172–96; T. R. S. Allan, 'Legislative supremacy and the rule of law: democracy and constitutionalism', *Cambridge Law Journal* 44 (1985), 111–43.

as each parliament is sovereign, and it is sovereign because it cannot be bound by another.[13]

Public opinion is divided. There are voices both on the right – Lord Hailsham, for example – and on the left – the Charter '88 movement, for example – in favour of a Bill of Rights, but they are usually raised when their own political family feels threatened by the prospect of a long spell in the opposition. There is nevertheless a wide current in favour of a Bill of Rights. At the time of writing, in the context of a long period of Conservative Party rule, the political right is not vocal in its defence,[14] whereas the left likes the idea on principle but is frightened by the prospect of judicial review and the concomitant impact of the judiciary, which it sees as a conservative force. Hence the expressions of alarm in readers' letters in the press about the enactment of an enforceable Bill of Rights meaning 'transferring political decisions from Parliament to the courts'.[15]

It is clear that the debate on a Bill of Rights for Britain – and judicial review – goes beyond academic comment, and concerns basic political views and options about that most sacred keystone of British life, the Parliament at Westminster.[16]

### FRANCE AFTER NAPOLEON

#### *Introductory remarks*

During the turbulent and creative quarter century between the fall of the Bastille and the battle of Waterloo the seeds of every later constitutional development were sown. All the main ideological families and national interests which fought each other from Louis

---

[13] Medieval parliaments have accepted the principle of higher laws that were binding for all time. Thus the Parliament of 1369 assented that 'the Great Charter and the Charter of the Forest be holden and kept in all points, and if any Statute be made to the contrary, that shall be holden for none' (Gough, *Fundamental law*, 15).

[14] It can be observed that politicians who are not happy with the way things are going in Parliament think of a Bill of Rights or a referendum as the last resort to put things right. It is not uncommon for them to reject the referendum as contrary to parliamentary democracy in one political context, and to want to resort to it in another.

[15] The *Independent* of 20 April 1989.

[16] Among recent publications, see the following: J. Jaconelli, *Enacting a bill of rights, The legal problems* (Oxford, 1980); R. Dworkin, *A bill of rights for Britain* (London, 1990); K. Ewing, *A bill of rights for Britain?* (London, 1990); A. Lester et al., *A British bill of rights* (London, 1990); F. Vibert (ed.), *Britain's constitutional future* (London, 1991); *A people's charter: liberty's bill of rights* (London, 1991). See also some remarks in R. C. van Caenegem, *Judges, legislators and professors. Chapters in European legal history* (Cambridge, 1987), 20–6.

XVIII to de Gaulle's Fifth Republic can be traced back to the great
revolution of 1789 and its immediate aftermath. The following
components come to mind.

Monarchism was a nostalgic movement, harking back to the
Ancient Regime and rejecting the revolution and all its works. The
kings of France were seen as the architects of the country's greatness.
Their disappearance was linked to the decline of the nobility and the
Church, the ancient elites who might have kept modern egalitarianism
at bay. A strong government was required as a dam against the
abominated democracy and the political wheeler-dealers and as the
guarantor of France's historical role. Monarchic traditionalism,
wedded to conservatism and nationalism, easily became xenophobic
and anti-Semitic. The vitality of this current was not only apparent
under Louis XVIII, Charles X and Louis-Philippe, but also after the
fall of the Second Empire, when France 'provisionally' became a
republic again, while the monarchist majority waited for the two
pretenders to the throne to settle their quarrel (it was only when this
proved impossible that the country became a republic for good).
Even in the first half of the twentieth century the chauvinist–royalist
*Action française* of the agitator Charles Maurras (*d.*1952) was a force to
be reckoned with.

Republicanism was a movement that saw itself as the true heir of
the revolution, and particularly of the National Convention. It was
progressive and attached to equality and the secular state. It was
bourgeois and parliamentarian. It distrusted a strong executive and
throve on the indirect democracy of the political parties and the all
powerful parliament. Its politicians would have preferred to dispense
with a head of state altogether, but when this seemed impossible, they
were prepared to put up with a presidential figure-head who was no
threat to their combinations and arrangements. The Third Republic
(of which the Fourth was a revised version) was their golden age.

Bonapartism, like monarchism, valued a strong executive and
forceful rule, but it lacked the traditional legitimist anchor of
kingship. It committed personal rule to a military leader, a saviour of
the fatherland in times of internal or external crises. It was not based
on parliament and parties, but on popular trust and acclaim,
expressed by plebiscite or election. It was plebeian and akin to direct
democracy in ways that were lacking both in monarchism and
republicanism. Bonapartism, the French version of Caesarism, appeared
on the political scene with the First Consul, Napoleon Bonaparte, as

one of the numerous experiments in the void left by the fall of the ancient monarchy. It reappeared after the debacle of the Second Republic under Emperor Napoleon III. It surfaced briefly at the time of the failed coup (more precisely, the coup that was never even attempted) of General Boulanger in 1889, and gained another chance after the inglorious demise of the Third Republic in the summer of 1940, with Marshal Pétain, to many Frenchmen the heroic saviour of France, and with General de Gaulle, to many other Frenchmen the liberator of Paris in 1944. De Gaulle had, however, to wait until 1958 for a Constitution that suited his ideas and his personality. His aim was a regime that would put an end to the rule of lobbies, such as the famous *féodalité de la betterave* (the sugar lobby), and the political parties, which he liked to call 'the factions'.

Socialism stood for working-class interests and fought bourgeois capitalism. It wanted to break the power of property-owners and extend equality before the law to social and economic equality, wedding economic to political democracy. Some adherents of this current viewed the state as the enemy and were converted to anarchism, whereas others saw in the state the most adequate machine for the foundation of economic democracy against the dominant capitalist interests. As industrialization came slowly and late in France, the proletariat only became a real force in the twentieth century. In the nineteenth it had surfaced in the brief but violent revolts of 1848 and 1871, but in the last phase of the Third Republic it attained governmental status at the time of the Popular Front and managed to obtain modest social benefits, such as yearly paid holidays and a shorter working week.

As the years after 1789 were the starting point of so many threads in the political and constitutional development of modern France, they were also responsible for the sharp and often bitter conflicts of the nineteenth and twentieth centuries. All great antagonisms go back to those dramatic years, which witnessed such extreme and unpardonable steps as Louis XVI's execution, the Terror and the persecution of Christianity.

The antagonism between monarchists and republicans was deep seated. Old-style kingship fell in 1830 and its more liberal version was driven out in its turn in 1848, whereas the expected restoration in the 1870s never materialized. Hence the Third Republic was abominated by the monarchists, a common name for conservatives and clericals, who campaigned relentlessly against it. The salient moments were the

Dreyfus affair, with the resultant nationalist and anti-democratic agitation of the *Action française*, directed by Léon Daudet (*d.*1942). Charles Maurras (*d.*1952) and Jacques Bainville (*d.*1936), and the fascist leagues after the First World War, responsible for the bloody demonstration in front of the parliament building in February 1934, together with various forms of collaboration during the Second World War.

The republic was threatened by replays of the Brumaire scenario. Napoleon's nephew put an end to the Second Republic, and General Boulanger's followers, who shouted '*A l'Elysée*' on 27 January 1889, would have liked to do the same to the Third. But the regime survived until it committed hara-kiri on 10 July 1940 and gave Philippe Pétain, a hero of the First World War, full powers to save France.

The estrangement of the Catholics, which started with the *Constitution civile du clergé* and was completed under the Convention (but to some extent reversed by Napoleon's Concordat), at times assumed a painful and bitter character. On various occasions the antagonism was violent and bloody, as under the Commune of 1871, when the archbishop of Paris was killed. At other times it was more civilized and organized, as during the bouts of anti-clericalism under the Third Republic, which led to the expulsion of the religious orders and the rupture of diplomatic relations with the Vatican. Republican anticlericalism had two faces. On the one hand it was caused by a genuine fear of the Church as the symbol of the Ancient Regime and the focus of various conservative tendencies. On the other it was a lightning rod used by the ruling parties to divert attention from social and economic demands from the left, which threatened bourgeois interests and were shelved while public opinion got worked up about the dangers of religious obscurantism.[17]

Agitation by the French extreme left was only taken seriously at a later date. In 1871 the army of the provisional government had given the Commune short shrift, and the Popular Front government of Léon Blum in 1936–7 was a brief episode. The left was only given a real chance during and after the Second World War, when the communists, after Hitler invaded the Soviet Union, joined the resistance against the Germans in large numbers and became a political force of the first magnitude. After the war the left carried governmental responsibility, as the Fourth Republic was dominated

---

[17] The problem is placed in a wider chronological perspective in N. Ravitch, *The Catholic Church and the French nation 1589–1989* (London, 1990).

by three parties of comparable strength, the communists, the socialists and the Christian democrats of the Mouvement Républicain Populaire (MRP). Later, the 'cold war' and Gaullist successes pushed back the left, until its comeback under President Mitterrand.

The successive Constitutions which we shall now present can only be understood against the political background, as the reverberations of the great revolution were always near the surface. Not only did opposing tendencies hark back to ideas and interests of 1789, but French political discourse is till this day full of references to personalities, pronouncements and events of the 'great years'. Some later Constitutions were not much more than new editions of the achievements of the heroic age: the regime of Napoleon III, for example, was based on a revised version of the Constitution of the Year VIII.

### The 'Charte octroyée' of 1814

The Restoration monarchy which succeeded the Napoleonic regime was no replay of the absolute kingship of bygone centuries: the past was buried for good. Indeed, the anointed kingship of Louis XVIII was a constitutional monarchy, even though the Constitution of 1814 had been *octroyée*, i.e. benevolently 'granted' by his majesty to his subjects, and, from 1816 onwards, it was in fact also a parliamentary monarchy even though the cabinet ministers were, according to the letter of the text of 1814, only accountable in the criminal sense of the word (*pénalement responsables*). The Constitution of 1814 was influenced by Benjamin Constant's ideas, as expressed in his *Réflexions sur les constitutions* of 1814,[18] where the king was depicted as a *pouvoir neutre* vis-à-vis the three traditional powers. The main elements of the Constitution can be summarized as follows.

A first panel, entitled *Droits publics des Français*, contained a declaration of the rights and liberties of the citizens, such as equality before the law (which excluded a return to the old privileged estates), the rule *nullum crimen sine lege* (excluding criminal laws with retroactive effect), a guarantee of due process of law, freedom of religion (although somewhat reduced by the stipulation that 'the Roman-Catholic religion is the religion of the state'), the inviolability of

---

[18] The full title was *Réflexions sur les constitutions, la distribution des pouvoirs et les garanties d'une monarchie constitutionnelle*, i.e. 'Reflections on the Constitutions, the distribution of powers and the guarantees of a constitutional monarchy'. The author proposed a return to the Constitution of 1791, but with less restricted royal powers.

property rights (with a clause excluding any return of the revolutionary *biens nationaux* to their Ancient-Regime owners), and also a form of amnesty for revolutionary activities (though in fact numerous 'regicides' fled abroad for fear of the 'white terror').

Executive power was in the hands of the king and his ministers, whose responsibility, as we have seen, was changed in 1816 from a criminal (before law courts) to a political accountability (before parliament). This took place after the elections had produced an ultra-royalist majority which wanted to make sure that the government would follow an ultra-conservative course and therefore demanded that after the British model, 'the ministers and the king himself should obey the will of the parliamentary majority'. This request was accepted through an interpretation of Article 18 of the Constitution, which said that on every law there had to be a free debate and a free vote by the majority of each chamber.[19] These two chambers, which wielded legislative power together with the king, were the Chamber of the Peers, an imitation of the House of Lords, for which La Fayette had pleaded in vain twenty-five years before and whose members were appointed by the king mostly from the ranks of the Ancient-Regime or Napoleonic nobility, and the Chamber of Deputies, elected by such a severely restricted suffrage that only landowners had the vote. The government had the exclusive right to propose bills.

Towards the end of the reign of Charles X, who had succeeded Louis XVIII in 1824, the liberal opposition gained influence and, in June 1830, won the elections. The refusal of the king to accept their results and the publication of ordinances to curtail freedom led to the July Revolution of that year and the abdication of the monarch.

### The 'Charte constitutionnelle' of 1830

The successor of Charles X was the 'bourgeois king' Louis-Philippe d'Orléans, son of the progressive Duke Philip of Orléans, called 'Philippe Egalité', who had been a member of the Estates General of 1789. The Constitution of 1814 was little changed. It was, however, no longer a 'granted charter' but a 'constitutional charter', and the monarch was styled 'king of the French' instead of 'king of France'; royal anointment, a religious element of the coronation which was deemed to recall too strongly the Ancient Regime, was abolished. Far

---

[19] This stipulation was literally repeated in Article 16 of the Constitutional Charter of 14 August 1830.

from 'granting' a Constitution out of the fullness of his power, the king was himself formally subjected to a fundamental law proclaimed by the Chamber of Deputies.

The following minor differences between the Constitutions of 1814 and 1830 deserve to be mentioned. The king's authority to issue ordinances, provided by Article 14 of the Charter of 1814, was abolished, and so was his right to veto or suspend laws. Catholicism was only recognized as the religion of the majority of the French people, but not of the state, and censorship was forbidden forever. The spirit of the new-style monarchy was more secular, modern, liberal, bourgeois and parliamentarian (it provided for ministerial accountability to parliament). The French *Charte constitutionnelle* lasted only till 1848, but it was the main model for the Belgian Constitution of 1831, which was much praised and imitated by liberal fundamental laws in Europe and elsewhere.

### *The Second Republic, 1848–52*

The July monarchy lost its popularity because of the reactionary policy of Louis-Philippe's prime minister, the historian François Guizot (*d.*1874). Liberal discontent led to the February Revolution of 1848, which easily conquered Paris and led to the flight of the king. The republic was proclaimed and a provisional government formed, containing liberal republicans, called 'radicals' (among whom the author Lamartine), and socialists (among whom the historian Louis Blanc). This was the beginning of a short but most dramatic phase, which ended with the seizure of power by Napoleon III, who bitterly disappointed both the liberal-republican and the socialist-republican movements. Liberals and socialists in the provisional government were initially in agreement, notably about the principle of universal suffrage, which was proclaimed. But soon dissension was created by socialist demands, unacceptable to the liberals. The great difference with the July Revolution of 1830 was precisely the impact of a strong socialist movement, which followed theories of C.-H. de Saint-Simon (*d.*1825), P. J. Proudhon (*d.*1865) and C. Fourier (*d.*1837) and was supported by the industrial proletariat of Paris, a product of advancing capitalism. Social unrest at the end of February and on 17 March 1848 radicalized the revolution and led to the recognition of the right to work, the creation of the *Commission pour les travailleurs* ('workers' commission') and the organization of the *Ateliers nationaux* ('national workshops'), where the workers were supposed to run production with state help, but which turned out to be places where the unemployed were kept busy and paid wages from the public purse.

In April elections took place for a Constituent Assembly, by universal male suffrage – a lasting feature of French elections.[20] To the amazement of many revolutionaries the resulting Assembly was very conservative. France was still an agricultural land, and the peasants had voted conservative in a massive way. In the late eighteenth century they had eagerly joined the revolution, taking their revenge on their old masters and hoping to grab land, but in 1848 they rejected the Parisian clubs of radicals and their attacks on property: many farmers had become small proprietors and all had profited from the abolition of tithes and servile services which had turned them and their forebears into revolutionaries in 1789. Now they were content and had no time for intellectuals who preached socialism and the expropriation of the means of production. The behaviour of the peasant masses in twentieth-century Russia was comparable, as they also supported the Bolshevik Revolution in 1917, in the hope of land, but turned against the new regime when it took the land from them under collectivization. Disappointed progressives in France blamed the electoral disaster on the village priests, who were supposed to have influenced the faithful in a conservative sense, but they overlooked the fact that the same village clergy had failed to keep their faithful in hand in 1789, so that its influence could not have been the decisive factor.

How conservative the Constituent Assembly was became clear as soon as it went into action and rejected various social demands out of hand. A motion to recognize the right to work, for example, was supported by 72 out of almost 900 members, and a proposal for a progressive income tax was supported by 110. The result was a left-wing coup under Armand Barbès (*d*.1870) and Louis-Auguste Blanqui (*d*.1881), the latter being a defender of the dictatorship of the proletariat and a follower of Babeuf. The coup was repressed without difficulty by the army and the National Guard, a bourgeois citizen militia, and various social initiatives, such as the national workshops, were liquidated in June 1848. This led to an angry explosion in working class areas, where some 20,000 men barricaded themselves. The revolt was smashed in bloody street fighting on 24–26 June 1848

---

[20] The female vote, as we have seen, was introduced in 1944.

by General Cavaignac with units of the army and the National Guard, strengthened by volunteers from the provinces who had had enough of Paris and its radical clubs. It was a clear-cut example of class warfare, the urban middle class and the peasants (mostly smallholders) fighting the anarchists and the *partageux*, i.e. people who defended the sharing of property.

In December 1848 presidential elections were held, which were won easily by Louis-Napoleon Bonaparte, a nephew of Napoleon. Bonapartism had reappeared, and the next step was the coup d'état of December 1851, when the president dissolved the National Assembly, elected in 1849, and arrested more than 200 of its members. The crowning achievement was the proclamation in December 1852 of Napoleon III as emperor: the Second Empire had begun. Thus the paradoxical consequence of the revolution and the workers' revolts of 1848 was the restoration of the Napoleonic regime, in which the peasants embodied conservatism and the army sustained the new order.

The main characteristics of the ephemeral Constitution of 1848 were the following. The separation of powers was made complete. The legislature consisted of a single assembly of 750 members, directly elected by universal suffrage. Executive power was in the hands of the president of the republic, elected for a four-year term by universal suffrage: he had no right of veto.[21]

### The Second Empire, 1852–70

The political consequences of the events of 1848–52 were as important as their constitutional impact was insignificant. The Constitution of 1848 was short-lived, as we have seen, and the Constitution of Napoleon III, of January 1852, was, as could be expected, not much more than a revised version of the Constitution of the Year VIII, the legal basis of his uncle's regime. The president of the republic, elected for ten years, received almost unlimited power, and a two-chamber parliament was reintroduced. The Legislative Corps, elected by universal suffrage, was a democratic motor, but the Senate, whose members were appointed by the president, acted as a forceful brake. The legislature was further restricted by the provision that it could

---

[21] The French February Revolution of 1848 was the signal for a series of revolts that shook many thrones in Europe. One of the best analyses of these events can be found in the classic of Sir Lewis Namier, *1848. The revolution of the intellectuals*, reissued with a new introduction by J. Joll (Oxford, 1992).

only accept or reject proposals worked out by the Council of State, whose members were appointed by the president, to whom cabinet ministers were also accountable.

At the proclamation of the empire, the Constitution of January 1852 was adapted to the new situation by the replacement of the title of president by that of emperor. The new regime was widely accepted, as appeared from the plebiscite where the new emperor received almost 8 million yes-votes, against about half a million no-votes. Popular Caesarism had proved its vitality. Once again the pendulum had swung between parliament and autocracy. The political consequences of 1848–52 were momentous, as the irreconcilable opposition between right and left led to bitter hatred. Leading republicans went into exile and Napoleon III's rule was repressive, numerous freedoms being abolished and the opposition harassed. The émigrés of the Second Empire bode their time and dreamt of revenge. They eventually got their chance, not because of the minor measures of liberalization in the 1860s but because of the military catastrophe in the French–German war of 1870 and the flight of the emperor.

## The Third and Fourth Republics, 1870–1958

One gains the impression that modern France, after much turbulence and experimentation, found stability at last in the regime of the Third Republic. Its most striking feature, at first sight, is its longevity by French standards: it lasted from 1870 till 1940 and, if one considers the Fourth Republic as a revised version of the Third, even till 1958. That is almost a century. The republic witnessed some critical moments, such as the episodes with Boulanger and the fascist leagues, but they were easily overcome. The crisis of 1940 was of the utmost gravity, but even then the system of the Third Republic – if not its Constitution – survived, as the Fourth Republic was basically the continuation of the Third. It was not until the Fifth Republic and the introduction of a presidential regime that French constitutional law took a new turn.

In 1875 the Third Republic said farewell to monarchy and Caesarism but also, and very markedly (as the repression of the Commune of Paris showed), to social radicalism. The republic was parliamentary, bourgeois and secular. Its party-political orientation was evident in the strong position of the legislature and the weakness of the president, a mere symbolic head of state and certainly no policy-maker; it also manifested itself in the unending succession of cabinets which were put on stage and sent packing again by the play of changing parliamentary majorities, as puppets in a Punch and Judy show. Its bourgeois character explains its attachment to economic liberalism and weak social consciousness. Its secularism led to religious indifference and occasionally to anti-religious animosity. The regime clearly suited society at large, as France was a nation of traditional and individualistic middle class town dwellers and peasants, keen on material gain and wary both of backward looking obscurantism and social and economic adventurism. These fundamental realities and the able national bureaucracy were the stable elements that kept the ship of state on an even keel and made possible the building of a large colonial empire; they also allowed France and the republic victoriously to survive the terrible ordeal of the First World War. In contrast to the political dramas in the years 1870–1958, the constitutional developments have been uneventful and the harvest of texts is meagre. In fact there are only two worth mentioning here, the Constitution of 1875, which was not a real Constitution but a set of three *lois constitutionnelles*, and the Constitution of the Fourth Republic of 1946.

The surrender of Napoleon III at Sedan, in September 1870, had immediate repercussions on the home front: the Paris mob demanded a republic, power was up for grabs. Two groups made a bid, the moderate and the revolutionary republicans, the latter marching behind the red flag. The moderates formed a Provisional Government of National Defence, containing Parisian republican members of the Legislative Corps and headed by the military governor of Paris. The provisional government proclaimed the republic and easily outflanked the extremists, who would return to the scene with a vengeance at the Commune of Paris the following year. The provisional government, which was also continuing the war against Germany, aimed at founding a stable regime at home. Elections were organized, which gave the conservative monarchists a clear lead. That in spite of this no restoration of the monarchy ensued was due to the uncompromising attitude of two pretenders and their followers: the legitimists, who marched behind the banner of the Count of Chambord, a grandson of Charles X, and the Orleanists, who adhered to the Count of Paris, a grandson of Louis-Philippe. Finally, after years of hesitation the (considerable) minority of republicans gained the upper hand and, to get out of the impasse, the republican regime was introduced in 1875, with a majority of one vote in the Assembly.

In the meantime, on 18 March 1871, the Paris Commune, a local left-wing revolt, anti-religious, Jacobin and proletarian had started. It was aimed against the conservative national government, which had appointed the historian Adolphe Thiers (*d.*1877) as *chef du pouvoir exécutif*, and resided at Versailles. The moderate republican regime suppressed the Commune *manu militari*, thus winning conservative support, and eventually the republican Constitution of 1875 was accepted as a lasting point of equilibrium. It consisted, as we said, of three 'constitutional laws', of 24 and 25 February and 16 July 1875, concerning respectively the Senate, the powers in the state, and their mutual relations. Paradoxically the French regime that lasted longest was based on the briefest legal texts, as if people remembered Napoleon's saying that the best Constitutions were 'short and obscure'. The main elements of the Constitution of the Third Republic were the following.

The head of state, the president of the republic, was elected for a term of seven years, not by the people, but by the two chambers of the legislature, which straight away highlighted the parliamentary character of the regime. The president, a sort of republican constitutional monarch, was inviolable and considered above party strife. The cabinet ministers, by contrast, were accountable, not to the president but to parliament. Consequently the legislative chambers – i.e. the capricious and changing party coalitions – always had the governments under control and could topple them with the greatest of ease (no constructive proposal for a replacement being required). This, together with the absence of a two-party system after the British or American models, led to the notorious instability of the governments of the Third Republic and, for that matter, of the Fourth (which counted twenty-one cabinets between 1947 and 1958).

Parliament was bicameral, with a Chamber of Deputies, elected by universal suffrage, and a Senate, elected since 1884 by the departmental councils – one more example of the role of the local notables (and comparable to the initial election of the United States Senate). Although there existed, generally speaking, a dichotomy in parliament – and in the country – between *la droite* and *la gauche*,[22] no two-party system, with one party grouping the left and the other the right, ever developed. French parties and mini-parties were too numerous and

---

[22] 'Right' and 'left' are notions which are indispensable in modern political history, even though their definition is extremely difficult. See the remarks in D. Caute, *The left in Europe since 1789* (London, 1966), 8–25.

divided for that, and it is even doubtful whether some of these 'parties' (particularly on the right) deserve that name, as they lacked even a minimum of party discipline and organization. Thus the 'radicals' (i.e. liberals) were split into doctrinaire, opportunist and progressive wings, whereas one section of their left formed, in 1893, the radical-socialist group, which for some time voted with the socialists. Among the latter also there was dissension. The Parti Ouvrier Français ('French Workers' Party'), founded in 1880, was more akin to Proudhon than Marx, but after it had won some fifty seats in parliament in 1893, it decided to adopt Marxism as its doctrine in 1895–6. Nevertheless there arose two socialist parties, one moderate and the other strictly Marxist and revolutionary, until Jean Jaurès (*d.*1914) managed to unite them in the Section Française de l'Internationale Ouvrière (SFIO), which was destined to a role of some importance between the World Wars and under the Fourth Republic. A communist party was founded shortly after the First World War, and a Christian-democrat party after the Second, with the foundation of the Mouvement Républicain Populaire (MRP), which we mentioned before. It is remarkable that France, where conservative opinion was influential, never gave birth to specifically Catholic parties, as happened in Germany, the Netherlands and Belgium.

In spite of various 'scandals', created by politicians' involvement with financial interests, and several 'affairs', caused by anti-Semitism and veneration for the military establishment, the Third Republic held out well until 1940, when it fell, like other regimes in the past, in the wake of a military disaster, i.e. the collapse of the French army and the armistice with the Germans, who already occupied a large part of the country. Legally speaking the regime was dissolved by a combined assembly of the senators and deputies which, in July 1940, at Vichy (in unoccupied France), gave a mandate to draft a new Constitution to Marshal Philippe Pétain, a hero of the First World War who had been placed at the head of the state in the vain hope of averting military defeat. The marshal was told that the new regime had to uphold the traditional values of *travail, famille et patrie* ('labour, family and fatherland'). The abolition of the Constitution of the Third Republic was implied in the mandate to draft a new one (which never materialized, although Pétain put some desultory work into it, and a few fragments were drafted). The constitutional law, which was passed on 10 July 1940 by a great majority and after an animated debate, contained a single article: 'The National Assembly gives full power to the government of the Republic, under the authority and signature of Marshal Pétain, in order to promulgate, by one or several acts, a new Constitution of the French state. This Constitution shall guarantee the rights of labour, the family and the fatherland. It will be ratified by the nation and applied by the Assemblies which it will have created'.[23] The first use which Pétain, as soon as 11 July 1940, made of his full powers was to abrogate the essential elements of the Constitution of 1875, by issuing his *Actes constitutionnels* nos. 1, 2 and 3. The legislative chambers were 'adjourned until further notice' and the new leader issued the proclamation: 'We, Philippe Pétain, Marshal of France, declare that we assume the functions of head of the French state'.[24] With the disappearance of the function of the president of the republic, the republic itself had been liquidated.

The 'head of the French state' assumed all executive and legislative powers until the new Constitution created the new Assemblies. It is noteworthy that in its gravest hour the Third Republic could think of nothing better than to recall an 84-year-old marshal, a hero of the previous war, to take over the ship of state. The republican Constitution had taken care to create an office of president without real influence, but in addition the politicians had systematically elected insignificant candidates, who could under no circumstances develop into new Napoleons. A weak executive, headed by weaklings, had led to a state of affairs where only a grey-haired marshal could be thought of to save the fatherland.[25]

At the liberation of France in 1944 a provisional government was formed under the leadership of General de Gaulle, who had worked with the allies against Germany during the war. De Gaulle and many members of the Resistance movement had conceived great hopes of a post-war France that would be rejuvenated and socially oriented. Various grandiose plans were launched, only to get stranded on ingrained habits. The disappointed de Gaulle left the political arena because his request for a strong government and a presidential regime

[23] See on the momentous events of 10 July 1940 the detailed work of E. Bcrl, *La fin de la IIIe République* (Paris, 1968). The constitutional law of that day was passed by 569 against 80 votes.

[24] The term head of the French state (and not president of the French Republic) is significant. It was presumably borrowed from the style of General Franco, *Jefe del Estado*; Pétain had been French ambassador in Madrid.

[25] For a classic survey of Pétain's regime, see R. O. Paxton, *Vichy France. Old guard and new order, 1940–1944* (New York, 1982).

was refused (a similar return to pre-war patterns was observed in other countries, where plans for a renovation of political life floundered). The communists could not stay in the government because of the cold war, so that the path was open for an unobtrusive return to the regime of the centre parties, which in those days were the socialists and the Christian democrats. The consequences for the Constitution can be described as follows.

From August 1944 till the referendum and the elections of October 1945 de Gaulle ruled in a way that has been called 'presidential and even authoritarian, rather than parliamentary'. The referendum of October 1945 put the choice before the country between the old – and universally condemned – Third Republic and a new Constitution for the Fourth, which would be drafted by a Constituent Assembly elected by the people. At the same time the country was to decide whether the new regime, if the old was rejected, would be based on an omnipotent or a limited assembly. It was the old alternative again between a strong or weak popular representation and a strong or weak executive. De Gaulle militated for a limited legislature, the communists against. The result of the referendum reflected popular disgust with the regime of the Third Republic, already deceased in 1940, for 96.4 per cent of the electors rejected it. This result had been expected, but that on the assembly came as a surprise: a clear majority of 65 per cent rejected the idea of an almighty assembly – a vote of confidence in de Gaulle and his plan for a strong executive. The parliamentary elections, held at the same time (and in which women had the vote), led to a Constituent Assembly where the major formation of the Third Republic, the radicals, was reduced to a relic of the past (with 28 seats), whereas three great parties shared victory, the communists with 152, the MRP with 150 and the SFIO with 143 seats.

The deliberations in the Constituent Assembly led in October 1946 to the proclamation of the Constitution of the Fourth Republic. Its elaboration had not been smooth, particularly since the Constituent Assembly followed a path not approved by de Gaulle, whom it had elected president of the republic in November 1945. He wanted a presidential regime, with a strong and stable cabinet, whereas the Assembly preferred an omnipotent parliament where the political parties ruled the roost. The conflict between president and Assembly was so acute that de Gaulle resigned at the beginning of 1946. The Assembly carried on, and the constitutional project was soon ready to be put before the country in a referendum. It provided for a unicameral parliament and left the election of the prime minister styled 'president of the Council of Ministers' to the National Assembly, which also elected the president of the republic (who was given a representative role). The spirit of the Constitution was clearly favourable to the Assembly and averse to an independent and strong cabinet and president. The project was narrowly defeated in the referendum of May 1946; it had been opposed by the MRP during discussions in the Assembly and was suspected by many as opening the gates to a totalitarian take-over by the left. Communist propaganda in its favour had created the impression that a vote for the projected Constitution was a vote for the communists.[26] The negative outcome of the referendum led to new elections in June 1946, but the resulting Constituent Assembly resembled its predecessor very closely and the same parties resumed the same talks. The predictable result was a slightly revised version of the rejected text of May. In the meantime de Gaulle had thrown himself into the battle for the Constitution, advocating a strong state and a *chef de l'Etat dûment et fortement armé* ('a head of state appropriately and strongly armed'). Who that strong head of state was meant to be was clear to everyone, including the politicians in parliament, who abominated the very idea of a 'strong man'. It was obvious that they were not going to change the project according to the wishes of de Gaulle, whose appeal was rejected outright by socialists and communists. The new text was subjected to a referendum in October 1946 and accepted, in spite of de Gaulle's warnings against the dangers of 'the parties disposing of all powers in the republic, directly, arbitrarily and without any checks'. There were (in round figures) 36 per cent yes-votes, 31 per cent no-votes and 31 per cent abstentions. It was a very weak popular majority, in sharp contrast with the massive majority for the project in parliament. Although the Constitution of the Fourth Republic of 27 October 1946 resembled closely that of the Third and lasted only a short time, it was not without some interest. We draw attention to the following points.

The Constitution adopted right from the start the leftist tone: 'France is an indivisible, secular, democratic and social republic'. It

[26] A comparable situation arose in France in the summer of 1992 when a referendum on the Maastricht Treaty on European Unification of 1991 was called. As President Mitterrand was strongly in favour of Maastricht, a vote against the treaty was felt by many to be a vote against the president and his government, although the real issue was totally different.

broke with the tradition of the older fundamental laws, which were almost exclusively concerned with the rights of the individual and strictly political matters, for it paid great attention to social and economic issues. Thus every enterprise which 'was in the nature of a national public service or enjoyed a factual monopoly was to become the property of the collectivity', a legitimation a posteriori of a series of nationalizations (coal, gas, electricity, banking and insurance, Renault, Air France). Article 25 announced a national plan for the economy, in order to ensure 'full employment and the rational use of material resources'. The Constitution declared that everyone had both the duty and the right to work, was free to join the trade union of his choice and to take part 'through the intermediary of his delegate' in the collective determination of the conditions of work and the policy of the enterprises. It also declared that it was the duty of the state to organize public education which was 'gratis and secular at all levels' – no mention was made of the free choice of education, a controversial question because it concerned possible state subsidies for free, mainly Catholic schools.

In the Constitution of 1946 the legislature ruled supreme. The legislative power was essentially in the hands of the Chamber of Deputies, which gave the regime the name of the 'republic of the deputies'. That Chamber alone carried the prestigious name of National Assembly, which used to be reserved for a common meeting of both the Chamber and the Senate. There was, however, a second chamber, not called Senate (because of conservative connotations), but Council of the Republic. Assembly and Council together constituted the Parliament of the Republic. The Council's role was real, but subordinate and 'reflective', even though on certain matters its advice was obligatory, but the Assembly had the last word '*définitivement et souverainement*'. The old Senate, where so many bills had died an inglorious death, was in its turn ingloriously sent to the museum of institutions. The Assembly was not only a legislative body, but also the real source of executive power, as appears from an analysis of the role of the president. The Constituent Assembly, though pretending to desire greater governmental stability, did not want to realize it through a presidential regime, which was associated or confused with personal rule. The idea was to obtain better results not by strengthening the position of the head of state but of the head of the government. Hence the prerogatives of the president of the Fourth Republic were little different from those of his predecessor and, just as in the Third

Republic, he was elected by parliament and not by the people. The leader of the government, called president of the Council (of Ministers), was appointed by the president of the republic at the beginning of each legislature and had to receive the confidence of the Assembly, whereupon he formed his cabinet. The prime minister, unknown by that name in the Constitution of 1875, was made the central figure in 1946, and expected to provide stability and efficiency (the event of a 'governmental crisis' was dealt with extensively in the Constitution).

All these fine intentions came to nothing. The omnipotence of the parties, constitutionally expressed in the Assembly, saddled France between 1946 and 1958 with an unstable regime and so many cabinet changes that the Fourth Republic was constantly in a state of latent or open crisis. The inglorious end came in 1958, with de Gaulle's Fifth Republic, which we will briefly touch upon in chapter 9.

### GERMANY FROM NAPOLEON TO WILHELM II

#### *Introductory remarks*

German constitutional development in the nineteenth century was unusually varied and dramatic, because the country was confronted with several fundamental problems at once. There was the struggle of the middle class for a liberal state, based on a Constitution and a parliament. This went hand in hand with efforts aimed at the unification of Germany, and the much debated problem whether it should be a 'little' or a 'greater' German unification[27] and what form of government the new Germany should have, unitary or federal. Another question concerned the role of the reunited Germany in Europe and the world, for even 'little' Germany would be a political and economic giant. In the course of one century Germany, which beat the French army in 1870, became a major power which not only caused the fall of the Second Empire in France, but developed global ambitions, as expressed by the term *Weltpolitik*. The crucial question in internal constitutional terms concerned the relations between monarchy and parliament, as was shown in all its sharpness in Prussia in the 1860s, when the crown felt entitled to raise revenue without the consent of parliament. While all this was going on, the old latent

---

[27] *Grossdeutsch* or great-German unification would have encompassed all ethnic Germans, including the Austrians; *kleindeutsch* or little-German unification left Austria out.

tension between Church and state became virulent and led under Bismarck to the *Kulturkampf*: in true enlightened-absolutism style the chancellor wanted to integrate the Catholic Church into the new empire, but met stiff opposition from the German Catholics and the Roman curia. To top it all, the spectacular industrialization of Germany and economic liberalism led to proletarian protest and the rise of a powerful social-democratic party. The establishment, again headed by Bismarck, tried to stem the tide with prohibitions of various sorts, but could not prevent the social-democrats from becoming even before the First World War the strongest party in the Reichstag.

What a perplexing imbroglio when compared with nineteenth-century Britain, where most such problems had been solved long ago. There national unity went back to the early Middle Ages, modern Church – state relations went back to Henry VIII, the struggle between crown and Parliament had been settled in Cromwell's day, and under Queen Victoria Britain was so used to world hegemony that hardly anyone questioned or even discussed it. Politically speaking labour problems were not acute yet, as before the First World War the Labour Party was of no consequence in Parliament; the only burning issue (except for the eternal Irish Question) was the modernization of Parliament and the franchise which, as we have seen, was solved gradually and peacefully.

We shall now present the public law which developed from the melting pot of nineteenth-century Germany.

### The period of the Vormärz

The period between Napoleonic rule and the revolution of 1848 is known as the *Vormärz* (literally before March, the month when revolution broke out in Germany) and was marked by hesitant moves towards German unification and the predominance of conservatism: it was the era of Metternich and the *Sainte Alliance* of the crowned heads of Russia, Prussia and Austria. The collapse of French hegemony in 1814–15 created a void which left all possibilities open. Germany could return to the Ancient Regime and total division, as in the days of the Holy Roman Empire, but a united German state, after the British or French mode, was also conceivable. In internal politics also one could turn the clock back and restore royal absolutism, or alternatively introduce a liberal form of government, marked by

Constitutions and parliaments. Public opinion ardently desired to live in a united and liberal Germany, but the major powers decided otherwise.

In June 1815 no single German state, but a German Bund ('Confederation') was created. This was no mere return to the old *Kleinstaaterei*, as the number of states was cut drastically: the great shake-up under Napoleon had not been in vain. After the Congress of Vienna, which concerned itself with German as well as European problems, only forty-one German states, all monarchies, except for the four urban republics of Hamburg, Bremen, Lübeck and Frankfurt, survived; among them there were one empire and five kingdoms. Although a confederation, not a federal state, the German Bund was more solidly organized than the old Reich. There was a Bundestag, residing at Frankfurt and chaired by the Austrian emperor, where delegates of the sovereign member states, appointed by their respective governments, met. Its main task was to guard the independence and integrity of the members' territories and the security of the whole of Germany (as Article 11 of the Constitution of the German Confederation excluded war between member states, the Prussian–Austrian war of 1866 signified the end of the Bund). The most tangible step towards German unity during that period was the *Zollverein* ('customs union'), which became effective on 1 January 1834 and turned seventeen states with a total population of 23 million into a common market (other states joined later, Austria doing so after its defeat in 1866: the *Zollverein* was terminated at the unification of Germany in 1871).

The liberal dream was not fulfilled. In Prussia and Austria absolute monarchy was restored, as there was not even a Constitution, and nowhere was a parliamentary regime introduced. Nevertheless, some progress was made, for in southern Germany a few constitutional monarchies were established, where the crown (which was not disputed) was limited by the norms of a fundamental law. This took place mostly through the 'granting' of a Constitution, after the model of the *Charte constitutionnelle* of Louis XVIII, considered as a happy *via media* between the extremes of absolutism and republicanism. Before 1830, in the era of 'early constitutionalism', written Constitutions were proclaimed, *inter alia*, in Nassau (the earliest of the series, dating from 1814), Bavaria, Württemberg and Baden. After the Parisian July Revolution of 1830 had caused some panic, other states followed, such as Saxony and Hanover. The five main constitutional monarchies in southern Germany, Bavaria, Württemberg, Baden, Hesse-Darmstadt and Nassau, formed a solid moderately progressive block, which could boast of bicameral representations of the people, with a first chamber of noblemen, bishops and notables appointed by the ruler, and a second that basically spoke for the bourgeoisie, even though it often contained some representatives of the nobility as well.

### The revolution of 1848 and its consequence

The example of the February Revolution in Paris was followed in several Central European countries. In Germany the liberal revolt aimed at unification and a liberal Constitution. It was almost purely bourgeois, which is not surprising if one considers that only 4.5 per cent of the population were factory workers. Its culminating point came with the parliament of Frankfurt, which gathered on 18 May 1848 in the Church of St Paul and proclaimed itself (following French inspiration even in the choice of words) the *Deutsche Verfassungsgebende Nationalversammlung* ('German Constituent National Assembly'). It contained 830 members, elected by the people in their respective states. Over 33 per cent were clerics or professional people, almost 40 per cent were higher civil servants or judges, whereas 0.49 per cent of the total came from the ranks of the manual workers. The 'revolutionaries' were in many ways marked by a deep latent conservatism, and remind one of Lenin's quip that when Germans decided to storm a railway station, they first bought platform tickets. They showed their attachment to the monarchy by first electing Archduke Johann of Austria, son of Emperor Leopold II, as *Reichsverweser* ('Reich Regent'), and in 1849 offering the German imperial crown to the king of Prussia, who declined to accept it from the hands of a popular assembly. Although the liberal dream of 1848 quickly vanished and the revolution was repressed in the following year, some ephemeral constitutional texts were drafted that influenced later developments in Germany and Austria. On 27 December 1848 the Frankfurt parliament proclaimed the *Grundrechte des deutschen Volkes* ('fundamental rights of the German people'), followed on 28 March 1849 by the Constitution, called *Reichsverfassung*, which was intended to turn Germany into a federal state and a constitutional monarchy. It provided, after the American model, for a two-chamber system, consisting of a Staatenhaus, with representatives of the states of the Union, and a Volkshaus, with representatives of the German people, elected by universal suffrage and a secret ballot. The Constitution went under with the revolution, but has had some influence on the public law of the twentieth century.[28]

At the moment of the proclamation of the Constitution of 1849 the revolution in the German states had already collapsed, and the king of Prussia and the emperor of Austria had diminished its impact by issuing Constitutions of their own. In Prussia this was done in December 1848, turning that country into a constitutional kingdom, but without recognition of popular sovereignty. In Austria, where Emperor Ferdinand had abdicated in December 1848 in favour of his nephew Francis Joseph, a Constitution was granted in March 1849, subjecting imperial legislation to the agreement of the Reichsrat – not a momentous step, as its members were appointed by the emperor.

The old monarchies soon reasserted themselves. An imperial letter patent of 31 December 1851 abolished the Austrian Constitution of March 1849, turning the empire again into an absolute monarchy. Prussia, which at that time was more progressive and only became arch-conservative in the second half of the century, did not go so far, as the Constitution of December 1848 was maintained and the kingdom consequently remained a *Verfassungsstaat*, a constitutional monarchy. The fundamental law of 1848 provided for a bicameral system with elected representatives in both chambers and a franchise that came to be considered too liberal and democratic, so that in May 1849 the king introduced, by way of an emergency measure, an involved plutocratic system known as the *Dreiklassenwahlrecht*, or three-class franchise. Its basic notion was that citizens who financially contributed most to the state should have the greatest say in its administration. This Prussian – not German – system was maintained until 1918 and based on indirect elections. It took the roll of tax-payers as the basis for the indication of bodies of electors. The highest taxpayers, who together accounted for one-third of the contributions in their circumscription, formed the first class, the next group, again accounting for one-third, formed the second class, and the rest formed the third. Each class indicated an equal number of electors, which resulted, for example, in 150,000 members of the first class choosing the same number of electors as 2.5 million of the third class: in other words 4.7 per cent of the citizens of the first class chose as many electors as 82.7 per cent of the third class (example taken from the year 1850). To present-day thinking the result was a grotesque

---

[28] See the classic study by F. Eyck, *The Frankfurt parliament* (London, 1968), translated as *Deutschlands grosse Hoffnung. Die Frankfurter Nationalversammlung 1848–1849* (Munich, 1973).

over-representation of the wealthy, all the more so if one realizes that the law of 1849 excluded all those on relief.

The composition of the first chamber was also tampered with: according to the 'revised Constitution' of 1850 only half its members were elected, the others were of noble birth or appointed. This measure was never put into practice, and in 1854 another change was carried out in the composition of the first chamber, called Herrenhaus ('House of Lords') since 1855: henceforth it would consist of hereditary members, plus a few members ex officio and some appointed for life by the king. Corporatist considerations played a role in the selection of this third group, as it contained members of important chapters, universities, cities and associations of landowners. In spite of various cosmetic adaptations, Prussia after 1848 was and remained a constitutional monarchy, where the traditional rights of the citizens were recognized – as were their duties, which were taken most seriously in matters of defence. Prussia, however, was no parliamentary monarchy in the sense of parliament being able to bring down the government. Nevertheless the king, in true medieval style, depended on the subsidies voted by the representatives of the country, more specifically the second chamber, the Haus der Abgeordneten ('House of Deputies').

In the 1860s a conflict broke out between the House of Deputies and the royal government. The conflict was like a leaf taken from the medieval history books, as the representatives of the people refused the credits demanded by the king and deemed indispensable for his policy and the national interest.[29] King Wilhelm I riposted by dissolving the House, but the new House resulting from the elections remained adamant. This cat and mouse game was repeated several times, until the king threatened to abdicate, which would have plunged the country into a deep crisis. It was the prime minister Otto von Bismarck, the later chancellor of the empire, who came up with a solution, making use of the *Lückentheorie* ('theory of the gap (in the Constitution)'). It alleged that, as Article 99 of the Constitution made no provision in case of parliamentary refusal to vote the yearly budget, this power gap, or void, had to be filled by the royal prerogative, allowing the state to function without the agreement of the elected assembly. It was no more than a legal fiction, but was accepted and allowed the crown for several years to raise revenue

---

[29] It should be realized that all this happened before the proclamation of the empire, so that it was a purely Prussian business.

without parliamentary consent and without seeming to violate the fundamental law. The Prussian monarchy, so the theory went, continued to possess all prerogative rights which had not been taken away by the Constitution or later laws. Thus the king simply continued to levy taxes without budget laws, until parliament gave in and the situation was normalized.

In the meantime Bismarck was involved with a more grandiose enterprise, the little-German unification under Prussian leadership: Austria had to disappear from the German scene and devote itself entirely to the Habsburg multinational, and German military success would prepare the path for a German empire, with Bismarck at the helm. His plan was realized by the Austrian defeat of 1866 in a short war with Prussia, and Napoleon III's defeat in 1870 in an equally short war with Germany,[30] followed in January 1871 by the proclamation of King Wilhelm I of Prussia as German emperor at Versailles, then under German occupation. The new empire only concerned Germany. Austria (which was previously part of the Reich) had disappeared in 1866 from the German constitutional scene and, as we have seen, put an end to the German Confederation. The short-lived North German Confederation (1866–70), which lasted till the foundation of the Second Reich, was a transitional construction between the German Confederation and the German empire.

The political organization of Austria, which in 1861 had at last and for good become a constitutional monarchy, quickly felt the consequence of its elimination from the German Confederation. As the Habsburgs were now on their own in their heterogeneous empire, they proceeded in 1867 to the historic *Ausgleich* ('Compromise') with Hungary. After the Hungarian revolt of 1848–9 (put down with Russian help) this ancient kingdom, under Habsburg rule since the sixteenth century, fell victim to imperial unification and simply became part of Austria. This policy was now reversed through a rare constitutional move, the separation of a unitary state into two autonomous parts, the empire of Austria and the kingdom of Hungary – a sort of 'federalism with two'. Both countries remained united through their common ruler, Francis Joseph, who was both emperor and king, but each had its own government, parliament and capital. The new construction was known as the Dual Monarchy and distinguished common affairs,

[30] Napoleon III was beaten by the North German Confederation, which had replaced the German Confederation and with which the southern Germans had concluded a military alliance.

called *kaiserlich und königlich,* from specifically Austrian or Hungarian business.[31] This bipartite arrangement was a success as far as Austro-Hungarian relations were concerned, but did not solve the nationality problem of the Danubian monarchy as a whole, since many other ethnic groups lived under the sceptre of Francis Joseph. The *Ausgleich* of 1867 was not followed by comparable arrangements – for Czechs and Germans, for example – and plans for a confederation of nation states under the House of Habsburg did not go beyond the discussion level. In the end the First World War caused the fall of the monarchy, where (in 1910) 12 million Germans, 10 million Hungarians and Slovaks, 6 million Czechs, 5 million Poles, 4 million Ruthenians, 3 million Romanians, 3 million Croats, 2 million Serbs, 1 million Slovenes and 800,000 Italians had lived together under one imperial sceptre.

### The Second German Empire (1871–1918)

On 18 January 1871, Bismarck's dream of a little-German unification came true, and King Wilhelm I of Prussia was proclaimed German emperor. The unification was far from radical and did not abolish existing kingdoms and principalities. Even the much debated new title was meant to make this clear: not 'emperor of Germany' (to which the other princes objected), but 'German emperor'.

We shall study the development of constitutional law on two levels, that of the relations between the new Reich and the old states, and that of the internal organization of Wilhelminian Germany. Expressions such as 'German unification' and 'the German empire' can easily be

---

[31] The following elements remained common: the monarch, foreign affairs, the army (with some reservations) and the finances concerning the common affairs, for which one common ministry was provided and whose expenses were to be borne 70% by Austria and 30% by Hungary. The two parliaments kept contact through delegates, the Hungarians being adamant against one central parliament. Some federal states arose from existing bases: the Seven Provinces existed before the Dutch Republic, and so did the Swiss cantons and cities and the thirteen American colonies. Other federal countries originated by the division of previously unitary states. Thus Brazil was a unitary empire till 1889, later becoming a federal republic with, at present, twenty-two states. The post-World War I kingdom of Yugoslavia was, according to the Constitution of 1921, a unitary state, dominated by the Serbs, but the Constitution of 1946 introduced the federal form, with six republics. After the unitarism of the Nazi era Germany went back to a federal form of government. In 1917–18 the unitary Russian empire became a federation of soviet socialist republics. Canada, which was a unitary British colony (Union Act of 1840), started experimenting with federalism as early as 1867 and eventually became a federal state, where the ten provinces have their own Constitutions and parliaments. Belgium, which was founded in 1830–1 as a unitary kingdom, has recently introduced a federal organization.

misleading, as they suggest a greater degree of unity than was in fact established in 1871. Numerous and important matters admittedly came under the authority of the emperor, chancellor and Reichstag: external relations, defence, currency (Reichsmark, Reichsbank); also the empire was a common market and, in course of time, came to live under unified codes of law. There remained nevertheless four kingdoms (Saxony, Bavaria, Württemberg and Prussia), six grand duchies, five duchies, seven princedoms and three free cities, all with their own rulers, governments and parliaments elected by different systems of suffrage. The Constitution stated that the empire was a federal state, and it might indeed have been better called the United States of Germany, as the analogy with America was unmistakable. Germany was nevertheless in many respects a case sui generis, *inter alia*, because, in contrast with America, one of the German states – the kingdom of Prussia – occupied a privileged position. It was not only exceptionally large and densely populated, but its king was also German emperor and its prime minister almost invariably chancellor of the Reich. Looking for a comparable situation in a federal state, one could point at the Republic of the United Netherlands and Holland's predominance.

The unification of 1871, which maintained the existing states while creating an overriding structure with a parliament and a bureaucracy of its own, can be compared with the European Community of our own time. In both cases the existing states and their institutions were maintained, but higher common organs placed above them, the Reichsgericht being comparable to the European Court of Justice, the Reichstag to the European Parliament and the Reich chancellor and his government to the European Commission. There are, of course, some interesting differences. The unification of all European legal systems is hardly conceivable. The Commission is a college of civil servants (heading an administration of some 10,000 officials) and is appointed by the national governments, whereas the imperial cabinet depended on the emperor, through the chancellor. Also, the European Parliament, in contrast with the Wilhelminian Reichstag, is no legislator and has little power: the Parliament can, as we have seen, force the Commission to resign, whereas the Reichstag could not topple the chancellor, but his power of the parliament is theoretical, and the imperial government, as we shall see, had to take the wishes of the Reichstag more seriously than the Commission those of the Parliament in Strasbourg.

The new empire was a constitutional monarchy: one of its first laws was the Constitution of 20 April 1871, called *Gesetz betreffend die Verfassung des deutschen Reiches* ('law concerning the Constitution of the German empire'), which was a revised version of the Constitution of the North German Confederation. Its principles were old-fashioned and fundamentally monarchic. The German emperor was an invaluable element of cohesion and deemed necessary to embody the newly found unity of a country where ordinary people were inclined to think and act first and foremost as Prussians or Bavarians. In this light one understands why Germany, although a constitutional monarchy, was not, strictly speaking, a parliamentary one. The possibility had not even been broached, Bismarck for one being adamant, as a convinced monarchist, that the Constitution had been a sufficient concession to democracy.

The government was headed by the chancellor and consisted properly speaking of *Reichsämter*, or imperial offices, directed by *Staatssekretäre*, or secretaries of state, depending on him. The chancellor was not accountable to the Reichstag, but to the emperor, who freely appointed and dismissed him. This happened on a famous and dramatic occasion, with the abrupt dismissal, in 1890, of the *éminence grise* of German and European politics, Bismarck, by the young Emperor Wilhelm II.[32] However, the emperor was far from almighty, and in reality there arose a situation which could be called crypto-parliamentarian, as the government had to ask parliament for the necessary finances for its policies, so that discussion and give and take between the chancellor and the Reichstag were the order of the day – a situation not unlike the relations between the White House and Capitol Hill in Washington, as described above. The changing majorities in parliament, which controlled the budget, definitely influenced the country's politics, and the chancellor had to take into account both the will of his imperial master and the feeling in the elected assembly. The emperor himself had (except in the extreme case of dismissal) to listen to his chancellor, who was an essential intermediary between crown and parliament and whose signature was needed for all imperial political acts. Nor should we forget that parliament had legislative powers: every piece of legislation proposed had to have the consent of the Reichstag and the Bundesrat, so that here again the government could not disregard parliament's wishes,

[32] A celebrated cartoon in *Punch* showed the aged and experienced pilot leaving the ship of state, while the silly new captain brazenly looked on.

as the rejection of bills desired by the government was an obvious way for the assembly to show its displeasure at the chancellor's policies.

The German parliament consisted of two houses. In the Bundesrat, the federal component of the empire, the states were represented proportionally to their importance. The Reichstag, whose composition reflected the demographic reality, represented the German people as a whole, and was elected directly by universal, equal, secret and male suffrage. After the Napoleonic era and its secularization the Church–state relation, an ancient point of controversy in European public law, had been no real problem in Germany, and the Constitution of 1871, which sanctioned the equality of all faiths, had nothing to say about it. The situation changed, however, when Bismarck started to interfere with the organization and educational activities of the Catholic Church, unleashing the *Kulturkampf* (1872–9). This was a bitter struggle, pushing the Catholic Centre Party into outright opposition and causing Bismarck to brand them as 'enemies of the Reich'. His action was an echo of the enlightened absolutism of the previous century, which also wanted to control the training of clerics and education in general. Ideologically the *Kulturkampf* was also caused by the *Syllabus Errorum* of Pope Pius IX (1864), which has been mentioned before, and by the declaration of papal infallibility at the First Vatican Council (1870), which many felt to be an outright declaration of war on modern thought. Bismarck believed that the Catholic Party was so dominated by the dictates of the Vatican that it was not a truly national, German party. The conflict led to the expulsion of religious orders, the abandonment of the Prussian legation at the Vatican and the severing of diplomatic relations between the Reich and the Holy See. But when clerics were being put in prison, the whole conflict was clearly getting out of control and Bismarck was happy to put an end to it, thanks to the conciliatory new pope, Leo XIII. In fact, he was trying to cope with a new and more ominous danger, socialism, against which the clergy was a useful dam which it would be unwise to undermine. In a speech to the Prussian Herrenhaus in March 1887 he admitted seeing the conclusion of the *Kulturkampf* in that light, when he declared: 'To a large extent the place of papal authority is taken by social democracy, wherever faith has disappeared'. And he added: 'Pope and emperor in this respect have the same interest and should present a common front against anarchy and revolution'.

The progress of the social democrats in the increasingly industrialized country worried Bismarck greatly and persuaded him to initiate a policy which was imitated much later in other European countries, i.e. compulsory social security. He saw this patriarchal state-socialism as a happy middle road between English-style economic liberalism and state capitalism which would abolish entrepreneurial freedom and destroy the market economy. Social security organized by the state preserved free enterprise, but relieved much of the misery and insecurity of the working class, while tying it closer to the provident and caring empire. This policy was more efficient as well as friendlier than the Prussian prohibition of workers' coalitions of 1845 and continued the *Gewerbeordnung* of the North German Confederation, which had permitted trade unions for more favourable working conditions and wages and had recognized the right of the workers to act collectively. At first Bismarck attempted to take back these concessions and to fight socialism outright, *inter alia*, by the *Sozialistengesetz* ('law against socialists') of October 1878 (a year of panic caused by attempts on the emperor's life), but in 1881 he changed course and began working on his social security plans. He drafted the 'First Imperial Message on the Social Question', by which the state not only declared its concern for the needy, but also its obligation, to some extent, to guarantee social security. After thorough study and extensive debates in the Reichstag, three important laws were passed, on insurance against sickness (1883), industrial accidents (1884) and old age and invalidity (1889). The measures failed, however, to halt the progress of social democracy in the Reichstag, where it advanced from 35 out of 397 seats in 1890 to 81 in 1903 and 110 in 1912, when it became the strongest single party (in that year the Catholic Centre, by comparison, had 91, the National Liberals 45, the Conservatives 43 and the left-wing Liberals 42 seats). The socialists played the constitutional game loyally, and hardly ever thought of subverting the existing political order – at least until the dramatic events of 1918.

Summing up these lines of development, we may formulate the following considerations. When the Germans founded their own nation state, they at last caught up with the European evolution. In the nineteenth century the sovereign national state seemed highly desirable as guaranteeing prosperity and security. German unification, which brought together the great majority of ethnic Germans in one state, had been achieved mainly by a peaceful and orderly process, and could be described as a success. Maybe it was even too successful, because weak and divided Germany suddenly developed into a political, intellectual and economic giant in the heartland of Europe – a position of newly found strength which, following the example of older European powers, could easily lead to expansion and imperialism.

German expansionism was supported by Prussian militarism. Ever since the eighteenth century *das Militär* had been most influential, and things were not different in the nineteenth century. The army, led by the General Staff, was a state within the state which owed and swore loyalty, not to the Constitution but to the emperor. It was also like the terribly expensive Battle Fleet, a political instrument that devoured such astronomical sums as to make the urge to use it almost irresistible.

In nineteenth-century Germany liberal principles were victorious: the form of government was constitutional, fundamental liberties were guaranteed and political parties influential and firmly organized. Germany was a *Rechtsstaat* and proud of it. There was admittedly no fully fledged parliamentary system after the western mode, but a strong monarchy and a forceful chancellor offered manifest advantages over governments which were totally dominated by the party-game, one illustration being the legislation on social security, which had no parallel in the classic parliamentary regimes at the time.

The observer cannot help being struck by the impact of the past. Germany had a tradition of small-scale politics and regionalism, accompanied by monarchic paternalism. Hence the impression that the 'federal' empire and the constitutional, but influential monarchy were the best possible forms of government at that time. Hence also the impression that Wilhelminian Germany was slowly but certainly moving towards a truly parliamentary form of government under a national dynasty that would more and more resemble the British model. The First World War interrupted this evolution, but that the potential for a thorough democratization was real was demonstrated in the years before 1914–18, in the good years of the Weimar Republic and, of course, in today's Federal Republic. There were no doubt anti-democratic and anti-Semitic currents at work in nineteenth-century Germany, but they were active, and virulently so, in other countries as well. It is not easy, in the light of what happened later, to realize that in nineteenth-century Germany they were marginal phenomena, in a free society where crazy ideas were not lacking.

BELGIUM AND THE NETHERLANDS

### The kingdom of the United Netherlands

When the Great Powers, in 1815, placed William I's kingdom of the Netherlands on the European map, the impression was justified that the Seventeen Provinces of Emperor Charles V gloriously were coming to life again. The ancient Netherlands had slowly been welded together by their common princes and, according to Charles V's pragmatic sanction, they were to remain united forever. The drama under his son Philip II had, however, caused their separation into a Protestant north and a Catholic south, one being an independent republic and the other a minor part of the Habsburg conglomerate. But in 1815, after more than two centuries, they were united, with the addition of the prince-bishopric of Liège, an ancient independent and successful principaltity of the Reichskirche, which had never fallen into Habsburg hands. Even the Constitution of the new kingdom appeared to hark back to old traditions.

In the past the Seventeen Provinces had lived under rulers who respected the rights and liberties of their subjects and accepted the participation of their representatives in the affairs of state. After the separation, consummated after the fall of Antwerp in 1585, freedom was saved in the north, but the monarchy was lost; in the south the monarchy survived, but freedom did not. Now north and south were united again, enjoying both monarchy and freedom under the Constitution.

The fundamental law of William I's kingdom had in fact been drafted in the north before the two parts were joined. After Napoleon's defeat at Leipzig French rule in the northern Netherlands collapsed, and in November 1813 William-Frederick of Orange-Nassau, son of the last stadholder, William V, who had fled to England, landed in Holland. He symbolized the liberated fatherland and was proclaimed sovereign prince. The country did not want to return to the old federal republic, but to become a national monarchy which, after the British model, would be constitutional. In March 1814 the Constitution of the new state was approved by the leading personalities of the land, and the sovereign prince of the United Netherlands (for such was his exact title) swore to uphold it. Shortly afterwards the Great Powers decreed the 'amalgam' of north and south (in present-day terms, Holland and Belgium) and the kingdom of the Netherlands was given international status as a unified state, headed by King William I. Attempts by conservative circles in the south to recall the Austrian Habsburgs had stranded on the lack of interest of Vienna. The Powers had added some constitutional provisions to their political decision, namely that the northern fundamental law would be valid for the whole kingdom (after possible adaptation, *d'un commun accord*, in north and south), that Protestants and Catholics would enjoy equal guarantees of freedom of worship and that the south would enjoy a *convenable* ('appropriate') representation in parliament, i.e. the States General of the new kingdom. Another stipulation concerned the financial burden of the new state, which was to be borne equally by north and south, although the northern public debt was much larger.

A commission equally composed of northern and southern members went to work from May to July 1815 on the adaptation of the northern Constitution of 1814. It maintained the latter's principles, but added a considerable number of new articles on a variety of topics. There was a change from a unicameral to a bicameral parliament, which was important enough in itself, but there was also the more explosive question whether the Second Chamber was to be composed of northern and southern members in equal numbers or proportionally to the demographic situation. The latter proposal, favourable to the south, with its 3.2 million inhabitants as against 2.2 million in the north, was narrowly defeated. The 'sovereign prince', of course, received the title of king.

As the northern notables had been given the opportunity of voting on the project of the Constitution, it was only just to give the south the same chance. However, the consultation went against the project and the king who supported it, because the Catholic bishops in the south combated it as providing for freedom of conscience and equal protection for all denominations and making education a responsibility of the state. The consultation of August 1815 was won by the no-votes but, using some far-fetched reasoning, the king nevertheless managed to declare that the text had been approved: he counted the abstentions as yes-votes because they had not voted against, and he also counted some hundred opponents as being partisans of the text, as they had only voted against because they rejected religious freedom (a point that was not under discussion and had been imposed by the Great Powers). So the Constitution of the new kingdom of the Netherlands was proclaimed by William I, who was solemnly received as the new ruler in Brussels.

The fundamental law of 1815, which we shall analyse presently, installed a regime that can best be described as enlightened absolutism after the eighteenth-century continental fashion, but tempered by the Constitution and a thin parliamentary veneer. Its main elements were the following. Various fundamental freedoms were guaranteed, not by a Bill of Rights or a Declaration of Human Rights (as requested by some southerners), but by the inclusion, throughout the text, of specific liberties. They concerned due process of law in case of arrest, the peaceful enjoyment of property rights and religious freedom, including public worship (except where order was disturbed). The freedom of the press was guaranteed, and state censorship forbidden 'in the interest of knowledge and enlightened progress'. The implementation of this article was, however, restricted in practice because the authorities continued, in time of peace, to apply a decree from the time of the war against Napoleon which made spreading false information an offence outside the jurisdiction of the ordinary courts. Thus in the period between 1827 and 1830 in particular, numerous Belgian journalists and authors were prosecuted for attacking the king's policy. The kingdom was unitary and centralized, and both the federalism of the republic in the north and the autonomy of the old principalities in the south belonged to the past. This was a consequence of French unitarism and centralism with which both Belgium and Holland had been familiar in the years before 1815. All powers in the state were ultimately in the hands of the king, assisted by his ministers and the representatives of the country.

Parliament, called the States General, consisted of two chambers, and was not really representative by present-day standards. The First Chamber consisted of an indefinite number of royal appointees for life, selected from the ranks of the 'leading personalities of the realm' – they were in fact 90 per cent recruited from the ranks of the nobility. Its purpose, in a country that ignored the aristocracy as a privileged estate, was to give the nobles, who still enjoyed considerable social prestige in the south, a political role in the new kingdom. The Second Chamber consisted, as we have seen, of an equal number of northern and southern members. They were elected by a complicated system conceived to accentuate their oligarchic, undemocratic character and ensure their loyalty to the crown. Indeed they were not chosen by the people, but by the provincial estates, which in their turn contained, in a corporatist vein, representatives of three social classes, the nobility, chosen by the provincial 'knights', the members from the cities, chosen by the 'regents' (who were themselves elected indirectly by a very restricted franchise) and the members of the 'rural estate', chosen by bodies of electors in rural districts. As even this unrepresentative body contained too many opponents for his liking, King William attempted to put a brake on its action through various legislative measures. Consequently the aristocratic element was very influential in the Second Chamber, and at times even in the majority. Legislation was, according to the Constitution, in the hands of the States General and the king. Bills were more specifically introduced by the king and the Second Chamber, although in fact most of them originated with the government. The questions for which the legislature was competent were limited and specified in the Constitution. They concerned the budget, taxation and major areas of civil and criminal law and procedure; the rest could be left to royal decrees. The budget was decennial, which drastically limited the impact of the States General.

In the exercise of his executive powers the king was assisted, or rather served, by a Council of State, with a counselling function and several ministers. These did not constitute a cabinet, headed by a prime minister and leading a political existence of its own. They were, on the contrary, each in his own department the executors of the king's will, and comparable to the secretaries of the president of the United States (a royal decree of 1823 installed a council of ministers, which never assumed any importance). The ministers naturally were only accountable to the king and not to the States General, so that there was no question of a parliamentary monarchy. As a consequence, so many ministers left because they objected to the king's policy, that only one, the minister of justice C. F. van Maanen (*d.*1846), kept his post throughout William's reign from 1813 till 1840. The ministers came both from the north and the south. Sometimes there were more from the north and at other times more from the south, but foreign affairs, justice, war and finance were always in northern hands.

## The kingdom of Belgium

The nineteenth-century edition of the Burgundian Netherlands was short-lived, and its fragile unity shattered by the Belgian Revolution of 1830. The reasons could be found in the Catholic opposition, which from the start had balked at religious equality and demanded a privileged position for the Catholic Church in the south. King William's interference with education, including the training of the clergy, inspired by his Enlightenment philosophy, met with a determined opposition by the influential clergy – Belgian governments would afterwards also find out that they could not unleash a 'school war' unpunished. Beside the Catholic, there was also the Liberal opposition, which objected to existing restrictions on freedom, notably of the press, and generally speaking grew restless under a regime marked by autocracy and conservatism.

That the revolt against the king came in 1830 and was so radical that it resulted in a complete separation was caused by a coincidence of various circumstances. The doctrine of F. R. de Lamennais (*d*.1854) on a 'free Church in a free state', condemned by Pope Gregory XVI in 1831, a year after the Belgian Revolution, became very popular with young Catholics from 1825 onwards. The ideas of such French neo-liberals as Guizot (who later became a leading conservative), who fought Charles X's absolutism, were most influential among liberal intellectuals in the south and prepared them for collaboration with the Catholics of Lamennais' camp. The alliance, translated into practical political terms by the Catholic–Liberal Union of 1828, was condemned by the pope in 1831, again a year after the fatal events: the revolution had profited from a very brief favourable juncture. The revolution of July 1830 in Paris, which toppled the old-fashioned regime of Charles X, inspired the malcontents in Brussels and Liège, who began to dream of a comparable success against King William. There was, moreover, social unrest with looting in Brussels on 24 August 1830, caused by rising prices and threatening mechanization of industry. The breakdown of public order was countered on 27–28 August by the armed forces of the well-to-do middle class, called *garde bourgeoise,* and exploited by the political opposition in the ranks of the bourgeoisie against King William. At first their demands merely aimed at reform within the existing legitimate order, but afterwards the tone became more radical and rebellious. Finally a pro-French current in certain sections of Belgian public opinion (soldiers who had fought under Napoleon, for example) also played a role, as did French ambitions to weaken the kingdom of the Netherlands, conceived by the British as a buffer state against France, and possibly to turn its southern half into a French satellite, if not to annex it outright (hence French financial and military support for the young Belgian state). Annexation was, however, out of the question because of determined British opposition; even a Belgian king of French origin was intolerable (there was no objection to a French queen for Leopold, the first king of the Belgians, who enjoyed British sympathy).

All these events and circumstances led to fighting in Brussels in September 1830 and the formation of the provisional government which on 4 October of that year proclaimed Belgian independence and announced the convocation of a Constituent National Congress. Various attempts to save the United Netherlands by introducing an administrative separation, keeping a common ruler from the House of Orange, failed. The Constitution of the new kingdom of Belgium was drafted in record time, which is understandable as 90 per cent of its articles were copied verbatim from other texts. A constitutional commission, created by the provisional government on 6 October 1830, prepared a project that was discussed between 25 November 1830 and 7 February 1831 and passed on that day by the National Congress, elected on 27 October and 3 November 1830. The Congress had already on 22 November 1830 decided that Belgium would be a hereditary monarchy. The Constitution was not put before the country for approval. Its main features were predictable in light of the events that led up to it. It contained numerous liberties, particularly those that had been curtailed in the preceding years: press, association, worship, education and language. The separation of powers was fundamental, as was ministerial responsibility before parliament, in other words the monarchy would be both constitutional and parliamentary, Article 25 stated that 'all powers emanate from the nation', which was represented by a bicameral parliament.

This is not the place for a detailed analysis of the Constitution of 1831, but some historical comments may be called for. The two main social forces, the Church and the liberal bourgeoisie, which made the Belgian Revolution, also profited most from the fundamental law drafted under their influence. Freedom of worship, education and association led in the decades after 1830 to an unparalleled expansion of the Catholic Church and its schools and religious orders. On the other hand the removal of royal autocratic control allowed the bourgeoisie, which to a large extent gained command of the state, to develop commercial and industrial enterprise so unrestrainedly that nineteenth-century Belgium was known as the paradise of capitalism.

The Constitution had no social and economic dimension and certainly no concern with labour problems. The state of 1831 was the state of the well-to-do bourgeoisie and the landowners, and no one thought of granting the vote to the man in the street who in Brussels in September 1830 had fought the troops of the government. Suffrage was a privilege to which, because of the very restricted franchise, just over 1 per cent of the population was entitled; those eligible for parliament were even less numerous, and the Senate was a club of landowners. The Constitution was a victory for the parliamentary oligarchy; there was no trace of democracy, either direct or indirect. Belgium was also a centralized kingdom. The Constitution granted no special powers to provinces and towns. The Provincial Law of 1836 underlined this anti-provincialism, whereas the Communal Law of the same year granted a good deal of autonomy to the elected administrations of towns and villages. Centralism was an important point of the programme of the Liberals, who hoped that the central government would make its secular influence felt in cities and countryside.

Belgium was also a unitary kingdom. The fundamental division of the country into two cultural communities, the Dutch-speaking Flemings in the north and the French-speaking Walloons in the south, was completely ignored. When French was imposed as the sole official language of the new state, it became clear which part of the country was going to pay the cost of unitarism. Even before the end of 1830 the provisional government decreed that 'although here and there various dialects existed, only one language was spoken in Belgium, French': the Dutch-speakers only spoke patois, the French-speakers spoke a language. For the higher classes this was no problem, as the nobility and well-to-do bourgeoisie in Flanders had learned to use French and found it useful as a social barrier against the mass of the people. They had fought King William's action in favour of the official use of Dutch and they objected to the idea that they might be obliged for official business to use the language of workers and peasants. The Flemish clergy, for its part, feared the entry of Protestant books from Holland and saw French as the language of the Catholic neighbour in the south. Just as William had hoped to elevate Dutch to the status of the common language of the realm and a unifying factor, so the same role was attributed to French in the new kingdom of Belgium, and with the same negative result. However, the merciless oppression of the Dutch language (then called *Vlaamsch*, or *Nederduitsch* or *Nederlandsch*) undertaken by the new masters of Belgium was much harsher than anything William had undertaken against French. The speed with which the elimination of the language of the people in the Flemish area was initiated is striking (it was, of course, also the language of the insurgents' Dutch enemy). On 5 October 1830 the provisional government decreed that the *Bulletin des arrêts et des actes du gouvernement provisoire de Belgique* would appear in French only, ten days later the Flemish Chambers of the Court of Appeal of Liège (with jurisdiction over Dutch-speaking Limburg) were abolished, twelve days later French became the sole language of the Belgian army and on 16 November the same government decided that all laws and decrees would be published in French only. The celebrated linguistic freedom, guaranteed by the Constitution, was applied in the law courts in the sense that the parties were only allowed to use their own language if the judges, the prosecuting magistrate and the barristers involved understood it; in other words, in a linguistic sense, the parties existed for the courts and not the other way round.

The Belgian Constitution, as we indicated, was based to a large extent on existing texts, but it was in its turn much imitated abroad. Its main sources were the Constitution of the kingdom of the Netherlands of 1815 and the French *Charte constitutionnelle* of 1830, which was itself, as we have seen, an adaptation of the *Charte octroyée* of 1814. Some articles were borrowed from the French Constitution of 1791 and from British constitutional practice. In any case, Britain, as the common model of all modern liberal monarchies, had a more profound impact than the limited literal borrowing would suggest. It has been calculated that the Belgian Constitution of 1831 borrowed 40 per cent of its articles more or less literally from the Constitution of the Netherlands of 1815, about 35 per cent from the French *Charte* of 1830 (itself almost invariably copied from the *Charte* of 1814), about 10 per cent from the French Constitution of 1791 and some 5 per cent from Britain. The remainder, some 10 per cent of new material, included ten articles on such important questions as the election of senators, the relations between Church and state and the freedom of association.

The Belgian Constitution found imitators, *inter alia*, in the Netherlands in 1848, as we shall see. Several other countries copied it more or less literally, still others took over the fundamental idea of the Belgian parliamentary monarchy without borrowing verbatim. The Belgian model clearly was attractive wherever a liberal monarchy was introduced, not only because of its substance, but also because of its concise and uncomplicated style and language. Among the imitations we mention the Constitutions of Spain (1837), Greece (1844 and 1864), Piedmont–Sardinia (1848), which itself in 1870 became the Constitution of the unified kingdom of Italy, Bulgaria (1864) and Romania (1866). It moreover exerted a considerable influence on the Constitution of Prussia of 1850 and, after the First World War, on those of Poland, Hungary and Czechoslovakia.[33]

### The kingdom of the Netherlands

The Belgian Revolution and the ensuing Constitution have not left the north untouched. Dutch public opinion – especially Protestant – welcomed the separation and was glad to be rid of the Belgian rebels: people were happy to return to their own national cocoon. The problem of ministerial accountability had, however, been sharply raised, and public opinion questioned the autocracy of its disappointed and stubborn king. This was no technical discussion for lawyers and academics, but a central issue in the political life of the country: ought the government to depend on the will of the sovereign, however enlightened, or be placed under the control of parliament and made accountable to the representatives of the nation (or the noble and bourgeois oligarchs who considered themselves the spokesmen of the silent mass of the people)? Many Dutch liberals believed William's enlightened absolutism to be untenable and wanted to introduce ministerial responsibility on the Belgian model, *inter alia*, because they had been struck by the disadvantage of personal rule at the time of the Belgian crisis. As early as January 1831 The Hague promised to take the introduction of ministerial responsibility into consideration, and a commission was installed to study the question, but the king was too busy with plans for the reconquest of Belgium, and nothing was achieved on the constitutional front. It was not until 1840 that a first step was made, with the introduction of criminal ministerial

---

[33] See on all this the work of a leading authority who taught legal history at Brussels for many years: J. Gilissen, 'Gouvernés et gouvernants en Belgique depuis 1815', *Receuils de la Société Jean Bodin* 26 (1965), 81–148; J. Gilissen, 'Die belgische Verfassung von 1831: ihr Ursprung und ihr Einfluss' in W. Conze (ed.), *Beiträge zur deutschen und belgischen Verfassungsgeschichte im 19. Jahrhundert* (Stuttgart, 1967), 38–69 (also published in French, under the title 'La Constitution belge de 1831. Ses sources, son influence', *Res publica* 10 (1968), 107–41); J. Gilissen, 'Le caractère collégial des premières formes de gouvernement et d'administration de l'état belge (1830–1831)', *Revue belge d'histoire contemporaine* 12 (1981), 609–39; J. Gilissen, 'De eerste administratieve organisatie van België ten tijde van de tijdelijke regering (Sept. 1830–Feb. 1831)', *Legal History Review* 52 (1984), 301–42.

responsibility (it was the first of eleven changes in the Constitution between 1840 and 1972 – a new Constitution was proclaimed in 1983, as we shall see); also the decennial budget became biannual. However moderate these changes were, the king found them unacceptable and he abdicated in favour of his son, William II, who accepted the innovations. Of much greater importance was the revision of 1848, realized under the impulse of the liberal professor J. R. Thorbecke (d.1872), for it at last introduced a parliamentary regime, with ministerial accountability to parliament. This was done after the Belgian model, which was copied verbatim. The competent commission stated in so many words that its project was an attempt 'to change our Constitution, not after the principles indicated previously, but those of the Belgian form of government'. Ten out of eighteen new articles were borrowed from the southern neighbour. We mention, among other innovations, the yearly budget and the direct election of the Second Chamber, the First being elected by the Provincial States. For the time being the suffrage remained the undemocratic taxation-restricted franchise, but the following constitutional revisions aimed at extending it (1887), and finally introduced universal male suffrage (1917) and female suffrage (1922).[34] Later revisions concerned mainly colonial and European affairs. All in all the Constitution of 1814–15 held out well and, except for ministerial responsibility and universal suffrage, this early nineteenth-century text has proved valuable and workable. The Dutch have not undergone the storm which wrought havoc in some other European nation states.

This remains true even after the introduction of a new Constitution in 1983, which was anything but a radical, let alone a revolutionary innovation (and consequently failed in any way to move public opinion). Indeed, although it took sixteen years to draft, the new fundamental law contains few elements to change day to day political life. It is no exaggeration to say that the new Constitution is old wine in new bottles and a vindication of Thorbecke's vision. Various bold plans, mooted at the early stages of the constitutional commission's activity, were quietly shelved. Nevertheless some antiquated features were scrapped, concerning, for example, the Protestant character of the country (which contains some 40 per cent Catholics). The prohibition of religious processions was abolished, but this ancient Catholic custom had anyway become unfashionable. Various social

---

[34] In 1917 a new article in the Constitution provided for the possible introduction of female suffrage, which was done in 1919; it was made an article of the Constitution in 1922.

features, such as full employment, social security and the fair distribution of wealth, were given a place in the Constitution. The role of the monarch was strongly reduced and his right to 'appoint or dismiss ministers at will' was scrapped, but ever since the middle of the nineteenth century this royal prerogative had been purely theoretical.

### Revisions of the Belgian Constitution

For a long time the Belgian Constitution underwent little change. Revision eventually concerned mainly two fundamental blemishes of the text of 1831, the disenfranchisement of the mass of the people and the negation of the evident reality that Belgium is inhabited by two communities, Flemings and Walloons. The first problem was tackled progressively from the later nineteenth century onwards and finally solved in the middle of the twentieth, when universal suffrage was extended to women.[35]

The solution of the second proved much more complicated and the necessary revisions of the Constitution were still going on at the time of writing. When in 1830, the unitary state was founded, one community imposed its language, French, on the other in all official business and to a large extent even in social relations, business, the army and education (the universities in the Dutch-speaking part, for example, exclusively used French). The ensuing discrimination against the mass of the Flemish people (i.e. those who did not belong to the bourgeoisie, which spoke or learned French) was oppressive and, with the progress of democracy, became intolerable. The unitary, French-dominated state had to go. Vague plans to make the whole country bilingual were unrealistic and were in any case rejected by the French speakers, who understandably wanted to preserve their own cultural identity. So the solution clearly was the division of the country into two autonomous parts, each with its own language, culture and way of life, but continuing to live together in one kingdom. In legal terms this meant the introduction, through successive revisions of the Constitution, of the federal form of government. This process is still going on, but there

---

[35] In 1893 universal plural male suffrage (not a right but, until today, a legal obligation) was introduced, in 1921 universal single suffrage was written in the Constitution, as was the principle of female suffrage, but the latter could only be realized in fact through a law voted with a two-thirds majority, and this did not happen until 1948.

are already fixed boundaries between the two halves of the federal state,[36] and separate Flemish and Walloon parliaments and governments, competent for various spheres which used to belong to the central government and parliament (which continue to run common affairs such as defence, currency and social security). The necessary adaptations of the Constitution, passed by the national parliament in Brussels in successive waves, started in 1970, and a fourth revision (following those of 1970, 1980 and 1988), the most radical in Belgian history, was passed by parliament in the summer of 1993. Article 1 of the new Constitution proclaims that 'Belgium is a federal state'.[37]

## SWITZERLAND

After the troubled years of the Helvetian Republic, a French vassal state with a centralized and unitary form of government based on the French model, Switzerland found tranquillity again. Its *neutralité perpétuelle* and the integrity and inviolability of its territory were recognized by the Great Powers, and it attained its present size when, in 1815, Geneva became a Swiss canton. The country returned to its ancient Constitution, with sovereign cantons allied in a confederation, but the power of the almighty leading lineages was broken (Article 7 of the *Bundesvertrag* of 1815 stated that the enjoyment of political rights could never be the exclusive privilege of one class of a canton's burghers). Swiss tranquillity was disturbed by the mini-war of secession of 1847, when seven Catholic cantons formed the *Sonderbund* ('separate confederation') and agitated for so much cantonal autonomy that the country might have broken up. The separatist movement was repressed in a military campaign that lasted for three weeks. The result was the more centralizing Constitution of 1848 which, in spite of partial adaptations and a more thorough revision in 1874, has remained the cornerstone of Swiss public law until the present day. In 1848 Switzerland became a federal state instead of a confederation of

[36] Two halves in a geographical sense, but not in terms of population, as roughly two-thirds of the inhabitants of Belgium are Flemish, and one-third Walloon.

[37] Professor Senelle, who used to teach constitutional law in Ghent, has devoted detailed surveys to these developments; see R. Senelle, *The Belgian Constitution. Commentary* (Brussels, 1974); R. Senelle, *The reform of the Belgian state* (5 vols., Brussels, 1978–90). See also on a more elementary level: A. Alen, *Belgium: bipolar and centrifugal federalism* (Brussels, 1990). A detailed analysis will be found in M. Uyttendaele, *Le fédéralisme inachevé*. For the repercussions on the law courts, see J. Sarot et al., *La jurisprudence de la Cour d'arbitrage* (Brussels, 1990); E. Orban et al., *Fédéralisme et cours suprêmes. Federalism and supreme courts* (Brussels, 1991).

states. Two striking features of the Swiss Constitution deserve our special attention here, the federal form of government and the mixture of direct and indirect democracy.

The federal organization combines federal institutions, competent for matters specifically assigned to them, with twenty-two sovereign cantons – not provinces, but mini-states – competent for all other affairs. The federal legislature is a bicameral parliament, called *Bundesversammlung* or *Assemblée fédérale*, and composed of a *Nationalrat* or *Conseil national* and a *Ständerat* or *Conseil des Etats*, the former being proportional to the demographic situation and the latter containing two members per canton. This serves to keep a balance between the will of the cantons and that of the entire Swiss nation. Federal executive power is in the hands of the government in Berne, called *Bundesrat* or *Conseil fédéral*, chosen by parliament; it is not liable to be toppled by parliament, but cannot dissolve it either. This provision ensures great stability, but specifies nothing in case parliament and government get involved in a frontal collision (a situation which has not so far arisen in any dramatic way). This Federal Council acts as collective head of state, the federal president being no more than the yearly elected chairman of the Federal Council. In the government, which contains seven members, the linguistic communities are not equally represented, as the custom has arisen that there are four German-speaking, two French-speaking and one Italian-speaking members. It is also customary to have one member from Berne, one from Zurich and one from the canton of Vaud.

Besides indirect democracy in the shape of elected federal and cantonal representatives, Switzerland also practises direct democracy in the form of frequent referendums, which can overrule the will of parliament. The mechanism is remarkable as it means that the representatives elected by the people can be disowned by them. In a few cantons there exists an unbroken continuity between the medieval democracy of the *Landgemeinde* and the present day. In Glarus, Unterwalden and Appenzell this primeval democracy has been in operation since the Middle Ages and the people decide in their annual spring gathering on all questions of legislation and administration. This is done publicly and after free discussion where everyone can speak up, under the chairmanship of the elected *Landammann* (this supersedes the cantonal parliament). Elsewhere the referendum is a nineteenth-century institution. In 1848 it was made compulsory for constitutional questions. In 1869 the canton of Zurich, followed by several neighbours, included the possibility of a referendum on legislative matters. Shortly afterwards this optional referendum on legislation was introduced at the federal level by the constitutional revision of 1874 (the right of initiative for a federal referendum was regulated in 1891).

At the federal level, leaving aside cantonal referendums, this means at present that for a law passed by the federal parliament 50,000 citizens or eight cantons can, within 90 days, demand that it be submitted to a popular consultation. And if at least 100,000 citizens request it, a proposal for a change in the Constitution can be entered. The variety of topics submitted to referendums is infinite, and varies from trivial to fundamental issues, but whatever the issue, the legislature has repeatedly been denied. Thus, to quote one example, a referendum in March 1986 rejected by a three to one majority the decision of the Swiss government to join the United Nations Organization. In light of our earlier discussion, one point may be specifically mentioned here: judicial control of the constitutionality of the laws was rejected by referendum in 1939.

It is moreover worth mentioning that the Constitution of 1848 recognizes the sovereignty of the cantons as a matter of principle, but only in so far as it is not restricted by the Constitution of the Confederation. This restricted sovereignty, which is in fact a contradiction in terms, reminds us of the European Community, whose 'sovereign' kingdoms, republics and duchies have accepted far-reaching limitations of their freedom of action in such fields as European legislation, jurisdiction and government. This has not turned them into vassal or satellite states, but there is no doubt that their total, nineteenth-century style of sovereignty has been lost.

# CHAPTER 9

# The liberal model transformed or rejected

## THE LIBERAL STATE TRANSFORMED

The twentieth century is so different from the previous one that the form of government could not remain unaffected. The oligarchic parliament was questioned, as was the capitalist economy. The role of the bourgeoisie, that relentless motor of the nineteenth century, was contested by new, politically conscious groups, but there was also displeasure within the ranks of the old middle class: the bourgeoisie was not without self-criticism, and the scions of well-to-do families played a conspicuous role in workers' parties. The demand for participation in the running of the economy, for social security and for a fairer share of the fruits of labour could not leave the old-style affluent liberalism and the governments that supported it untouched. Nor could the ambition of previously inarticulate classes to take part in the political power game be ignored, particularly after the old leading groups had seen their world collapse in the terrible conflagration of the First World War. At the same time the proclamation of the right of self-determination by the smaller nations led many to oppose existing governments, which were blamed for oppressing minorities: the time had come for the latter to take their political fate into their own hands.

Discontent was universal, but the forms it took and their impact on the state differed widely. In several countries the liberal state continued on its old foundations, albeit not without some more or less radical adaptations. The parliamentary regime, dominated by political parties, was maintained, and so were the traditional freedoms and ideological pluralism (including the freedom of the press and trade unions). In all those countries the *Rechtsstaat* survived, but underwent or carried out profound social and economic changes, such as a state-controlled economy, compulsory social security imposed and partially funded by the state and a conscious policy aiming at social and economic (and not only legal) equality through direct taxation. This was the road taken in most Western-European countries, by socially motivated parties, hesitantly after the First World War and resolutely after the Second. Some were social democratic (reformist but inspired by Marxism), others Christian democratic, and some were pragmatic, as the Labour parties of British inspiration. Conservative governments often followed the prevailing trend. Thus, when the British Conservatives took over from Labour in 1951, they maintained the principal outlines of the changes introduced in 1945–51. The blueprint for the welfare state and full employment had in any case already been elaborated during the Second World War in Churchill's coalition government. Even in the United States, the most capitalist of all western countries, President Roosevelt's New Deal had taken the road to massive state intervention in the economy.

Existing Constitutions were little affected by these vast mutations. The fundamental change was, of course, the introduction of universal suffrage. This was usually sufficient, because the desired fiscal, social and economic improvements could be introduced by way of ordinary legislation, and for this the necessary parliamentary majorities were made available by the new working-class electorate. All these changes – universal franchise in France, social security in Germany – had admittedly already been initiated in the nineteenth century, but the massive breakthrough came in the twentieth, as did the organized action of the proletariat. The result was the present-day liberal welfare state, a mixed product (as is the economy) of free market and private enterprise checked by state intervention and trade union influence (in an uncertain balance following the ups and downs of party politics).

Few constitutional changes, as we have pointed out, were needed to keep pace with these developments. Existing fundamental laws appeared to be adequate for the peaceful transformation of the political landscape. We should, however, not close our eyes to reality, for even if in many countries the text of the Constitution remained unchanged, the existing political institutions assumed different roles: it was clearly possible to alter a political regime without changing the letter of the Constitution. It could be argued that this does not interest the legal historian, who is attached to the text of the law, and that shifts in the political power game within the framework of the existing Constitution belong to political and not legal history. To us this seems a narrow and legalistic approach, as legal reality does not only consist of words and articles of law and decrees, but also of custom and the application of the texts in everyday life. If one accepts this point of view, it becomes clear that the public law of our time has sometimes changed noticeably, without a jot of the Constitution being altered. Take, for example, the transformation of parliament in some western democracies. In the nineteenth century it was the meeting place of the people's elected spokesmen, where after a free debate, laws were passed and budgets voted under the critical eye of the nation from which 'all powers emanated', and where the government and the civil service were questioned on the affairs that moved public opinion. Nowadays this same parliament is often a meeting place, frequently empty (particularly when some sports event is being broadcast on television), where people appointed by the central offices of the parties (i.e. placed on the top places on the lists of candidates or in safe seats) pass all the bills wanted by the government (whose members have been appointed by the party offices and by organized pressure groups). These parliamentarians moreover vote the budget which the government desires (and may in fact already have spent). If the cabinet thinks it needs full powers, again these parliaments will meekly grant them. No wonder that some observers ask themselves what the difference is between this sort of assembly and the rubber-stamp parliaments of the dictatorships of the recent past.

If in some countries this power shift in favour of the executive has taken place unobtrusively and unavowedly, in France the strengthening of the government came about through the proclamation of a new Constitution which introduced the presidential regime of the Fifth Republic.[1] It was drafted on the basis of a mandate given to General de Gaulle in 1958 and gave the president the leading position he had advocated in 1946.[2] In 1962, through a constitutional change, approved by referendum, the president, who in 1958 was chosen by politicians from the national parliament and regional and local councils, became a leader elected by the people. This brought the French form of government closer to the American model,[3] and greatly strengthened the executive vis-à-vis the legislature, as the

---

[1] As this is not a book on comparative law we can be very brief on the present French Constitution.
[2] See the section on France after Napoleon in chapter 8.
[3] The presidential system of the Fifth Republic is less radical than the American. In the United States the government is not accountable to Congress and cannot be brought down by it; on the other hand the American head of state cannot dissolve Congress.

president's legitimacy was henceforth based directly on the popular vote.[4]

## THE LIBERAL STATE REJECTED

In various countries the 'wind of change' which blew over the twentieth century acquired hurricane force and left no stone of the old Constitutions unturned. We shall now study the states – or rather two of them in particular – that have rejected the existing model most radically. In the West the victim of the hurricane was liberal democracy, in Russia it was the autocracy of the tsars. Although Russia was experimenting with liberal forms of government at the end of tsarism and even more between the two revolutions of 1917, it may safely be stated that in November 1917 Russia really passed from imperial absolutism to proletarian dictatorship, missing out the intermediate stage of bourgeois capitalism. The novel regimes in East and West were inspired by different ideologies and had different aims, but they shared several negative features in their rejection of the classic liberal model (which is why we discuss them here together).

They rejected the division of powers which was considered a cause of weakness for the state, and they defended the concentration of all controls in the hands of one party and even one leader. They also rejected ideological pluralism and saw the state as the instrument of one doctrine. If 'lies had no rights' and falsehood could not claim the same rights as truth, there was no room for the traditional freedom of thought and expression. They rejected the *Rechtsstaat*, or rule of law, as no individual could possibly have the right to stand up to the state and its ideology, putting personal interest above the collective needs of nation, class or race. They put an end to bourgeois byzantine disputes about the correct balance of power between government and parliament. Henceforth both were instruments of the one ruling party and its leadership, which determined both the composition of the government and of the national assembly. The latter was, moreover, only expected to applaud the decrees of the almighty leadership on particular occasions and following a hallowed ritual. There was no room for a 'loyal opposition', as this was equated with rebellious treason and lese-majesty against the state.

The gamut of these monolithic and intolerant regimes is wide and

---

[4] See J.-L. Quermonne, *Le gouvernement de la France sous la Ve République* (Paris, 1981).

varied, but it is possible to distinguish two species, which may be called left and right, or communist and fascist. The former is more easily defined, as it was Marxist-inspired and on the whole internationally-minded (although Stalin's doctrine of 'socialism in one country' and his foreign policy betrayed a national, Russian outlook), while the latter's inspiration was clearly nationalistic. The former camp aimed at a new system of government, based on the dictatorship of the proletariat and the creation of a Marxist society all over the world. The latter thought in strictly national terms. The right-wing parties regretted the weakness of their countries, blamed existing regimes and wanted to build a strong state and bring about a national rebirth. This narrow, strictly national starting point explains why these regimes were anti-Marxist (possibly the only ideological trait they had in common), as they abhorred the cosmopolitanism of the *vaterlandlose Gesellen* ('comrades without a fatherland'). It also explains why the diversity in the fascist and Nazi camp is so bewildering. In some cases (such as Spain), this sort of regime was forced upon the country by the army and the generals, in others by plebeian agitators, such as Hitler and Mussolini (the latter started as a socialist leader). In some cases the regime was close to the Church (Salazar in Portugal, Franco in Spain), in others, such as Mussolini's Italy, relations with the Church could be described as neutral and correct, but in Germany the ideological antagonism between Nazism and the Church (particularly the Catholic Church) was unbridgeable, even though Hitler, for tactical reasons, desired to wait until after the war to settle accounts with his ecclesiastical opponents: it was obvious that there was complete incompatibility between universalist Christianity and the racist mystique of national socialism.[5]

From this wide spectrum we shall select two examples for further study, the Soviet Union and Nazi Germany. In 1917 the Bolshevik Revolution founded a regime that denied and rejected the western form of government: it lasted for about three-quarters of a century. It is too early to assess the historical significance of this experiment, which ended a few years ago. It was certainly a sign of contradiction, exciting great hopes in Russia and elsewhere, but also bitter opposition.

[5] The reader will find the following works useful. D. Clarke, *Conservatism* (London, 1950); E. Weber (ed.), *The European right* (Berkeley, Los Angeles, 1965); K. Epstein, *The genesis of German conservatism* (Princeton, 1966); F. L. Carsten, *The rise of fascism* (London, 1967); S. J. Woolf (ed.), *Fascism in Europe* (London, 1968); F. Glum, *Konservatismus im 19. Jahrhundert* (Bonn, 1969).

It led to untold suffering under a harsh dictatorship, forced industrialization and agricultural collectivization. It resisted the onslaught of the German army but in the end succumbed to inherent contradictions, impoverishment and lack of freedom. Nevertheless, the Soviet Union for several decades enjoyed the status of second world power and won the loyalty of the mass of its people. Germany deserves our special attention because Hitler's brief dictatorship, which went against the country's cultural traditions and its attachment to the *Rechtsstaat*, established a regime of terror and unleashed a world-wide conflagration whose consequences are still with us.

## THE BOLSHEVIK REVOLUTION AND THE CONSTITUTION OF THE SOVIET UNION

### *Historical background*

The international role of the Soviet Union, now called the Commonwealth of Independent States, and its very size (about half of Europe and a third of Asia) would alone justify our special attention. More importantly, its political institutions were of exceptional significance for two reasons. They were a novel departure, as they rejected both the Russian past and western models, and they were the fruits of the only left-wing revolution that lasted long enough – some three generations – to prove itself in the field, and not only in the blueprints of social scientists. In order to understand the origins of this extraordinary experiment – in constitutional as in so many other respects – it is necessary to grasp the situation of tsarist Russia at the beginning of the twentieth century, a vast country that was modern in comparison with its southern and eastern neighbours, but backward in western eyes.

Russia was socially and economically underdeveloped. Around 1900 some 80 per cent of the population consisted of mostly illiterate peasants, who had been freed from serfdom in 1861,[6] but without becoming owners of their land and therefore still dependent on their old masters. Modern capitalism was expanding, mainly through foreign investment, and led to the concentration of an industrial proletariat in cities such as Moscow and St Petersburg, which was then the capital. In Russia the urban bourgeoisie, the main motor in the West of the transition

---

[6] D. Field, *The end of serfdom. Nobility and bureaucracy in Russia 1855–1861* (Cambridge, Mass., 1977).

from feudalism to capitalism, was a small group, curbed by the almighty state and its bureaucracy, and politically insignificant except on the local level. Russia was also intellectually backward. Speculative thought was dominated by the orthodox Church, which was itself subjected to the state. The country had experienced neither humanism and renaissance, nor the tension between reformation and counter-reformation, which in the West had ultimately led to pluralism and tolerance: in Russia the doctrine of the national Church was the only true faith and no others were tolerated. The oldest Russian university was founded in 1755 in Moscow. Tsar Peter the Great (*d.*1725) admittedly opened his country to foreign influence, but not indiscriminately: modern technology and industry were welcome, but western political and religious ideas were subversive and taboo. Consequently Russian intellectuals were divided into two camps, the progressives, liberals or Marxists, inspired by the West, and the Slavophiles, who preferred their native traditions. The impact of this intelligentsia was in any case very limited in a country that even at the beginning of the twentieth century conserved its ancient monolithic character, i.e. of a single Russian peasant mass, inspired by one true faith and governed by one venerated father figure.

Russian political institutions were equally backward. The country still lived in the Ancient Regime, ruled by an emperor who was bound by no Constitution and accountable to no parliament. Powerful cities as autonomous political centres were unheard of, and the unorganized peasant millions were governed by noble landowners, who had given up their national political role in exchange for local social privilege. To western observers this regime was a monstrous anomaly. Russia was also a strictly unitary state, where ethnic diversity was ignored and non-Russian nations subjected to a central policy or Russification. Several tsars had deplored this backwardness and had, under western influence, attempted to modernize and liberalize the country to some extent, but these liberal phases had always been followed by reactionary backlashes during which the state police struck mercilessly.

The regime was not only criticized in the West, but judged intolerable in the long run by many observers at home. The nineteenth century produced various oppositionist movements, all of which remained important in the twentieth century and particularly in the fateful year 1917. Some people found the western model superior and wanted to transform tsardom into a constitutional and parliamentary monarchy, as had happened in England and France in the seventeenth and eighteenth centuries. This current was popular with western-inspired intellectuals and the nascent bourgeoisie. They saw autocracy as a barrier to economic progress and the maximum utilization of the country's natural resources, which should be left to free enterprise and individual efforts instead of state capitalism. Others saw the solution, not in the transformation but in the downfall of autocracy via the emancipation of the peasants and particularly land reform which would turn the farmers into smallholders. The *narodniki* (*narod* = the people) expected salvation from the agrarian masses and the liberation of the countryside, which they glorified. To their great disappointment they won no success in the nineteenth century, as the peasant population proved very difficult to mobilize and was devoted to the great father figure in imperial St Petersburg (on whose life the *narodniki* made several attempts). In the following century the movement lived on in the party of the Social Revolutionaries (SRs) who, in 1917, before the Bolshevik Revolution, briefly played an important role under A. F. Kerensky (*d.*1970), but afterwards were dominated and finally, as early as 1918, liquidated by the victorious Bolsheviks. The *narodniki* were a social phenomenon of the non-urban, non-proletarian type, comparable to some liberation movements in present-day Latin America.

Capitalist industry, a recent actor on the Russian scene, had concentrated a proletariat that was susceptible to the Marxist gospel, as preached by some intellectuals. In 1898 the social democratic party was founded after the German model, but it was soon racked by internal division, the main bone of contention being the movement's strategy for victory. In Germany and other western countries the reformist view predominated, based on belief in parliament and the hope of victory through the ballot box (which indeed was achieved in a few countries after the First and particularly the Second World War). While this approach had its followers in Russia, others remained sceptical, as was understandable in a country without any parliamentary tradition and where the state police waged a merciless war against the opposition. As V. I. Lenin (*d.*1924), their most eloquent spokesman put it : 'Only knaves and fools can imagine that the proletariat is obliged first to obtain a majority in elections organized under the yoke of the bourgeoisie, under the yoke of wage-slavery, and only afterwards to gain power ... We maintain on the contrary that the proletariat must first bring down the bourgeoisie and seize power, and afterwards use that power, i.e. the dictatorship of the proletariat, as the instrument of its class in such a way as to gain the sympathy of the great majority of working people'.[7] In 1903 the division led to a final rupture, when the radical wing headed by Lenin won against the reformists under P. B. Axelrod (*d.*1928), who after the October Revolution were driven out and in the end eliminated. As, in 1903, in Brussels and London, at the Second Congress of what was later called the Russian Communist Party, the radicals happened to be in the majority and their opponents in the minority, the two wings became known as the Bolsheviks (*bolshiy* = larger) and the Mensheviks (*menshiy* = smaller).

The tsarist regime received a first serious warning in 1905, when the Russian defeat in the war against Japan led to riots, strikes, mass demonstrations and the organization of soviets (= councils) of workers. In 1906 Tsar Nicholas II gave in to some extent to the demand for liberalization by granting a Constitution[8] that guaranteed freedom of conscience, assembly and association, and by introducing a bicameral parliament, composed of the Duma, a popular assembly of elected members, and the Diet, whose members represented various regions and were partly appointed by the emperor and partly elected by the people. On paper this was a major breakthrough: Russia had a Constitution – a total innovation – and a national parliament, which had not existed in living memory. In reality the two-pronged modernization was less momentous, as the persecution of opponents to the regime continued relentlessly and the Duma was very docile. Not docile and conservative enough, however, for the tsar did not hesitate to dissolve it when the representatives of the people appeared to have a will of their own. From 1908 onwards Nicholas II stopped convoking it and retracted various concessions, so that Russia in 1914 in fact still lived in the Ancient Regime.[9]

The second – and fatal – crisis was caused by the disasters of the First World War. Russian defeats, corruption in leading circles and the misery of soldiers and civilians led in the crucial year of 1917 to food riots, revolt and mutiny. The Duma, which had been called several times after August 1914, demanded political and social reforms, and when for that reason it was dissolved in 1917, it refused

[7] *Collected Works*, XVI (Moscow, 1919), 336 (reprinted 1992).
[8] M. Szeftel, *The Russian Constitution of April 23, 1906. Political institutions of the Duma monarchy* (Brussels, 1976); K. Fröhlich (ed.), *The emergence of Russian constitutionalism 1900–1904* (Leiden, 1981).
[9] G. A. Hosking, *The Russian constitutional experiment. Government and Duma 1907–1914* (Cambridge, 1973); A. Levin, *The Third Duma. Election and profile* (London, 1974).

to obey and leave; the leader of the resistance was the liberal Constitutional Democratic Party ('Cadets'). In March 1917 rebellion and mutiny became so widespread, mainly under the impulse of the aforementioned SRs, that the Duma finally took an openly revolutionary step and founded the Provisional Committee with Executive Power. It was composed of various opposition parties, but mainly supported by pro-western liberals. On 15 March 1917 their regime, which came to be called the provisional government, induced Tsar Nicholas II to abdicate. In the subsequent months the government, composed of liberals and moderate socialists (SRs and Mensheviks), moved closer to socialism: bourgeois ministers resigned and the SR leader Kerensky became prime minister of the provisional government. On 16 September 1917 he proclaimed the republic, putting an end to four centuries of tsarist rule.

While this moderate government tried to bring some sort of order in the turmoil, to continue the war with the western allies and to organize a constitutional and parliamentary regime along western lines, the Bolshevik Party chose a more radical course. It prepared a take-over and sought to establish the dictatorship of the proletariat, a form of government of a totally different type. Its aim was not only to change the Constitution, but the social and economic order as well. The Bolsheviks acted principally via the soviets of workers, peasants and soldiers, which sprang up and gained control in many places. At first the soviets were mainly SR-orientated, but in the summer of 1917 the impact of the Bolsheviks became stronger, and they managed to gain the majority in the soviet of the capital. This swing to the left weakened the provisional government, whose leader Kerensky wanted to continue the war against Germany at least until the election of a Constituent Assembly, whereas the Bolsheviks promised to end the war as soon as they came to power. This probably tipped the balance in their favour and led the all important garrison of St Petersburg to take Lenin's side. On 6 November 1917 the Bolsheviks under Lenin's leadership rose against the provisional government and stormed its seat in the Winter Palace. In the night of 7 November the government surrendered and the Bolsheviks were in control[10]: the second Russian Revolution of 1917, known as the October Revolution, had entered history. It is not superfluous, considering the confusion one sometimes

---

[10] As Russia had at that time not yet introduced the Gregorian calendar, these events according to the old chronology took place in the month of October, hence the name October Revolution for the rising of the Bolsheviks.

meets in popular works, to point out that the Bolshevik Revolution was not directed against the tsar, who had already abdicated (and was under arrest together with his family), and took place some seven weeks after the republic had been proclaimed. The October Revolution was aimed against the bourgeois regime of the provisional government, judged too liberal and western and not radical enough in its social and economic policy. The weak and vacillating rule of Kerensky and massive popular unrest had created a void which gave Lenin's temerity its chance. As in France in 1792, so in Russia in November 1917 a more radical revolution overtook its bourgeois predecessor. After 8 November 1917 power was in the hands of Lenin and his government, which was called the Council of People's Commissars and composed of Bolsheviks and a few left-wing SRs, who were ousted after their Moscow revolt of July 1918. It counted fifteen members, of whom eleven were intellectuals and four workers. It took various social measures, such as the Land Decree that expropriated landowners and put the land provisionally at the disposal of peasant soviets; it also nationalized various industries and banks and placed them under the authority of a Higher Council for the National Economy. The existing legal order was eliminated, and attempts were made at once to end the war with Germany and Austria: in March 1918 the peace of Brest–Litowsk was signed, in spite of its harsh conditions.

In the meantime the question of a new Constitution was posed. In December 1917 elections were already held for a Constituent Assembly, which gave a clear victory to the SRs, to the disappointment of the Bolsheviks, who gained only 183 out of a total of 715 seats. As the Constituent Assembly in January 1918 rejected Bolshevik demands for a transfer of all power to the soviets, the Council of Commissars dissolved it and ordered the Red Army to disperse its members. In July 1918 the Bolsheviks proclaimed a Constitution of their own for Russia, which implemented Lenin's idea on the necessity of the dictatorship of the proletariat. In the following years the new regime and its military instrument, the Red Army, vanquished not only the White Russian counter-revolution, but also the revolt of the sailors at Kronstadt in 1921, who demanded more power for the soviets and resisted the claim to absolute and exclusive control of the Communist Party.[11]

The suppression of the 1921 revolt was a crucial turning point, as

---

[11]  P. Avrich, *La tragédie de Cronstadt 1921* (Paris, 1975); I. Getzler, *Kronstadt 1917–1921. The fate of a Soviet democracy* (Cambridge, 1983).

the rebels had wanted to put an end to the dictatorship of the Bolshevik Party and return to a government by the soviets, according to Bolshevik promises. In fact the Tenth Party Congress of that year not only forbade all other parties, but also banned all opposition within its ranks. From then onwards for almost seventy years the omnipotence of the one party in power was never seriously challenged. Lenin's death in 1924 unleashed a bitter struggle for the succession, which was won by the general secretary of the party, Joseph Stalin (*d.*1953), who got rid of his main rival, L. D. Trotsky (*d.*1940). Stalin established in what in 1924 had become the Soviet Union a reign of terror that assumed proportions which had been unthinkable even in imperial Russia. Millions were sent to their deaths, with or without mock trials, by execution or by deportation to Siberia. Among the victims was the almost entire old Bolshevik leadership of the October Revolution and Lenin's entire Politburo.[12]

Two closely related economic developments were brought about under Stalin's guidance, the collectivization of agriculture and a massive industrialization. Private agricultural enterprise, run by well-to-do peasants (kulaks), was condemned and the entire peasantry forced to work in state or collective farms (called respectively sovkhoz and kolkhoz). As a result, by 1936 some 97 per cent of the peasantry were employed in one or another of these enterprises, which were more and more mechanized in order to produce food for the expanding industrial centres.[13] These arose as a consequence of a series of five-year plans for the industrialization of the country, under the guidance of a state committee ad hoc. The main objective was not the production of consumer goods, but the expansion of heavy industry. Although the hard hand of Stalin could be felt everywhere, there was also a good deal of enthusiasm for making the Soviet Union a powerful and socialist industrial country. Stalin had given up hope for a world-wide proletarian revolution (a dream entertained for a few years after the October Revolution) and pursued 'socialism in one country'. Afterwards a mighty and modern Soviet Union would be able to support or impose socialism elsewhere. His vision was not shared by Trotsky, who maintained his belief in a world-wide 'permanent revolution' and whose ideas provided the ideological

---

[12] R. Conquest, *Kolyma: the Arctic death camps* (Oxford, 1979); A. Bullock, *Hitler and Stalin. Parallel lives* (London, 1991), 511–71.

[13] The 'genocide' of the recalcitrant peasantry assumed terrible proportions. See R. Conquest, *The harvest of sorrow* (London, 1986); Bullock, *Hitler and Stalin*, 285–340.

background to his quarrel with Stalin. The strength of the Soviet Union was demonstrated when it resisted the German invasion of 1941 and, after the war, became one of the two superpowers on the international scene.

After Stalin's death there was a thaw of sorts, with a lessening of police terror and growing respect for 'socialist legality'. This came forcefully into the open at the Twentieth and Twenty-Second Party Congresses of 1956 and 1961, when Stalin's terror was officially denounced and his personal responsibility for the unjustified torture and killing of numerous innocent people.[14]

In 1956 the emergency law which had formed the legal basis for Stalin's persecution of the 'enemies of the people', i.e. the so-called Kirov-law of 1934, whereby an exceptional criminal procedure was introduced, denying the accused any rights, was repealed.[15] This form of permanent emergency can be compared to the one created in Nazi Germany by the *Notverordnung* ('emergency decree') of 1933, which we shall study later in the chapter. Stalin, speaking for the Central Committee, had personally authorized torture because it was also applied by 'bourgeois services' against the 'representatives of the socialist proletariat', as his circular letter to local party secretaries of 20 January 1939 put it.[16]

### Constitutional law

Constitutions have taken an important place in the life of the Soviet Union, and we will briefly present them, devoting special attention to the last, proclaimed in 1977 (and abolished in November 1991). But first we would like to make a more general remark about the internal contradictions in the Soviet Union's constitutional development. They can, we believe, be explained by the fact that the new regime pursued several different and even contradictory goals at the same time and through means that were sometimes incompatible with its professed ideals. On the one hand the Soviet Constitutions attached great importance to human liberty, expressed in the freedom of thought

---

[14] B. Lazitch, *Le rapport Khrouchtchev et son histoire* (Paris, 1976).

[15] S. M. Kirov joined the Bolsheviks before the First World War, became a member of the Central Committee of the Party in 1922 and in 1926 succeeded Zinoviev as party boss in Leningrad. In 1930 he became a member of the Politburo. His murder in Leningrad on 1 December 1934 in mysterious circumstances (Khrushchev in his 1956 speech hinted that Stalin was involved) was the start of the great purges of the following years.

[16] A. Rossi, *Autopsie du stalinisme* I (Paris, 1957), 102.

and the press, assembly and demonstration, which flowed from the official ideology, Marxism being a philosophy of liberation. On the other hand Lenin consciously established the exclusive dictatorship of the proletariat, i.e. its own political party, leaving unanswered the question how a dictatorship, by definition the denial of personal freedom, could be compatible with the liberation of the people.

The Soviet Union and other socialist regimes liked to call themselves people's democracies, but how could this popular character be combined with the leading role of the only permissible political formation, the Communist Party (and the single party list at elections), when the party was openly elitist, its membership rising after many years to a mere 6 per cent of the population? This strictly selected minority considered itself the one politically conscious leader of the masses, a claim that brings to mind the attitude of the seventeenth-century 'saints' in Puritan England.

The Soviet Union was from the start confronted with the problem of the relation between the party and the soviets. Judging from its name the Soviet Union should have been run by spontaneous soviets of peasants, workers and soldiers, as was indeed the case in the heady days of the revolution. But in reality all power belonged to the party, which was a strictly centralized formation, and the 'councils', which existed on paper till the end, were anything but spontaneous, as they simply served to enforce the election of party candidates. In the political life of the Soviet state the soviets counted for little and the party controlled everything, a contradiction which, as we have seen, as early as 1921 led to the drama of Kronstadt.

From the start the Soviet regime paid attention to the problem of nationalities in tsarist Russia, and the name Union of Soviet Socialist Republics expressly referred to its federal character. In contrast to the old imperial unitarism the Bolsheviks promised to recognize ethnic diversity and to respect the cultural identity of the numerous nationalities, which the tsars had conquered in the course of the centuries, through the creation of a federation of sovereign republics. In the first Bolshevik government this concern was given expression by the creation of a ministry for the nationalities, led by the people's commissar Joseph Stalin, a Georgian whose father barely spoke Russian. However, reality again looked rather different. Indeed, the dominating role of the Russian language and the Russian republic was accepted or imposed throughout the Union and the 'sovereignty' of the republics was a sham for, whereas the Constitution gave them the right to secede, the criminal code forbade any initiative which could weaken the Union. More importantly the *prokuratura*, the public prosecutor's office, was unitary and centralized, and so, of course, was the Communist Party, where real power resided (Stalin spoke of a 'centralized federation'). In true Jacobin vein 'proletarian centralism' was predominant, and the diversity of national or ethnic groups ignored. The situation inside the Soviet Union had a parallel in international affairs, where the leading role of Moscow was legitimized as 'proletarian internationalism' and defended against 'national deviations', branded as 'bourgeois nationalism', which led fatally to 'bourgeois liberalism.[17]

It seems appropriate to open an excursus here on the nationality problem in general, which is at present at the centre of much political debate. The desire for independence of numerous nationalities in the ex-Soviet Union led to the creation of the Commonwealth of Independent States. The final breakdown of Tito's communist Yugoslavia led several ethnic groups to political autonomy while others were, at the time of writing, locked in battle. In the European Community at the same time a war of words was being waged about the need to save national identities in an *Europe des patries* and to protect the sovereignty of national parliaments against the onslaught of the supranational bureaucracy in Brussels. The terms 'national' and, even more, 'nationalism' are emotionally charged. Most people are naturally attached to their own country and find national feeling not only not reprehensible, but even a virtue. But when it develops into xenophobic nationalism, which makes everything and everybody subservient to national grandeur and expansion, it meets with disapproval. As in every debate on sensitive issues, there is a good deal of verbal confusion between such terms as national identity, nationalism and separatism. Thus when a large country defends itself against a powerful enemy, its courage and patriotism are praised; but when small nations rise against oppression by the central government in order to assert their political as well as their cultural nationhood, they are easily accused of separatism and disruption of the existing order. Yet, why should only large nationalities be entitled to statehood,

---

[17] There were lively discussions on this point at the Twenty-Fifth Party Congress in Moscow in 1976, where the Italian and French communist parties were criticized for their resistance to Moscow's leadership. Also, in February 1976, a few days after the congress of the French Communist Party, *Pravda* attacked its leader, Georges Marchais, reminding him of the fundamental principle of proletarian dictatorship.

when this is clearly the best guarantee of cultural survival? National diversity is a fact of life, in Europe as in the Commonwealth of Independent States. Nevertheless, some people feel that the multiplication of independent states is a threat to peace, but so is oppression by imperial governments that deny minorities the right to live their own lives.[18]

Historically, four main solutions to the nationality problem can be discerned. The first is the imperial approach, where all ethnic groups live together in a vast multinational superstate under one powerful central government and share a single citizenship. In modern history the classic examples are the Danubian monarchy and imperial Russia. The advantages of empire in terms of security, power and wealth are real, but so are the negative aspects, stifling of cultural diversity, overcentralization and domination by one ethnic group and its language. The second solution is the unlimited multiplication of states, allowing every country, region or even city to organize itself politically and run its own business. This total sovereignty *ad infinitum* existed in modern Europe at the level of the nation states, and inside Germany and Italy at the level of principalities and cities. Here again there are positive and negative points, as the *Kleinstaaterei* ('system of mini-states') guarantees 'nearness' and offers smaller groups the scope to live their own lives fully, but it can give them neither large markets nor protection against powerful neighbours (as the small republics created after the collapse of the Habsburg empire have experienced). The third solution is the federal form of government. This is an attempt to combine local with central statehood, of which there is no lack of successful examples in past and present. The advantages of this form of government are obvious enough, as it combines the large market and the security of a great power with a government that is not too remote from the citizens (at least in a genuine federalism, which the old Soviet Union did not offer). On the negative side we find the multiplication of governmental organs and disputes about the exact definition of federal and non-federal matters (the 'subsidiarity' in the discussions about the 1991 Treaty of Maastricht). The fourth solution, which may lie in a remote future, would consist in the creation of a true world order, allowing all states,

---

[18] The term minority should be taken with a grain of salt, as some of these discriminated minorities, the 50 million Ukrainians, for example, are as large as the greater nation states in Western Europe, while others are indeed very small, possibly containing no more than a million people.

however small (and some present member states of the United Nations are very small indeed), to enjoy independence under the protection of a global authority – something that was in President Woodrow Wilson's mind, but proves very hard to realize.

But let us return to the contradictions in Soviet constitutional law, especially that between the power of the state and the protection offered by the law. The Soviet Union was based on Marxist ideology, which branded law and the state as class instruments for the oppression of the workers and doomed to disappear together with capitalist exploitation. In spite of this philosophy, however, the state and its organs became increasingly powerful in the Soviet Union, which in its later stages acquired more respect for the law and the courts, in the name of 'socialist legality'. This important issue posed the much debated question as to whether the Soviet Union was a *Rechtsstaat*, and again revealed some glaring internal contradictions. It is on the one hand undeniable that the Soviet Union wanted to be considered a *Rechtsstaat*. Thus when the Constitution of 1977 declared that all persons in authority were under the law and that the 'Constitution is the highest authority, so that all laws and other acts of state organs must be based on and in conformity with the fundamental law' (Articles 4 and 173), it proclaimed the rule of law. There was admittedly no court empowered to control the constitutionality of the laws, but that does not per se exclude the rule of law, as the case of Britain and some other western countries demonstrates. Nevertheless Soviet jurists have maintained that the rule of law was a bourgeois concept and that their country was no *Rechtsstaat*, but a sovereign state. It seems to us that two concepts are confused here, sovereignty and the rule of law. The former concerns the autonomy of a country to decide its own internal and external policies, the latter concerns the subjection of government to the law, and the example of the United States shows that a country can at the same time be a sovereign state and a law-based state. By proclaiming respect for 'socialist legality' as a fundamental principle, the Soviet Union declared itself a *Rechtsstaat*. And in this connection yet another contradiction deserves to be mentioned. The rule of law presupposes the separation of powers and more particularly the independence of the judiciary. Yet the Bolshevik regime declared from the start in so many words that the *Rechtsstaat* was an objectionable bourgeois notion which crippled the state. I. M. Reisner (*d.*1958), a member of the People's Commissariat of Justice from 1917 to 1919, put it as follows in 1918, during the preparation of the Constitution of that year: 'The separation of powers in legislative, executive and judicial branches corresponds to the structure of the state of the bourgeoisie . . . The Russian Soviet Republic . . . has only one aim, the establishment of a socialist regime, and this heroic struggle needs unity and concentration of power rather than separation'. Nevertheless Article 155 of the Constitution of 1977 expressly proclaimed the independence of the judiciary: 'the judges and people's assessors are independent and only subjected to the law'.

The first Constitution of the Bolshevik regime was proclaimed in July 1918. It was a Russian law, valid for the Russian lands under Bolshevik rule, leaving out huge areas of the old tsarist empire where the red writ did not run. It introduced a regime based on the soviets, moving up from the smallest local ones to the supreme assembly, the All Russian Congress of Soviets. The government was in the hands of the Council of People's Commissars.

The following Constitution was not purely Russian any more, but valid for the territories beyond historic Russia that had been reconquered from counter-revolutionary forces. Consequently the federal organization of this Eurasian superstate was an important feature. This first fundamental law of the Union of Soviet Socialist Republics was approved by the Congress of Soviets in January 1924, shortly after Lenin's death. Following the American model, a number of matters were attributed to the Union, such as foreign relations, defence, general economic policy and essential legal principles. The rest, such as interior affairs, justice, agriculture, education, health and social security, were being left to the republics. The federal character was reflected in the bicameral composition of the Supreme Soviet of the Union, the Congress of Soviets. Its central executive committee contained a Council of the Union, reflecting the demographic reality, and the Council of Nationalities, representing the republics as such. The daily running of affairs remained in the hands of the Council of People's Commissars.

The next fundamental law was the so-called Stalinskaia of December 1936, issued because the party judged that socialism had finally been established. The irony, however, was that this Constitution, full of individual freedoms, was promulgated while the Stalinist terror with the great purges and their mock trials was raging, and that two of the authors of this democratic Constitution fell victim themselves to the fury of their leader, namely Nikolai Bukharin who was executed in

1938[19] and Karl Radek, who was condemned in 1937 and perished, probably in 1939, in the camps. The Constitution was a political manifesto rather than a legal document. The separation of powers was rejected as a factor of weakness at a moment when the workers needed unity and the consolidation of their forces. The state received important economic tasks, and offences against official economic policy were punishable by death. This strong state, however, was only a machine that received its ideological impulse from the party, the political elite consisting, as the Constitution put it, of 'the most active and politically conscious citizens from the ranks of the working class, labouring peasants and intellectuals': they were united in the Communist Party of the Soviet Union, which was 'the vanguard of the workers in their struggle to build a communist society and the leading core of all organizations, social as well as political, of the working people'. The federal structure was preserved, as was the organization of soviets, forming a pyramid of councils from the villages at the bottom to the Soviet of the USSR at the summit. In reality the top decisions were taken by the Politburo, chosen by the Central Committee of the Party, and by its General Secretary, who at that time was Stalin.

By 1977 the moment was judged ripe for a new Constitution. Its drafting was preceded by a wider popular consultation and, although it brought no fundamental change, it placed some significant new accents, relating to foreign policy, the omission of the dictatorship of the proletariat, the importance attached to the supremacy of the law (called the principle of socialist legality) and the express declaration that the state belonged to the people as a whole and not to the party, the bureaucracy or the leadership alone. There were in the Constitution of 1977 numerous articles which sounded familiar to the western jurist, concerning the federal nature of the Union, the composition and competence of the organs of the state, the freedom of the citizens and the rule of law.

The USSR was a federation of fifteen sovereign union-republics, twenty autonomous republics, eight autonomous regions and ten autonomous districts.[20] The population figures of the fifteen basic republics varied greatly, from about 135 million for the Russian and fifty million for the Ukrainian republics, to less than two million for Estonia. All these sovereign union-republics, provided with Constitu-

---

[19] S. F. Cohen, *Bukharin and the Bolshevik Revolution* (2nd edn, Oxford, 1980).
[20] The last three types were situated within the borders of one of the union-republics, and constituted a federalism within the federation.

tions of their own, had complete residual competence, i.e. over all affairs not attributed to the central organs of the Soviet Union itself. However, as the Constitution also stipulated that as well as eleven specifically named matters, decisions 'on all other problems of importance to the Union' fell under the competence of the highest organs of the USSR, the role of the republics could be severely eroded. Nevertheless the constitutional recognition of the cultural identity of large numbers of nations or ethnic groups on the territory of the USSR was a far cry from the absolute unitarism of the old tsarist empire.

Political power was vested in the aforementioned pyramid of elected soviets. The Supreme Soviet was bicameral and reflected the federal organization of the country, as it contained the Soviet of the Union, whose membership was proportional to population, and the Soviet of Nationalities, where the ethnic components were represented irrespective of demographic data, but taking into account their status as union-republic, autonomous republic, autonomous region or autonomous district. The Supreme Soviet was the 'highest organ of state power', wielding, *inter alia*, the highest legislative authority. Its Presidium was given various specific tasks and could be considered the collective head of state, and its president the individual head of the USSR. The government was called the Council of Ministers of the Soviet Union, the 'highest executive and decreeing organ of the state'. This very large body contained a core of about twelve members who carried out the day to day business of ruling the country; it was called the Presidium of the Council of Ministers and whereas previously it had only existed in fact, it was now given constitutional recognition. The Constitution of 1977 guaranteed the familiar freedoms of thought, press, assembly, association and conscience, i.e. 'the right to profess any religion or none, to worship or to make atheistic propaganda' – the 'excitement of feelings of enmity and hatred against religious convictions being forbidden'. Personal inviolability was also guaranteed in the following terms: 'nobody can be arrested except by judicial decision or the agreement of the prosecuting magistrate'. All organs of the state were, as mentioned before, placed under the authority of the law, and the old cornerstone of Bolshevik rule, the dictatorship of the proletariat, was given up: 'having entirely accomplished the task of the dictatorship of the proletariat, the Soviet state has become the state of all the people', claimed the general introduction to the Constitution. The text went on: 'the activity of the Soviet state and all its organs is based on socialist legality: they guarantee legal order' (Article 4). Even the leading role of the Communist Party was placed under the law, in the words of Article 6: 'the operation of all party organizations takes place within the framework of the fundamental law of the USSR', the 'strengthening of the legal foundation of the life of the state and society' being, in the words of Article 9, one of the fundamental tendencies in the country's political system.

Review of the legality of governmental decrees was attributed to parliament or, as Article 121(7) put it: 'the Presidium of the Supreme Soviet annuls the decisions and decrees of the Council of Ministers of the USSR and of the Councils of Ministers of the Union Republics, if they conflict with the law'. In the same context we find the familiar declaration on the citizens' equality before the law, the prohibition of discrimination on the basis of race, sex, language, nationality or religious attitude, whereas proclaiming the superiority of a particular race or nation was made an offence (Articles 33–8).

Besides these, to western ears, familiar themes, the Constitution contained another set of articles which were unknown in the classic western texts of the nineteenth century (even though they had made some headway there in the twentieth). We mention the economic articles in chapter II, entitled *the economic system* (Articles 10–18), directly following chapter I, entitled *the political system*. Here we read that 'the economic system of the USSR is based on the socialist property of the means of production in the shape of state property (of all the people) and the property of kolkhozes and sovkhozes'. Individual ownership was accepted in so far as it was based on income from labour or savings from that income; as private ownership of the means of production led, in the Marxist view, to exploitation, it was proscribed. In this connection the Constitution of 1977 also contained a set of provisions on the economic safety and social security of the citizens. Personal liberties and the rule of law were deemed useless if the people enjoying them lived in poverty or economic serfdom: what sense did the traditional freedoms make to someone without a roof over his head? These articles concerned the right to work, free medical care, provisions for old age, sickness and disablement as well as free education at all levels. To these rights various duties corresponded (the famous 'duties of the citizens' of which the French Constituent Assembly in 1789 did not want to hear). The duty to work went hand in hand with the right to work; there was no 'right to laziness', but a 'right to relax'. Article 60 put it as follows: 'It is for every able bodied citizen of the USSR a duty and a point of honour to work conscientiously . . . and strictly to obey the discipline of the workplace, as desisting from socially useful labour goes against the principles of a socialist community'. On the other hand the state had the duty to encourage physical fitness and sport (Article 24) and to take care of the 'protection, the advancement and wide diffusion of spiritual values, educating the Soviet people morally and aesthetically, and raising their cultural level' (Article 27).

A third, and possibly the most interesting group of articles was most strange to western jurists, who either did not expect to meet them in a piece of legislation, let alone a fundamental law, or found them alien to their own experience. The Constitution was indeed not only a law, but also a programme, a profession of faith and the proclamation of the millenarian mission of the state of the soviets, at home and abroad. In the introductory declaration promises were held out 'of democracy and peace in the whole world'. The Constitution of 1977 was the fundamental law of an ideologically motivated state, carrying out an historic and universal mission – a very different stance from the ideologically neutral states in the West, that are no more than legal shells for citizens to lead their personal lives in, according to their own beliefs and values. The very first lines of the Constitution declared: 'The great Socialist October Revolution, carried out by the workers and peasants of Russia under the guidance of the Communist Party led by V. I. Lenin, smashed the power of capitalists and big landowners, established the dictatorship of the proletariat, broke the chains of oppression and created the Soviet State, a state of a new type'. And the paragraph ended, on a similar messianic tone, with the declaration that 'in this way the historic world-wide transition of mankind from capitalism to socialism was initiated'.

In order to safeguard this heritage and to continue on the road to communism a strong state was indispensable. At the end of the road, after socialism had given way to the ultimate achievement of communism, the state would be meaningless and doomed to disappear. In the meantime, however, its power was needed to keep the forces of reaction in check. When exactly this disappearance would take place was a moot point that used to pop up in theoretical journals. The date was, like that of the coming of the Lord for the early Christians, constantly pushed into a more distant future. It was precisely because a strong state was necessary and capitalism meant bondage for the workers that the constitutional freedoms had to be limited, as they could not be invoked against the workers and their state. We are faced here with a philosophical conception of freedom that was totally different from its western counterpart. Freedom in the Soviet Union was a guided, teleological freedom, not to do what one liked, but to co-operate in the construction of socialism. It was comparable to the Christian doctrine that true liberty consists in doing God's will. Consequently Article 50, which guaranteed freedom of the press and of the expression of opinion, stated that Soviet citizens enjoyed those liberties 'in accordance with the interests of the people and in order to strengthen and develop the socialist regime'. No aimless, unbridled, but a targeted and meaningful freedom! In this light one understands that there was no room for 'lies' in the media and that western-style freedom of the press was rejected by Lenin as a fiction: what could the workers expect from a press that called itself free, but was owned by capitalists and financial interests? Hence in the USSR, control of the media was absolute, as there was not only a bureaucracy of some 70,000 officials in the censorship department, but private ownership of printing presses and other equipment for the multiplication of texts was excluded.[21] Hence also the severe punishments meted out to authors who had offended against Article 70 of the criminal code, which forbade 'anti-soviet propaganda', even though 'criticism' was allowed by the Constitution and 'prosecution because of criticism' forbidden (Article 49). Hence also the prohibition of strikes for higher wages and of free trade unions beside, let alone against, the existing official ones. Article 8 of the Constitution stated that it was the task of the 'associations of working people' to ensure the 'strengthening of labour discipline' and the education of their members 'in the spirit of communist morality'. A few isolated attempts in the 1980s to found independent unions ended with the initiators being sent to psychiatric hospitals: to the official mind founding a union of workers against the state of workers and peasants must indeed have seemed an act of madness. Article 51 granted the citizens the right 'to organize themselves in social organizations', but it added that this was to be

---

[21] It is not surprising that clandestine publications flourished, called *samizdat* ('own publication'), a term that appeared around 1966 in contrast to *gosizdat* ('government publication'). They were typed and circulated secretly, the best known being the *Chronicle of current events*, the organ from April 1968 onwards of the Movement for Human Rights (an English translation was published in London by Amnesty International). See P. Reddaway (ed.), *Uncensored Russia* (London, 1972); M. Meerson-Aksenov and B. Shragin (eds.), *The political, social and religious thought of Russian 'Samizdat'. An anthology* (Belmont, Mass., 1978); A. Boiter (ed.), *Sobranie dokumentov samizdata* (Zug, 1979).

done 'in accordance with the aim of the construction of communism'.[22]

The state in all its sections, governments, soviets, law courts, army and police, had to pursue one historic goal; it was no blind mechanism, but an inspired community of people. In order to ensure correct decisions and the right orientation of all these activities an organization was needed, operating outside the state but inspiring and animating it. This was the role of the Communist Party of the Soviet Union, the only authorized political formation. It was the party that had the final word in all fundamental questions and decisions, as it was the keeper of Marxism–Leninism, the ideological cornerstone and philosophical justification of the very existence of the Soviet state. The situation recalled medieval society, based on the Christian faith, whose guardian and expositor was the Church. Not only were all important functions in the Soviet Union held by members of the Politburo or at least the Central Committee, so that the party directly controlled the corridors of political power, but it also dominated the selection and training of the bureaucracy and the judicature.[23] For this purpose the party secretariat disposed of a list of all key posts in the party, the state and the enterprises called the *nomenklatura*, i.e. an elite of members or confidants of the party who enjoyed various privileges.

The leading role of the party was not just a factual situation, but a constitutional principle, as appeared from Article 6: 'The leading and guiding force of Soviet society and the nucleus of its political system, of all state organizations and public organizations is the Communist Party of the Soviet Union ... Armed with Marxist–Leninist doctrine, it determines the central line of development of society, the internal and external political course of the USSR, it guides the great constructive activity of the Soviet people and provides a planned and scientifically founded character to their struggle for the victory of communism'. As the party was the all powerful formation, its general secretary was the key figure in the Soviet Union.

The single party consisted, as we said, of an elite, an eminent minority to which one acceded through co-optation and which excelled by its exceptional dedication and personal morality. Hence

---

[22] S. Bloch and P. Reddaway, *Russia's political hospitals. The abuse of psychiatry in the Soviet Union* (London, 1977); *Syndicat libre en URSS. Dossier réuni par le comité international contre la répression* (Paris, 1978).

[23] By 1937 some 90% of the judges were party members. In the West also there are democracies where access to the Bench and promotion require the support of political parties, the idea being that the judicature should roughly reflect the power relations in parliament.

the crucial role of the party in the elections for the soviets, the people's representatives at all levels and the pillars of the state. Articles 89–102, devoted to this matter, showed again a marked difference with the western approach, in spite of superficial similarities. Suffrage was universal for all citizens over eighteen years of age without discrimination, everyone having one vote in a direct and secret ballot. However, the electorate only had a very limited choice, as there was only one list to vote on, that of the 'Block of communists and those without a party affiliation', and when, as usually happened, this single list contained only one name, the choice lay between acceptance or rejection of the official candidate. There were no opposition parties, because the western notion of opposition was unknown in the Soviet Union, where it was equated with sabotage, treason and anti-soviet propaganda. So everything depended on who got on to the list of candidates and that decision was in the hands of a restricted committee of the Communist Party, which saw to it that only party members or sympathizers received that honour. Article 100 of the Constitution put it as follows: 'The right to propose candidates for the office of people's representative belongs to the organizations of the Communist Party of the Soviet Union, the trade unions, the national league of the communist Lenin-Youth, the co-operatives and their social organizations, to the associations of working people and the general assemblies of soldiers in their units'. In the local soviets non-party members were numerous, but they became rarer as one went up the ladder. These elections clearly made sense only when they were understood as mass manifestations of adhesion and support for the leadership and as festive demonstrations of loyalty to the Soviet Union and socialism. The elections regularly showed that this was the case with the majority of the people, so that the elections could be seen as ritual plebiscites in favour of the state and its trustees.

There were more surprising elements in the Constitution of 1977, which one would expect in a civil code rather than in a fundamental law: they concerned, for example, the duty of children to care for their parents. Other articles would have been more suited to a governmental declaration or a law on the preservation of historic monuments, such as the duty of the citizens to protect their cultural heritage. Equally amazing was the attention paid to international relations. In one of those contradictions that we mentioned before it was stated on the one hand that the Soviet Union aimed at 'strengthening the position of socialism in the world and supporting the struggle of the peoples for national liberation and social progress' (Article 28), but on the other hand it was said that 'non-interference in the internal affairs' of other countries was the foundation of the external relations of the USSR (Article 29). Here we find the old dream of a world revolution and the universal victory of Marxism (with reminiscences of the Comintern of 1919–43) combined with growing respect for the legal order in general and the law of nations in particular.[24]

The appearance of M. Gorbachev on the Soviet scene and its world-wide repercussions belong to political history and need not detain us here, but their constitutional fall-out deserves all our attention. Gorbachev's policy of glasnost led to freedom of information, his policy of perestroika opened the way to a market economy, whereas his foreign policy put an end to decades of confrontation with the West and led to the collapse of the Soviet empire. It all amounted to a veritable revolution, even though it was initiated from above and, so Gorbachev hoped, would be carried out under the guidance of the party. But the movement of liberation soon got out of hand and turned against the one-party system. The collapse of communism became visible in the wonder year 1989, when Gorbachev was general secretary of the party and president of the Soviet Union. There were changes in the Central Committee of the Party and in the Politburo, the elections for the congress of people's representatives of April 1989 went badly for the old leaders and brought B. Yeltsin to the fore, and the scheduled revision of the Constitution failed to materialize. The nationality problem reappeared in strength. Lithuania abolished the one-party system. The anniversary of the October Revolution in Red Square in Moscow was celebrated without reference to Marxism-Leninism. After the failed conservative coup of August 1991 things went from bad to worse for the Communist Party, which was not only banned but, in 1992, came under judicial scrutiny as a criminal organization accused of robbery, oppression and murder. Its general secretary, Gorbachev, who had initiated the momentous transformation, was stripped of public office. At the time of writing the old Soviet Union had left the historical stage, through a process that, in comparison with many other changes of regime, was amazingly peaceful. The ancient nationality problem was provisionally solved by granting the nations and ethnic groups so much autonomy

---

[24] We would like to express our thanks to the late Professor J. Gilissen and his successor in the University of Brussels, Professor F. Gorlé, for information and commentary on the Soviet Constitution of 1977.

that the new Commonwealth of Independent States is an alliance of states rather than a federal Union.[25]

## GERMANY AND THE THIRD REICH

### *Introductory remarks*

The short period of Adolf Hitler's Nazi regime (1933–45) is known as the Third Reich, the Holy Roman Empire being the first, and the empire of the Hohenzollerns the second. Its violent world-wide impact has produced a vast historical literature and a never ending debate. One question that is often posed concerns the roots of Nazism: was it the normal outcome of age-old tendencies and permanent characteristics, or was it a momentary aberration, caused by an extraordinary concurrence of circumstances, an unforeseen and unforeseeable catastrophe in German history? The defenders of the former thesis allege the traditional German submissiveness to the authority of strong rulers, and refer to the historic roots of German anti-Semitism, a glaring feature of Martin Luther's writings, for example. Their opponents argue that ever since the *Aufklärung* there was a strong liberal tradition in Germany, with marked respect for the 'law abiding state'. They point out that anti-Semitism is an ancient European phenomenon, which was particularly virulent in nineteenth-century France and Austria, and that absolutist rule was widespread outside Germany. In our own view Nazism was not a typical German product, nor was it the natural outcome of the preceding centuries: similar authoritarian nationalist regimes have been known elsewhere in twentieth-century Europe, and modern German society until Hitler had shown attachment to critical thought, free research and the *Rechtsstaat*. The victory of the Nazi Party was the result of an extraordinary conjunction of dramatic developments, the great economic depression of 1929 and following years being the decisive one. The results of the Reichstag elections speak for themselves. As late as 1928 Hitler's party was an eccentric side-show, as disreputable as it was negligible, and disposing of a

---

[25] On the rising importance of constitutional thought and the increasing role of the lawyers in the later stages of the Soviet Union, Gorbachev being the most conspicuous example, see R. S. Wortman, *The development of a Russian legal consciousness* (Chicago, 1977); J. N. Hazard, *Managing change in the USSR. The politico-legal role of the Soviet jurist* (Cambridge, 1983). For the earlier years, see E. Huskey, *Russian lawyers and the Soviet state. The origins and development of the Soviet bar 1917–1939* (Princeton, 1986).

paltry twelve seats in parliament. But in September 1930, hardly one year after the great panic on Wall Street, it jumped to 107 seats, and the 'marginal phenomenon' became the second largest party in the Reichstag; in July 1932 it was the biggest, with 230 seats. It is clear that the internal weakness of the Weimar Republic also paved the way for Nazi rule. The failure of this first democratic regime and the first republic on German soil now deserves our attention.

## The Weimar Republic

When, in November 1918, the war looked hopeless for Germany, the home front collapsed. Just as in Russia a year before, strikes, mutiny and popular revolts betrayed massive discontent with the war and the regime. Kaiser Wilhelm II abdicated and left the country. The socialist leader P. Scheidemann (*d*.1939) proclaimed the republic on 9 November 1918, and a provisional government was installed that decided to respect the legal order. This contrasted with the *Räterepublik* (i.e. 'republic of councils') proclaimed on the same day, after the model of the Russian soviets, by the communist leader Karl Liebknecht (*d*.1919) and called the Freie Sozialistische Republik Deutschland. Both the attempts of the councils of workers and soldiers to seize power and the revolt of the German Communist Party (the Spartacus League), founded on 31 December 1918, were suppressed after prolonged street fighting. It was mainly thanks to the efforts of the moderate, reformist social democrats that a government on western lines survived and elections were organized, in January 1919, for a National Constituent Assembly. The parties and their respective strengths looked traditional enough. The social democrats with 163, the liberals (Deutsche Demokratische Partei and Deutsche Volkspartei) with 94, and the Catholic German Centre Party with 73 seats were and remained the pillars of the new Germany until the thirties. The Constituent Assembly met in Weimar, which was safer than turbulent Berlin, and debated about the Constitution, which was proclaimed in August 1919. Germany was a democratic, constitutional and parliamentary republic. It was also a federal state, even though the balance between the federal powers and those of the Länder was clearly tilted in favour of the former. The ancient dynasties, often of medieval origin and without which public life seemed hardly thinkable – such as the Bavarian House of Wittelsbach – disappeared following local revolts, but attempts to replace them by *Räterepubliken* were foiled.

While the Constitution was being discussed in Weimar, the victorious allies met at the Conference of Paris to draft a peace treaty with Germany and, incidentally, with Austria and Hungary. Strangely enough this was no meeting where the ex-belligerents, who had concluded an armistice on 11 November 1918, sat around the table to discuss peace terms, but a conference of the victors who debated and drafted the terms of a treaty in Germany's absence. After the allied powers had agreed on the text, it was communicated to the German government, composed of socialists and Catholics and led by the socialist Gustav Bauer (*d*.1944). The National Assembly accepted it and it was signed at Versailles, under the threat of renewed hostilities and a blockade of Germany. The conditions were harsh. Germany lost territory, had to pay damages amounting to an unrealistic 226 billion gold marks and was forced to acknowledge exclusive guilt for the First World War. This most unusual clause in a peace treaty was not only historically incorrect (Austrian keenness on punishing the Serbs, for example, was also to blame), but was an unnecessary humiliation of a great power. Right from the start the Weimar Republic was abominated both by the extreme right and the extreme left. The former never forgave its leaders for the signing of the Treaty of Versailles and reproached the socialists with betraying the unconquered army by proclaiming the republic; the latter never forgot the suppression, with the help of bayonets, of the radical left.

The first years of the new regime were miserable. The currency became worthless, ruining millions of citizens, and the French and Belgian armies occupied the Ruhr area in order to force the Germans, who offered passive resistance, to pay the war damages. One putsch followed another: the Kapp putsch in Berlin in 1920, and those of the Rhineland separatists, the national-socialists and the Hamburg communists, all three in 1923. However, in the mid-twenties the sky looked brighter, as the Treaties of Locarno caused an international détente and Germany entered the League of Nations. National politics also entered calmer waters, but not for long: the great economic depression hit Germany particularly hard, and quickly led to massive unemployment, with 3 million jobless by the end of 1929, almost 5 million early in 1931 and over 6 million at the beginning of 1932. The traditional parties hoped to muddle through, but political instability took on alarming proportions (twenty governments in fourteen years). Parliament abdicated in favour of the president, Field Marshal Paul von Hindenburg, a hero of the First World War, born in 1847, who was supposed to overcome the crisis with emergency decrees and full powers. When all this failed, the country rejected the regime, lost trust in the centre parties that were loyal to the republic and gave its confidence to the two extremist movements that had sworn to bring down the existing social and political order, the Nazis and the communists. On 30 January 1933 President Hindenburg appointed Hitler as chancellor, i.e. head of government, thus initiating Nazi rule and sealing the fate of the existing regime.

The Constitution of the Weimar Republic was an interesting document whose main outlines we shall now present. As was so often the case in the past, so here again the fundamental issue concerned the balance of power between the executive and parliament, a situation that went back, as we have seen, to the medieval give and take between the crown and the assemblies of estates. To be more precise, two republican models vied with each other, the American, with a president heading the government and ministers only responsible to him, and that of the French Third Republic, where the president was a figure-head and the government depended utterly and solely on parliament. Weimar constituted a compromise between those two options. On the one hand the republic was not only constitutional, but also fully parliamentary, as the cabinet and every single minister depended on the confidence of the Reichstag, which could bring down governments without producing an alternative cabinet (in contrast with the 'constructive motion of censure' of present-day Germany). On the other hand the president's position was greatly strengthened by the fact that he was elected by the people and that he appointed both the head of government and – on the latters's proposal – the other members of the cabinet. Executive power was, of course, in the hands of president, chancellor and cabinet.

Legislation belonged to the Reichstag, which was elected directly by general male and female suffrage. Corresponding to the federal structure of the republic, there was also a Reichsrat, representing the Länder and composed of members of the latter's governments. Its legislative role was restricted and mainly advisory.

Besides the traditional freedoms the Constitution also mentioned various duties of the citizens. Some were rather unexpected in a fundamental law, such as the duty of parents to provide a good physical and spiritual education for their children, or the duty of every German to dispose of his property in view of the 'common good', an expression of the lawgiver's social preoccupation, referring in particular to the idea that the land should be tilled and made useful. Equality before the law was also proclaimed and advantages and disadvantages at public law, based on birth or social position, were proscribed. Marriage was placed 'under the special protection of the fundamental law' and motherhood was placed under the protection of the state.

The Constitution also provided for a form of direct democracy in the shape of the referendum. However, as direct democracy is the eternal cinderella of European public law, it comes as no surprise that the articles in question have remained a dead letter. They deserve nevertheless to be briefly presented because of their academic interest and because they show how difficult it is to make direct democracy work in those countries – and they are the great majority – where popular decision making has no historical tradition. Article 73 of the Constitution of Weimar provided that every law passed by the Reichstag had to be submitted to a referendum if the president so decided within one month. Article 74 laid down that in case the Reichsrat objected, the bill was sent back to the Reichstag and if the two houses maintained their dissension, the president could organize a referendum; if the Reichstag had rejected the Reichsrat's objections with a two-thirds majority, the president could either proclaim the disputed law or organize a referendum. All these provisions were based on the philosophy of Article 1 of the Constitution which said that the authority of the state emanated from the people.

A whole section of the text, Articles 151–65, was a rather elaborate attempt to proclaim both free enterprise and the 'socialization' (to quote Article 156) of the economy. This squaring of the circle proved so difficult that the lawgiver only managed to produce vague generalizations. Thus Article 151 stated that 'freedom of commerce and trade is guaranteed according to the laws of the republic', but added that 'the organization of economic life must respect fundamental justice and provide a humane existence for everyone'. No practising lawyer knew what to do with that sort of message and, in the early thirties, a humane existence was in any case out of the question for the millions of unemployed.

The Constitution, of course, defined the nature of the republic, but did so in such obscure terms that endless discussions among jurists were the result. The name Deutsches Reich, for example, did not exactly evoke a federal country, and the old crowned heads and their kingdoms and dukedoms had all gone. Nevertheless Germany had to be a federal rather than a unitary state, because regional patriotism – in Bavaria, for example – was so strong. Hence Weimar Germany consisted – at least initially – of twenty-five Länder, each with a parliament and a government of its own, and repeated conflicts broke out between Berlin and separatist movements, especially in Bavaria and the Rhineland. However, the power of the president, the chancellor and the Reichstag was so great all over the republic that one might be justified in speaking of a decentralized unitary state. The old pre-eminence of Prussia, and the special relationship between Prussia and the German state had gone, so that, strictly speaking, Prussia was a Land like any other. In reality its political weight was still very considerable, because of its large population and economic preponderance: Prussia contained some 37 million inhabitants, whereas the Land Schaumburg-Lippe, for example, had no more than 50,000.

In the fundamental relationship between the executive and legislative branches the last years of the Weimar regime witnessed a striking shift away from parliament and towards the president, albeit without any formal change in the Constitution. It is clear that the Constituent Assembly of 1919 definitely wanted to create a parliamentary republic, and Article 52 stated expressly, speaking of the chancellor and the members of the cabinet: 'each one of them shall resign, whenever the Reichstag withdraws its confidence by an express decision', whereas Article 50 held that all decrees and decisions of the president needed the counter-signature of the chancellor or the competent minister, who by doing so assumed responsibility. Parliament, and more precisely the Reichstag, was the cornerstone of the political edifice, or at least this was the case in the eyes of the lawgiver. In fact, things turned out quite differently as, especially in the later years under President Hindenburg (who assumed office in 1925), parliament lost its impact and the president took effective power, or rather, power was handed to him on a plate. The numerous political parties and their changing majorities in parliament did not succeed in producing governments capable of carrying out long-term policies.

The parliamentarians often failed to find the courage for necessary but unpopular measures, especially in the financial field, and were grateful when Hindenburg, whose prestige was unassailable, was prepared to take the blame upon himself. The legal mechanism by which this was done was based on two articles of the Constitution.

Article 48 laid down that whenever public order was threatened, the president could 'take the necessary measures to ensure public safety and order' and that in view of this aim he could also 'temporarily' completely or partially suspend the fundamental freedoms of Articles 114, 115, 117, 118, 123, 124 and 153 concerning personal liberty, the inviolability of the home, privacy of letters, freedom of the press and of association and assembly, and respect of property. The commentators interpreted Article 48 as providing for a *Diktaturgewalt* ('dictatorial power') and justified it as a necessary but temporary means of saving the Constitution itself in times of grave crisis: ancient Rome was quoted as an example and authority! The decrees issued on the strength of Article 48, which came to be known as *Notverordnungen* ('emergency decrees'), were so frequent that the republic, even before 1933 and the notorious *Verordnung zum Schutz von Volk und Staat* ('decree for the protection of the people and the state') of February of that year, had slipped into a permanent regime of emergency decrees, while parliament looked on passively. The decrees under Article 48 had admittedly to be notified to parliament and had to be revoked if parliament requested it, but the politicians were too divided to take this step and were all too happy to let the president govern the country, while they devoted themselves to their favourite pastime, forming coalitions and making ideological speeches. The country saluted this *Diktaturgewalt* of the old president as a stabilizing factor and to many his rule was a surrogate monarchy: at public manifestations Hindenburg always spoke with great veneration of the monarchy and loved to present himself as the emperor's loyal soldier. He also consciously strove to expand his power, as was made clear at his swearing in as president in 1925: he demanded the recognition of the president of the Reich as a political factor on an equal footing with the Reichstag.

The president was in a truly strong position, both vis-à-vis the government and parliament, as he appointed and dismissed the leader of the cabinet and could dissolve the Reichstag and organize new elections, a prospect that held little attraction for the sitting members. The Reichstag also, even before 1933, sometimes gave the government full legislative powers by passing *Ermächtigungsgesetze* ('Enabling Acts') and temporarily eliminating itself. These precursors of Hitler's *Gesetz zur Behebung der Not von Volk und Reich* ('law for the relief of the distress of the people and the state'), the famous Enabling Act of March 1933, concerned, *inter alia*, the great economic reforms of 1923–4, the stabilization of the currency and the financial reorganization of the state. It can be said without exaggeration that from 1930 onwards the parliamentary regime came to a grinding halt. It was unfortunate that the first German experiment with a parliamentary republic coincided with a deep European crisis of parliamentarianism.

The Weimar Republic did not survive the shock of the early thirties. Why this was so is a problem of political history, which should not detain us here. What we are concerned with is a question of legal history: when and how did the Constitution of 1919 go under? We consciously did not ask when it was 'abolished', because it was never expressly and legally cancelled (as happened, for example, with the French Third Republic): it died a quiet death, so quiet that the exact time of its demise is hard to determine.

If one accepts that a Constitution is clinically dead as soon as the majority of the people reject it, the year 1932 can be considered as the date of the Weimar Republic's end. Indeed at the Reichstag elections of 31 July 1932 the two extreme parties that had sworn to kill the republic, Nazis and communists, together obtained a majority of 318 seats out of a total of 608: their combined votes could prevent any Weimar-loyal government. Socialists, liberals and Catholics, who had supported the republic from the start, had lost the confidence of the majority of the German electorate. Formally speaking, however, the Constitution was still in force, and when President Hindenburg in January 1933 appointed the Nazi leader Adolf Hitler as chancellor in order to form a 'government of national union', he acted on the strength of Article 53 of the fundamental law. Similarly, when in February 1933 the emergency decree suspending constitutional rights was issued which was the legal basis for the Nazi police-state for twelve years, it was done 'on the strength of Article 48(2) of the Constitution of the Reich'. And when the Reichstag passed the Enabling Act of March 1933, handing over legislative power to the government for four years, it again was done in the form of a constitutional amendment and with the two-thirds majority required by Article 76 of the fundamental law.[26]

The Enabling Act of 1933 consisted of five articles, but the first two said all. Article 1 stated: 'Reich laws can, besides the procedure laid

---

[26] The Enabling Act was renewed in 1937, 1939 and 1943, an interesting indication of the new regime's schizophrenic combination of legal formalism with ruthless violence and basic contempt of the rule of law.

down by the Constitution, also be passed by the government. This applies equally to the laws referred to in Articles 85(2) and 87 of the Constitution' (i.e. budget laws). Article 2 laid down: 'The Reich laws passed by the government may deviate from the Constitution, in so far as they do not concern the organization of the Reichstag and the Reichsrat as such. The rights of the President of the Reich remain unaffected'.

Even this formalistic respect of the fundamental law was finally abandoned in August 1934 on the death of President Hindenburg. According to the Constitution new presidential elections should have been held, but Hitler caused the government to pass a law uniting the functions of head of state and head of government in his own hands. This clearly violated the Constitution and also the Enabling Act of March 1933 which stipulated, as we have seen, that the rights of the president were to remain unaffected. The crowning achievement of the coup d'état of August 1934 was the replacement of the army's oath of loyalty to the Constitution by one to the person of the 'Führer of the German Reich and people, Adolf Hitler'. It must have been clear even to those who loved to think that legality was at least formally being observed that the Constitution of 1919 had become a worthless bit of paper. No Nazi law mentions the Constitution of Weimar, not even to state that it was abolished or amended. The de facto elimination of the Constitution by the events of 1933 and 1934 was called 'the legal revolution' by Nazi jurists, and it was indeed obvious to everyone that a revolution had truly taken place.

### Nazi Germany

We have seen how in 1933 the Weimar Republic gave itself up to Hitler. Before presenting the public law during his years in office it is fitting to analyse his political aims and underlying beliefs. Adolf Hitler was born in Austria in 1889, and in 1907 went to Vienna to lead an errant life. In this cosmopolitan capital of the multiracial Habsburg empire, where the Germans were a dominant but threatened minority, he became a convinced racist and a champion of German and Germanic supremacy against the menace of Jews and Slavs (many Viennese Jews came from Slav countries). During the First World War Hitler fought as a volunteer in the Bavarian army and afterwards entered politics in Munich. He never accepted the

German defeat, attributing it and the hated *Diktat* of Versailles to Jewish and left-wing traitors who, in his view, had stabbed Germany in the back. The Weimar Republic was the object of his scorn because it had signed the Treaty of Versailles and he blamed its parliamentary regime for the division and weakness of Germany. He turned an existing mini-party into a mass-movement, called the National-sozialistische Deutsche Arbeiterpartei ('National Socialist German Workers' Party' – NSDAP). As the name indicated, the party was meant to bring together the two great currents with mass appeal of the twentieth century, socialism and nationalism, i.e. the desire for social justice and the exaltation of national pride. Nationalism, lifting Germany to the leading position to which she was entitled, was Hitler's prime motive. It would be wrong, however, to underestimate the plebeian and anti-capitalist ingredients, i.e. the struggle for the liberation of the people from the 'stranglehold of Jewish plutocracy' and 'interest-slavery'.[27] It is, however, clear that this second component in Hitler's eyes lost its importance as his international objective, for which he needed the army and the industrialists, gained the upper hand. But, however strongly anti-capitalist the Nazis may have been, they always remained fanatical anti-Marxists, not only because Karl Marx was a Jew, but also because he had preached international solidarity, whereas the Nazis dreamed of a German socialism of their own and despised everything cosmopolitan and supranational. They were prepared to collaborate with the communists temporarily and for tactical reasons, against the Weimar Republic, for example, or against Poland and the western democracies at the time of the Ribbentrop–Molotov pact of August 1939, when both parties pursued their own objectives: Germany hoped for safety at her back while she tackled the western powers before conquering Russia, whereas the Soviet Union hoped that Germany and her enemies would exhaust themselves in a protracted war, after which Stalin would dominate the world.

Convinced as he was of the innate superiority of the German

---

[27] All social layers were represented in the Nazi Party and not only the middle class, as is sometimes maintained. See on this controversial point the following studies. D. Gessner, *Agrarverbände in der weimarer Republik* (Düsseldorf, 1977); R. F. Hamilton, *Who voted for Hitler?* (Princeton, 1982); M. Kater, *The Nazi Party. A social profile of members and leaders 1919–1945* (Oxford, 1983); Z. Sternhell, *Ni Droite ni Gauche. L'idéologie fasciste en France* (Paris, 1983) (deals with France but contains generalizations on proletarian nationalism and anti-democratic, anti-Marxist anti-capitalism); H. Trevor-Roper, *Was nazism unique?* (Opladen, 1983); P. Manstein, *Die Mitglieder und Wähler der NSDAP 1919–1933. Untersuchungen zu ihrer schichtmässigen Zusammensetzung* (3rd edn, Berne, Frankfurt, 1990).

people, Hitler could only explain their misery by blaming external factors, i.e. an alien race – the Jews – and a feeble state – the Weimar Republic and its party politics. Consequently both anti-Semitism and anti-parliamentarianism were fundamental to his movement. Hitler also believed in violence and he created his own party-army, where numerous disgruntled ex-soldiers found refuge. It was called the *Sturmabteilungen* (SA), whereas his personal bodyguards, a Nazi elite corps, were called the *Schutzstaffeln* (SS).

In 1923 Hitler attempted a coup in Munich that was foiled by the police. He was imprisoned and wrote *Mein Kampf* ('my struggle'), in which he rejected the existing order and outlined what a future, greater Germany should undertake, i.e. to build a strong *Führerstaat*, ensure racial purity and let 'the German sword conquer land for the German plough' in Eastern Europe. After 1923 Hitler refrained from further coups d'état, although not from street violence, and announced his intention to obtain power by legal means. The NSDAP took part in parliamentary elections and he himself stood as a candidate for the presidency. He was unable to beat Hindenburg, but the NSDAP gained, as we have seen, an impressive number of seats in the Reichstag after the great depression had hit the world, and eventually became the largest party, so that on 30 January 1933 Hindenburg appointed him as chancellor. Initially everyone seemed to respect the law, as Hitler formed a coalition government with the Deutschnationale Volkspartei, in which both parties had three members,[28] whereas five departments were run by non-political experts. As the new cabinet had no majority in the Reichstag, new elections were held on 5 March 1933, which gave the Nazis 43.9 per cent and the German Nationalist Party 8 per cent of the vote. Conservatives like Vice-Chancellor Franz von Papen (*d.*1969) lived in the illusion that they could use Hitler and his mass-following in their struggle against communism. One should indeed never forget that Western Europe between the two World Wars was haunted by the Bolshevik peril. Hitler had promised to gain power in a legal way, but not that he would go on respecting the law once he was in control and patiently hope for the required vote of confidence in parliament. The emergency decree of 28 February 1933, following the fire of the Reichstag building, and the Enabling Act of 24 March 1933, which we mentioned before, opened the way to a complete political take-over. Within a short

---

[28] For the NSDAP: Hitler, W. Frick and H. Göring, and for the DVP: A. Hugenberg, F. Seldte and F. Guertner.

while totalitarian rule was established. The traditional freedoms, including that of the press, were curtailed, all other parties than the NSDAP forbidden,[29] the existing trade unions dissolved without a blow and the monopoly of the Deutsche Arbeitsfront ('German Labour Front') introduced.

The Weimar Republic was replaced by a *völkischer Führerstaat*, and public life was quickly transformed in accordance with Nazi ideology. On 12 November 1933 elections took place for a new Reichstag, the people being invited to vote for the one prearranged list of candidates, known as the 'Führer's list'. The 'elections' were in fact a plebiscite for the Führer, who received a 95 per cent support. In 1934, as we have seen, Hitler became head of state as well as leader of the government, and in the same year he overcame a grave crisis within the Nazi movement. The armed forces of the party and their leaders, especially Ernst Roehm, disagreed with Hitler's policy that veered away from social radicalism and towards a *rapprochement* with such traditional centres of influence as heavy industry and the army and its Prussian officer corps. Hitler decided to liquidate his rivals, and in the 'night of the long knives' the leaders of the SA, together with some old enemies of the Nazi Party, were shot without any form of process. Hitler tried to justify his extra-judicial action in a Reichstag speech, where he invoked the necessity to save the state from a mortal conspiracy and called himself the 'supreme justiciar of the German people'. There was in fact a widespread feeling of relief that the SA gangs had been taught a lesson, and Hitler was hailed as a peacemaker and the saviour of the fatherland. People were apparently less concerned with the blow to the rule of law than with the end of mob rule. Nothing could henceforth stop Hitler's ascendancy, and his popularity with all sections of public opinion was confirmed by several plebiscites: order was restored, the economic depression was overcome and unemployment fell back spectacularly. It would, however, be simplistic to attribute Hitler's success merely to the improved economy, for the attraction of the Nazi movement went much deeper. Indeed, for the first time in many years public order was restored and the streets safe again – a situation that many people could hardly remember. The country had the impression that it was being governed at last, after drifting rudderlessly for many years: effective government, even

---

[29] The *Gesetz gegen die Neubildung von Parteien* ('law against the foundation of new parties') of 14 July 1933 declared the NSDAP the only permitted party and made founding new parties a punishable offence.

inspired by a wrong-headed ideology, seemed better than no government at all.

The NSDAP had more in mind than purely political reforms and wanted to create a new society and a new man. Traditional Christian morality was decried as 'bourgeois', and in 'the people's Germany' the chasm between the classes would be bridged, as the individualism of the liberal past was replaced by community feeling and camaraderie. The virtues of labour – particularly on the land – were extolled (this was the inspiration for compulsory labour service). Nazism fascinated the young, many of whom for the first time had the feeling that they had a task to fulfil. Great messianic and millenarian expectations were in the air. And, last but not least, there was the spellbinding personality of Hitler, an orator who could whip the masses up to a frenzy of faith and enthusiasm. He was not the only European dictator from the right, but neither Mussolini, Franco nor Salazar was comparable to Hitler in will power, belief in his own mission and grip on the people. Hitler's gift as a speaker was first noticed when, immediately after the First World War, he was given a job as a political educator in the army. From then onwards his German listeners underwent his charisma time and again, either in their dozens in small beer halls in Munich or, later on, in their hundreds of thousands at the mass meetings of the party in Nuremberg, and in their millions over the radio, at that time a new medium. His voice kept the German people spellbound up till the bitter end as, except for a few unrepresentative conspirators (mainly connected with the failed attempt on Hitler's life of 20 July 1944), all sections of the German people loyally followed their leader. Under Hitler's impulse Germany again became a European power of the first magnitude. His political programme was carried out to the very limits, both internally – with dictatorship and persecution of the Jews – and externally – with the unleashing of the Second World War, and the final catastrophe of the Thousand Years' Reich came in 1945, a bare twelve years after the Nazi seizure of power.

After this brief survey, meant to provide some background information, we shall now undertake the study of German public law in the period 1933–45. The preliminary question should be posed whether one is justified in speaking of 'law' and particularly 'public law' in a regime where the law was quite simply the will of the leader. Can we truly speak of law when the *bene placitum* of one person is absolute? Or is this pure arbitrariness and therefore the very negation of law? Modern jurists, educated in 'the western legal tradition',[30] will predictably be inclined to answer that arbitrary will and the rule of law are impossible bedfellows. One should, nevertheless, beware of simplistic reactions, determined by our present-day outlook. World history knows numerous civilizations that considered the will of the ruler as a valid and even the supreme source of the law, without lapsing into utter lawlessness. In the Roman empire 'what pleased the emperor had force of law'. Jean Bodin maintained that the will of the monarch was law, and various medieval jurists explained that the king was the *fons et origo iuris* ('the fountain and mainspring of the law') and that the pope held the law *in pectore suo* ('in his breast'). That the will of a ruler – legitimized by God's grace or the people's confidence – often has been a primordial and legitimate source of law is an undeniable historical fact. Just as, according to the *lex regia*, the Roman people had transferred their power to their kings, so the German people had vested their power in their leader, as appeared from plebiscites and jubilant mass-acclamations. This meant that several jurists of the Nazi era could even argue – oddly to present-day thinking – that Nazi Germany was a *Rechtsstaat*. Their success was, however, limited, as the very idea of the *Rechsstaat* was tainted with nineteenth-century liberalism. Other names were more successful, such as *völkischer Staat, völkischer Führerstaat,* or 'authoritarian democracy'. Whatever name jurists used, there undoubtedly was, in the light of the reigning ideology, law in Germany in 1933–45, but it stemmed from quite different sources from the traditional ones and was politically determined.[31] Private law was least affected and, as could be expected, public law most. Its dominant features can be analysed as follows.

Just as in the Soviet Union, the separation of powers was rejected

---

[30] We borrow the expression from the encyclopedic work of H. J.Berman, *Law and revolution. The formation of the western legal tradition* (Cambridge, Mass., 1983).

[31] In E. R. Huber's *Verfassungsrecht des Grossdeutschen Reichs* (2nd edn, Hamburg, 1939), for example, we read: 'All public authority both in the State and in the Movement stems from that of the Führer. The correct term for political authority in the People's Reich is therefore not "the authority of the State" but "the authority of the Führer". This is so because political authority is wielded not by an impersonal entity, the State, but by the Führer as executor of the united will of the people' (we quote the translation in Bullock, *Hitler and Stalin,* 479). See also G. Feder, *Der deutsche Staat auf nationaler und sozialer Grundlage* (13th edn, Munich, 1933); O. Koellreutter, *Der deutsche Führerstaat* (Tübingen, 1934); H. Krüger, *Führer und Führung* (Breslau, 1935); H. Frank, *Nationalsozialistisches Handbuch für Recht und Gesetzgebung* (2nd edn, Munich, 1935).

radically and on principle, because it was blamed for the inner division and weakness of the state. It was replaced by the concentration of powers in the hands of one party and, above all, its one and only leader, in whom the people put their hope and their trust. Thus at the Day of the German Lawyers on 2 October 1933 Hitler spoke of the total state and its 'comprehensive claim to power, destroying all liberal forms of autonomy'.

The Führer led the executive branch. He was head of state, represented Germany vis-à-vis other countries and was commander-in-chief of the armed forces. He also headed the government, or rather, he was the government, as the ministers led their departments in order to execute his policy. The cabinet as such had no will or responsibility of its own and met less and less frequently. No counter-signature was required for the Führer's acts of government, as he was accountable to no one. The foundation of this system was called the *Führerprinzip*.

The leader also exercised legislative power: his will was law. The Reichstag admittedly passed *Beschlüsse*, but they were all based on initiatives from the Reich Chancellery. No bill could be introduced in the Reichstag without the Führer's agreement. Besides the *Beschlüsse* from the Reichstag there were others from the government, as well as laws passed by referendum, *Ausführungsverordnungen* ('executive decrees') and *Führererlasse* ('instructions from the Führer'). All these were, however, surpassed by the notorious *Führerbefehle* ('Führer's commands'), which were issued on secret affairs of state, sometimes by word of mouth only. The extermination of the Jews during the Second World War must have been based on such an oral command, whose written text was never found, for the obvious reason that there never was one. It is remarkable that medieval descriptions of the king as source of the law were occasionally applied to Hitler. Thus Dr Hans Frank, the president of the Akademie für deutsches Recht, in a book of 1938 spoke of Hitler as 'the source and representative of the law', adding for good measure that the Führer belonged to the 'greatest lawgivers of universal history'.

As the Reichstag had been left neither legislative power nor control of the budget, it had undergone a complete metamorphosis. After the exclusion of the other parties all its seats were occupied by selected members of the ruling NSDAP, who from time to time were assembled to pass laws required by the government and to acclaim the Führer's speeches (lustily singing national and party songs).

These exhilarating occasions will remind the reader of the famous acclamations in the Roman senate.[32]

The Führer was the supreme judge. The courts gave sentence in his name and, as we have seen, he had proclaimed himself in 1934 'the supreme justiciar of the German people', claiming the right to proceed to executions when he believed them to be rightful, and to bypass the law courts and their procedures. As is the case in all regimes that reject the principles of the *Rechtsstaat* or are in the process of doing so, respect for lawfully acquired rights and vested interests went overboard. A most illuminating expression of this attitude can be found in a law passed by the Grossdeutsche Reichstag on 26 April 1942, which said: 'There can be no doubt that . . . the Führer . . . must have the right to do anything which serves or contributes to the achievement of victory. He therefore must, in his capacity as Führer of the nation . . . supreme justiciar and leader of the party, always be in a position, without following prescribed procedures, to mete out due punishment . . . to every German . . . who fails to fulfil his duties, regardless of so-called well-acquired rights'.[33]

As supreme judge Hitler could intervene in the ordinary administration of justice. This interference with the courts, an abomination to people attached to the rule of law, could take several forms. What was, in 1934, only a claim made in a Reichstag speech became a formal law in the *Änderungsgesetz* ('modifying act') of 16 September 1939, where the Führer appeared as *oberster Gerichtsherr und Richter* ('supreme justiciar and judge'), empowered, by his objection, to annul a criminal sentence passed by the courts.

The aforementioned law of 26 April 1942 gave Hitler, *inter alia*, the unlimited right to dismiss judges. A *Führererlass* of 20 August of the same year went a step further and appointed a new minister of justice, who on the same day was also authorized to dismiss judges via the ordinary administrative channels. Some Nazi jurists rejected the independence of the judges on principle, alleging that it was a relic of

---

[32] Thus the *Gesta senatus Romani de Theodosiano publicando* (eds. T. Mommsen and P. M. Meyer, 1, 2, Berlin, 1905, 1–4) record that various acclamations by the senators on the occasion, in AD 438, of the promulgation of the Theodosian Code, were repeated up to 14 and even 28 times, reaching a grand total of 352 ovations (D. A. Bullough, 'Games people played: drama and ritual as propaganda in medieval Europe', *Transactions Royal Historical Society* (1974), 102). See also A. H. M. Jones, *The later Roman empire 284–602. A social, economic and administrative survey*, 1 (Oxford, 1964), 329–31.

[33] *Reichsgesetzblatt 1942*, no. 44, Part 1, p. 247. For an official, slightly different English translation, see the Documents of the Nuremberg Trials, *Nazi conspiracy and aggression* IV (Washington, 1946).

nineteenth-century liberalism, leading to a lack of ideological engagement and the protection of individual rights, regardless of the requirements of the state. They felt that there was no room for that sort of freedom in the national-socialist state, where the greatest possible reliance on the Führer was required. Thus Dr C. Rothenberger declared that the term 'judicial independence' was out of place in an authoritarian state and might as well be scrapped.[34]

Direct interference by the party was not accepted.[35] Nevertheless, whenever a party office believed a sentence to contradict national socialist ideas of justice, it could, via the legal services of the party, bring the matter to the attention of the Führer's deputy, who could contact the ministry of justice. A frequent technique for intervening in the operation of the courts was the *Nichtigkeitsbeschwerde* ('complaint of nullity') introduced by the Competence Decree of 21 February 1940 to be used within a year by the Supreme Reich Procurator against sentences that in the ordinary courts had become final.

Citizens' freedoms, human rights and Constitutions were anathema to the Nazis. Individual basic rights could hamper the action of the Reich, an intolerable notion in the new Germany, where the very idea of an individual standing up to the state and placing his own interests above those of the nation was monstrous. There was therefore no question of a Constitution that might restrain the Führer: his will was the fundamental law and no other was required. Consequently there was never a Constitution of the Third Reich:[36] such was the inescapable logic of the regime. Some jurists even argued that a Constitution could never be a pact between equal partners, but only an 'expression of the faithful trust' of the people.

We have already seen how often illiberal Caesarist regimes are popular with the masses. This was, for example, the case with Napoleon, and the same applies to Hitler's Germany. In the second round of the presidential elections in April 1932 Hitler obtained only

---

[34] Rothenberger became secretary of state in the Reich ministry of justice in August 1942. He was the author of a book entitled *Der deutsche Richter*, published in Hamburg in 1943.

[35] J. Meinck, 'Justiz und Justizfunktion im Dritten Reich', *Zeitschrift für Neuere Rechtsgeschichte* 3 (1981), 28–49; H. Rüping, *Staatsanwaltschaft und Provinzialjustizverwaltung im Dritten Reich. Aus den Akten der Staatsanwaltschaft bei dem Oberlandesgericht Celle als höherer Reichsjustizbehörde* (Baden-Baden, 1990).

[36] For certain spheres there existed a sort of organic law, such as the *Grundgesetz* of 30 January 1935 which eliminated municipal autonomy: see H. Matzerath, *Gemeinde im Nationalsozialismus* (Berlin, 1973). Hitler once spoke of a possible *unvergängliches Grundgesetz aller Deutschen* ('everlasting fundamental law of all Germans'), but nothing was heard any more of this verbal hint.

36.8 per cent of the vote and at the Reichstag elections of 5 March 1933 (shortly after the 'seizure of power' of 30 January and the emergency decree of 28 February) his party obtained only 44 per cent of the vote, but soon afterwards the era dawned of successful plebiscites (after the occupation of the demilitarized Rhineland and after the Austrian Anschluss) and of referendums on changes in the law, where majorities of 99 per cent were common. Possibly the strangest show of massive adoration Hitler ever received occurred on 1 May 1933 in Berlin's Tempelhof district, where hundreds of thousands of members of the powerful association of trade unions ADGB turned up, at the behest of their leaders, for a gigantic workers' demonstration of support for the new regime. They were addressed by the leader of the Nazi Party, who spoke of Germany's rebirth and of taming capitalist exploitation in order to make way for the creation of a new social and economic order. What made the whole spectacle even weirder was that the following day the trade unions were dissolved, their offices occupied by SA and SS and their leaders arrested.[37]

It was obvious that the concentration of all authority at the centre of the Reich would affect its federal structure: in no time Germany was turned into a unitary centralized state. The separate governments and parliaments of the Länder – with their different political colouring – were abolished. The Länder themselves became provinces of the Reich and were placed under the authority of a *Statthalter* ('lieutenant'), usually the highest regional party leader (*Gauleiter*). On 30 January 1934 a law on 'the reconstruction of the Reich' was published transferring the public assignments of the Länder to the Reich, subordinating their governments to that in Berlin and abolishing their parliaments. The *Reichsstatthalter*, until then exclusively a representative of the chancellor, was placed under the administrative authority of the ministry of the interior, so that the last vestiges of the autonomy of the Länder were wiped out. And it was only logical that the Reichsrat, the expression of the federal nature of the Weimar Republic, was simply abolished by a law of 14 February 1934.

The reborn Germany had to be inspired by a new ideology, which the state was expected to impose in everyday life. The keeper of that ideology was the party, which necessarily exercised a strong influence on the apparatus of the state. Consequently officials were required to

[37] G. Goriely, *Hitler prend le pouvoir* (Brussels, 1983).

become party members, which they did en masse after 30 January 1933, and those who were recalcitrant could be dismissed. The law of 7 April 1933 'for the restoration of professional officialdom' fixed the rules for their removability on racial or political grounds. The definitive law on the status of public officials, of 26 January 1937, maintained their irremovability on principle, but threatened functionaries who were not unconditionally loyal to the national socialist state with enforced early retirement. Thus German officials were freed from the choice of party membership which could make life difficult for their colleagues in the western democracies, for a law of 14 July 1933 had, as we have seen, instituted the one-party regime. The matter was finally settled on 1 December of the same year by the Law for Securing the Unity of Party and State, which threatened dissenters with severe sentences of forced labour or imprisonment and proclaimed the NSDAP the 'sole political party' and the *Trägerin des deutschen Staatsgedankens* ('the bearer of German political thought'). The single party state was, of course, no German monopoly, and is still in favour in various Third World countries. It should be realized that in a world-historical perspective the multi-party state is an exception, or even a deviation from the normal pattern.

As the Nazi gospel was expected to transform and inspire the whole of German society, it could not limit its impact to the organs of the state. Everything was affected, social life, the arts, science, trade unions and, of course, the media. This process was called *Gleichschaltung*, not an easy word to translate. It could be rendered as 'centralized levelling', but it concerned, of course, political and cultural but not social levelling (as in the case of the English levellers of the seventeenth century). To achieve this 'homogeneity' on a massive scale, old social organizations were dissolved and new, compulsory ones founded. Here are some examples. The press was placed under the control of the propaganda minister, Joseph Goebbels. All liberal professions were encapsulated in Nazi bodies. A *Kulturkammer* was created to supervise and guide the arts and cultural life in general. Youth had to join the *Hitler-Jugend*, and the existing trade unions were dissolved and replaced by a single *Arbeitsfront*, while *Kraft durch Freude* ('strength through joy') took care of the leisure of the workers. The attempt to found a pro-Hitler Reichskirche, headed by a Reichsbischof, was a flop and, except for a few individual dissenting clerics, the churches were left in relative peace.

However great the country's approval or at least acquiescence, the regime met with opposition. The police took care of this internal enemy, for Hitler-Germany, like any other totalitarian state, needed the weapon of terror. This was in the hands of the *Geheime Staatspolizei* (Gestapo), which developed – as the SS would do somewhat later – into a state within the state and resorted to internment in concentration camps and extra-judicial executions. Pronouncements have been recorded of police chiefs at meetings of lawyers to the effect that the police considered themselves justified in operating outside the law whenever the security of the state was at risk. The police did indeed interfere with criminal justice in various ways and managed to bypass the courts. One technique was the long-term *Schutzhaft* ('protective custody') in the course of a trial or even outside any judicial procedure. The police even used *Schutzhaft* in cases where the accused had been acquitted by the courts; they were simply arrested *polizeilich* as they left the court room, and carted off to a camp. During discussions on this point in the official Commission for Criminal Justice the representative of the police frankly maintained that *Schutzhaft* in criminal cases was the police's good right and that they themselves decided on its use: they happened to have their own ideas and norms, and they did not feel bound by what the courts said. In other words, the police was a state within the state and that state was *legibus solutus*.

Anti-Semitism was a crucial feature of the Nazi creed, which saw the struggle against the Jews and even their extermination as a service to mankind and an act of racial cleansing for which later (Arian) generations would be thankful. As soon as the NSDAP came to power it put its ideas into action, but the systematic and massive genocide, the Holocaust in the extermination camps, only took place during the war. The persecution of the Jews assumed two forms, legal and illegal. The legally organized action was based on racist legislation, such as the Nuremberg Laws of 1935 and the Thirteenth Decree of 1 July 1943, which amended the law on citizenship. The Nuremberg Laws were proclaimed on the occasion of the party rally in that city on 15 September 1935. They contained the prohibition of marriages and extra-marital sexual relations between Jews and subjects of German or related blood. A distinction was introduced between *Staatsangehörigen* ('subjects of the state') and *Reichsbürger* ('citizens of the Reich'). The former only had public duties, the latter also had political rights, and only people of German or related blood could be *Reichsbürger*. Thus the German Jews were made helots in their own country. Various decrees closed several professions to them, and a decree of 1 July 1943 deprived them of the protection of the courts and completely handed them over, as rightless individuals, to the police. Its Article 1(1) stated: 'Criminal actions by Jews are punished by the police'. It was moreover laid down that after their death their property was confiscated by the state.[38]

As well as this persecution, based on official law texts, violence was perpetrated against German and European Jews without any known basis in legislation. Before the war it consisted of the destruction of shops and even, in the *Kristallnacht* of 9 November 1938, the burning of synagogues and large-scale organized vandalism (a revenge for the assassination in Paris of a German diplomat by a German Jew). It was, however, only during the war, after America became a belligerent, that the Nazi top finally decided to proceed to the systematic killing of millions of European Jews who were in German hands. The plan was carried out without the German people being told and without any legislative text being issued. This '*Endlösung* ("final solution") of the Jewish problem' was entrusted to the SS and authorized, as we have seen, by an oral *Führerbefehl*, given by Hitler personally to a very few confidants, probably Goering, Himmler and Heydrich.[39] The practical details of this genocide were discussed at a meeting of top officials of the SS and SD (*Sicherheitsdienst*, 'security service') which Heydrich convened on 20 January 1942 at Wannsee, a suburb of Berlin.[40] It is hardly believable that while the Holocaust was going on, the jurists of the regime were busy publishing the aforementioned decree of 1 July 1943 in the *Reichsgesetzblatt*, dealing with the byzantine question as to whether the Jews fell under the competence of the police or the law courts.

After the Second World War Germany was under allied occupation and, as no peace treaty was concluded, the occupation zones developed into two Germanies, the pro-western German Federal Republic and the Soviet-oriented German Democratic Republic. Both received a Constitution in 1949. That of West Germany followed to a large extent the pattern of the Constitution of Weimar,

---

[38] Confiscatory death duties are not unknown in western democracies, but they at least afflict all heirs and legatees, without discrimination.

[39] W. Laqueur, *The terrible secret. An investigation into the suppression of information about Hitler's 'final solution'* (London, 1980); G. Fleming, *Hitler und die Endlösung: Es ist des Führers Wunsch* (Munich, 1982).

[40] The minutes were conserved and placed before the judges at the Nuremberg Trials: *Trials of war criminals before the Nuremberg military tribunals*, XIII, 210–19.

notably as far as the federal form of government was concerned, whereas East Germany espoused the familiar constitutional concept of the socialist countries. Article 67 of the West German Constitution built in an efficient guarantee of governmental stability, as parliament could only bring down the government – more precisely the chancellor, who heads the cabinet – if there was an alternative cabinet with the necessary majority (experience has proved the wisdom of this provision). The Constitution of the Federal Republic of 1949 made good another shortcoming of the Weimar era by severely restricting the power of the president (not directly elected by the people any more), thus eliminating the possibility of dictatorial rule. Article 20 of the same Constitution called the country a 'democratic and social federal state' and Article 100 attributed the review of the constitutionality of the laws to a special constitutional court, the Bundesverfassungsgericht. It is also worth mentioning that political parties were expressly mentioned in the Constitution. Article 21 said that they might be organized freely, that their internal organization must be democratic and that they must publicly account for their financial resources. Parties that combat the 'free democratic basic order' were declared unconstitutional. The Constitution also posited the reunification of the two Germanies as an aim to be striven for, or as the text put it: 'It remains a requirement for the whole body of the German people to accomplish the unity and freedom of Germany in free self-determination' – a stipulation that for many years looked like a pipe dream. The same paragraph also insisted on the Federal Republic's duty to serve the peace of the world as an equal partner in a united Europe.

# Epilogue

Reflecting on fifteen centuries of constitutional experiment readers may feel as if they were visiting a vast churchyard and reading the inscriptions on the tombstones which recall, extol or curse bygone regimes. Some of the dinosaurs in the cemetery, such as the hallowed medieval kingdoms, have been dead for a long time. Others, such as the Nazi or communist empires, were alive and kicking only a few decades or even a few years ago. Not all Constitutions are dead, however. Indeed, some old and venerable political systems are still flourishing but, in this changing world, nobody knows for how long. The variety of Constitutions the West has produced is bewildering. There was the personal rule of monarchs by God's grace in Charlemagne's or Frederick II's post- or pseudo-Roman empires, or in Henry VIII's or Francis I's sovereign nation-states at the time of the Renaissance. There was royal absolutism of the obscurantist or of the enlightened variety, but also modern constitutional and parliamentary kingdoms. There were city-states, democratic or aristocratic, like Florence or Venice, but also confederations of free peasant communities, like Switzerland, and federal, city-based sovereign nations, like the Republic of the United Netherlands. And if the First French Republic was run by the violent ideologues of the *comité de salut public*, the Third was a sedate regime where a contented population maintained the *paix bourgeoise*. Is this endless list, which must, of course, include the plebeian totalitarian regimes of our own century, more than a chaotic and meaningless succession of failed, futile or precarious attempts, a 'tale told by an idiot, full of sound and fury, signifying nothing'? Is our cemetery not only the burial ground of all those Constitutions, but also of the beliefs and illusions that inspired them? What has become of the millenarian expectations, either of the City of God ruled by the Lord and his saints, or of the golden age of peace prophesied by Isaiah, or the new man and the new society built on science and universal brotherhood? What has happened to the Grand Design and the vision of history as the assertion of the human spirit through a logical sequence of dialectic stages? Is it possible, desirable or allowed, in our post-modern, illusion-free age, to detect some sense or a pattern in the history of western constitutional law?

One such long-term line of development seems to be the shift – the reader will decide whether it was progress – from personal rule to the law-based state. The former was embodied in paternalistic and autocratic kingship, steeped in religion and allied to Church and nobility; it ignored, or rather rejected equality, constitutional limitation and government answerable to the electorate. The latter, which took shape in some parts of Europe in the seventeenth century (notably in Holland and England), was embodied in the rule of law, an abstract and secular state, with legal equality, a free-market economy, constitutional limitations and parliamentary control. The eighteenth and nineteenth centuries witnessed the advance of this younger model, against the resistance of the ancient monarchies, enlightened or otherwise, and we have described its triumph in America. In France it made little progress for a long time but when it arrived, it was with the force of a hurricane: we have seen after what dramatic vicissitudes it finally gained the upper hand at the time of the Third Republic. In Central Europe, where benevolent and philosophically-minded autocrats had enjoyed a good deal of success, the new model progressed more slowly. Bismarck's paternalism still harked back to eighteenth-century ideas of the caring state, and whereas the German empire of his day had a written Constitution and an influential Reichstag, elected by general suffrage, the head of the government was still responsible to the emperor and not to the representatives of the people. Nevertheless, in the early twentieth century the prospect of the new model looked good, and even tsarist Russia acquired a Constitution and an elected Duma. The progress of the liberal paradigm was interrupted but not halted by the First World War and its aftermath of Bolshevik, Fascist and Nazi regimes, which rejected bourgeois democracy. After the fall of these messianic regimes the liberal free-trade democracies seemed to have everything their own way. They owed this, *inter alia*, to their social security safety nets, which made the slings and arrows of the market forces acceptable or at least bearable.

Nobody knows what forms of government will prevail in the lands of the ex-Soviet Union, particularly, of course, in Russia, where a new

Constitution was being prepared at the time of writing. A popular shibboleth holds that freedom and democracy have no future there, since the Russians have not experienced them in the past and have only been exposed to autocracy and oppression. We should, however, not forget that the West has also for hundreds of years lived under such regimes and has been so slow to develop the rule of law, freedom and democracy that as late as the eighteenth century the prospect for constitutional and parliamentary government looked hazardous. So why could Eastern Europe not undertake now what the West realized in the past two centuries? After all, even the general franchise was only achieved there in the previous century, and not even in every country. Some people think that 'Byzantine' Europe is unfit for democracy because of the autocratic tradition that linked the late Roman empire to Byzantium and Moscow, the 'Third Rome'. They write as if democracy has always come naturally to the western world and they conveniently forget about such 'minor accidents' as Philip II and Louis XIV (not to mention certain aberrations of our own century). Nor do they seem to realize that Russian communism was rooted more in the Western Enlightenment than in Byzantine ideology. The idea of an absolute division between pure democracy in the West and sheer serfdom in the East belongs to the realm of phantasy. Nor should we forget that as far as decentralization and religious tolerance are concerned the record of Greek Christianity easily outshines that of the Latin Church.

Whatever the outcome of events in Eastern Europe may be, the world seems less and less interested in political regimes built on religion, philosophy or dogmatic utopianism, whereas rational pragmatism, securing the greatest prosperity for the greatest number, is the order of the day: neither the heavenly nor the earthly paradise provides inspiration any longer. If the world-wide victory of this political approach is only a question of time and if there is no valid alternative, is it – to speak with Francis Fukuyama – the end of history, including constitutional history? Some commentators are certainly inclined to think so, worthy followers of Edward Gibbon who, in the enlightened eighteenth century, was convinced that the world-wide domination of western civilization was around the corner. It is indeed conceivable that the Occident has discovered – or stumbled upon – certain constitutional formulas which are valuable and permanent acquisitions for mankind, but this does not mean the end of the debate, either outside the western tradition (what will future developments bring in China, or in the Muslim world where benevolent autocracy and religiously-inspired government are very much alive?) or even within it. The reader will be aware, for example, of the debate caused by the 'social chapter' in the Treaty of Maastricht, this possible embryo of a European Constitution, and he knows that the 'social chapters' in the Constitutions of Weimar and the French Fourth Republic were equally controversial and proved difficult to implement. This discussion is, of course, connected with the question as to how much or how little state and bureaucracy is needed or desirable. The bureaucratization has gone so far that in some countries even top politicians are recruited from the state-run school of administration, so that Europe seems to follow in the footsteps of the ancient Chinese mandarinate. The choice between social security and personal freedom may not be so easy to make. And the never-ending nationality problem is still with us, as is the debate about federalism: unitary states become federal under our very eyes or split up peacefully into independent nations, whereas some pseudo-federal states do the same amid much bloodshed. Some ancient countries still pretend to fight for a national sovereignty which they gave up to the European Community years ago. The controversies about the power-shift from parliament to cabinet, the necessity of a written Constitution and a Bill of Rights and the desirability of constitutional courts will, no doubt, go on. And so will the debate on human rights: do they belong to the heritage of mankind or are they a western invention that only spread world-wide in the wake of intellectual imperialism? Some twenty-three centuries ago Aristotle posed the speculative question as to which was, under varying circumstances, the best Constitution (*politeia*): the discussion is still open.

# Select bibliography

## INTERNATIONAL

Anderson, E. N. and Anderson, P. R., *Political institutions and social change in continental Europe in the nineteenth century*, Berkeley, Los Angeles, 1967

Aretin, K. O. von (ed.), *Der aufgeklärte Absolutismus*, Cologne, 1974

Asbeck, F. M. van (ed.), *The universal declaration of human rights and its predecessors (1679–1949)*, Leiden, 1949

Ashford, D. E., *The emergence of the welfare states*, Oxford, 1987

Baratta, A., 'Zur Entwicklung des modernen Rechtsstaatsbegriffs', *Festschrift B. C. H. Aubin*, Kehl, Strasbourg, 1979, 1–14.

Birtsch, G. (ed.), *Grund- und Freiheitsrechte im Wandel von Gesellschaft und Geschichte. Beiträge zur Geschichte der Grund- und Freiheitsrechte vom Ausgang des Mittelalters bis zur Revolution von 1848*, Göttingen, 1981
*Grund- und Freiheitsrechte von der ständischen zur spätbürgerlichen Gesellschaft*, Göttingen, 1987

Blom, H. W., Blockmans, W. P. and De Schepper, H. (eds.), *Bicameralisme. Tweekamerstelsel vroeger en nu. Bicameralism in past and present*, The Hague, 1992

Blythe, J. M., *Ideal government and the mixed constitution in the Middle Ages*, Princeton, 1992

Böckenförde, F.-W., 'Entstehung und Wandel des Rechtsstaatsbegriffs', *Festschrift für A. Arndt*, Frankfurt, 1969, 53–73

Bogdanor, W. (ed.), *The Blackwell encyclopaedia of political institutions*, Oxford, 1987

Brinkmann, K., *Freiheit und Verfassung. Das Wesen der Freiheit und Unfreiheit und ihre Berücksichtigung in einer Verfassung*, Bonn, 1963

Brinton, C., *The anatomy of revolution*, 2nd edn, New York, 1965
*A decade of revolution, 1789–1799*, New York, 1934

Brownlie, J. (ed.), *Basic documents on human rights*, Oxford, 1971

Bullock, A., *Hitler and Stalin. Parallel lives*, London, 1991

Burns, J. H. (ed.), *The Cambridge history of medieval political thought c. 350–c. 1450*, Cambridge, 1988

Carsten, F. L., *Revolution in Central Europe 1918–19*, London, 1972

Chapman, B., *Police state*, London, 1970

Chianéa, G., *Les droits de l'homme et la conquête des libertés. De l'antiquité aux révolutions de 1848*, Grenoble, 1988

Chittolini, G. and Willoweit, D., *Statuten, Städte und Territorien zwischen Mittelalter und Neuzeit in Italien und Deutschland*, Berlin, 1992

Cohn, H. J. (ed.), *Government in Reformation Europe 1520–1560. The major European states facing reformation, wars and price revolution*, London, 1971

Conze, W. (ed.), *Beiträge zur deutschen und belgischen Verfassungsgeschichte im 19. Jahrhundert*, Stuttgart, 1967

Cooper, J. P., 'Differences between English and continental government in the early seventeenth century' in G. E. Aylmer and J. S. Morrill (eds.), *Land, men and beliefs. Studies in early-modern history*, London, 1983, 97–114

Cortese, E., *La norma giuridica*, Milan, 1962–4; 2 vols.

Dareste, F., *Les constitutions modernes*, Paris, 1928–34; 6 vols.

David, M., 'Le serment du Sacre du IXe and XVe siècle. Contribution à l'étude des limites juridiques de la souveraineté', *Revue du Moyen Age Latin* 6 (1950), 5–272

*La souveraineté et les limites juridiques du pouvoir monarchique du 9e au 15e siècle*, Strasbourg, 1954

Dennewitz, B. with collaboration of B. Meissner, *Die Verfassungen der modernen Staaten. Eine Dokumentensammlung*, Hamburg, 1947–9; 4 vols.

Dietze, G., *Kant und der Rechtsstaat*, Tübingen, 1982

*I diritti fondamentali della persona umana e la libertà religiosa: Atti del V colloquio giuridico, 1984*, Vatican, 1985

Dogan, M. (ed.), *The mandarins of Western Europe. The political role of the civil servants*, New York, 1975

Dufau, P. A., Duvierger, J. B. and Guadet, J., *Collection des constitutions, chartes et lois fondamentales des peuples de l'Europe et des deux Amériques*, Paris, 1821–3; 6 vols., Suppl., 1830

Dufour, A., *Droits de l'homme, droit naturel et histoire: droit, individu et pouvoir de l'Ecole du Droit naturel à l'Ecole du Droit historique*, Paris, 1991

Duverger, M., *Constitutions et documents politiques*, Paris, 1957

Ely, J. H., *Democracy and distrust. A theory of judicial review*, Cambridge, Mass., 1980

Foerster, R. H., *Europa. Geschichte einer politischen Idee. Mit einer Bibliographie von 182 Einigungsplänen aus den Jahren 1306 bis 1945*, Munich, 1967

*Die Idee Europa, 1330–1946. Quellen zur Geschichte der politischen Einigung*, Munich, 1963

Forsthoff, E., *Der totale Staat*, 2nd edn, Hamburg, 1934

Franz, G., *Staatsverfassungen. Eine Sammlung wichtiger Verfassungen der Vergangenheit und der Gegenwart in Urtext und Übersetzung*, 2nd edn, Munich, 1964

Friedrich, C. J., *Der Verfassungsstaat der Neuzeit*, Berlin, Göttingen, Heidelberg, 1953

Gasser, A., *Geschichte der Volksfreiheit und der Demokratie*, 2nd edn, Aarau, 1949

*Gegenstand und Begriffe der Verfassungsgeschichtsschreibung. Tagung der Vereinigung für Verfassungsgeschichte 1981*, Berlin, 1983

Genet, J.-P. (ed.), *L'Etat Moderne. Genèse, bilans et perspectives*, Paris, 1990 (papers of Paris colloquium of 1989)

Gilissen, J. (ed.), *Introduction bibliographique à l'histoire du droit et à l'ethnologie juridique. Bibliographical introduction to legal history and ethnology*, Brussels, 1964–88; 10 vols.

Gladden, E. N., *A history of public administration*, London, 1972; 2 vols.

Gouron, A. and Rigaudière, A. (eds.), *Renaissance du pouvoir législatif et genèse de l'état*, Montpellier, 1988

Gress, D., *The rise of the state*, Oxford, 1988

Griffiths, G., *Representative government in Western Europe in the sixteenth century. Commentary and documents for the study of comparative constitutional history*, Oxford, 1968

Grimm, D., 'Entstehungs- und Wirkungsbedingungen des modernen Konstitutionalismus' in D. Simon (ed), *Akten des 26. Deutschen Rechtshistorikertages*, Frankfurt, 1987, 45–76
*Recht und Staat der bürgerlichen Gesellschaft*, Frankfurt, 1987

Guenée, B., *L'Occident aux XIVe et XVe siècles. Les Etats*, 4th edn, Paris, 1991

Haberkern, E. and Wallach, J. F., *Hilfswörterbuch für Historiker. Mittelalter und Neuzeit*, 2nd edn, Berne, Munich, 1964

Hall, J. A. (ed.), *States in history*, Oxford, 1986

Hartung, F., *Die Entwicklung der Menschen- und Bügerrechte von 1776 bis zur Gegenwart*, 3rd edn, Göttingen, 1964

Hattenhauer, H., *Europäische Rechtsgeschichte*, Heidelberg, 1992
*Geschichte des Beamtentums*, Cologne, 1980

Hawgood, J., *Modern constitutions since 1787*, London, 1939

Heidelmeyer, W. (ed.), *Die Menschenrechte. Erklärungen, Verfassungsartikel, Internationale Abkommen*, 3rd edn, Munich, 1982

Henshall, N., *The myth of absolutism. Change and continuity in early modern European monarchy*, London, 1992

Heyen, E. V. (ed.), *Geschichte der Verwaltungsrechtswissenschaft. Stand und Probleme der Forschung*, Frankfurt, 1982

Jellinek, G., *Die Erklärung der Menschen- und Bürgerrechte*, 2nd edn, Leipzig, 1904

Kaufmann, A. (ed.), *Widerstandsrecht*, Darmstadt, 1972

Kelly, J. M., *A short history of western legal theory*, Oxford, 1992

Klatt, R., *Die Menschenrechte in geschichtlichen Dokumenten bis zur Gegenwart*, Hagen, 1950

Köck, H. F., *Der Beitrag der Schule von Salamanca zur Entwicklung der Lehre von den Grundrechten*, Berlin, Munich, 1987

Koenigsberger, H. G., *Estates and revolutions. Essays in early modern European history*, Ithaca, London, 1971

Lapeyre, A., de Tinguy, F. and Vasak, K., *Les dimensions universelles des droits de l'homme*, Brussels, 1990–1; 3 vols.

Lutaud, O., *Des Révolutions d'Angleterre à la Révolution française*, The Hague, 1973

MacCormick, D. N., 'Der Rechtsstaat und die rule of law', *Juristenzeitung* 39 (1984), 65–70

McIlwain, C. H., *Constitutionalism: ancient and modern*, Ithaca, 1940
McKitterick, R., *The Frankish kingdoms under the Carolingians, 751–987*, London, New York, 1983
Mager, W., *Zur Entstehung des modernen Staatsbegriffs*, Wiesbaden, 1968
Mandrou, R., *L'Europe 'absolutiste'. Raison et raison d'Etat 1649–1775*, Paris, 1977
Meinecke, F., *Die Idee der Staatsräson in der neueren Geschichte*, Munich, 1963; 3rd edn by W. Hofer
Melville, G. (ed.), *Institutionen und Geschichte. Theoretische Aspekte und mittelalterliche Befunde*, Cologne, Weimar, Vienna, 1992
*Menschenrechte und Menschenwürde. Historische Voraussetzungen, Säkuläre Gestalt. Christliches Verständnis*, Stuttgart, 1987
Meyer, J., *Noblesses et pouvoirs dans l'Europe de l'Ancien Régime*, Paris, 1974
Mirkine-Guetzevitch, B., *Les constitutions européennes*, Paris, 1951; 2 vols.
Mohnhaupt, H., 'Potestas legislatoria und Gesetzesbegriff im Ancien Régime', *Ius Commune. Veröffentlichungen des Max-Planck-Instituts für Europäische rechtsgeschichte* 6 (1972), 188–239
Moore, B., *Social origins of dictatorship and democracy. Lord and peasant in the making of the Modern World*, London, 1967
Myers, A. R., *Parliaments and Estates in Europe to 1789*, London, 1975
Näf, W. (ed.), *Staatsverfassungen und Staatstypen 1830/31*, 2nd edn, Berne, 1968
Newton, A. P., *Federal and unified constitutions*, London, 1923
Nolte, E., *Die Krise des liberalen Systems und die faschistischen Bewegungen*, Munich, 1968
Oestreich, G., *Geschichte der Menschenrechte und Grundfreiheiten im Umriss*, Berlin, 1968
Orban, E. (ed.), *Fédéralisme et cours suprêmes. Federalism and supreme courts*, Brussels, 1991 (concerns the USA, Canada, Germany, Belgium and the European Community)
Palmer, R. R., *The age of democratic revolution. A political history of Europe and America*, Princeton, 1959
Paravicini, W. and Werner, K. F. (eds.), *Histoire comparée de l'administration (IVe–XVIIe siècles). Actes du XIVe colloque historique franco-allemand Tours 27 mars-1er avril 1977 organisé en collaboration avec le Centre d'Etudes Supérieures de la Renaissance par l'Institut Historique Allemand de Paris*, Munich, 1980
Quaritsch, H., *Souveränität. Entstehung und Entwicklung des Begriffs in Frankreich und Deutschland vom 13. Jahrhundert bis 1806*, Berlin, 1986
*Staat und souveränität*, 1: *Die Grundlagen*, Frankfurt, 1970
Raab, H., *Kirche und Staat. Von der Mitte des XV. Jahrhunderts bis zur Gegenwart*, Munich, 1966
Raeff, M., *The well-ordered police state. Social and institutional change through law in the Germanies and Russia 1600–1800*, Yale, 1983
*Recueils de la Société Jean Bodin pour l'histoire comparative des institutions. Transactions of the Jean Bodin Society for comparative institutional history*, Brussels, Paris, 1936 ff. (by 1992 65 vols. were published)

Reibstein, E., *Volkssouveränität und Freiheitsrechte. Texte und Studien zur politischen Theorie des 14.–18. Jahrhunderts*, Munich, 1972; 2 vols. ed. by C. Schott

Roggen, H. and Weber, E. (eds.), *The European right*, Berkeley, 1965

Rowen, H. H., *From absolutism to revolution, 1648–1848*, New York, London, 1963.

Scheiber, H. M. and Feeley, M. M., *Power divided: essays on the theory and practice of federalism*, Berkeley, 1989

Schieder, T., *Der Nationalstaat in Europa als historisches Phänomen*, Cologne, 1964

Schieder, W. (ed.), *Faschismus als soziale Bewegung. Deutschland und Italien im Vergleich*, Göttingen, 1983

Schlochauer, H. J., *Die Idee des ewigen Friedens. Ein Überblick über Entwicklung und Gestaltung des Friedenssicherungsgedankens*, Bonn, 1953

Schnur, R. (ed.), *Die Rolle der Juristen bei der Entstehung des modernen Staates*, Berlin, Munich, 1986

Schulze, R. (ed.), *Europäische Rechts- und Verfassungsgeschichte. Ergebnisse und Perspektiven der Forschung*, Berlin, 1991

Scupin, H. U. and Schevner, U., *Althusius-Bibliographie. Bibliographie zur politischen Ideengeschichte und Staatslehre, zum Staatsrecht und zur Verfassungs-geschichte des 16. bis 18. Jahrhunderts*, Berlin, 1973; 2 vols.

Seibt, F., *Revolution in Europa. Ursprung und Wege innerer Gewalt. Strukturen, Elemente, Exempel*, Munich, 1984

Senellart, M., *Machiavélisme et raison d'Etat. XIIe–XVIIIe s.*, Paris, 1989

Shennan, J. H., *Liberty and order in early modern Europe. The subject and the state, 1650–1800*, London, New York, 1986

   *The origins of the modern European state, 1450–1725*, London, 1974

Stollberg-Rilinger, B., *Der Staat als Maschine. Zur politischen Metaphorik des absoluten Füstenstaates*, Berlin, Munich, 1986

Stolleis, M., 'Condere leges et interpretari. Gesetzgebungsmacht und Staatsbildung im 17. Jahrhundert', *Savigny Zeitschrift für Rechtsgeschichte*, G. A. 100 (1984), 89–116

Thomann, M., 'Rechtsphilosophische und rechtsgeschichtliche Etappen der Idee der Menschenrechte im 17. u. 18. Jahrhundert', *Festkolloquium H. Thieme*, Sigmaringen, 1983, 73–83

Tierney, B., ' "The prince is not bound by the laws". Accursius and the origins of the modern state', *Comparative Studies in Society and History* 5 (1962), 378–400

   *Religion, law, and the growth of constitutional thought 1150–1650*, Cambridge, 1982

Tilly, C. (ed.), *The formation of national states in Western Europe*, Princeton, 1975

Torstendahl, R., *Bureaucratisation in Northwestern Europe 1880–1985*, London, 1990

Tuck, R., *Natural rights theories. Their origin and development*, Cambridge, 1979

Ullmann, W., *Principles of government and politics in the Middle Ages*, 2nd edn, London, 1966

Unger, A. L., *The totalitarian party. Party and people in Nazi-Germany and Soviet Russia*, Cambridge, 1974

Vierhaus, R. (ed.), *Herrschaftsverträge, Wahlkapitulationen, Fundamentalgesetze*, Göttingen, 1977

Vile, J. C., *Constitutionalism and the separation of powers*, Oxford, 1967
Watts, M. R., *The dissenters. From the Reformation to the French Revolution*, Oxford, 1978
Weinacht, P.-L., *Staat. Studien zur Bedeutungsgeschichte des Wortes von den Anfängen bis ins 19. Jahrhundert*, Berlin, 1968
Wheare, K. C., *Federal government*, 4th edn, Oxford, 1963
Wheeler-Bennett, J. and Nicholls, A., *The semblance of peace: the political settlement after the Second World War*, London, 1972
Wolf-Phillips, L. (ed.), *Constitutions of modern states*, London, 1968
Wormuth, F. D., *The origins of modern constitutionalism*, New York, 1949
Würtenberger, T., *Die Legitimität staatlicher Herrschaft. Eine staatsrechtlich-politische Begriffsgeschichte*, Berlin, 1973
Wyduckel, D., *Princeps legibus solutus. Eine Untersuchung zur frühmodernen Rechts- und Staatslehre*, Berlin, 1979
Ybema, S. B., *Constitutionalism and civil liberties*, Leiden, 1973
Zurcher, A. (ed.), *Constitutions and constitutional trends since World War II*, 2nd edn, New York, 1955

## AUSTRIA

Baltl, H., *Österreichische Rechtsgeschichte. Von den Anfängen bis zur Gegenwart*, 3rd edn, Graz, 1977
Brauneder, W., *Geschichte der Grundrechte in Österreich*, Vienna, Cologne, Weimar, 1993
Dickson, P. G. M., *Finance and government under Maria Theresa 1740–1780*, Oxford, 1987; 2 vols.
Hellbling, E. C., *Österreichische Verfassungs- und Verwaltungsgeschichte. Ein Lehrbuch für Studierende*, Vienna, 1956
Macartney, C. A., *The Habsburg Empire 1790–1918*, London, 1968
Pauley, B. F., *Hitler and the forgotten Nazis. A history of Austrian national socialism*, London, 1981
Schambeck, H. (ed.), *Österreichs Parlamentarismus. Werden und System*, Berlin, Munich, 1986
Walter, F., *Österreichische Verfassungs- und Verwaltungsgeschichte von 1500 bis 1955*, ed. by A. Wandruszka, Vienna, 1972

## BELGIUM AND THE NETHERLANDS

Bouchat, P., *Le Tribunal des XXII au XVIIIe siècle*, Kortrijk, 1986 (concerns the prince-bishopric of Liège)
Broeck, J. van den, *De rechten van de mens omstreeks 1789 in de Oostenrijkse Nederlanden*, Antwerp, 1986
Dievoet, G. van (ed.), *Patrice de Neny (1716–1784)*, Kortrijk, 1987
Fockema Andreae, S. J., *De Nederlandse Staat onder de Republiek*, Amsterdam, 1961
Fruin, R., *Geschiedenis der staatsinstellingen in Nederland tot de val der republiek*,

2nd edn by H. T. Colenbrander, The Hague, 1922

Geelen, A. A. B. van, *Geschiedkundige aantekeningen ten dienste van de studie van het staatsrecht*, 4th edn, Deventer, 1973

Gosses, I. H. and Japikse, N., *Handboek tot de staatkundige geschiedenis van Nederland*, 3rd edn by R. R. Post and N. Japikse, The Hague, 1946–7 (Post's 4th edn, The Hague, 1959, does not go beyond the Middle Ages)

Grolle, J. J., *Weg met de koning. 's Konings zegel gebroken. Het ontstaan van de Nederlandse Staat in 1581*, The Hague, 1981

Hansotte, G., *Les institutions politiques et judiciaires de la principauté de Liège aux Temps Modernes*, Brussels, 1987

Henrion, R., 'Le Parlement belge, pouvoir de législation et de contrôle', *Académie Royale de Belgique, Bulletin de la Classe des Lettres*, 5th ser., vol. 71 (1985), 99–111

Jacob, M. C. et al. (eds.), *The Dutch Republic in the eighteenth century: decline, enlightenment and revolution*, Ithaca, 1992

Monté Ver Loren, J. P. de, *Hoofdlijnen uit de ontwikkeling der rechterlijke organisatie in de Noordelijke Nederlanden tot de Bataafse omwenteling*, 6th edn by J. E. Spruit, Deventer, 1982

Stallaert, K., *Glossarium van verouderde rechtstermen*, completed by F. Debrabandere, Leiden, Handzame, 1886–1977; 3 vols.

Steene, L. van den, *De Belgische grondwetcommissie (oktober–november 1830)*, Brussels, 1963

Tamse, C. A. and Witte, E. (eds.), *Staats- en natievorming in Willem I's koninkrijk (1815–1830)*, Brussels, 1992

Uyttendaele, M., *Le fédéralisme inachevé. Réflexions sur le système institutionnel belge issu des réformes de 1988–1989*, Brussels, 1991

## FRANCE

Antoine, M., *Le Conseil du Roi au XVIIIe siècle*, Paris, 1970

Ardant, P., *Histoire de l'impôt*, Paris, 1972; 2 vols.

Azema, J.-P. and Winock, M., *La IIIe République*, Paris, 1970

Barbey, J., *Etre roi. Le roi et son gouvernement en France de Clovis à Louis XVI*, Paris, 1992

Bastid, P., *Doctrines et institutions politiques de la Seconde République*, Paris, 1945; 2 vols.

*Les institutions politiques de la monarchie parlementaire française (1814–1848)*, Paris, 1954

Bourquin, J., *La liberté de la presse*, Paris, 1950

Bruguière, M.-B., Gilles, H. and Sicard, G., *Introduction à l'histoire des institutions françaises des origines à 1792*, Toulouse, 1983

Chevallier, J. J., *Histoire des institutions et des régimes politiques de la France de 1789 à nos jours*, 4th edn, Paris, 1972

Contamine, P., *Des Pouvoirs en France, 1300–1500*, Paris, 1992

Deslandres, M., *Histoire constitutionnelle de la France*, Paris, 1932–7; 2 vols

Duguit, L., Monnier, H. and Bonnard, R., *Les constitutions et les principales lois politiques de la France depuis 1789*, 7th edn by G. Berlia, Paris, 1952

Duhamel, O. and Merry, Y. (eds.), *Dictionnaire constitutionnel*, Paris, 1992 (monumental work, with extensive historical coverage)

Dupont-Ferrier, G., *La formation de l'Etat français*, Paris, 1934

Durand, G., *Etats et Institutions. XVIe–XVIIIe siècles*, Paris, 1969

Ellul, J., *Histoire des institutions*, I–II: *L'Antiquité*, Paris, 1972, III: *Le Moyen Age*, 6th edn, 1969, IV: *XVIe–XVIIIe siècles*, 6th edn, 1969, V: *Le XIXe siècle*, 6th edn, 1969

Esmein, A., *Cours élémentaire d'histoire du droit français*, 15th edn, Paris, 1925

Fauré, C., *Les déclarations des droits de l'homme de 1789*, Paris, 1988 (text and commentary)

Fougère, L., (ed.), *Le Conseil d'Etat (1799–1974). Son histoire à travers les documents d'époque*, Paris, 1975

Furet, F. and Richet, D., *La Révolution française*, 2nd edn, Paris, 1973

Garrisson, F., *Histoire du droit et des institutions. Le pouvoir des temps féodaux à la révolution*, Paris, 1977

Godechot, J., *Les institutions de la France sous la Révolution et l'Empire*, 3rd edn, Paris, 1985

Goubert, P., *L'Ancien Régime*, 3rd edn, Paris, 1971–3; 2 vols.

Hamaoui, E., *Les régimes politiques de la France de 1789 à 1958*, Paris, 1970

Hanley, S., *The Lit de Justice of the kings of France. Constitutional ideology in legend, ritual and discourse*, Princeton, 1984

Harouel, J.-L., Barbey, J., Bournazel, E. and Thibaut-Payen, J., *Histoire des institutions de l'époque franque à la Révolution*, Paris, 1987

Henry, J.-P., 'Vers la fin de l'état de droit?', *Revue du Droit Public et de la Science Politique* 93 (1977), 1208–35

Hincker, F., *Les Français devant l'impôt sous l'Ancien Régime*, Paris, 1971

Holtzmann, R., *Französische Verfassungsgeschichte: von der Mitte des neunten Jahrhunderts bis zur Revolution*, Munich, 1910

Imbert, J., Sautel, G. and Boulet-Sautel, M., *Histoire des institutions et des faits sociaux*, I: *Des origines au Xe siècle*, 2nd edn, Paris, 1963, II: *Xe–XIXe siècles*, 3rd edn, 1970

Kelley, D. R., *François Hotman. A revolutionary's ordeal*, Princeton, 1973

Knecht, R. J., 'Francis I and the "Lit de Justice": a "legend" defended', *French History* 7 (1993), 53–83

Lanjuinais, J. D. de, *Constitutions de la nation française*, Paris, 1819, 2 vols.

Lefebvre, G., *Napoléon*, Paris, 1953
*La révolution française*, Paris, 1951

Legendre, P. (ed.), *La bureaucratie et le droit*, Paris, 1975
*Trésor historique de l'Etat en France. L'administration classique*, 2nd edn, Paris, 1992

Lepointe, G., *Histoire des institutions du droit public français au 19e siècle (1789–1914)*, Paris, 1953
*Histoire des institutions et des faits sociaux*, 2nd edn, Paris, 1963 (concerns the period 987–1875)

Lepointe, G., Boulet-Sautel, M. and Vandenbossche, A., *Bibliographie en langue française d'histoire du droit 987–1875*, Paris, 1961 ff.

Lepointe, G. and Vandenbossche, A., *Eléments de bibliographie sur l'histoire des institutions et des faits sociaux. 987–1875*, Paris, 1958

Lloyd, H. A., *The state, France and the sixteenth century*, London, 1983

Lot, F. and Fawtier, R. (eds.), *Histoire des institutions françaises au moyen âge*, I: *Institutions seigneuriales*, II: *Institutions royales*, III: *Institutions ecclésiastiques*, Paris, 1957–62; 3 vols.

Maillet, J., *Histoire des institutions publiques depuis la Révolution française*, Paris, 1968

Malafosse, J. de, *Histoire des institutions et des régimes politiques de la Révolution à la IVe République*, Paris, 1975

Malettke, K., 'Frankreich und Europa im 17. und 18. Jahrhundert. Der französische Beitrag zur Entfaltung des frühmodernen, souveränen staates', *Francia* 3 (1975), 321–45

Mandrou, R., *L'Europe 'absolutiste'. Raison et raison d'Etat 1649–1775*, Paris, 1977 (first publ. as vol. III of the *Geschichte Europas*, Frankfurt, 1976, under the title *Staatsräson und Vernunft*)

Marion, M., *Dictionnaire des institutions de la France aux XVIIe et XVIIIe siècles*, Paris, 1923

Mathiez, A., *La révolution française*, 2nd edn, Paris, 1959

Merriman, J. M., *The agony of the republic. Repression of the left in revolutionary France, 1848–1851*, New Haven, Conn., 1978

Miaille, M., *L'état du droit. Introduction à une critique du droit constitutionnel*, Grenoble, 1978

Mousnier, R. (ed.), *Le Conseil du Roi de Louis XIII à la Révolution*, Paris, 1970
  *Les institutions de la France sous la monarchie absolue*, I: *Société et Etat*, Paris, 1974
  *La plume, la faucille et le marteau. Institutions et Sociéte en France du Moyen Age à la Révolution*, Paris, 1970

Neré, J., *La IIIe République, 1914–1940*, Paris, 1973

Parker, D., *The making of French absolutism*, London, 1983

Ponteil, F., *Les institutions de la France de 1814 à 1870*, Paris, 1966

Portemer, J., 'Recherches sur l'enseignement du droit public au XVIIIe siècle', *Revue historique de droit français et étranger*, 4th ser. 37 (1959), 341–97

Prelot, M., *Institutions politiques et droit constitutionnel*, 8th edn by J. Boulouis, Paris, 1980 (Ch. II: *Histoire des institutions politiques françaises*, pp. 295–582, contains an excellent survey of French public law from 1789 to 1958)

Purtschet, C., *Histoire des institutions. Xe–XVIIIe siècle*, Paris, 1972

Regnault, H., *Manuel d'histoire du droit français*, 5th edn, Paris, 1947

Rémon, R., *Introduction à l'histoire de notre temps*, I: *L'Ancien Régime et la révolution, 1750–1815*, Paris, 1988

Richet, D., *La France moderne: l'esprit des institutions*, Paris, 1973 (deals with the Ancient Regime, i.e. from the sixteenth to the eighteenth century)

Rousselet, M., *Le souverain devant la Justice de Louis XVI à Napoléon III*, Paris, 1946

Rowen, H. H., *The king's state: proprietary dynasticism in early modern France*, New Brunswick, N.J., 1980

Russell Major, J., *Representative government in early modern France*, New Haven, Conn., 1983

Sautel, G., *Histoire des institutions publiques depuis la révolution française. Administration, justice, finances*, 7th edn, Paris, 1990

Schramm, P. E., *Der König von Frankreich. Das Wesen der Monarchie vom 9. bis zum 16. Jahrhundert. Ein Kapitel aus der Geschichte des abendländischen Staates*, 2nd edn, Darmstadt, 1960; 2 vols.

Shennan, J. H., *Government and society in France 1461–1661*, London, New York, 1969
*The Parlement of Paris*, London, 1968

Soboul, A., *La révolution française*, I: *De la Bastille à la Gironde*, II: *De la Montagne à Brumaire*, Paris, 1962; 2 vols.

Soulé, C., *Les Etats généraux en France, 1302–1789. Etude historique, comparative et doctrinale*, Heule (Belgium), 1968

Sparwasser, R., *Zentralismus, Dezentralisation, Regionalismus und Föderalismus in Frankreich. Eine institutionen, theorien- und ideengeschichtliche Darstellung*, Berlin, Munich, 1986

Sternhell, Z., *La Droite révolutionnnaire 1885–1914. Les origines françaises du fascisme*, Paris, 1978

Sueur, P., *Histoire du droit public français: la genèse de l'Etat contemporain*, I: *La constitution monarchique*, II: *Affirmation et crise de l'Etat sous l'Ancien Régime*, Paris, 1989; 2 vols.

Szramkiewicz, R. and Bouineau, J., *Histoire des Institutions 1750–1914. Droit et société en France de la fin de l'Ancien Régime à la Première Guerre Mondiale*, 2nd edn, Paris, 1992

Timbal, P.-C. and Castaldo, A., *Histoire des institutions publiques et des faits sociaux*, Paris, 1979

Villard, P., *Histoire des institutions publiques de la France (de 1789 à nos jours)*. 3rd edn, Paris, 1983

Vovelle, M. (ed.), *L'état de la France pendant la révolution 1789–1799*, Paris, 1988
*La révolution et l'ordre juridique privé: rationalité ou scandale? Actes du Colloque d'Orléans 11–13 Sept. 1986*, Orleans, 1988; 2 vols.

Wallace-Hadrill, J. M. and McManners, J. (eds.), *France: government and society. An historical survey*, 2nd edn, London, 1970

# GERMANY

Angermeier, H., *Die Reichsreform 1410–1555. Die Staatsproblematik in Deutschland zwischen Mittelalter und Gegenwart*, Munich, 1984

Apelt, W., *Geschichte der Weimarer Verfassung*, 2nd edn, Munich, 1964

Baum, D., *Bürokratie und Sozialpolitik. Zur Geschichte staatlicher sozialpolitik im Spiegel der älteren deutschen Staatsverwaltungslehre*, Berlin, 1988

Böckenförde, E. W., *Moderne deutsche Verfassungsgeschichte 1815–1918*, 2nd edn,

Konigstein/Ts, 1981

Bornhak, C., *Deutsche Verfassungsgeschichte. Vom Westfälischen Frieden*, Stuttgart, 1934

Bracher, K. D., *Die Deutsche Diktatur. Entstehung und Folgen des Nationalsozialismus*, Berlin, 1969

Brunner, H., *Grundzüge der deutschen Rechtsgeschichte*, 8th edn, Leipzig, 1930

Brunner, O., Conze, W. and Koselleck, R. (eds.), *Geschichtliche Grundbegriffe. Historisches Lexikon zur politisch-sozialen Sprache in Deutschland*, Stuttgart, 1974 ff.

Bryce, J., *The Holy Roman Empire*, 2nd edn, London, New York, 1904

Bussi, E., *Il diritto pubblico del Sacro Romano Impero alla fine del XVIII secolo*, 2nd edn, Milan, 1970

Christmann, T., *Das Bemühen von Kaiser under Reich um die Vereinheitlichung des Münzwesens. Zugleich ein Beitrag zum Rechtsetzungsverfahren im Heiligen Römischen Reich nach dem Westfälischen Frieden*, Berlin, Munich, 1988

Coing, H., *Epochen der Rechtsgeschichte in Deutschland*, 2nd edn, Munich, 1971

Coing, H. (ed.), *Handbuch der Quellen und Literatur der neueren europäischen Privatrechtsgeschichte*, I: *Mittelalter*, II: *Neuere Zeit*, 1: *Wissenschaft*, Munich, 1973–7 (although mainly devoted to private law, these volumes contain a good deal of information on political organization)

Conrad, H., *Deutsche Rechtsgeschichte*, I: *Frühzeit und Mittelalter*, 2nd edn, Karlsruhe, 1962, II: *Neuzeit bis 1806*, 1966

*Der deutsche Staat. Epochen seiner Verfassungsentwicklung (843–1945)*, Frankfurt, 1969

*Richter und Gesetz im Übergang vom Absolutismus zum Verfassungsstaat*, Graz, 1971

Conway, J. S., *Die nationalsozialistische Kirchenpolitik*, Munich, 1969

*Deutsches Rechtswörterbuch. Wörterbuch der älteren deutschen Rechtssprache*, dir. by R.Schröder and E. von Künssberg, Weimar, 1914 ff.

Dilcher, G. and Diestelkamp, B. (eds.), *Recht, Gericht, Genossenschaft und Policey. Studien zu Grundbegriffen der germanistischen Rechtstheorie. Symposion für A. Erler*, Berlin, 1986

Eisenhardt, U., *Deutsche Rechtsgeschichte*, Munich, 1984 (the author leaves out the Germanic and Frankish periods in order to have more space for the nineteenth and twentieth centuries)

Erler, A. and Kaufmann, E. (eds.), with collaboration of W. Stammler, *Handwörterbuch zur deutschen Rechtsgeschichte*, Berlin, 1964ff. (by 1992 the letter u was reached)

Feine, H. E., *Deutsche Verfassungsgeschichte der Neuzeit*, 3rd edn, Tübingen, 1943

*Das Werden des deutschen Staates seit dem Ausgang des Heiligen Römischen Reiches 1800 bis 1933*, 2nd edn, Stuttgart, 1944

Fest, J. C., *Hitler. Eine Biographie*, Frankfurt, 1973

Fioravanti, M., *Giuristi e costituzione politica nell'ottocento tedesco*, Milan, 1979

Forsthoff, E., *Deutsche Verfassungsgeschichte der Neuzeit*, 4th edn, Stuttgart, 1972

Frei, N., *National socialist rule in Germany. The Führer state 1933–1945*, Oxford, 1993

Friedrich, C. J., *Der Verfassungsstaat der Neuzeit*, Berlin, Göttingen, 1953

Funk, A., *Polizei und Rechtsstaat. Die Entwicklung des staatlichen Gewaltmonopols in Preussen 1848–1914*, Frankfurt, 1986

Grimm, D., *Deutsche Verfassungsgeschichte 1776–1866. Vom Beginn des modernen Verfassungsstaats bis zur Auflösung des Deutschen Bundes*, Frankfurt, 1988

Groeben, K. von der, *Die öffentliche Verwaltung im Spannungsfeld der Politik, dargestellt am Beispiel Ostpreussens*, Berlin, Munich, 1979

Gross, H., *Empire and sovereignty. A history of public law literature in the Holy Roman Empire 1599–1804*, Chicago, 1974

Gürtler, P., *Nationalsozialismus und evangelische Kirchen im Warthegau*, Göttingen, 1958

Hamel, W., *Deutsches Staatsrecht*, II: *Verfassungsgeschichte. Ideologie und Wirklichkeit*, Berlin, 1974

Hammerstein, N., 'Jus Publicum Romano-Germanicum', *Diritto e Potere nella Storia Europea*, Florence, 1982, 717–53

Hartung, F., *Deutsche Verfassungsgeschichte vom 15. Jahrhundert bis zur Gegenwart*, 9th edn, Berlin, 1969

Heinig, P.-J., *Reichsstädte, Freie Städte und Königtum 1389–1450. Ein Beitrag zur deutschen Verfassungsgeschichte*, Wiesbaden, 1983

Hirschfield, G. and Kettenacker, L. (eds.), *Der 'Führerstaat': Mythos und Realität. Studien zur Struktur und Politik des Dritten Reiches*, Stuttgart, 1981

Hubatsch, W., *Grundlinien preussischer Geschichte. Königtum und Staatsgestaltung 1701–1871*, Darmstadt, 1983

Huber, E. R., *Deutsche Verfassungsgeschichte seit 1789*, Stuttgart, 1963–85; 7 vols. (reaches the end of the Republic of Weimar)
*Nationalstaat und Verfassungsstaat. Studien zur Geschichte der modernen Staatsidee*, Stuttgart, 1965

Hughes, M., *Early modern Germany 1477–1806*, London, 1992

Jeserich, K. G. A., Pohl, H. and Unruh, G.-C. von (eds.), *Deutsche Verwaltungsgeschichte*, Stuttgart, 1983–8; 6 vols.

Kehr, H. and Langmaid, J., *The Nazi era 1919–1945. A select bibliography of published works from the early roots to 1980*, London, 1982

Kern, E., *Geschichte des Gerichtsverfassungsrechts*, Munich, Berlin, 1954

Kimme, J., *Das Repräsentativsystem unter besonderer Beachtung der historischen Entwicklung der Repräsentation und der Rechtsprechung des Bundesverfassungsgerichts*, Berlin, 1988

Kimminich, O., *Deutsche Verfassungsgeschichte*, Frankfurt, 1970

Klessmann, C., *Zwei Staaten, eine Nation. Deutsche Geschichte 1955–1970*, Göttingen, 1988

Köbler, G., *Deutsche Rechtsgeschichte. Ein systematischer Grundriss*, 4th edn, Munich, 1990

Koch, H. W., *A constitutional history of Germany in the nineteenth and twentieth centuries*, London, 1984

Köhler, M., *Die Lehre vom Widerstandsrecht in der deutschen konstitutionellen Staatstheorie der 1. Hälfte des 19. Jahrhunderts*, Berlin, 1973

Kroeschell, K., *Deutsche Rechtsgeschichte*, I: *bis 1250*, 7th edn, Hamburg, 1985,

II: *1250–1650*, 6th edn, 1986, III: *seit 1650*, Opladen, 1989 (from Germanic times to the present)

Lambsdorff, H. G., *Die Weimarer Republik*, Frankfurt, 1990

Langewiesche, D. (ed.), *Liberalismus im 19. Jahrhundert. Deutschland im europäischen Vergleich*, Göttingen, 1988

Löw, K., *Ursachen und Verlauf der deutschen Revolution 1989*, Berlin, 1991

Lübbe-Wolff, G., 'Das wohlerworbene Recht als Grenze der Gesetzgebung im neunzehnten Jahrhundert', *Savigny Zeitschrift für Rechtsgeschichte*, G. A. 103 (1986), 104–39

Meier, K., *Der evangelische Kirchenkampf*, Göttingen, 1984; 3 vols.

Menger, C. F., *Deutsche Verfassungsgeschichte der Neuzeit*, 5th edn, Vienna, Leipzig, 1986

Mitteis, H., *Deutsche Rechtsgeschichte*, 7th edn, Munich, 1961
*Der Staat des hohen Mittelalters*, 7th edn, Weimar, 1962

Mosse, G. L., *Nazism. A historical and comparative analysis of national socialism*, Oxford, 1979

Müller, I., *Furchtbare Juristen. Die unbewältigte Vergangenheit unsrer Justiz*, Munich, 1987

Neumaier, K. *Jus Publicum. Studien zur barocken Rechtsgelehrsamkeit an der Universität Ingolstadt*, Berlin, 1974

Noakes, J., *The Nazi Party in Lower Saxony 1921–1933*, Oxford, 1973

Oestreich, G., *Geist und Gestalt des frühmodernen Staates. Ausgewählte Aufsätze*, Berlin, 1969
*Verfassungsgeschichte vom Ende des Mittelalters bis zum Ende des alten Reiches*, Munich, 1974

Orlow, D., *The history of the Nazi Party*, Newton Abbot, 1973–4; 2 vols.

Planitz, H. and Buyken, T., *Bibliographie zur deutschen Rechtsgeschichte*, Frankfurt, 1952

Rüfner, W., *Verwaltungsrechtsschutz in Preussen von 1749 bis 1842*, Bonn, 1962

Scheyhing, R., *Deutsche Verfassungsgeschichte der Neuzeit*, Cologne, 1968.

Schmidt, E., *Beiträge zur Geschichte des preussischen Rechtsstaates*, Berlin, 1980

Schneider, O., *Rechtsgedanken und Rechtstechniken totalitärer Herrschaft aufgezeigt am Recht des öffentlichen Dienstes im Dritten Reich und der DDR*, Berlin, 1988

Schorn, H., *Die Gesetzgebung des Nationalsozialismus als Mittel der Machtpolitik*, Frankfurt, 1963
*Der Richter im Dritten Reich. Geschichte und Dokumente*, Frankfurt, 1959

Schubert, E., *König und Reich. Studien zur spätmittelalterlichen deutschen Verfassungsgeschichte*, Göttingen, 1979

Schulz, H., *Das System und die Prinzipien der Einkünfte im werdenden Staat der Neuzeit dargestellt anhand der kameralwissenschaftlichen Literatur (1600–1835)*, Berlin, 1982

Schuster, R. (ed.), *Deutsche Verfassungen*, 11th edn, Munich, 1979

Schwennicke, A., *Die Entstehung der Einleitung des Preussischen Allgemeinen Landrechts von 1794*, Frankfurt, 1993

Schwerin, C. von, *Grundzüge der deutschen Rechtsgeschichte*, 4th edn by H. Thieme, Munich, 1950

Shirer, W. L., *The rise and fall of the Third Reich. A history of Nazi Germany*, London, 1960

Stolleis, M., *Geschichte des öffentlichen Rechts in Deutschland*, i: *Reichspublizistik und Policeywissenschaft 1600–1800*, ii: *Staatsrechtslehre und Verwaltungswissenschaft 1800–1914*, Munich, 1988–92; 2 vols.

Stolleis, M. and Simon, D. (eds.), *Rechtsgeschichte im Nationalsozialismus. Beiträge zur Geschichte einer Disziplin*, Tübingen, 1989

Süle, T., *Preussische Bürokratietradition. Zur Entwicklung von Verwaltung und Beamtenschaft in Deutschland 1871–1918*, Göttingen, 1988

Vann, J. A. and Rowan, S. W. (eds.), *The Old Reich. Essays on German political institutions 1495–1806*, Brussels, 1974

Watt, R. M., *The kings depart. The tragedy of Germany: Versailles and the German Revolution*, London, 1968

Willoweit, D., *Deutsche Verfassungsgeschichte. Vom Frankenreich bis zur Teilung Deutschlands. Ein Studienbuch*, 2nd edn, Munich, 1992

    *Rechtsgrundlagen der Territorialgewalt, Landesobrigkeit. Herrschaftsrechte und Territorium in der Rechtswissenschaft der Neuzeit*, Cologne, Vienna, 1975

Wunder, B., *Geschichte der Bürokratie in Deutschland*, Frankfurt, 1986

Wyduckel, D., *Ius Publicum. Grundlagen und Entwicklung des öffentlichen Rechts und der deutschen Staatsrechtswissenschaft*, Berlin, 1984

Zipfel, F., *Kirchenkampf in Deutschland*, Berlin, 1965

## GREAT BRITAIN

Arthurs, H. W., *'Without the Law'. Administrative justice and legal pluralism in nineteenth-century England*, Toronto, 1985

Beauté, J., *Un grand juriste anglais: Sir Edward Coke 1552–1634. Ses idées politiques et constitutionnelles ou aux origines de la démocratie occidentale moderne*, Paris, 1975

Brewer, J. and Styles, J. (eds.), *An ungovernable people? The English and their law in the seventeenth and eighteenth centuries*, London, 1980

Cannon, J., *Parliamentary reform 1640–1832*, Cambridge, 1973

Chandaman, C. D., *The English public revenue 1660–1688*, Oxford, 1975

Chester, N., *The English administrative system 1780–1870*, Oxford, 1981

Conacher, J. B., *The emergence of British parliamentary democracy in the nineteenth century: The passing of the Reform Acts of 1832, 1867 and 1884–5*, Chichester, 1971

Eichler, H., *Verfassungswandel in England. Ein Beitrag zur europäischen Rechtsgeschichte des 17. und 18. Jahrhunderts*, Berlin, Munich, 1988

Fry, G. K., *The growth of government: the development of ideas about the role of the state and the machinery and functions of government in Britain since 1780*, London, 1979

Gough, J. W., *Fundamental law in English constitutional history*, Oxford, 1955

Hanham, H. J., *The nineteenth century constitution. Documents and commentary*, Cambridge, 1969

Holdsworth, W. S., *A history of English law*, London, 1903–72; 16 vols. and 1 vol. index

Keeton, G. W. (ed.), *The British Commonwealth. The development of its laws and constitutions*, London, 1955 ff. (England by G. W. Keeton and O. Lloyd, 1955; Scotland by T. B. Smith, 2nd edn, 1962)

Keir, D. L., *The constitutional history of modern Britain since 1485*, 8th edn, London, 1966

Keller, E. (ed.), *Die englischen Freiheitsrechte des 17. Jahrhunderts*, 2nd edn, Berne, Frankfurt, 1962

Kleinhenz, R., *Königtum und parlamentarische Vertrauensfrage in England 1689–1841*, Berlin, 1991

Krautheim, U., *Die Souveränitätskonzeption in den englischen Verfassungskonflikten des 17. Jahrhunderts. Eine Studie zur Rezeption der Lehre Bodins in England von der Regierungszeit Elisabeths I. bis zur Restauration der Stuartherrschaft unter Karl II.*, Berne, Frankfurt, 1977

Lyon, B., *A constitutional and legal history of medieval England*, 2nd edn, New York, 1980

Moodie, G. C., *The government of Britain*, 3rd edn, London, 1971

Parris, H., *Constitutional bureaucracy*, London, 1969

Plucknett, T. F. T., *A concise history of the common law*, 5th edn, London, 1956

Pocock, J. G. A. (ed.), *Three British revolutions: 1641, 1688, 1776*, Princeton, 1980

Pollock, F. and Maitland, F. W., *The history of English law before the time of Edward I*, 2nd edn, Cambridge, 1898 (reprinted with introduction and bibliography by S. F. C. Milsom)

Radbruch, G., *Der Geist des englischen Rechts*, 3rd edn, Heidelberg, 1956

Sedgemore, B., *The secret constitution. An analysis of the political establishment*, London, 1980

Smith, E. A., *The House of Lords in British politics 1815–1911*, London, 1992

Sommerville, J. P., *Politics and ideology in England 1603–1640*, London, New York, 1986

Taswell-Langmead, *English constitutional history from the Teutonic Conquest to the present time*, 11th edn by T. F. T. Plucknett, London, 1960

Veitch, G. S., *The genesis of parliamentary reform*, London, 1913

Weston, C. C. and Greenberg, J. R., *Subjects and sovereigns: the grand controversy over legal sovereignty in Stuart England*, Cambridge, 1981

## HUNGARY

D'Eszlary, C., *Histoire des institutions publiques hongroises*, Paris, 1959–65; 3 vols.

Hantos, E., *The Magna Carta of the English and the Hungarian Constitution*, London, 1904

Timon, A. von, *Ungarische Verfassungs- und Rechtsgeschichte. Mit Bezug auf die Rechtsentwicklung der westlichen Staaten*, trans. F. Schiller, Berlin, 1909

# ITALY

*L'amministrazione nella storia moderna*, Milan, 1985 (concerns mainly Italy, but contains bibliographical introductions for France, Germany, Austria and Spain)

Bellomo, M., *Società e istituzioni in Italia tra medioevo ed età moderna*, 2nd edn, Catania, 1977

Besta, E., *Storia del diritto italiano. Diritto pubblico*, I, 2nd edn, Milan, 1949, II, 3rd edn, Milan, 1950

Colliva, P., *Ricerche sul principio di legalità nell' amministrazione del Regno di Sicilia al tempo di Federico II*, I: *Gli organi centrali e regionali*, Milan, 1964

Guidi, G., *Il governo della città-repubblica di Firenze del primo quattrocento*, Florence, 1981; 3 vols.

Haverkamp, A., *Herrschaftsformen der Frühstaufer in Reichsitalien*, Stuttgart, 1970–1; 2 vols.

Hyde, J. K., *Society and politics in medieval Italy 1000–1350*, London, 1975

Litchfield, R. B., *Emergence of a bureaucracy. The Florentine patricians 1530–1790*, Princeton, 1986

Marongiu, A., *Storia del diritto italiano. Ordinamenti e istituti di governo*, 2nd edn, Milan, 1977

Martines, L., *Lawyers and statecraft in Renaissance Florence*, Princeton, 1968

Monti, G. M., *Lo stato normanno svevo. Lineamenti e ricerche*, Naples, 1934

Tabacco, G., *The struggle for power in medieval Italy: structures of political rule*, Cambridge, 1989 (translation of *Egemonie sociali e strutture del potere nel Medioevo Italiano* (2nd edn 1979), with new material)

Wickham, C. J., *Early medieval Italy: central power and local society 400–1000*, London, 1983

# POLAND

Dany, C., *Les idées politiques et l'esprit public en Pologne à la fin du XVIIIe siècle*, Paris, 1901 (contains an incomplete translation of the Polish Constitution of 1791)

Fedorowicz, J. K. (ed. and trans.), *A republic of nobles: studies in Polish history to 1864*, Cambridge, 1982

Gieysztor, A. et al., *History of Poland*, 2nd edn, Warsaw, 1979, 23–143 (analysis of Polish medieval political institutions)

Kutrzeba, S., *Grundriss der polnischen Verfassungsgeschichte*, 3rd edn trans. Christiani, Berlin, 1912

Siekanowicz, P. (ed.), *Legal sources and bibliography of Poland*, New York, 1964

Wagner, W. J. (ed.), *Polish law throughout the ages*, Stanford, 1970

Wojciechowksi, Z., *L'état polonais au moyen-âge. Histoire des institutions*, Paris, 1949

## PORTUGAL

Gama Barros, H. da, *Historia da Administraçao publica em Portugal nos seculos XII à XV*, 2nd edn by I. de Sousa Soares, Lisbon, 1945–54; 11 vols.

## RUSSIA AND THE SOVIET UNION

Adams, A. E., *The Russian Revolution and Bolshevik victory: causes and processes*, New York, 1972
Berman, H. J., *Justice in the USSR. An interpretation of Soviet law*, 2nd edn, Cambridge, Mass., 1963
  *Soviet criminal law and procedure*, Oxford, 1966
Blakeley, T. J., *Soviet scholasticism*, Dordrecht, Stuttgart, 1961
Bloch, S. and Reddaway, P., *Soviet psychiatric abuse: the shadow over world psychiatry*, London, 1984
Brown, A. (ed.), *The Cambridge encyclopedia of Russia and the Soviet Union*, Cambridge, 1981
Carmichael, J., *Trotsky. An appreciation of his life*, London, 1975
Carr, E. H. and Davies, R. W., *A history of Soviet Russia*, London, 1950–78: *The Bolchevik Revolution 1917–1923*, 1950–4; 3 vols.; *The Interregnum 1923–1924*, 1954; *Socialism in one country 1924–1926*, 1958–64; 3 vols.; *Foundations of a planned economy 1926–1929*, 1969–78; 3 vols.
Chambre, H., *L'évolution du marxisme soviétique. Théorie économique et droit*, Paris, 1974
  *Le marxisme en Union Soviétique. Idéologie et institutions. Leur évolution de 1917 à nos jours*, Paris, 1955
  *Le pouvoir soviétique. Introduction à l'étude de ses institutions*, Paris, 1959
Charvin, R., *Les états socialistes européens. Institutions et vie politique*, Paris, 1975
Collignon, J. G., *La théorie de l'Etat du peuple tout entier en Union Soviétique*, Paris, 1967
Conquest, R., *The great terror. Stalin's purge of the thirties*, London, 1968
  *The harvest of sorrow*, London, 1986 (deals with collectivization in the Soviet Union)
Daniels, R. V. (ed.), *The Stalin revolution: foundations of Soviet totalitarianism*, 2nd edn, Lexington, Mass., 1972
  *The Stalin revolution. Fulfillment or betrayal?*, Lexington, Mass., 1965
Dekkers, R., *Introduction au droit de l'Union Soviétique et des républiques populaires*, 2nd edn, Brussels, 1971
Deutscher, I., *Russia after Stalin*, London, 1969
  *Stalin. A political biography*, 2nd edn, London, 1967
  *Trotsky*, I: *The prophet armed, 1879–1921*, II: *The prophet unarmed, 1921–1929*, III: *The prophet outcast, 1929–1940*, London, 1954–63; 3 vols.
Elleinstein, J., *Histoire du phénomène stalinien*, Paris, 1975
Fejtö, H., *Histoire des Démocraties populaires*, I: *L'ère de Staline 1945–1952*, II: *Après Staline 1953–1968*, Paris, 1952–69; 2 vols.

Feldbrugge, F. J. M., 'The constitution of the USSR', *Review of Socialist Law* 16 (1990), 163–224.

Ferro, M., *La Révolution de 1917: Octobre. Naissance d'une société*, Paris, 1977

Fitzpatrick, S., *The Russian Revolution*, Oxford, 1982

Gill, G. J., *Peasants and government in the Russian Revolution*, London, 1979

Gsovksi, V. and Grzybowski, K, *Government, law and courts in the Soviet Union and Eastern Europe*, London, The Hague, 1959

Hammond, T. T. (ed.), *The anatomy of Communist takeovers*, Yale, 1975

Haupt, G. and Marie, J. J., *Les Bolchéviks par eux-mêmes*. Paris, 1969 (trans. by C. I. P. Ferdinand and D. M. Bellos, *Makers of the Russian Revolution*, London, 1974)

Hazard, J. N., *The Soviet system of government*, 5th edn, Chicago, 1980

Heller, M. and Nekrich, A., *L'Utopie au pouvoir. Histoire de l'URSS de 1917 à nos jours*, Paris, 1982

*Histoire de l'URSS*, I: *Depuis les origines jusqu'à 1917*, II: *De 1917 à nos jours*, Moscow, 1977

Hough, J. F. and Fainsod, M., *How the Soviet Union is governed*, Cambridge, Mass., 1979

Kadlec, K., *Introduction à l'étude comparative de l'histoire du droit public des peuples slaves*, Paris, 1933

Kaiser, D. H., *The growth of law in medieval Russia*, Princeton, 1980

Keep, J. L. H., *The rise of social democracy in Russia 1898–1907*, Oxford, 1963

Leggett, G., *The Cheka. Lenin's political police*, Oxford, 1981

Leideritz, P. M., *Key to the study of East European law*, Antwerp, 1978

Leontovitsch, V., *Geschichte des Liberalismus in Russland*, 2nd edn, Frankfurt, 1974

Lesage, M., *Le droit soviétique*, Paris, 1975

*Les régimes politiques de l'URSS et de l'Europe de l'Est*, Paris, 1971

Liebman, M., *Leninism under Lenin*, London, 1975

Meder, W., *Das Sowjetrecht. Grundzüge der Entwicklung 1917–1970*, Frankfurt, 1971

Medvedev, R. A., *All Stalin's men*, Oxford, 1984

*Let history judge. The origins and consequences of Stalinism*, 2nd edn, Oxford, 1989

Meeus, A. de, *Livre Blanc sur l'internement psychiatrique de dissidents sains d'esprit en URSS*, Brussels, 1974

Mouskhely, N. and Jedryka, R., *Le gouvernement de l'URSS*, Paris, 1961

Nogee, J. L., *Man, state and society in the Soviet Union*, London, 1972

Pipes, R., *Russia under the old regime*, London, 1975

Radkey, O. H., *The agrarian foes of bolshevism: promise and default of the Russian socialist revolutionaries*, Oxford, 1958

Rauch, G. von, *Geschichte der Sowjetunion*, Stuttgart, 1969

Riasanovsky, N. V., *A history of Russia*, 3rd edn, Oxford, 1977

Rigby, T. H., *Lenin's government: Sovnarkom 1917–1922*, Cambridge, 1979

Rubenstein, J., *Soviet dissidents. Their struggle for human rights*, Boston, 1980

Ryavec, K. W. (ed.), *Soviet society and the Communist Party*, Amherst, 1979

Saunders, D., *Russia in the age of reaction and reform 1801–1881*, London, 1992

Schapiro, L., *The Communist Party of the Soviet Union*, 2nd edn, London, 1970

*The origins of the communist autocracy. Political opposition in the Soviet state, 1917–1922*, 2nd edn, London, 1976

*1917: The Russian Revolutions and the origins of present-day Communism*, London, 1983

Scott, D. J. R., *Russian political institutions*, London, 1969

Seton-Watson, H., *The Russian Empire 1801–1917*, Oxford, 1967

Shanin, T., *The awkward class. Political sociology of peasantry in a developing society: Russia 1910–1925*, Oxford, 1972

Shukman, H. (ed.), *The Blackwell encyclopedia of the Russian Revolution*, Oxford, 1988

*Sowjetsystem und Ostrecht. Festschrift für Boris Meissner*, Berlin, 1985

Szamuely, T., *The Russian tradition*, London, 1975

Szeftel, M., *Russian institutions and culture up to Peter the Great*, London, 1975

Tatu, M., *Le pouvoir en URSS*, Paris, 1967

Tökes, R. L., *Dissent in the USSR. Politics, ideologies and people*, Baltimore, 1975

Tucker, R. C., *Stalin as revolutionary 1879–1929. A study in history and personality*, New York, 1973

Tucker, R. C. (ed.), *Stalinism. Essays in historical interpretation*, New York, 1977

Unger, A. L., *Constitutional development in the USSR. A guide to the Soviet Constitution*, New York, 1981 (comprises the texts of the Constitutions of 1918, 1924, 1936 and 1977, with notes)

Zaslavsky, V., *The new Stalinist state*, Brighton, 1983

Zile, Z. L. (ed.), *Ideas and forces in Soviet legal history. A reader on the Soviet state and law*, New York, Oxford, 1992

## SCANDINAVIA

Herlitz, N., *Grundzüge der schwedischen Verfassungsgeschichte*, Rostock, 1939

Orfield, L. B., *The growth of Scandinavian law*, Philadelphia, 1953

Stjernquist, N. (ed.), *The Swedish Riksdag in an international perspective*, Stockholm, 1989

## SPAIN

Beneyto Perez, J., *Historia de la administración española e hispanoamericana*, Madrid, 1958

Bisson, T. N., *The medieval crown of Aragon*, Oxford, 1986

Clavero, B., *Manual de historia constitucional de España*, Madrid, 1989

*Las cortes de Castilla y León en la edad media. Actas ... congreso ... historia de la corte de Castilla*, Valladolid, 1988; 2 vols.

Engels, O., *Reconquista und Landesherrschaft. Studien zur Rechts- und Verfassungsgeschichte Spaniens im Mittelalter*, Paderborn, Munich, 1989

Garcia Gallo, A., *Manual de historia del derecho español*, 2nd edn, Madrid, 1964; 2 vols.

Gibert, R., *Historia general del derecho español*, Granada, 1968

Iglesia Ferreirós, A., *La creación del derecho. Una historia de la formación de un derecho estatal español*, Barcelona, 1992; 2 vols.

Lalinde Abadía, J., *Iniciación historica al derecho español*, Barcelona, 1970 'Perspectiva europea de la monarquia hispana', *Anuario de historia del derecho español* 58 (1988), 205–76

Lynch, J., *Spain under the Habsburgs*, Oxford, 1965–9; 2 vols.

O'Callaghan, J. F., *The Cortes of Castile-León 1188–1350*, Philadelphia, 1993

Payne, S. G., *The Spanish Revolution*, London, 1970

Pérez-Prendes, J. M., *Curso de historia del derecho español*, Madrid, 1973

Tomas y Valiente, F., *Manual de historia del derecho español*, Madrid, 1979


### SWITZERLAND

Aubert, J. F., *Petite histoire constitutionnelle de la Suisse*, 2nd edn, Berne, 1975

Bluntschli, J. C., *Geschichte des schweizerischen Bundesrechtes von den ersten ewigen Bünden bis auf die Gegenwart*, 2nd edn, Stuttgart, 1875; 2 vols.

Curti, T., *Geschichte der schweizerischen Volksgesetzgebung, zugleich eine Geschichte der schweizerischen Demokratie*, Berne, 1882

Gignoux, C.-J., *La Suisse*, Paris, 1960

Heusler, A., *Schweizerische Verfassungsgeschichte*, Basle, 1920

His, E., *Geschichte des neueren schweizerischen Staatsrechts*, Basle, 1920–38; 3 vols.

Kölz,A., *Neuere schweizerische Verfassungsgeschichte. Ihre Grundlinien vom Ende der Alten Eidgenossenschaft bis 1848*, Berne, 1992

Kölz, A. (ed.), *Quellenbuch zur neueren schweizerischen Verfassungsgeschichte. Vom Ende der Alten Eidgenossenschaft bis 1848*, Berne, 1992

La Roche, E. P., *Das Interregnum und die Entstehung der schweizerischen Eidgenossenschaft*, Berne, Frankfurt, 1971

Peyer, H. C., *Verfassungsgeschichte der alten Schweiz*, Zurich, 1978

Poudret, J.-F., *Libertés et franchises dans les pays romands au moyen âge. Des libertés aux droits de l'homme*, Lausanne, 1986

Wernli, F., *Die Entstehung der schweizerischen Eidgenossenschaft: Verfassungsgeschichte und politische Geschichte in Wechselwirkung*, Uznach, 1972


### UNITED STATES OF AMERICA

Acheson, P. C., *The Supreme Court. America's judicial heritage*, New York, 1961

Bailyn, B., *The ideological origins of the American Revolution*, Cambridge, Mass., 1967

Becker, C., *The Declaration of Independence*, 2nd edn, New York, 1942

Beeman, R., Botein, S. and Carter, E. C., II, *Beyond confederation: origins of the Constitution and American national identity*, Houston, 1987

Berger, R., *The Fourteenth Amendment and the Bill of Rights*, Norman, Okla., 1989 *Government by judiciary: the transformation of the Fourteenth Amendment*, Cambridge, Mass., 1977

Carroll, P. N. and Noble, D. W., *The free and the unfree. A new history of the United States*, New York, 1977

Charles, J. E., *Origins of the American party system*, Magnolia, Mass., 1956

Clinton, R. L., *Marbury v. Madison and judicial review*, Laurence, Kans., 1989

Currie, D. P., *The Constitution in the Supreme Court. The first hundred years 1789–1888*, Chicago, London, 1985

*The Constitution in the Supreme Court. The second century 1888–1986*, Chicago, London, 1990

Curtis, M. K., *No state shall abridge: the Fourteenth Amendment and the Bill of Rights*, Durham, N.C., 1986

Farrand, M., *The framing of the Constitution of the United States*, New Haven, Conn., 1913

Fraenkel, E., *Das amerikanische Regierungssystem. Eine politische Analyse*, Cologne, 1960

Freedman, J. O., *Crisis and legitimacy. The administrative process and American government*, Cambridge, 1979

Freidel, F., *America in the twentieth century*, 23rd edn, New York, 1970

Gilmore, G., *The ages of American law*, New Haven, Conn., 1977

Greene, J. P. (ed.), *The American Revolution. Its character and limits*, New York, 1987

Griffith, E. S., *The American system of government*, 3rd edn, London, 1976

Hall, K. L., *A comprehensive bibliography of American constitutional and legal history, 1896–1979*, Millwood, N.Y., 1984; 5 vols.

*The magic mirror: law in American history*, Oxford, New York, 1989

*The Supreme Court and judicial review in American history*, Bloomington, Ill., 1985

Hall, K. L. (ed.), *United States constitutional and legal history*, New York, 1986; 21 vols. (collection of more than 450 previously published articles, in a systematic order and with introductions, public law receiving extensive attention)

Hargrove, E. C., *The power of the modern presidency*, New York, 1974

Haskins, G. L., 'The English Puritan Revolution and its effects on the rule of law in the early American colonies', *Legal History Review* 54 (1986), 323–34

Haskins, G. L. and Johnson, H. A., *Foundations of power: John Marshall 1801–15*, New York, 1981

Hickok, E. W., Jr (ed.), *The Bill of Rights: original meaning and current understanding*, Charlottesville, Va., 1991

Hill, C. P., *A history of the United States*, 3rd edn, London, 1974

Hofstadter, R., *The American political tradition*, New York, 1948

Hyman, H. and Bruchey, S. (eds.), *American legal and constitutional history*, New York, 1987; 55 vols. (collection of monographs, not previously published and presented here often in a revised form)

Jeffreys-Jones, R. and Collins, B., *The growth of federal power in American history*, New York, 1983

Jensen, M., *The Articles of Confederation*, Madison, 1940

*The founding of a nation. A history of the American Revolution 1763–1776*, New York, 1968

Kammen, M., *A machine that would go of itself: the constitution in American culture*, New York, 1986

Kelly, A. H. and Harbison, W. A., *The American constitution. Its origins and development*, 3rd edn, New York, 1963

Kurland, P. B. and Lerner, R. (eds.), *The founders' constitution*, Chicago, 1987; 5 vols.

Lambert, E., *Le gouvernement des juges et la lutte contre la législation sociale aux Etats-Unis*, Paris, 1921

Lees, J. D., *The political system of the United States*, London, 1975

Levy, L. W., Karst, K. L. and Mahoney, D. J. (eds.), *Encyclopedia of the American Constitution*, New York, London, 1986; 4 vols.

Maccloskey, R. G., *The modern Supreme Court*, Cambridge, Mass., 1972

McDonald, F., *Novus ordo seclorum. The intellectual origins of the Constitution*, Laurence, Kans., 1985

Maltz, E. M., *Civil rights, the Constitution, and Congress, 1863–1869*, Laurence, Kans., 1990

Merriam, C. E. and Merriam, R. E., *The American government. Democracy in action*, Chicago, 1954

Morison, S. E., Commager, H. S. and Leuchtenburg, W. E., *The growth of the American republic*, 6th edn, Oxford, 1969–70; 2 vols.

Morris, R. B. and Morris, J. B. (eds.), *Encyclopedia of American history*, 6th edn, New York, 1982

Murphy, P. L. (ed.), *The Bill of Rights and American legal history*, New York, 1990; 20 vols. (collection of reprints, each volume being devoted to one theme; vol. 1 is entitled *The historic background of the Bill of Rights*)

Nedelsky, J., *Private property and the limits of American constitutionalism. The Madisonian framework*, Chicago, 1990

Nelson, W. E., *The Fourteenth Amendment. From political principle to judicial doctrine*, Cambridge, Mass., 1988

*The roots of American bureaucracy 1830–1980*, Cambridge, Mass., 1982

Nelson, W. E. and Reid, J. P., *The literature of American legal history*, New York, 1985

Phillips, M. J., *The dilemmas of individualism: status, liberty, and American constitutional law*, New York, 1983

Reid, J. P., *Constitutional history of the American Revolution.* I: *The authority of rights*, II: *The authority to tax*, III: *The authority to legislate*, Madison, 1986–91 (4 vols. planned)

Schwartz, B., *The new right and the constitution: turning back the legal clock*, Boston, 1990

*The reins of power: a constitutional history of the United States*, New York, 1963

*Super chief. Earl Warren and his Supreme Court: a judicial biography*, New York, 1983

Smith, P., *The constitution. A documentary and narrative history*, New York, 1980

Snowiss, S., *Judicial review and the law of the constitution*, New Haven, Conn., 1990

Stimson, S. C., *The American Revolution in the law: Anglo-American jurisprudence before John Marshall*, Princeton, 1990

Swisher, C. B., *American constitutional development*, 2nd edn, Boston, 1954

Thorpe, F. N., *The constitutional history of the United States*, Chicago, 1898–1901; 3 vols.

Tucker, R. W. and Hendrickson, D. C., *The fall of the first British Empire. Origins of the War of American Independence*, Baltimore, 1983

Tunc, A. and Tunc, S., *Le système constitutionnel des Etats-Unis d'Amérique*, 2nd edn, Paris, 1954

Urofsky, M. I. (ed.), *Documents of American constitutional and legal history*, New York, 1989; 2 vols.

*Webster's guide to American history. A chronological, geographical and biographical survey and compendium*, Springfield, Mass., 1971; 3 vols.

Wiecek, W. W., *Liberty under law. The Supreme Court in American life*, Baltimore, 1988

Wood, G. S., *The creation of the American republic 1776–1787*, Chapel Hill, N.C., 1969

# Index

319